SAS/FSP® Software:
Usage and Reference

Version 6
First Edition

SAS Institute Inc.
SAS Campus Drive
Cary, NC 27513

The correct bibliographic citation for this manual is as follows: SAS Institute Inc., *SAS/FSP® Software: Usage and Reference, Version 6, First Edition*, Cary, NC: SAS Institute Inc., 1989. 451 pp.

SAS/FSP® Software: Usage and Reference, Version 6, First Edition

1st printing, November 1989
2nd printing, September 1991
3rd printing, October 1993
4th printing, March 1995
5th printing, June 1996

Note that text corrections may have been made at each printing.

Doc S19F, Ver 1.17, 090889

Contents

Part 3 ▪ Usage: Developers' Tools   133

Reference Aids

Displays

Figures

Tables

Special Topics

Credits

Documentation

Composition	Gail C. Freeman, Cynthia Hopkins, Blanche W. Phillips, Pamela A. Troutman, David S. Tyree
Illustrations	Laura B. Hill, Ginny Matsey
Proofreading	Beth A. Heiney, Beryl C. Pittman, Josephine P. Pope, Toni P. Sherrill, Michael H. Smith, John M. West, Susan E. Willard
Technical Review	Melissa A. Atkinson, Scott L. Bass, Patricia L. Berryman, John C. Boling, Patti M. Brideson, Cathy L. Brinsfield, Ann E. Carpenter, Thomas E. Disque, James H. Goodnight, Sue Her, William S. Hopkins, LanChien Hsueh, Angela V. Huggins, Bernadette H. Johnson, K. Deva Kumar, Anna R. Kushner, Carl L. LaChapelle, Jama A. Lidral, Richard A. Ragland, Carol M. Thompson, Sue B. Watts, Linda L. Wharton
Writing and Editing	Amy E. Ball, Ottis R. Cowper, Kathryn A. Restivo

Software

The procedures in Release 6.06 of SAS/FSP software were developed by the Display Products Division. Product development includes design, programming, debugging, support, and preliminary documentation. In the following list, developers who currently support the procedure or feature are indicated with an asterisk. Others provide specific assistance for this release or assisted in the development of the procedure or feature in previous releases.

FSBROWSE and FSEDIT procedures	James H. Goodnight*
FSLETTER procedure	Patti M. Brideson, Carl L. LaChapelle*
FSLIST procedure	Sue Her*
FSVIEW procedure	Patti M. Brideson, Carl L. LaChapelle*
HELP windows	Melissa A. Atkinson, Angela V. Huggins, Elly Sato*, Melissa L. Stevenson, Carol M. Thompson
PMENU action bars and menus for SAS/FSP windows	Tracy C. Byrd, Pamela A. Katchuk, Elly Sato*
Printer support	Patti M. Brideson, Carl L. LaChapelle*
Sample library	Melissa A. Atkinson*, Linda L. Wharton
Screen Control Language	Christopher D. Bailey, Gary W. Black, Yao Chen*, Sue Her, K. Deva Kumar

Testing	Melissa A. Atkinson, Patti M. Brideson, Thomas E. Disque, LanChien Hsueh, Angela V. Huggins, Carol M. Thompson, Linda L. Wharton

Support Groups

Technical Support	Ann E. Carpenter, Annette T. Harris
Quality Assurance Testing	Scott L. Bass, Patricia L. Berryman, Anna R. Kushner, Richard A. Ragland

Using This Book

Purpose

SAS/FSP Software: Usage and Reference, Version 6, First Edition provides both tutorial and reference information about the procedures, windows, and commands provided in Release 6.06 of SAS/FSP software. The two types of information are presented in separate parts of this book:

☐ The tutorial (usage) portion focuses on common tasks and explains how these can be accomplished using the procedures and windows in SAS/FSP software. It does not attempt to cover all the options and commands of each procedure.

☐ The reference portion provides complete descriptions of all the statements, options, windows, and commands that can be used with the procedures in SAS/FSP software. It does not attempt to teach you how to use the software.

If you have been using a previous release of SAS/FSP software, this book replaces *SAS/FSP User's Guide, Version 5 Edition* or *SAS/FSP User's Guide, Release 6.03 Edition* for Release 6.06.

You should read the remainder of "Using This Book" to learn what assumptions *SAS/FSP Software: Usage and Reference* makes about readers and what conventions it uses in presenting information about SAS/FSP software. The information provided in this section will help you use both this book and SAS/FSP software more effectively.

Audience

SAS/FSP Software: Usage and Reference is intended for end users who want to use the data editing and browsing facilities provided in SAS/FSP software and for applications developers who want to use the procedures in SAS/FSP software as the basis for data entry, editing, or browsing applications. This book assumes that readers are familiar with basic SAS System concepts such as creating SAS data sets using the DATA step and manipulating SAS data sets with the procedures in base SAS software.

Prerequisites

The following table summarizes the SAS System concepts that you need to understand in order to use SAS/FSP software:

You need to know how to	Refer to
invoke the SAS System at your site	instructions provided by the SAS Software Consultant at your site
use base SAS software	*SAS Introductory Guide, Third Edition* for a brief introduction, or *SAS Language and Procedures: Usage, Version 6, First Edition* for a more thorough introduction
allocate SAS data libraries and assign librefs	documentation for using the SAS System under the operating system for the hardware at your site
create and manipulate SAS data sets using the DATA step use formats and informats with variable values manipulate SAS Display Manager System windows use the SAS text editor to enter and edit text	*SAS Language: Reference, Version 6, First Edition*
manipulate SAS data sets using SAS procedures	*SAS Procedures Guide, Version 6, Third Edition*

Refer to "Additional Documentation" later in this section for a listing of other books that provide information about related SAS System topics.

How to Use This Book

The following sections provide an overview of what information is contained in this book and how it is organized.

Organization

This book is divided into five parts. Each part of this book (except for Part 1) includes an overview chapter that serves as a roadmap to the information contained therein. Consult these overviews for guidance in finding the information you need.

Part 1: Introduction to SAS/FSP Software

Part 1 provides a brief overview of the procedures in SAS/FSP software and of the SAS System concepts you need to understand to use the procedures.

Chapter 1, "Introduction to SAS/FSP Software"

Part 2: Usage: User's Tools

Part 2 is for end users. It provides examples showing how to perform basic data manipulations using SAS/FSP software.

Chapter 2, "Overview: Part 2"

Chapter 3, "Browsing and Editing SAS Data Sets Using the FSBROWSE and FSEDIT Procedures"

Chapter 4, "Browsing and Editing SAS Data Sets Using the FSVIEW Procedure"

Chapter 5, "Preparing Letters Using the FSLETTER Procedure"

Chapter 6, "Browsing External Files Using the FSLIST Procedure"

Part 3: Usage: Developer's Tools

Part 3 is for applications developers. It provides examples showing how to build data entry and presentation applications using SAS/FSP software. The examples in these chapters are useful as models for creating your own applications.

Chapter 7, "Overview: Part 3"

Chapter 8, "Creating Data Entry Applications Using the FSEDIT Procedure"

Chapter 9, "Creating Data Entry Applications Using the FSVIEW Procedure"

Chapter 10, "Enhancing Data Entry Applications Using Screen Control Language"

Part 4: Reference: SAS/FSP Software Procedures

Part 4 describes the individual procedures in alphabetical order. The syntax for all procedure statements, options, and commands is presented in a uniform format.

Chapter 11, "Overview: Part 4"

Chapter 12, "The FSBROWSE Procedure"

Chapter 13, "The FSEDIT Procedure"

Chapter 14, "The FSLETTER Procedure"

Chapter 15, "The FSLIST Procedure"

Chapter 16, "The FSVIEW Procedure"

Part 5: Reference: Global Features

Part 5 describes global commands and other features that are common to all procedures in SAS/FSP software.

Chapter 17, "Overview: Part 5"

Chapter 18, "Command Reference"

Chapter 19, "The PMENU Facility"

Chapter 20, "Forms"

What You Should Read

Refer to the following table to determine which sections of *SAS/FSP Software: Usage and Reference* are appropriate for your level of experience with SAS/FSP software.

Level of Experience	Suggested Reading
no previous experience with SAS/FSP software	Begin by reading Chapter 1, "Introduction to SAS/FSP Software," for an overview of the available procedures.
	See the chapters in Part 2 for introductions to the basic features of particular SAS/FSP procedures.
	When you are ready to learn how to develop applications for your own use or for others, see Part 3 for an introduction to that process.
experience with an earlier release of SAS/FSP software	Begin by reading "Changes and Enhancements" for a list of features that are new or changed from the version of SAS/FSP software you used previously.
	Scan the tables of contents for the chapters in Parts 2 and 3 to locate the areas of the usage material that discuss new or changed features and read those sections.
all experience levels	Refer to Parts 4 and 5 whenever you need to see a list of the available statements, options, and commands; to check the exact syntax of a statement, option, or command; or to learn how the various commands and statement options interact.

Reference Aids

SAS/FSP Software: Usage and Reference includes a variety of features to help you locate the information you need. The following sections at the front and back of this book provide information about special SAS/FSP software topics:

Changes and Enhancements

provides information about features of SAS/FSP software that have been added or modified since Release 5.18.

Glossary

provides definitions of SAS/FSP terms and general SAS terms used in the book.

Index

provides a cross-reference of the pages where specific topics, procedures, statements, commands, or options are discussed.

The chapters in Part 4, "Reference: SAS/FSP Software Procedures," have a uniform structure that makes information easy to find. The following list shows the elements of this structure. Some elements may appear more than once.

Note: In the following list, FS*XXXX* can be replaced with the name of a SAS/FSP software procedure and *YYYY* can be replaced with the name of a subsidiary statement for that procedure.

Overview

provides a brief description of the types of tasks that can be performed using the procedure.

This element also includes a "Terminology" section that lists any special terms that appear in the chapter. These terms are defined in the Glossary.

FS*XXXX* Procedure Syntax

provides the following information:

- the syntax of the PROC statement for the procedure

- the syntax for any subsidiary statements that can be used in conjunction with the PROC statement

- brief descriptions of each statement

- discussion of the information that must be specified when the procedure is invoked

- the syntax for the global command that can be used in lieu of the PROC statement.

PROC FS*XXXX* Statement

provides complete descriptions of all required arguments and all options for the procedure's PROC statement.

YYYY Statement   provides the following information:

    □ a description of the purpose of a subsidiary statement

    □ the complete syntax for the statement

    □ discussion of any restrictions on the use of the statement.

    This element is repeated for each subsidiary statement that can be used with the procedure.

FS*XXXX* Command   provides the following information:

    □ a description of the global command that can be used to invoke the procedure from any SAS System window

    □ the complete syntax for the command

    □ descriptions of all command arguments

    □ discussion of any restrictions on the use of the command.

Using the FS*XXXX* Procedure   provides descriptions of each window used in the procedures and of the commands that are valid in each window. For windows used to set parameters or attributes for the procedure, this section also includes descriptions of the parameters or attributes.

Definitions of statements, options, and commands in the reference chapters of this book are presented in alphabetical order.

The graphic on the inside front cover of this book provides a functional overview of the SAS System. The graphic on the inside back cover provides an overview of SAS/FSP software and of the uses of each procedure. You can use these graphics as aids in determining which SAS software products or SAS/FSP software procedures you should use to accomplish particular data management tasks.

Conventions

This section explains the various conventions used in presenting text, SAS language syntax, command execution, and file and library references in this book. The following terms are used in the discussions of procedure syntax:

keyword   is a literal that is a primary part of the SAS language. Keywords in this book are procedure names, statement names, and command names.

argument   is an element that follows a keyword. It may be either a literal or user-supplied. It has a built-in value or accepts a value assignment. Arguments that you must use are *required arguments*. Other arguments are *optional arguments*, or simply *options*.

value   is an element that follows an equal sign in an argument and provides a value for the argument. It may be either literal or user-supplied.

Typographical Conventions

You will see several type styles used in this book. The following list explains the meaning of each style:

roman   is used for most text in this book.

UPPERCASE ROMAN   is used for SAS statements, commands, variable names, and other SAS language elements when they appear in the text. However, you can enter these elements in your own SAS code in lowercase, uppercase, or a mixture of the two.

italic   is used for generic terms that represent values you supply. Italic is also used for special terms defined in the text or in the glossary.

monospace   is used for examples of SAS program code and commands. Monospace is also used for character values when they appear in text.

Syntax Conventions

Type styles have special meanings when used in the presentation of SAS/FSP procedure syntax in this book. The following list explains the style conventions for the syntax sections:

UPPERCASE BOLD   identifies SAS keywords such as the names of statements and procedures.

UPPERCASE ROMAN   identifies command names, arguments, and literal values that must be spelled exactly as shown (although they do not necessarily have to be entered in uppercase).

italic   identifies arguments or values that you supply. Italic is also used for generic terms that represent classes of arguments.

The following symbols are used to indicate other syntax conventions:

⟨ ⟩ (angle brackets)   identify optional arguments. Any argument not enclosed in angle brackets is required.

| (vertical bar)   indicates that you can choose one argument or value from a group. Items separated by bars are either mutually exclusive or aliases.

. . . (ellipsis)   indicates that the argument or value following the ellipsis can be repeated any number of times.

The following example illustrates these syntax conventions:

PROC FSLETTER LETTER=*SAS-catalog*⟨*.catalog-entry*⟩
            ⟨DATA=*data-set*⟩
            ⟨PRINTFILE=*fileref* | '*actual-filename*'⟩;

☐ **PROC FSLETTER** is in bold uppercase because it a SAS keyword, the name of a statement. The remaining elements are arguments for this statement.

☐ LETTER= is not enclosed in angle brackets because it is a required argument. It is in uppercase to indicate that it must be spelled as shown.

☐ *SAS-catalog* is in italic because it represents a value that you supply. In this case, the value must be the name of a SAS catalog.

☐ *.catalog-entry* is enclosed in angle brackets because it is optional.

☐ The DATA= and PRINTFILE= arguments are enclosed in angle brackets because they are also optional. Optional arguments are called simply options.

☐ The *fileref* and *actual-filename* values are separated by a vertical bar to indicate that they are mutually exclusive. You must choose one or the other. If you use *actual-filename*, it must be enclosed in quotes. (Notice that the quotes are not italic.)

☐ The ending semicolon (;) is outside the angle brackets for the PRINTFILE= argument because it is required to mark the end of the PROC FSLETTER statement.

Here is another example:

STRING ⟨*variable* ⟨. . . *variable-n*⟩⟩

☐ STRING is in uppercase because it is a command name. Notice that the names of the commands used in SAS/FSP windows are not shown in boldface (except for the global commands that invoke SAS/FSP procedures).

☐ All the arguments for the STRING command are enclosed in angle brackets because all arguments for this command are optional. (The STRING command can be used alone, with no arguments.)

□ *variable* and *variable-n* are in italic because they represent values that you supply. In this case, the value must be the name of a variable.

□ The *variable-n* value is enclosed in angle brackets because it is optional, but the ellipsis (. . .) before the value indicates that, if it is used, it can be repeated as many times as desired. For example, the following STRING commands are all valid (assuming that the specified variables exist):

```
string var1
string var1 var2
string var1 var2 var3 var4
```

Windowing Systems

In this book, displays show SAS/FSP windows as they appear in the default SAS Display Manager System. The displays were produced using Release 6.06 of the SAS System in the MVS environment using a 3270-class terminal with a 24-line display. What you see on your display may look different, depending on what windowing system you are using and whether you use the PMENU facility.

Choice of Windowing Systems

Under some operating systems, you have the choice of running the default display manager or running it as part of a different windowing system. The following display shows the default display manager; the following figure shows the display manager in the DECwindows™ windowing system that is available on the VMS™ operating system.

SAS Display Manager System Windows

```
┌LOG──────────────────────────────────────────────────────┐
│ Command ===>                                             │
│                                                          │
│                                                          │
│                                                          │
│                                                          │
│                                                          │
│                                                          │
│                                                          │
│                                                          │
└──────────────────────────────────────────────────────────┘
┌PROGRAM EDITOR───────────────────────────────────────────┐
│ Command ===>                                             │
│                                                          │
│ 00001                                                    │
│ 00002                                                    │
│ 00003                                                    │
│ 00004                                                    │
│ 00005                                                    │
│ 00006                                                    │
└──────────────────────────────────────────────────────────┘
```

DECwindows and VMS are trademarks of Digital Equipment Corporation.

Display Manager Windows in DECwindows

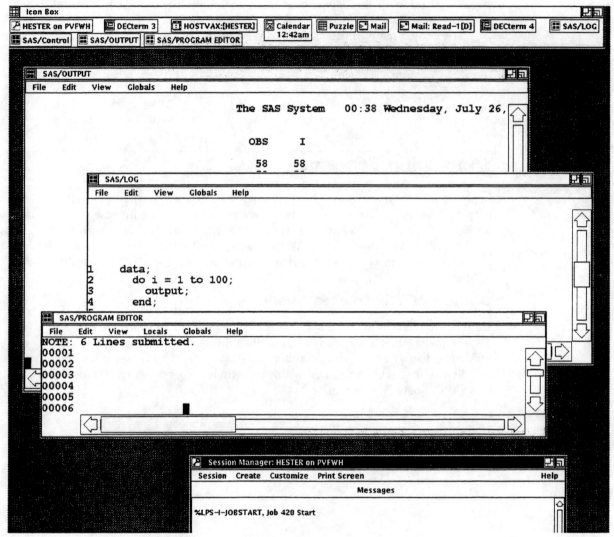

As the labels show, the command line may be in a different place, and there may be different tools available for scrolling, moving, and sizing the windows. Consult your host operating system documentation for more details.

The PMENU Facility

The PMENU facility substitutes a set of pull-down menus for the command line in each window. Refer to Chapter 19 for more details about the PMENU facility.

Command Execution

Most of the command examples in this book assume that you execute the command by typing the command on the window's command line and pressing ENTER. However, if the PMENU facility is active, an action bar of menu items is presented in place of the command line. Refer to Chapter 19 for information on how you can use action bars and pull-down menus to execute commands. You can also assign commonly used commands to function keys. In general, when this book instructs you to issue a given command, any of the following alternatives are equally valid:

□ Type the command on the command line and press ENTER.

□ Locate and select the menu item that corresponds to the command.

□ Press the function key to which the command has been assigned.

If your terminal or workstation supports a mouse or other pointing device, you can use that in lieu of the keyboard's cursor keys to move the cursor in SAS/FSP windows. Wherever this book instructs you to press ENTER, you can press the mouse button instead.

References to Libraries and Files

The examples in this book do not specify actual names for the file structures used for SAS data libraries or for external (non-SAS) files. This is because different operating systems and different computing installations use different conventions for naming files and directories. Instead, the examples refer to storage locations generically. For example, a LIBNAME statement to assign the libref STORE is shown as

```
libname store 'location';
```

For *location*, you should supply the complete specification for the storage location of the data library (for example, directory, MVS data set, or CMS minidisk), using the form required by your operating system.

If you are unsure of the requirements at your site, see your SAS Software Consultant for more information.

Information You Need

This section provides a place to record important information you need to use the SAS System effectively at your site. You should gather the information in this section before you attempt to use the examples in this book.

Support Personnel

Record the name of the SAS Software Consultant and system administrator at your site in the space provided. Also, record the names of anyone else you regularly turn to for help with problems you encounter while using SAS/FSP software.

SAS Software Consultant: _____ Phone: _____

Other systems personnel: _____ Phone: _____

_____ Phone: _____

_____ Phone: _____

_____ Phone: _____

Printers

You need to know the type and system destination of printers available at your site before you can use some of the examples in this book. Ask your SAS Software Consultant or system administrator what printers are available at your site. For future reference, record this information in the space provided.

Printer type: _____ Destination: _____ Location: _____

Printer type: _____ Destination: _____ Location: _____

Printer type: _____ Destination: _____ Location: _____

Printer type: _____ Destination: _____ Location: _____

Sample Library

Although most examples in this book are short enough to be easily entered, the source code for longer examples is provided in the SAS Sample Library. The sample library is provided to each site along with the SAS System.

The naming convention for sample library members is FU*cc*N*nn*, where *cc* is the chapter number and *nn* is the example number. For example, the code to create the example data set in Chapter 1 is stored in member FU01N01.

If you use the SAS Display Manager System, you can use the INCLUDE command to bring the source code into the display manager PROGRAM EDITOR window. Refer to Chapter 18, "Display Manager Commands," in *SAS Language: Reference* for more information about using the INCLUDE command.

Ask your SAS Software Consultant for the location of the SAS Sample Library at your site. For your reference, record the location in the space provided.

Sample Library location: _____

Additional Documentation

SAS Institute provides many publications about SAS System products. For a complete list of available publications, refer to the current issue of the SAS Institute *Publications Catalog*. The catalog is published twice yearly. You can obtain a free copy of the catalog by writing to the following address:

SAS Institute Inc.
Book Sales Department
SAS Campus Drive
Cary, NC 27513

The following publications update the information in *SAS/FSP Software: Usage and Reference* for versions subsequent to Release 6.06:

☐ SAS Technical Report P-216, *SAS/AF Software, SAS/FSP Software, and SAS Screen Control Language: Changes and Enhancements, Release 6.07* (order #A59133) provides information about the features of SAS/FSP software and SAS Screen Control Language that were added or modified in Release 6.07 of the SAS System.

☐ SAS Technical Report P-242, *SAS Software: Changes and Enhancements, Release 6.08* (order #A59159) provides information about the features of SAS/FSP software and SAS Screen Control Language that were added or modified in Release 6.08 of the SAS System.

In addition to *SAS/FSP Software: Usage and Reference*, you will find these other documents helpful when using SAS/FSP software:

☐ *SAS Introductory Guide, Third Edition* (order #A5685) provides information if you are unfamiliar with the SAS System or any other programming language.

☐ *SAS Language: Reference, Version 6, First Edition* (order #A56076) provides detailed reference information about SAS language statements, functions, formats, and informats; the SAS Display Manager System; the SAS text editor; or any other element of base SAS software except for procedures.

☐ *SAS Procedures Guide, Version 6, Third Edition* (order #A56080) provides detailed reference information about the procedures in base SAS software.

☐ *SAS Language and Procedures: Usage, Version 6, First Edition* (order #A56075) provides task-oriented examples of the major features of base SAS software.

- *SAS Screen Control Language: Reference, Version 6, First Edition* (order #A56030) provides detailed reference information about the statements, functions, and other elements of Screen Control Language, including the SCL debugger.

- *SAS Screen Control Language: Usage, Version 6, First Edition* (order #A56031) provides detailed conceptual and tutorial information about Screen Control Language, including the SCL debugger.

- *SAS/AF Software: Usage and Reference, Version 6, First Edition* (order #A56011) provides tutorial and reference information about the applications development facilities available in SAS/AF software.

- *SAS/GRAPH Software: Reference, Version 6, First Edition* (order #A56020) provides detailed reference information about the graphical presentation facilities available in SAS/GRAPH software.

- *SAS/ACCESS Interface to DB2: Usage and Reference, Version 6, First Edition* (order #A56060)
  SAS/ACCESS Interface to ORACLE: Usage and Reference, Version 6, First Edition (order #A56061)
  SAS/ACCESS Interface to Rdb/VMS: Usage and Reference, Version 6, First Edition (order #A56062)
  SAS/ACCESS Interface to SQL/DS: Usage and Reference, Version 6, First Edition (order #A56063)

  These interface guides provide tutorial and reference information about the facilities that allow database management system tables to be viewed as SAS data sets.

- *SAS Guide to the SQL Procedure: Usage and Reference, Version 6, First Edition* (order #A56070) provides tutorial and reference information about the Structured Query Language facility in Release 6.06 of the SAS System.

- The SAS companion or other SAS documentation for your operating system provides information about the operating-system-specific features of the SAS System under your operating system.

Changes and Enhancements

Introduction

This section lists the major changes and enhancements made to SAS/FSP software since Release 5.18. It is intended for users who have previous experience with SAS/FSP software. If you are a new user of the SAS System, you may skip this section.

Note: Although this section does not separately identify which of the changes and enhancements were available in Release 6.03, it does point out which Release 6.03 features are no longer valid in Release 6.06.

Overview of Changed or Enhanced Features

Version 6 SAS/FSP software contains many new features including

□ a windowing environment for executing SAS/FSP procedures

□ global commands for invoking SAS/FSP procedures from any SAS System window

□ global commands shared by all SAS/FSP procedures

□ the capability to specify SAS data set options with any procedure argument that takes a SAS data set name

□ the capability to route messages generated by SAS/FSP procedures to the MESSAGE window rather than to the SAS log

□ full integration of the SAS text editor with the FSLETTER window

□ a new procedure, FSVIEW, that replaces the FSPRINT procedure and provides editing capabilities and the handling of computed variables

□ Screen Control Language, a powerful new programming language for driving FSBROWSE, FSEDIT, and FSVIEW applications.

Two of the procedures in Version 5 SAS/FSP software are not available in Release 6.06:

□ The FSCALC procedure will be available in a later release of the SAS System.

□ The FSCON procedure is obsolete. This procedure converted special screen and letter data sets from earlier versions of SAS/FSP software into Version 5 catalog entries. The Version 6 facility for converting Version 5 catalog entries into Version 6 catalog entries is the V5TOV6 procedure in base SAS software. Refer to the *SAS Procedures Guide, Version 6, Third Edition* for details.

The following sections provide details of the changes and enhancements to the individual procedures in SAS/FSP software.

The FSBROWSE and FSEDIT Procedures

The behavior of the FSEDIT and FSBROWSE procedures in Version 6 differs from Version 5 in the following ways. For complete details, see Chapter 12, "The FSBROWSE Procedure," and Chapter 13, "The FSEDIT Procedure."

□ The FSBROWSE and FSEDIT procedures can read and update Version 5 SAS data sets without conversion. However, the format for catalog entries has changed. As a result, you must use the V5TOV6 procedure in base SAS software to convert Version 5 screen entries into Version 6 screen entries before you can use them with the Version 6 FSBROWSE and FSEDIT procedures.

□ The PROC FSBROWSE and PROC FSEDIT statements now accept the following additional options:

DEBUG	turns on the Screen Control Language debugger facility.
KEYS=	selects a specific set of function key definitions for the session.
MODIFY	opens the FSBROWSE Menu or FSEDIT Menu window when the procedure begins.
NC=	specifies the width (in columns) of the FSBROWSE or FSEDIT window.
STCOL=	selects the display column for the left margin of the FSBROWSE or FSEDIT window.
STROW=	selects the display row for the top margin of the FSBROWSE or FSEDIT window.

□ The Version 5 DDNAME= option has been renamed PRINTFILE=. (DDNAME= is still accepted as an alias for PRINTFILE=.)

□ The Release 6.03 CMENU option is no longer valid in the PROC FSBROWSE or PROC FSEDIT statements. Use the global PMENU command to turn on menus in Release 6.06.

□ WHERE statements can now be used in conjunction with PROC FSBROWSE and PROC FSEDIT statements to view subsets of the input data set.

□ The following new commands are available in the FSBROWSE and FSEDIT windows:

OVERRIDE	overrides error conditions so that observations can be stored even if they contain values outside the allowed range or lack values for required fields.
WHERE	restricts processing of the input data set to only those observations that meet specified criteria.

□ The LETTER command now replaces the Version 5 CATALOG command. (In Version 6, CATALOG is a global command to open the display manager CATALOG window.)

□ When a search command (FIND, FIND@, LOCATE, LOCATE:, SEARCH, or SEARCH@) fails to find a match, the last observation in the data set is now displayed. In Version 5, the procedure remained at the observation from which the search command was issued.

□ The ADD and DUP commands in the FSEDIT procedure no longer automatically add the new observation to the data set. Observations created by these commands are not added to the data set until you move to another observation, issue a SAVE command, or end the procedure. You can use the CANCEL command to cancel the new observation before it is added to the data set.

□ The FSBROWSE and FSEDIT windows have a border, so their text area is slightly narrower than the FSBROWSE and FSEDIT screens in Version 5. For example, fields in a Version 5 FSEDIT screen could occupy up to 79 columns of an 80-column display, while fields in an 80-column FSEDIT window in Version 6 can be no more than 76 columns wide. Any Version 5 screen entries that use more columns than are allowed in Version 6 must be modified before the Version 6 procedures can use them.

□ Field identification is no longer available as a separate option in the modification menu. It is still available as a step of the display modification process (option 2).

□ In the FSBROWSE Identify or FSEDIT Identify window, the UNWANTED command replaces the Version 5 HOME command, and the WANTED command replaces the Version 5 FREE command.

□ Three new field attributes are available:

JUSTIFY   determines how values are positioned in the field.

NONDISPLAY   makes values entered in the field invisible.

NOAUTOSKIP   prevents the cursor from automatically skipping to the next field when the current field is filled.

Also, the Version 5 field attributes COLOR and ATTR have been renamed FCOLOR and FATTR.

□ A new programming language, Screen Control Language (SCL), is now available to drive FSBROWSE and FSEDIT applications. SCL provides a rich set of functions and statements that give you complete control over the user's interaction with the procedure. SCL programs are entered in the FSBROWSE Program or FSEDIT Program window, which can be opened from the modification menu for either browsing or editing.

□ The general parameters for FSBROWSE and FSEDIT sessions have been enhanced:

□ Color and highlighting attributes can be assigned to more areas of the display.

□ Applications developers can control users' ability to override errors with the OVERRIDE command.

□ Specific sets of function key definitions can be assigned to the FSBROWSE or FSEDIT application.

The FSLETTER Procedure

The behavior of the FSLETTER procedure in Version 6 differs from Version 5 in the following ways. For complete details, see Chapter 14, "The FSLETTER Procedure."

☐ Because of a change in catalog structure, the Version 6 FSLETTER procedure cannot read Version 5 letter or form entries. Before you can use Version 5 catalog entries, you must convert them to Version 6 entries using the V5TOV6 procedure in base SAS software.

   Note: When you convert Version 5 letter entries to Version 6 format, convert the associated form entries for the documents also. (By default, the V5TOV6 procedure converts all entry types in a catalog.) If you have forms stored in your Version 5 SASUSER.PROFILE catalog, convert those forms to Version 6 format before converting any letter entries that use those forms.

☐ The PROC FSLETTER statement now accepts the following additional option:

   DATA=   specifies a SAS data set used to automatically fill the fields in your documents. A separate copy of the document is created for each observation in the data set.

☐ The Version 5 option DDNAME= has been renamed PRINTFILE=. (DDNAME= is still accepted as an alias for PRINTFILE=.)

☐ The following Version 5 options are no longer valid in the PROC FSLETTER statement:

   CPRO=
   CUNPRO=

☐ The Release 6.03 CMENU option is no longer valid in the PROC FSLETTER statement. Use the global PMENU command to turn on menus in Release 6.06.

☐ The FSLETTER window now uses the SAS text editor exclusively; you no longer use the EDIT command to switch between FSLETTER text editing and the SAS text editor. As a result, the following Version 5 FSLETTER editing commands are no longer valid:

   CHI
   CPRO
   CUN
   DASH
   DELETE
   HIGHLITE
   INSERT
   MOVE

☐ You can now set text editor parameters that control your editing environment for each individual letter. You can also define default editor parameters for an entire catalog or for all catalogs. This default information is stored in a new catalog entry type called EDPARMS. You create and edit EDPARMS entries in the FSLETTER window.

☐ The spelling checker feature of the SAS text editor can be used to check the correctness of your documents.

☐ The following new commands are available in the FSLETTER window:

DATA   opens a SAS data set for filling fields in the document when the SEND command is issued.

CLOSE   closes the data set opened by the DATA command.

WHERE   specifies conditions that observations in the data set opened with the DATA command must meet in order to be used.

☐ The EDIT command now opens additional FSLETTER windows, so you can now display more than one document or form at a time.

☐ The SEND command has been enhanced. It now provides options for selecting a data set to fill fields in the document and for specifying a print file destination.
   Also, the print queue or print file is now freed automatically when the FSLETTER SEND window is closed. You no longer need to use the FREE command to explicitly free FSLETTER documents. (This may change in future releases.)

☐ A new field attribute, FLOW LINE, is available. This attribute flows the text on a single line.

☐ The color and highlighting attributes of fields are now specified in the document text itself rather than in the FSLETTER ATTR window.

☐ Forms are now an element of base SAS software, although you can still create and modify FORM entries from the FSLETTER procedure. Complete information on creating and editing forms is now in *SAS Language: Reference, Version 6, First Edition* rather than in this book.

The FSLIST Procedure

The behavior of the FSLIST procedure in Version 6 differs from Version 5 in the following ways. For complete details, see Chapter 15, "The FSLIST Procedure."

☐ The procedure now lets you browse external files with variable-length records, as well as files containing the native carriage-control characters of the host operating system.

☐ You can now identify the file to browse by its actual filename as well as with a fileref.

☐ The PROC FSLIST statement now accepts the following additional options:

CC | FORTCC | NOCC   controls the type of carriage-control information recognized by the procedure.
　　　　　　　　　　　Note: The Release 6.03 CC option is equivalent to the Release 6.06 FORTCC option.

OVP | NOOVP   controls whether the procedure honors control codes for overprinting lines.

☐ The following Version 5 options are no longer valid in the PROC FSLIST statement:

CMD | NOCMD
CPROTECT=
PAGE=

☐ The following Release 6.03 options are no longer valid in the PROC FSLIST statement:

CMENU
LINESIZE=
PAGESIZE=

☐ The following new commands are available in the FSLIST window:

BFIND   searches for a specified string from the current cursor position toward the top of the file.

BROWSE   closes the current file and displays another external file without closing the FSLIST window.

COLUMN   displays a column ruler at the top of the FSLIST window.

HEX   displays the file contents in hexadecimal format.

NUMS   turns line numbering on or off.

VSCROLL   sets the default vertical scrolling increment.

☐ The following Version 5 commands are no longer valid in the FSLIST window:

CMD
CURSOR
ECHO

The FSVIEW Procedure

The FSVIEW procedure replaces the FSPRINT procedure in earlier releases of SAS/FSP software. The FSVIEW procedure provides the capabilities of the FSPRINT procedure but also allows you to edit and sort SAS data sets. The FSVIEW procedure gives you more control over the display of the data set than the FSPRINT procedure allowed, and it allows you to open multiple FSVIEW windows. You can also use the FSVIEW procedure to create new empty SAS data sets as well as complete or partial copies of the displayed SAS data set.

Note: For compatibility with existing programs, the PROC FSPRINT statement is accepted as an alias for PROC FSVIEW.

In addition to data set variables, the FSVIEW procedure can display *computed variables*. The values for computed variables are calculated from SAS expressions called *formulas*. Formulas can also include Screen Control Language functions and statements (except for those that are valid only in SAS/AF entries). You can use SCL in FSVIEW formulas to manipulate the FSVIEW window and to control the user's interaction with the FSVIEW application.

Formulas are stored in *formula entries*, which are SAS catalog entries with the new type FORMULA. Formula entries also store other information about the FSVIEW session, including

☐ the size, position, and colors of the FSVIEW window

☐ the names and order of the variables displayed in the FSVIEW window

☐ general parameters such as the current HSCROLL and VSCROLL settings.

With the addition of these new features, the FSVIEW procedure can serve as the basis for data entry or presentation applications as well as a tool for browsing data sets.

The behavior of the FSVIEW procedure differs from that of the Version 5 FSPRINT procedure in the following ways. For complete details, see Chapter 16, "The FSVIEW Procedure."

☐ The PROC FSVIEW statement accepts the following additional options:

AUTOADD	adds a new blank observation automatically each time the previous new observation is filled.
BROWSEONLY	prevents editing of the displayed data set.
DEBUG	turns on the Screen Control Language debugger, which can be used in debugging formulas.
EDIT | MODIFY	opens the FSVIEW window for editing rather than for browsing.
FORMULA=	names the formula entry associated with the data set.
LIKE=	names an existing data set used as a template when creating a new blank data set.
NEW=	opens the FSVIEW NEW window for creating a new blank data set when the procedure begins.
NOADD	prevents adding observations to the displayed data set.
NODELETE	prevents deleting observations from the displayed data set.
NOMSG	routes procedure messages to the SAS log rather than to the MESSAGE window.

☐ The following Version 5 options are not valid in the PROC FSVIEW statement:

CPRO=
CUNPRO=

□   The Release 6.03 CMENU option is not valid in the PROC FSVIEW
    statement. Use the global PMENU command to turn on menus in Release
    6.06.

□   WHERE statements can now be used in conjunction with the PROC FSVIEW
    statement to view subsets of the input data set.

□   The following new commands are available in the FSVIEW window:

AUTOADD	creates a new blank observation automatically each time the previous new observation is added to the data set.
AUTOSAVE	sets the frequency with which the procedure automatically saves changed observations.
BROWSE	opens additional FSVIEW windows for browsing.
CREATE	creates a new data set containing some or all of the variables (and variable values) in the displayed data set.
DEFINE	defines the formulas and attributes for computed variables.
DELETE	deletes observations from the displayed data set.
DROP	removes variable columns from the FSVIEW window.
DUP	creates new copies of existing observations.
EDIT	opens additional FSVIEW windows for editing.
FORMAT	assigns formats to variable columns.
FORMULA	loads an existing formula entry.
INFORMAT	assigns informats to variable columns.
INITIAL	selects an existing observation to provide default values for autoadded observations.
MODIFY	changes the FSVIEW window from browsing to editing.
MOVE	rearranges the order of variable columns in the FSVIEW window.
NEW	opens the FSVIEW NEW window for creating a new blank data set.
PARMS	opens the FSVIEW Parameters window for setting general parameters of the FSVIEW session.
PROTECT	prevents changes to the values in one or more variable columns.
RENAME	renames variable columns in the FSVIEW window.
RESET	erases some or all of the current formula definitions.
REVIEW	opens the FSVIEW REVIEW window to display current formula definitions.

SAVE	saves changed observations to the data set.
SAVE FORMULA	saves current formula definitions and FSVIEW parameter settings to the specified formula entry.
SETWSZ	records the current size and position of the FSVIEW window.
SHOW	adds variable columns to the FSVIEW window.
SORT	sorts the displayed data set.
WHERE	restricts processing to only those observations that meet specified criteria.

In addition, the behavior of the CURSOR command has changed. In Version 5 the CURSOR command moved the cursor to the command line. In Version 6 it specifies the variable column where the cursor is initially positioned when a new observation is autoadded.

☐ The following Version 5 FSPRINT procedure commands are not valid in the FSVIEW window:

BODY
ID
NAME

Note: In Version 6, colors are set with the global COLOR command or in the FSVIEW Parameters window.

xl

Part 1

Introduction to SAS/FSP® Software

Chapter 1   **Introduction to SAS/FSP® Software**

Chapter 1 Introduction to SAS/FSP® Software

Introduction

The procedures in SAS/FSP software provide convenient interactive facilities for data entry, editing, and retrieval. Using SAS/FSP software you can

□ browse and edit the contents of SAS data sets

□ enter data into existing SAS data sets

□ create new SAS data sets

□ browse and edit SAS data views created with SAS/ACCESS software

□ browse SAS data views created with the SQL procedure in base SAS software

□ create, edit, and print form letters and reports

□ browse the contents of files external to the SAS System

□ build and customize end-user applications.

If your device has color and highlighting capabilities, SAS/FSP software can take advantage of these.

SAS/FSP Procedures

Table 1.1 shows the procedures included in Release 6.06 of SAS/FSP software.

Table 1.1
Procedures in
Release 6.06 of
SAS/FSP Software

Procedure	Uses
FSBROWSE	Displaying the contents of SAS data sets one observation at a time
	Displaying the contents of SAS data views one row at a time
	Building custom end-user data presentation applications
FSEDIT	Displaying, entering, and changing data values in SAS data sets one observation at a time
	Displaying, entering, and changing data values in SAS/ACCESS views one row at a time
	Creating new SAS data sets
	Building custom end-user data entry applications
FSLETTER	Creating, editing, and printing form letters and reports
FSLIST	Browsing external (non-SAS) files, including files containing SAS source lines or output from SAS procedures
FSVIEW *	Browsing or editing SAS data sets displayed in tabular format
	Browsing or editing SAS/ACCESS views displayed in tabular format
	Browsing PROC SQL views displayed in tabular format
	Creating new SAS data sets
	Building custom end-user data entry applications

* The FSVIEW procedure in Release 6.06 replaces the FSPRINT procedure in earlier releases of SAS/FSP software.

In addition to the facilities of each procedure used individually, you can also use the FSEDIT or FSBROWSE procedures in conjunction with the FSLETTER procedure to customize form letters and reports with information from a SAS data set. For example, you can generate personalized letters using names and addresses from a SAS data set.

Important SAS Software Concepts

The remainder of this introduction briefly presents some basic SAS software concepts used in the procedure descriptions in this book. Complete details are given in *SAS Language: Reference, Version 6, First Edition.*

SAS Data Libraries

The SAS System uses specially structured files called *SAS files*. All SAS files reside in *SAS data libraries*. The SAS data library is the highest level of file organization used by the SAS System. The SAS System places no restrictions on the type or number of SAS files that can be stored in a SAS data library, although your operating system may impose some restrictions.

To use a SAS data library, you must link a storage location on your system with a nickname called a *libref*. The physical structure of the storage location varies according to the operating system under which the SAS System runs. For example, under directory-based operating systems, the storage location is a directory. Under the MVS operating system, the storage location is an MVS data set. Under the CMS operating system, the storage location is defined by a particular filetype on a minidisk.

The LIBNAME statement links librefs with storage locations. For example, the libref MYLIB is defined with a statement of the form

```
libname mylib 'location';
```

where *location* is the complete specification for the storage location as defined by your operating system (called the fully qualified pathname on some systems).

The complete name of any SAS file begins with the libref of the data library in which the file resides. At least one SAS data library, the default library with the libref WORK, is always allocated when a SAS session is started. If you omit the libref in a SAS filename specification, the default libref WORK is used.

See Chapter 6, "SAS Files," in *SAS Language: Reference* for more information on SAS data libraries and librefs.

Access to SAS Libraries

The Multiple Engine Architecture implemented in Release 6.06 of SAS software provides a variety of access methods, or *engines*, for accessing files in SAS data libraries. Engines allow you to access data libraries that contain data sets from older versions of the SAS System as well as data libraries written in special formats.

Some aspects of SAS/FSP procedure behavior depend on the engine used to access the file. For example, some engines do not support access by observation number, so commands to move to specific observations do not work for data sets accessed with these engines. Such restrictions are noted in this book.

See Chapter 6 in *SAS Language: Reference* for more information on SAS engines.

SAS Data Sets

A *SAS data set* is a SAS file that allows the SAS System to access stored data as rows of observations and columns of variables. SAS data sets include *SAS data files*, which physically contain the information in this form, and *SAS data views*, which contain directions that allow the SAS System to access information from other files as if it was stored in this form.

Most SAS procedures manipulate SAS data sets in one way or another. The following SAS/FSP procedures use SAS data sets:

□ The FSBROWSE procedure displays values from a SAS data set, one observation at a time, for browsing only.

□ The FSEDIT procedure displays values from a SAS data set, one observation at a time, for editing. It also allows you to add observations to the data set and delete observations from the data set.

□ The FSLETTER procedure can customize the text of a letter or report for each observation in a SAS data set.

□ The FSVIEW procedure displays values from a SAS data set as a table for browsing or editing. It also allows you to add observations to the data set and delete observations from the data set.

As you become familiar with SAS/FSP software, you will learn to create, list, and change data sets with appropriate SAS/FSP procedures.

SAS Data Files

A *SAS data file* is a file created by the SAS System to store your data. SAS data files reside in SAS data libraries and have the library member type DATA. They are created with the DATA step in base SAS software. Some SAS procedures can also create data files, including the FSEDIT and FSVIEW procedures in SAS/FSP software.

SAS data files are identified using two-level names of the form

libref.file-name

The first element, *libref*, specifies the SAS data library in which the data file resides. The second element, *file-name*, gives the name of the data file within the data library. If you omit the libref, SAS/FSP procedures use the default libref WORK (unless the libref USER has been defined, in which case that library is used by default).

See Chapter 6 in *SAS Language: Reference* for more information on SAS data files.

SAS Data Views

A *SAS data view* is a special type of SAS file that enables procedures to interpret another type of file as if it were a SAS data file. SAS data views reside in SAS data libraries and have the library member type VIEW. Release 6.06 of the SAS System supports two types of views:

□ views created using SAS/ACCESS software

□ views created using the SQL procedure in base SAS software.

SAS/ACCESS views are descriptor files that enable the SAS System to interpret the information in rows of a database management system (DBMS) table as if it were in observations of a SAS data set. Using SAS/ACCESS views, you can browse, edit, and otherwise use the underlying DBMS table as if it were a SAS data set. PROC SQL views are Structured Query Language (SQL) queries that are given names and stored for repeated use. The views can derive data from SAS data files, other PROC SQL views, or SAS/ACCESS views. However, unlike SAS/ACCESS views, PROC SQL views are read-only; you cannot update the information underlying the PROC SQL view.

SAS/FSP procedures that use SAS data files can also use SAS data views (except that the FSEDIT procedure cannot use PROC SQL views because they are read-only). Unless otherwise noted, SAS data view names can be specified for any option or command that lists *data-set* as a valid argument. For example, you can specify a view name as the argument for the DATA= option in any of the PROC statements that support that option.

SAS data views are identified using two-level names. The names have the form

  libref.view-name

The first element, *libref*, specifies the SAS data library in which the view resides. The second element, *view-name*, gives the name of the view within the data library. If you omit the libref, SAS/FSP procedures use the default libref WORK (unless the libref USER has been defined, in which case that library is used by default).

For additional information about SAS data views, refer to Chapter 6 in *SAS Language: Reference*. For complete details of PROC SQL views, see the *SAS Guide to the SQL Procedure: Usage and Reference, Version 6, First Edition*. For complete details of SAS/ACCESS views, see the SAS/ACCESS documentation (a separate document is provided for the SAS/ACCESS interface to each supported DBMS).

SAS Catalogs

A *SAS catalog* is a SAS file used to store another special class of data objects called SAS catalog entries. SAS catalogs reside in SAS data libraries and have the library member type CATALOG. SAS catalogs have a special structure; procedures do not use catalogs in the same way that they use SAS data sets.

Catalog entries are used to store a variety of utility information. Different types of information are stored in different types of catalog entries. Procedures that use catalogs generally require a particular type of catalog entry. This book discusses six catalog entry types used by SAS/FSP software. These types are listed in Table 1.2.

	Catalog Entry Type	Description	Documentation
Table 1.2 *Catalog Entry Types Used in SAS/FSP Software*	EDPARMS	text editor parameter settings	FSLETTER procedure
	FORM	instructions for printing FSLETTER procedure output and SPRINT pictures	*SAS Language: Reference*
	FORMULA	computed variable formulas and environment parameters created with the FSVIEW procedure	FSVIEW procedure

(continued)

	Catalog Entry		
Table 1.2 (continued)	**Type**	**Description**	**Documentation**
	KEYS	function key assignments	*SAS Language: Reference*
	LETTER	text created with the FSLETTER procedure	FSLETTER procedure
	SCREEN	custom features created with the FSEDIT or FSBROWSE procedures	FSEDIT procedure

SAS catalog entries are identified by four-level names of the form

libref.catalog-name.entry-name.entry-type

□ The first level, *libref*, identifies the SAS data library in which the catalog resides. SAS/FSP procedures that use catalog entries assume the default libref, WORK, if you omit this element of the name.

□ The second level, *catalog-name*, identifies the catalog within the SAS data library in which the catalog entry resides. SAS/FSP procedures that use catalog entries create a new catalog if you specify a catalog name that does not already exist.

□ The third level, *entry-name*, identifies the entry within the catalog.

□ The fourth level, *entry-type*, identifies the type of catalog entry. It is permissible to have two entries with the same entry name in one catalog if the two have different entry types. SAS/FSP procedures that use catalog entries assume a default entry type if you omit this element of the name. (The default type depends on the procedure.)

Although each type of catalog entry stores a different kind of information, different entry types can be stored in the same SAS catalog. See Chapter 6 in *SAS Language: Reference* for more information on SAS catalogs.

External Files

In addition to the special files created and managed by the SAS System, your operating system's file structure is used to store certain types of information. For example, *external* (non-SAS) *files* are used to store

□ lines of raw data

□ your SAS program statements

□ the SAS log

□ procedure output, including the contents of the SAS Display Manager System's OUTPUT window.

In SAS/FSP software, the FSLIST procedure lets you browse external files without leaving your SAS session. You can copy text from a file displayed in the FSLIST window into an FSLETTER window, NOTEPAD window, or any other window that uses the SAS text editor.

To use an external file with the SAS System, you identify it to your SAS session by its full name or, in some instances, by using a nickname called a *fileref*. Filerefs are assigned with the FILENAME statement. For example, the fileref MYFILE is defined with a statement of the form

```
filename myfile 'location';
```

where *location* is the complete file specification (fully qualified path and filename) for the file on your operating system. See *SAS Language: Reference* for more information on the FILENAME statement.

Example Data Set

Most of the examples in this book use a data set of magazine subscriber information named SUBSCRIB. If you want to create this data set to follow along with the examples in the book (before you learn to do this with the FSEDIT or FSVIEW procedures), execute the SAS statements below.

In the LIBNAME statement, replace *location* with the proper operating system specification for the permanent SAS data library in which you want to store the data set.

Note: The source code for this example is available in member FU01N01 of the SAS/FSP sample library. See "Using This Book" for information on accessing the SAS/FSP sample library at your site.

```
libname master 'location';

data master.subscrib;
    input fullname $25.
          #2 addr1 $25.
          #3 addr2 $25.
          #4 begdate monyy5. +1 yrs 1. +1 new $1.;
    informat begdate monyy5.;
    format begdate monyy5.;
    cards;
Adams, Ms. Debra
1414 S. 20th St.
Arlington, VA 22202
APR89 2 0
Bailey, Mr. Mark
2721 1/2 Van Dyke
Logan, UT 84322
MAR90 2 1
Bertram, Ms. Mary
701 Catawba
Raleigh, NC 27609
AUG89 2 0
Carroll, Mr. Herman
6122-A Smithdale Dr.
```

```
Raleigh, NC 27606
OCT88 2 0
Dilley, Mr. Matthew
420 Polk St.
Ithaca, NY 14853
MAY87 5 0
Marvin, Ms. June
Route 7, Box 482
Durham, NC 27714
AUG90 1 0
Stiller, Mr. Allan
Route 2, Box 22-B
Moyock, NC 27958
JAN90 1 1
Vance, Ms. Martha
424-204 Navaho Dr.
Raleigh, NC 27609
NOV89 1 1
Womble, Mr. Kenneth
702-F Walden Dr.
Wilmington, NC 28401
FEB90 1 1
Ziller, Mr. Paul
P.O. Box 94
Burlington, CA 90406
MAY90 3 0
;
run;

proc print data=master.subscrib;
run;
```

Output 1.1 shows the data set as printed by the PRINT procedure.

Output 1.1
SAS Data Set for
Examples

```
                                                                    1
              F
              U
              L
              L       A                       A            B
              N       D                       D            E
   O          A       D                       D            G
   B          M       R                       R            A Y N
   S          E       1                       2            T R E
                                                           E S W

   1 Adams, Ms. Debra   1414 S. 20th St.      Arlington, VA 22202  APR89 2 0
   2 Bailey, Mr. Mark   2721 1/2 Van Dyke     Logan, UT 84322      MAR90 2 1
   3 Bertram, Ms. Mary  701 Catawba           Raleigh, NC 27609    AUG89 2 0
   4 Carroll, Mr. Herman 6122-A Smithdale Dr. Raleigh, NC 27606    OCT88 2 0
   5 Dilley, Mr. Matthew 420 Polk St.         Ithaca, NY 14853     MAY87 5 0
   6 Marvin, Ms. June   Route 7, Box 482      Durham, NC 27714     AUG90 1 0
   7 Stiller, Mr. Allan Route 2, Box 22-B     Moyock, NC 27958     JAN90 1 1
   8 Vance, Ms. Martha  424-204 Navaho Dr.    Raleigh, NC 27609    NOV89 1 1
   9 Womble, Mr. Kenneth 702-F Walden Dr.     Wilmington, NC 28401 FEB90 1 1
  10 Ziller, Mr. Paul   P.O. Box 94           Burlington, CA 90406 MAY90 3 0
```

Part 2
Usage: Users' Tools

Chapter **2** Overview: Part 2

Introduction

Many of the most common data management tasks you perform with base SAS software can be accomplished more easily in the interactive environment provided by SAS/FSP software, including

☐ reviewing the contents of SAS data files and SAS data views

☐ editing and updating SAS data files and SAS data views
   Note: Only SAS data views created using SAS/ACCESS software can be edited.

☐ creating new SAS data files.

Chapters 3 through 6 show you how to use SAS/FSP procedures for all of these tasks, as well as for

☐ creating personalized form letters and reports

☐ browsing external files.

Other features of SAS/FSP software are more useful for applications developers. For example, SAS/FSP software provides tools for creating custom data entry applications. These features are explained in Part 3, Chapters 7 through 10.

For detailed reference information on SAS/FSP software, turn to Parts 4 and 5, Chapters 11 through 20.

Selecting the Proper SAS/FSP Procedure

Table 2.1 tells you which SAS/FSP procedure to select to accomplish a given task. It also directs you to the chapter that illustrates each procedure.

Table 2.1	Task	Solutions
Procedure Selection Guidelines: Users' Tools	Review the contents of an existing SAS data set	Use the FSBROWSE procedure to display observations one at a time. See Chapter 3 for details.
		Use the FSVIEW procedure to display observations in a tabular format. See Chapter 4 for details.
	Edit or add observations in an existing SAS data file or in a SAS data view created with SAS/ACCESS software	Use the FSEDIT procedure to interactively edit or update one observation at a time. See Chapter 3 for details.
		Use the FSVIEW procedure to interactively edit or update observations displayed as a table of rows and columns. See Chapter 4 for details.
	Create a new SAS data file	Use either the FSEDIT procedure or the FSVIEW procedure to create an empty SAS data file and add observations. See Chapters 3 or 4, respectively, for details.
		Use the FSVIEW procedure to create a new SAS data file that duplicates the structure and contents of an existing data set. See Chapter 4 for details.
	Create personalized form letters and reports	Use the FSLETTER procedure to prepare a letter or report containing fields that can be filled (either manually or with values from a SAS data set) before printing. See Chapter 5 for details.
		Use either the FSEDIT procedure or the FSBROWSE procedure to produce letters or reports customized with information from a SAS data set. See Chapter 5 for details.
	Review the contents of an external file	Use the FSLIST procedure. See Chapter 6 for details.
	Copy text from an external file into a SAS text editor window	Use the FSLIST procedure. See Chapter 6 for details.

Chapter 3 Browsing and Editing SAS® Data Sets Using the FSBROWSE and FSEDIT Procedures

Introduction

The FSBROWSE procedure provides an interactive environment for browsing the contents of SAS data sets. In addition to scrolling commands that allow you to move among observations, the procedure provides a full range of commands for locating specific observations based on the values they contain.

The FSEDIT procedure provides the same interactive environment as the FSBROWSE procedure. However, the FSEDIT procedure also allows you to modify the displayed data, greatly simplifying the tasks of updating existing information and adding new information to the data sets. In addition to commands for scrolling and searching, the procedure includes commands for editing, adding, and deleting observations.

The FSEDIT procedure also provides a way to create SAS data sets without running a DATA step. Using the FSEDIT New window, you enter variable names and attributes to define a new data set. You then use the FSEDIT procedure to add observations and enter values.

This chapter illustrates the browsing and editing features of the FSBROWSE and FSEDIT procedures and shows how to use the FSEDIT procedure to create a new data set. For details of individual commands, refer to Chapter 12, "The FSBROWSE Procedure," and Chapter 13, "The FSEDIT Procedure."

Note: The FSBROWSE procedure can also be used to browse SAS data views created with SAS/ACCESS software and with the SQL procedure in base SAS software. The FSEDIT procedure can also be used to edit SAS data views created with SAS/ACCESS software. See SAS/ACCESS documentation for information on using the FSBROWSE and FSEDIT procedures to browse and edit SAS/ACCESS views. See *SAS Guide to the SQL Procedure: Usage and Reference, Version 6, First Edition* for more information on browsing PROC SQL views with the FSBROWSE procedure.

How Data Are Displayed

The FSBROWSE and FSEDIT procedures display one observation at a time in FSBROWSE and FSEDIT windows, respectively. Display 3.1 shows the default FSEDIT window for a blank observation in the SAS data set MASTER.SUBSCRIB, described in Chapter 1, "Introduction to SAS/FSP Software." The default FSBROWSE window would be the same except for the window title.

Display 3.1
Default Display
for the Example
Data Set

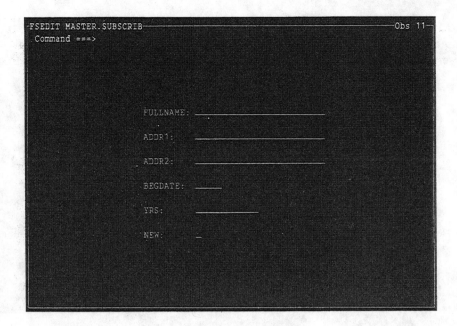

The current observation number is displayed in the upper-right corner of the window border. (For newly added observations, the word *New* appears in lieu of an observation number.)

Note: The observation number is not displayed when the access method used to read the data set does not support access by observation number.

Enter variable values for the observation in the variable fields, indicated by underscores. In the default display, variable fields are arranged in the order in which the variables appear in the data set and are identified by the corresponding variable names. Use the VAR statement to choose other orderings and the LABEL statement (in conjunction with the LABEL option) to provide more descriptive labels. See the discussions of these statements in Chapters 12 and 13 for details.

Notice the vertical display format in Display 3.1. If the data set contains more variables than fit in a single vertical column, multiple columns are used if the variable fields are short enough. Otherwise, the contents of the window are partitioned into units called *screens*. Each screen contains as much information as will fit in the window.

FSBROWSE or FSEDIT sessions that use more than one screen are called multiscreen applications. Display 3.2 shows the FSEDIT window display for a new observation in a multiscreen application. The current screen number is shown in the upper-right corner of the window border following the observation number.

Display 3.2
*Default Display
for a Multiscreen
Application*

```
┌─FSEDIT MASTER.MULTISCR──────────────────────────────Obs 1  Screen 1─┐
│ Command ===>                                                        │
│ NOTE: This application uses 2 screens.                              │
│   VAR1:  _____         VAR2:  _____        VAR3:  _____     │
│   VAR4:  _____         VAR5:  _____        VAR6:  _____     │
│   VAR7:  _____         VAR8:  _____        VAR9:  _____     │
│   VAR13: _____    │
│   VAR14: _____    │
│   VAR15: _____    │
│   VAR16: _____    │
│   VAR17: _____    │
│   VAR18: _____    │
│   VAR19:     ·   _____    │
│   VAR20: _____    │
│   VAR21: _____         VAR22: _____        VAR23: _____     │
│   VAR24: _____         VAR25: _____        VAR26: _____     │
│   VAR27: _____         VAR28: _____        VAR29: _____     │
│   VAR30: _____    │
│   VAR31: _____    │
│   VAR32: _____    │
│   VAR33: _____    │
│   VAR34: _____    │
│   VAR35: _____    │
└─────────────────────────────────────────────────────────────────────┘
```

Browsing SAS Data Sets

This section demonstrates the browsing features of the FSBROWSE and FSEDIT procedures. Although the examples in this section use the FSBROWSE procedure, all the commands are equally applicable to the FSEDIT procedure. The commands used in the following examples are described in detail in Chapters 12 and 13.

A Sample Session: Browsing Features

Suppose the circulation department of a monthly magazine, *The News Monthly*, stores subscriber list information in a SAS data set. When a subscriber calls, you need to display the correct observation from the data set so that you can refer to the account information. The FSBROWSE procedure lets you

□ view observations for current subscriptions

□ locate observations meeting specific criteria.

The data set used in this example, MASTER.SUBSCRIB, is described in Chapter 1. To begin viewing the data in the sample data set, submit the following statements:

```
proc fsbrowse data=master.subscrib;
run;
```

The PROC FSBROWSE statement initiates an FSBROWSE session and opens the FSBROWSE window. The DATA= option names the SAS data set that is displayed.

You can also initiate an FSBROWSE session for this data set by issuing the following command in any SAS System window:

```
fsbrowse master.subscrib
```

Display 3.3 shows the FSBROWSE window display for the first observation in the data set.

Display 3.3
FSBROWSE
Window for the
First Observation
in
MASTER.SUBSCRIB

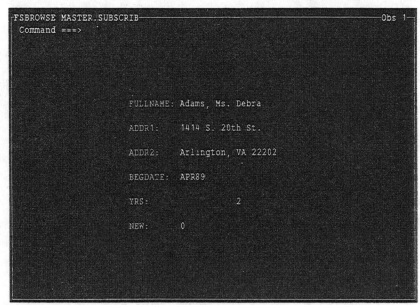

Fields are identified by their corresponding variable names. Values for character variables are left-aligned in the fields, and values for numeric variables are right-aligned. Variables with assigned formats, such as BEGDATE in this example, are displayed using their formats.

Moving from One Observation to Another

To move from one observation to another, use the BACKWARD and FORWARD commands or the function keys to which the BACKWARD and FORWARD commands have been assigned. If you know the number of the observation you want to view, type the observation number on the command line and press ENTER to move directly to that observation.

For example, suppose you want to check the fourth observation. Type 4 on the command line and press ENTER to display that observation. To move to the first observation in the data set, type 1 on the command line and press ENTER. If you use a number that is greater than the number of observations in the data set, the last observation in the data set is displayed. Thus, you can deliberately enter a very large number to move to the end of the data set.

Note: Scrolling by observation number is not allowed under the following conditions:

□ when a WHERE clause is in effect

□ when the data set is compressed

□ when the access method used to read the data set does not support access by observation number.

Scrolling in Multiscreen Applications

Because the MASTER.SUBSCRIB data set has only six variables, all the variable fields fit within the FSBROWSE window. In cases where the variable fields for a data set do not all fit within the window, the fields are partitioned into groups called screens. Each screen contains as many fields as will fit in the window at one time. If the FSBROWSE session uses multiple screens, use the LEFT and RIGHT commands, or the function keys to which these commands have been assigned, to move among the screens for each observation.

Two other scrolling commands are useful in multiscreen applications. To move directly to any screen within an observation, type an equal sign (=) followed by the screen number on the command line. For example, the following command displays screen 4 of the current observation:

```
=4
```

This command has no effect in the current example because the example does not use multiple screens.

If you know the name of the variable you want to display, but not the number of the screen on which it appears, type an equal sign (=) followed by the variable name on the command line to move to the screen containing that variable. For example, if you know that the data set you are browsing contains the variable TOTQTR1, but the variable is not in the current screen, you can issue the following command to move directly to the screen containing that variable:

```
=totqtr1
```

Locating Observations by Content

Often you need to locate records based on information they contain rather than by their observation numbers. The FSBROWSE procedure provides a variety of commands to help you locate observations that contain particular values.

Finding an Exact Match

When you know the exact value that one of the variables in an observation contains, use the NAME and LOCATE commands to find and display the observation. The NAME command identifies the variable that is searched, and the LOCATE command specifies the value searched for.

For example, suppose you want to locate Herman Carroll's observation. Enter the following on the command line to identify which variable in MASTER.SUBSCRIB contains subscriber names:

```
name fullname
```

Move to the first observation; then use the LOCATE command to search forward for the desired observation. Specify the value you want to locate in the exact form in which it is stored:

```
locate 'Carroll, Mr. Herman'
```

The value must be enclosed in quotes because it contains special characters (the comma and period) and embedded blanks. This command locates and displays observation 4. See Display 3.4.

Display 3.4
Observation Found
Using the LOCATE
Command

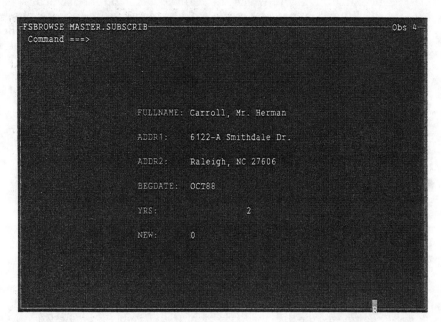

Finding a Partial Match

On many occasions you have only part of the information you need to identify a subscriber. For example, you may be unsure of the exact spelling of the name, or you may not have the complete name. In these cases, the LOCATE: command (note the colon) is useful. Unlike the LOCATE command, which requires an exact match, LOCATE: requires only that the starting characters of the variable value match the specified value. Like LOCATE, the LOCATE: command requires a NAME command to identify the variable to be searched.

For example, if you were unsure of the exact spelling of Herman Carroll's name but knew that his last name begins with the letters *Carr*, you could use the following command to locate observations whose FULLNAME value begins with the letters *Carr*:

```
locate: Carr
```

This assumes that you have previously used a NAME command to identify FULLNAME as the search variable. If you use the LOCATE or LOCATE: commands when no NAME variable has been specified, you will get a warning to this effect on the window's message line.

Repeating a Search Command

Once an observation has been located and displayed, use the RFIND (repeat find) command to display the next observation meeting the same criterion. The RFIND command repeats the most recently executed search command (LOCATE, LOCATE:, or any of the others introduced in following sections).

Note: For greater convenience, you can assign the RFIND command to a function key. Then you can repeat the most recent search command simply by pressing the key to which the RFIND command is assigned.

When you use any of the search commands to look for observations in the data set, the procedure begins the search at the observation following the one currently displayed. Thus, you should initiate searches from the first observation in the data set if you want to ensure that all matches are found. If the end of the data set is reached without finding an observation that meets the criterion, you see the message "End of file reached without a match," and the last observation in the data set is displayed. Use the RFIND command to continue the search at the beginning of the data set.

As an example, type 9 on the command line and press ENTER to move to observation 9, Kenneth Womble's observation. If you have not already done so, enter the NAME command to identify the search variable:

```
name fullname
```

Now enter the LOCATE: command described earlier:

```
locate: Carr
```

The last observation in the data set is displayed, along with a message telling you that you have reached the end of the data set without finding an observation that meets the specified criterion. (See Display 3.5.) Between Kenneth Womble's observation and the end of the data set, no observation has a FULLNAME value starting with *Carr*.

Display 3.5
When the Search
Value Is Not
Found

```
┌FSBROWSE MASTER.SUBSCRIB────────────────────────────────────────Obs 10─┐
│ Command ===>                                                           │
│ NOTE: End of file reached without a match.                            │
│                                                                        │
│                                                                        │
│                                                                        │
│                                                                        │
│                 FULLNAME: Ziller, Mr. Paul                             │
│                                                                        │
│                 ADDR1:    P.O. Box 94                                  │
│                                                                        │
│                 ADDR2:    Burlington, CA 90406                         │
│                                                                        │
│                 BEGDATE:  MAY90                                        │
│                                                                        │
│                 YRS:                      3                            │
│                                                                        │
│                 NEW:      0                                            │
│                                                                        │
└────────────────────────────────────────────────────────────────────────┘
```

Now issue the RFIND command (or press the RFIND key) to begin the search again at the beginning of the data set. This time observation 4 is displayed because its FULLNAME variable value begins with *Carr*.

Improving Search Efficiency with Indexes

Under certain circumstances, the efficiency of searches in the FSBROWSE and FSEDIT procedures can be enhanced by creating one or more *indexes* for the data set. Indexes are a new feature in Release 6.06 of the SAS System. They store the sorted values of one or more variables along with pointers to the observation containing each value. Using this information, the SAS System can locate an observation containing a particular value more quickly than if it had to search every observation for the desired value. For indexes to be useful, the key variables in the index must match the variables being searched.

Indexes are created using the DATASETS procedure in base SAS software, the display manager SERVICES window, or the ICREATE function in Screen Control Language. Once an index is created for a data set, the SAS System maintains the index automatically, adding, updating, and deleting index entries as observations are added, updated, and deleted in the corresponding data set. If indexes are available, the SAS System decides for itself whether using the indexes would improve the efficiency of the operation. No special commands are required.

For more information on indexes, see Chapter 6, "SAS Files," in *SAS Language: Reference, Version 6, First Edition*.

Finding Observations that Meet Specific Criteria

The LOCATE and LOCATE: commands search only one variable for one value. To locate observations based on more than one criterion, use the FIND or FIND@ command instead. Unlike the LOCATE and LOCATE: commands, the FIND and FIND@ commands let you specify both the search variable and search value in one command. The FIND and FIND@ commands also allow you to specify a comparison operator, so you can search for observations containing values greater than, less than, or unequal to the search value, rather than just searching for equivalent values. And the FIND and FIND@ commands let you search more than one variable simultaneously.

Finding an Exact Match

Suppose you want to identify those subscribers whose subscriptions lapse in a particular month. You must look at both the BEGDATE and YRS variables in the data set. For example, a two-year subscription beginning in August 1989 ends in July 1991. To find the two-year subscriptions that expire in July of 1991, move to observation 1 and then issue the following command:

```
find begdate=AUG89 yrs=2
```

This command locates only those observations that satisfy both of the specified criteria. Display 3.6 shows the first observation meeting both conditions.

Display 3.6
*Using the FIND
Command*

```
┌─FSBROWSE MASTER.SUBSCRIB─────────────────────────────────────────Obs 3─┐
│  Command ===>                                                          │
│                                                                        │
│                                                                        │
│                                                                        │
│                                                                        │
│                     FULLNAME: Bertram, Ms. Mary                        │
│                                                                        │
│                     ADDR1:    701 Catawba                              │
│                                                                        │
│                     ADDR2:    Raleigh, NC 27609                        │
│                                                                        │
│                     BEGDATE:  AUG89                                    │
│                                                                        │
│                     YRS:               2                              │
│                                                                        │
│                     NEW:      0                                        │
│                                                                        │
│                                                                        │
└────────────────────────────────────────────────────────────────────────┘
```

To continue the search for the next observation meeting the specified criteria, use the RFIND command.

Finding a Partial Match

In situations where you want to find observations that satisfy at least one, but not necessarily all, of a list of criteria, use the FIND@ command. In contrast to the FIND command, the FIND@ command locates any observation that satisfies at least one criterion in the list.

Suppose you want to locate observations for subscribers who last renewed for more than two years or who last renewed after May 1990. Move to the first observation in the data set; then issue the following command:

```
find@ yrs>2 begdate>MAY90
```

Display 3.7 shows the first observation that meets at least one of the conditions.

Display 3.7
Using the FIND@
Command

```
┌─FSBROWSE MASTER.SUBSCRIB─────────────────────────────────────Obs 5─┐
│  Command ===>                                                       │
│                                                                     │
│                                                                     │
│                                                                     │
│                                                                     │
│                 FULLNAME: Dilley, Mr. Matthew                       │
│                                                                     │
│                 ADDR1:    420 Polk St.                              │
│                                                                     │
│                 ADDR2:    Ithaca, NY 14853                          │
│                                                                     │
│                 BEGDATE:  MAY87                                     │
│                                                                     │
│                 YRS:               5                                │
│                                                                     │
│                 NEW:      0                                         │
│                                                                     │
│                                                                     │
│                                                                     │
│                                                                     │
│                                                                     │
│                                                                     │
└─────────────────────────────────────────────────────────────────┘
```

Use the RFIND command to repeat the search.

Searching for Embedded Text Strings

The SEARCH and SEARCH@ commands are the FSBROWSE procedure's most
flexible searching tools. The SEARCH command locates observations that contain
a specified string embedded in the values of any of a list of variables. The
SEARCH@ command locates observations that contain any of a list of strings
embedded in the values of any of a list of variables. Use the STRING command
to specify the list of variables to be searched, and then use the SEARCH or
SEARCH@ commands to specify the character string or strings to search for.

   Note: The SEARCH and SEARCH@ commands can only be used to search
character variables.

Finding a Particular String

Suppose *The News Monthly* is preparing a special issue of interest only to North
Carolina subscribers and you want to search the data set for observations of
subscribers from that state. A subscriber's state is embedded in the value of the
ADDR2 variable, so issue the following command to identify the search variable:

```
string addr2
```

Move to observation 1; then issue the following command to identify the string
to be searched for:

```
search NC
```

   Note: The search value (NC) must be entered in uppercase because that is
the way the corresponding value is stored in the data set. The SEARCH and
SEARCH@ commands are case-sensitive; they only match variable characters in
the same case as the search characters.

The first observation whose ADDR2 value contains the string NC is displayed, as shown in Display 3.8. Use the RFIND command to display the next subscriber in that state. Continue using the RFIND command until you have found all North Carolina subscribers.

Display 3.8
Locating an Embedded String Using the SEARCH Command

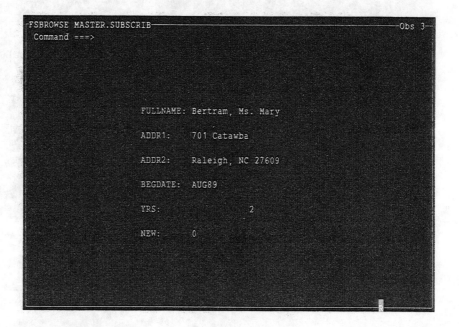

Finding Any of a List of Strings

In contrast to the SEARCH command, which allows only a single search string, the SEARCH@ command can include a list of search strings. The SEARCH@ command locates the first observation that contains any one of the specified search strings embedded in the value of the specified STRING variable or variables.

Suppose *The News Monthly* is preparing a special issue of interest to subscribers in both North Carolina and Virginia. To search the data set for observations of subscribers from either of those two states, substitute the following command for the SEARCH command in the previous example:

```
search@ NC VA
```

This command locates the first observation that contains either NC or VA in the ADDR2 variable value.

Ending the FSBROWSE Session

To end your browsing session, use the END command. The FSBROWSE window is closed and you exit the FSBROWSE procedure.

Editing SAS Data Sets

This section demonstrates the editing features of the FSEDIT procedure. Unlike the previous section, the information that follows applies only to the FSEDIT procedure. You cannot use editing commands in an FSBROWSE session. See Chapter 13 for detailed descriptions of the commands used in the examples that follow.

▶ *Caution* . . . . ***The FSEDIT procedure edits a data set in place.***
The FSEDIT procedure does not leave an unedited copy of the original. If you need to preserve a copy of the original data, be sure to make one before you begin editing the data set. ▲

A Sample Session: Basic Editing Features

Suppose that the circulation department of a monthly magazine, *The News Monthly*, stores its subscriber list information in a SAS data set. This data set must be updated frequently as new subscribers are added and old subscribers move, renew their subscriptions, cancel their subscriptions, or allow them to lapse. The FSEDIT procedure lets you

□   update observations to record renewals and address changes

□   add observations for new subscribers .

□   delete observations for canceled or lapsed subscriptions.

In addition, the FSEDIT procedure provides all the browsing features described earlier for the FSBROWSE procedure.

The data set used in the following examples, MASTER.SUBSCRIB, is described in Chapter 1. To begin editing the sample data set, submit the following statements:

```
proc fsedit data=master.subscrib;
run;
```

The PROC FSEDIT statement initiates an FSEDIT session and opens the FSEDIT window. The DATA= option specifies the data set to display.

You can also initiate an FSEDIT session for this data set by issuing the following command from any SAS System window:

```
fsedit master.subscrib
```

Display 3.9 shows the FSEDIT window display for the first observation in the data set.

Display 3.9
FSEDIT Window
for the First
Observation in
MASTER.SUBSCRIB

```
┌FSEDIT MASTER.SUBSCRIB────────────────────────────────────────────Obs 1─┐
│ Command ===>                                                            │
│                                                                         │
│                                                                         │
│                                                                         │
│             FULLNAME: Adams, Ms. Debra                                  │
│                                                                         │
│             ADDR1:    1414 S. 20th St.                                  │
│                                                                         │
│             ADDR2:    Arlington, VA 22202                               │
│                                                                         │
│             BEGDATE: APR89                                              │
│                                                                         │
│             YRS:                    2                                   │
│                                                                         │
│             NEW:      0                                                 │
│                                                                         │
│                                                                         │
│                                                                         │
│                                                                         │
└─────────────────────────────────────────────────────────────────────────┘
```

As in the FSBROWSE procedure, fields are identified by variable names. Values for character variables are left-aligned in the field, and values for numeric variables are right-aligned. Variables with assigned formats, such as BEGDATE in this example, are displayed with the specified formats.

Updating Observations

To update a variable value in an existing observation, simply display the desired observation, move the cursor to the field you want to modify, and type the new value over the current value.

For example, suppose you want to update the subscriber list to show that Herman Carroll has renewed his subscription for one year. Use any of the scrolling or searching commands described in the section on browsing data sets to locate Herman's observation (observation 4). Once the proper observation is displayed, type the new values in the BEGDATE and YRS fields.

Because the current BEGDATE value for this observation is OCT88 and the current YRS value is 2, the new starting date is two years beyond the current starting date. Enter OCT90 in the BEGDATE field. Since the subscription is being renewed for one year, enter 1 in the YRS field. Display 3.10 shows the updated observation.

Display 3.10
Updating an
Observation

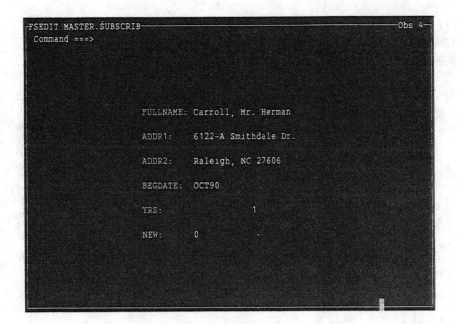

```
┌─FSEDIT MASTER.SUBSCRIB─────────────────────────────────────Obs 4─┐
│ Command ===>                                                     │
│                                                                  │
│                                                                  │
│                                                                  │
│                                                                  │
│             FULLNAME: Carroll, Mr. Herman                        │
│                                                                  │
│             ADDR1:    6122-A Smithdale Dr.                       │
│                                                                  │
│             ADDR2:    Raleigh, NC 27606                          │
│                                                                  │
│             BEGDATE:  OCT90                                      │
│                                                                  │
│             YRS:              1                                  │
│                                                                  │
│             NEW:      0                                          │
│                                                                  │
│                                                                  │
└──────────────────────────────────────────────────────────────────┘
```

Canceling Changes to a Displayed Observation

If you make a mistake while updating an observation, use the CANCEL command to cancel all changes made to the current observation.

For example, suppose you are entering change-of-address information for Kenneth Womble (observation 9) and incorrectly type `2120 Lakshore Dr.` as the new ADDR1 value and `Highpoint, MC` as the ADDR2 value, as shown in Display 3.11. Cancel your changes by issuing a CANCEL command. All fields are restored to their original values, as shown in Display 3.12.

▶ *Caution* .... ***You must issue the CANCEL command before moving to another observation or executing a SAVE command.***
Once you take either of these actions, you cannot cancel changes. You must instead re-enter the correct information. ▲

Display 3.11
Canceling Changes
to an Observation

```
┌FSEDIT MASTER.SUBSCRIB─────────────────────────────────────────Obs 9─┐
│ Command ===> cancel                                                  │
│                                                                      │
│                                                                      │
│                                                                      │
│                                                                      │
│                  FULLNAME: Womble, Mr. Kenneth                       │
│                                                                      │
│                  ADDR1:    2120 Lakshore Dr.                         │
│                                                                      │
│                  ADDR2:    Highpoint, MC                             │
│                                                                      │
│                  BEGDATE:  FEB90                                     │
│                                                                      │
│                  YRS:                   1                            │
│                                                                      │
│                  NEW:      1                                         │
│                                                                      │
│                                                                      │
│                                                                      │
│                                                                      │
└──────────────────────────────────────────────────────────────────  ┘
```

Display 3.12
Observation with
Original Values
Restored

```
┌FSEDIT MASTER.SUBSCRIB─────────────────────────────────────────Obs 9─┐
│ Command ===>                                                         │
│                                                                      │
│                                                                      │
│                                                                      │
│                                                                      │
│                  FULLNAME: Womble, Mr. Kenneth                       │
│                                                                      │
│                  ADDR1:    702-F Walden Dr.                          │
│                                                                      │
│                  ADDR2:    Wilmington, NC 28401                      │
│                                                                      │
│                  BEGDATE:  FEB90                                     │
│                                                                      │
│                  YRS:                   1                            │
│                                                                      │
│                  NEW:      1                                         │
│                                                                      │
│                                                                      │
│                                                                      │
│                                                                      │
└──────────────────────────────────────────────────────────────────  ┘
```

Adding Observations

Use the ADD command to add a new blank observation to the data set. Display
3.13 shows the FSEDIT window with blank fields ready for entering data for a
new observation. Notice that for a new observation the label in the upper-right
corner of the window border is *New* rather than an observation number.

Display 3.13
Adding an
Observation

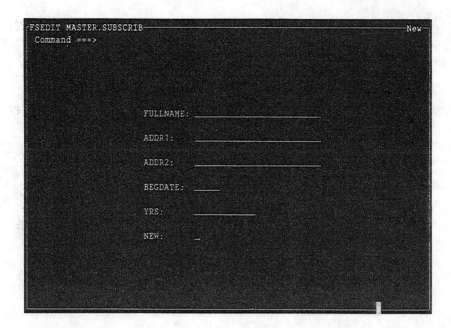

```
┌FSEDIT MASTER.SUBSCRIB─────────────────────────────────────────New─┐
│ Command ===>                                                      │
│                                                                   │
│                                                                   │
│                                                                   │
│                                                                   │
│              FULLNAME: _____                     │
│                                                                   │
│              ADDR1:    _____                     │
│                                                                   │
│              ADDR2:    _____                     │
│                                                                   │
│              BEGDATE:  _____                                       │
│                                                                   │
│              YRS:      _____                                  │
│                                                                   │
│              NEW:      _                                           │
│                                                                   │
│                                                                   │
│                                                                   │
│                                                                   │
└───────────────────────────────────────────────────────────────────┘
```

Note: Your position in the data set when you issue the ADD command does not affect where in the data set the new observation is added. The position of the new observation depends on the access method used.

If you want to create a new observation that is similar to an existing one, use the DUP command instead of the ADD command. Like ADD, the DUP command adds a new observation to the data set, but DUP copies all the values from an existing observation into the new observation. You can then edit any of the values displayed in the fields of the new observation.

To use the DUP command, scroll to the observation you want to copy, type DUP on the command line, and press ENTER. The copy of the observation is added to the data set and is displayed for editing.

Entering Values in the Fields

The underscores in a new blank observation indicate where you enter values. To enter values for variables in the new observation, simply type values into the spaces indicated by the underscores after the variable names. When you press ENTER or issue another command, the field values are verified and the observation is updated.

For example, add an observation for Jennette McRay, a new subscriber, by filling in a value for each variable, as shown in Display 3.14.

Display 3.14
Entering Data for
a New Observation

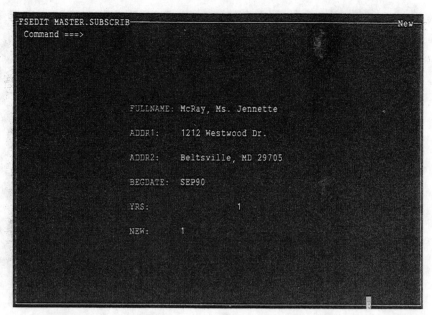

```
┌─FSEDIT MASTER.SUBSCRIB──────────────────────────────────────────New─┐
│ Command ===>                                                         │
│                                                                      │
│                                                                      │
│                                                                      │
│            FULLNAME: McRay, Ms. Jennette                             │
│                                                                      │
│            ADDR1:    1212 Westwood Dr.                               │
│                                                                      │
│            ADDR2:    Beltsville, MD 29705                            │
│                                                                      │
│            BEGDATE:  SEP90                                           │
│                                                                      │
│            YRS:               1                                      │
│                                                                      │
│            NEW:      1                                               │
│                                                                      │
└─────────────────────────────────────────────────────────────────────┘
```

Note: New observations displayed by the ADD or DUP commands are not actually added to the data set until you move to another observation or use the SAVE or END commands. Even if you have entered values in variable fields, you can use the CANCEL command to cancel the new observation as long as you have not moved to a different observation or saved the data set.

Entering Data with Informats

To enter the subscriber's name and address, you simply type the information in any form you want. However, the variable for starting date, BEGDATE, has special requirements. BEGDATE was assigned an informat and a format when the data set was created (see Chapter 1). The informat tells the SAS System how to interpret values entered in the field; the format determines how values are displayed in the field. Refer to Chapter 3, "Components of the SAS Language," in *SAS Language: Reference* for details of formats and informats.

BEGDATE has the informat and format MONYY., so you must enter the date value the same way it is displayed. The MONYY. informat requires that values for BEGDATE be entered as the first three characters in the name of the month followed by the last two digits of the year. A value entered using any other informat is flagged as an error.

Suppose you enter the value 09/90 instead of SEP90 in Jennette's observation. When you issue a command or press ENTER, an error message is displayed below the command line and the cursor is positioned on the field with the bad value, as shown in Display 3.15.

Display 3.15
Entering Data with an Incorrect Informat

```
┌FSEDIT MASTER.SUBSCRIB──────────────────────────────────────New──┐
│ Command ===>                                                     │
│ ERROR: Data value is not valid.  Please reenter.                │
│                                                                  │
│                                                                  │
│                                                                  │
│              FULLNAME: McRay, Ms. Jennette                       │
│                                                                  │
│              ADDR1:    1212 Westwood Dr.                         │
│                                                                  │
│              ADDR2:    Beltsville, MD 29705                      │
│                                                                  │
│              BEGDATE:  09/90                                     │
│                                                                  │
│              YRS:                    1                           │
│                                                                  │
│              NEW:      1                                         │
│                                                                  │
│                                                                  │
│                                                                  │
│                                                                  │
└──────────────────────────────────────────────────────────────┘
```

You must re-enter the data value before you can continue. If you are unsure of how to enter the value, use the HELP command. Either type HELP on the command line, place the cursor on the BEGDATE field, and press ENTER, or place the cursor on the BEGDATE field and press a function key to which the HELP command has been assigned. The variable's attributes are displayed on the window's message line, as shown in Display 3.16.

Display 3.16
Getting Help on a Variable's Attributes

```
┌FSEDIT MASTER.SUBSCRIB──────────────────────────────────────New──┐
│ Command ===>                                                     │
│ VAR: BEGDATE  TYPE: NUM    INFORMAT: MONYY    FORMAT: MONYY      │
│                                                                  │
│                                                                  │
│                                                                  │
│              FULLNAME: McRay, Ms. Jennette                       │
│                                                                  │
│              ADDR1:    1212 Westwood Dr.                         │
│                                                                  │
│              ADDR2:    Beltsville, MD 29705                      │
│                                                                  │
│              BEGDATE:  09/90                                     │
│                                                                  │
│              YRS:                    1                           │
│                                                                  │
│              NEW:      1                                         │
│                                                                  │
│                                                                  │
│                                                                  │
│                                                                  │
└──────────────────────────────────────────────────────────────┘
```

The message tells you that the BEGDATE variable has been assigned the informat MONYY., so the variable value must be entered in the form SEP90.

Positioning the Cursor

By default, the cursor is positioned on the command line whenever an observation is displayed. (If you are using action bars rather than the command line, the cursor is positioned on the first item in the action bar.) When you need to edit the same field in several observations, you can specify that the cursor automatically move to that field when an observation is displayed.

For example, suppose you have several renewals to record and want to position the cursor on the BEGDATE field when an observation is displayed. Type CURSOR on the command line, position the cursor anywhere on the BEGDATE field, and press ENTER; or position the cursor on the field and press the function key to which the CURSOR command has been assigned. Now each time an observation is displayed, the cursor is automatically positioned on the BEGDATE field.

To reset the cursor to its default initial position, type CURSOR on the command line, leave the cursor on the command line, and press ENTER.

Deleting an Observation

Use the DELETE command to delete an observation from the data set. When you issue the DELETE command, the displayed observation is marked for deletion from the data set and you can no longer edit it.

For example, suppose Mary Bertram has canceled her subscription. Her observation now needs to be deleted from the data set. First move to Mary's observation (number 3); then type the following on the command line and press ENTER:

```
delete
```

Display 3.17 shows the result, a deleted observation. Notice that the word DELETED has replaced the word Obs in the upper-right corner of the window border. All fields are cleared, and you can no longer modify field values in this observation.

***Display* 3.17** *An Observation Marked for Deletion*

```
-FSEDIT MASTER.SUBSCRIB-----------------------------------------DELETED 3-
 Command ===>
 NOTE: Observation has been deleted.




                    FULLNAME: _____


                    ADDR1:    _____


                    ADDR2:    _____


                    BEGDATE:  _____


                    YRS:      _____


                    NEW:      _
```

Once you issue the DELETE command no further editing is allowed, and once you move to another observation you cannot return to a deleted observation.

Special Topic: Removing Deleted Observations

When you use the DELETE command, the deleted observation may or may not be physically removed from the data set, depending on the way the data set is accessed.

For uncompressed Version 6 data sets and for Version 5 data sets, the deleted observation is not physically removed from the data set. For example, if you delete observation 3 as shown in the previous example, end the FSEDIT session, and then later edit this data set again in another FSEDIT session, observation 3 will be inaccessible. Likewise, if you use the PRINT procedure to print the contents of the data set, nothing is printed for observation 3.

To actually remove the deleted observation, you must create a new copy of the data set. You can do this with the DATA step or with any of the SAS procedures that writes a new copy of the data set—the SORT procedure, for example. See "Managing an Edited Data Set" later in this chapter for details.

Ending the FSEDIT Session

To end your editing session, use the END command. The data set is saved, the FSEDIT window is closed, and you exit the FSEDIT procedure.

Managing an Edited Data Set

After editing a data set with the FSEDIT procedure, you can use any of the other data management tools provided by the SAS System to further manipulate the data set. For example, you can sort or print the revised version.

The following statements print the edited version of the example data set. Output 3.1 shows the results.

```
options linesize=120 pagesize=60 nodate;


proc print data=master.subscrib;
run;
```

Output 3.1   Updated MASTER.SUBSCRIB Data Set

```
                                       The SAS System                                                          1

      OBS      FULLNAME           ADDR1              ADDR2               BEGDATE    YRS    NEW

       1     Adams, Ms. Debra    1414 S. 20th St.     Arlington, VA 22202    APR89     2     0
       2     Bailey, Mr. Mark    2721 1/2 Van Dyke    Logan, UT 84322        MAR90     2     1
       4     Carroll, Mr. Herman 6122-A Smithdale Dr. Raleigh, NC 27606      OCT90     1     0
       5     Dilley, Mr. Matthew 420 Polk St.         Ithaca, NY 14853       MAY87     5     0
       6     Marvin, Ms. June    Route 7, Box 482     Durham, NC 27714       AUG90     1     0
       7     Stiller, Mr. Allan  Route 2, Box 22-B    Moyock, NC 27958       JAN90     1     1
       8     Vance, Ms. Martha   424-204 Navaho Dr.   Raleigh, NC 27609      NOV89     1     1
       9     Womble, Mr. Kenneth 702-F Walden Dr.     Wilmington, NC 28401   FEB90     1     1
      10     Ziller, Mr. Paul    P.O. Box 94          Burlington, CA 90406   MAY90     3     0
      11     McRay, Ms. Jennette 1212 Westwood Dr.    Beltsville, MD 20705   SEP90     1     1
```

Herman Carroll's subscription has been renewed, and Jennette McRay has been added to the end of the data set.

Notice that nothing is printed for observation 3. The deleted observation has not been physically removed from the data set. To remove deleted observations, use the following simple DATA step:

```
data master.subscrib;
   set master.subscrib;
run;
```

With the added observation, the data set is now in unsorted order. The following statements sort the data set into alphabetical order again:

```
proc sort data=master.subscrib;
   by fullname;
run;
```

The SORT procedure orders the data set according to the value of the FULLNAME variable, then writes the sorted version back to the file MASTER.SUBSCRIB. The sorted version of the data set replaces the old version of MASTER.SUBSCRIB.

Note: Because you are sorting the data set, you could have omitted the previous DATA step to remove deleted observations. The SORT procedure also eliminates deleted observations as it sorts the data set.

To view the results of the sorting, submit the following statements:

```
proc print data=master.subscrib;
run;
```

Output 3.2 shows the new sorted version as printed by the PRINT procedure.

Output 3.2   *Sorted Version of Updated Data Set*

```
                                   The SAS System                                         2

    OBS       FULLNAME          ADDR1                    ADDR2              BEGDATE   YRS   NEW

     1    Adams, Ms. Debra      1414 S. 20th St.      Arlington, VA 22202    APR89    2     0
     2    Bailey, Mr. Mark      2721 1/2 Van Dyke     Logan, UT 84322        MAR90    2     1
     3    Carroll, Mr. Herman   6122-A Smithdale Dr.  Raleigh, NC 27606      OCT90    1     0
     4    Dilley, Mr. Matthew   420 Polk St.          Ithaca, NY 14853       MAY87    5     0
     5    Marvin, Ms. June      Route 7, Box 482      Durham, NC 27714       AUG90    1     0
     6    McRay, Ms. Jennette   1212 Westwood Dr.     Beltsville, MD 20705   SEP90    1     1
     7    Stiller, Mr. Allan    Route 2, Box 22-B     Moyock, NC 27958       JAN90    1     1
     8    Vance, Ms. Martha     424-204 Navaho Dr.    Raleigh, NC 27609      NOV89    1     1
     9    Womble, Mr. Kenneth   702-F Walden Dr.      Wilmington, NC 28401   FEB90    1     1
    10    Ziller, Mr. Paul      P.O. Box 94           Burlington, CA 90406   MAY90    3     0
```

Using WHERE Clauses

Sometimes you only need to process a subset of the observations in a SAS data set, rather than the entire data set. For such occasions, the SAS System provides WHERE clauses. A WHERE clause is a set of conditions that observations in a data set must meet in order to be processed. Observations that do not satisfy the conditions cannot be viewed or edited. They are effectively excluded from the data set while the WHERE clause is in effect.

Two types of WHERE clauses are available in FSBROWSE and FSEDIT sessions:

□   those established by WHERE statements when the procedure is started. These are called permanent WHERE clauses because they cannot be modified or canceled while the procedure is executing.

□   those established by WHERE commands during the editing or browsing session. These are called temporary WHERE clauses because they can be modified or canceled while the procedure is executing.

The data set used in the following examples is MASTER.SUBSCRIB, the example data set described in Chapter 1, as updated in the previous FSEDIT procedure editing exercises. The following examples show the use of WHERE clauses with the FSEDIT procedure, but all the information on WHERE clauses is equally applicable to the FSBROWSE procedure.

Using Permanent WHERE Clauses

Suppose *The News Monthly* wants to process only observations for first-time subscribers. These subscribers are identified by the value 1 in the variable NEW. Use a WHERE statement to begin an FSEDIT session with a permanent

WHERE clause applied that selects the desired subset of the updated MASTER.SUBSCRIB data set:

```
proc fsedit data=master.subscrib;
   where new='1';
run;
```

Notice that the value 1 in the WHERE statement must be enclosed in quotes to identify it as a character value rather than numeric. NEW is a character variable.

Display 3.18 shows the initial FSEDIT window display after these statements are submitted. The word *Subset* in parentheses following the window title tells you that a permanent WHERE clause is in effect. Notice that the first observation displayed is observation 2. Observation 1 (Debra Adams) is not accessible because the NEW variable value in that observation is 0, not 1.

Display 3.18
FSEDIT Window with Permanent WHERE Clause in Effect

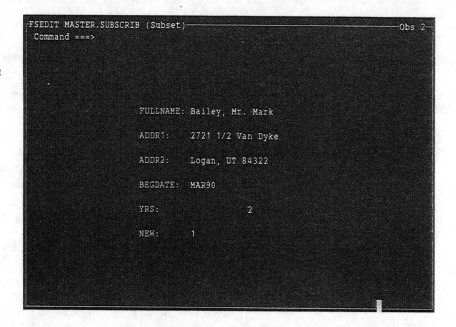

If you use the FORWARD command to scroll to the next observation, observation 6 (Jennette McRay) is displayed. Observations 3 through 5 are skipped because they do not meet the condition imposed by the WHERE clause.

While a WHERE clause (permanent or temporary) is in effect, you cannot scroll by entering observation numbers on the command line. An error message appears if you attempt to return to the first observation in the subset by entering 2 on the command line, even though observation 2 meets the WHERE condition.

If you edit an observation so that it no longer satisfies the conditions defined in the WHERE clause, the observation remains accessible. You can still scroll back to that observation after moving to a different observation. However, each time the edited observation is displayed, a warning appears on the message line indicating that the observation no longer meets the WHERE conditions.

If you add a new observation and enter values in that observation that do not satisfy the conditions of the WHERE clause, the observation is added to the data set, but it is not accessible after it is added. Once you move to another observation, you will not be able to scroll back to the added observation.

Using Temporary WHERE Clauses

Use the WHERE command in an FSEDIT or FSBROWSE session to create subsets of the input data set. The following examples show the use of the WHERE command in an FSEDIT session that also has a permanent WHERE clause applied by a WHERE statement. However, this is not a requirement; the WHERE command can be used independently of the WHERE statement.

Suppose the FSEDIT session with the previously described permanent WHERE clause is still executing and you want to further restrict processing to those new subscribers who began their subscriptions after December 31, 1989. The following command establishes a temporary WHERE clause that imposes the desired restriction:

```
where begdate>'31dec89'd
```

As shown in Display 3.19, the word *Where...* appears in the upper-right corner of the window border to indicate that a temporary WHERE clause is in effect.

Display 3.19
*FSEDIT Window
with Temporary
WHERE Clause in
Effect*

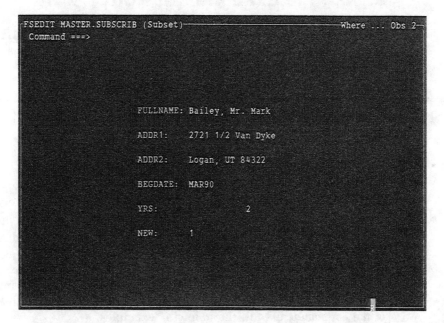

```
┌─FSEDIT MASTER.SUBSCRIB (Subset)──────────────────────Where ... Obs 2─┐
│ Command ===>                                                         │
│                                                                      │
│                                                                      │
│                                                                      │
│           FULLNAME: Bailey, Mr. Mark                                 │
│                                                                      │
│           ADDR1:    2721 1/2 Van Dyke                                │
│                                                                      │
│           ADDR2:    Logan, UT 84322                                  │
│                                                                      │
│           BEGDATE:  MAR90                                            │
│                                                                      │
│           YRS:               2                                       │
│                                                                      │
│           NEW:      1                                                │
│                                                                      │
│                                                                      │
└──────────────────────────────────────────────────────────────────────┘
```

Once this command is issued, observation 8 (Martha Vance) can no longer be processed because its BEGDATE value does not meet the WHERE condition.

The WHERE command has several additional options. For example, each WHERE command by default replaces the temporary WHERE clause established by the previous WHERE command. However, if you use the ALSO option, the specified condition is instead added to the current clause. To further restrict processing to those observations for new subscribers who began after December 31, 1989 and who subscribed for only one year, issue the following command:

```
where also yrs=1
```

Once this command is issued, observation 2 (Mark Bailey) can no longer be processed because the YRS variable value for that observation does not satisfy the new WHERE condition.

You can use the UNDO option with a WHERE command to remove the most recently added condition in the current temporary WHERE clause. For example, the following command removes the restriction that limits processing to one-year subscriptions (YRS=1):

```
where undo
```

To completely cancel the current temporary WHERE clause, enter WHERE alone on the command line or use the following command:

```
where clear
```

Canceling the temporary WHERE clause has no effect on the permanent WHERE clause established by the WHERE statement.

Ending the Example Session

Issue the END command to end the FSEDIT session for the WHERE clause example. The permanent WHERE clause has no effect on the data set beyond the end of the current FSEDIT session.

Creating a New SAS Data Set

In addition to editing and browsing SAS data sets, you can also use the FSEDIT procedure to create a new, empty SAS data set. Once the data set is created, you use the FSEDIT procedure to add observations and enter values.

The structure of the new data set is defined in the FSEDIT New window. You fill in the fields provided to name variables and to specify their characteristics. When the FSEDIT New window is closed, the data set is created. The FSEDIT window is then opened for adding observations.

The following sections discuss how to create a new SAS data set, how to define variables, and how to create a SAS data set like an existing one without entering all the information yourself. See Chapter 13 for complete descriptions of the commands used in the following examples.

Opening the FSEDIT New Window

The FSEDIT New window is opened when you invoke the FSEDIT procedure with the NEW= option, rather than with the DATA= option, in the PROC FSEDIT statement. For example, submit the following statements to open the FSEDIT New window to create a data set named MASTER.QTR1REV:

```
proc fsedit new=master.qtr1rev;
run;
```

The initial display looks like Display 3.20.

Display 3.20
The FSEDIT New Window

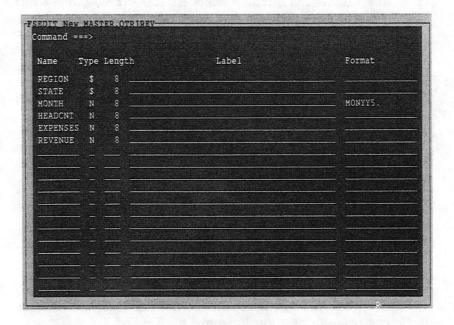

You define the structure of the new data set by entering values in the fields of the FSEDIT New window. You must specify at least a name for each variable. You can also specify a type, length, label, format, and informat. See Chapter 13 for the rules for defining variables in the FSEDIT New window.

Display 3.21 shows typical definitions for six variables in the FSEDIT New window.

Display 3.21
Variable Definitions in the FSEDIT New Window

Displaying the Format and Informat Columns

The Format and Informat columns share the same display area at the far-right side of the window. The Format column is displayed initially. (See Display 3.21.) Use either the RIGHT or LEFT command to display the Informat column, as shown in Display 3.22. The RIGHT and LEFT commands both alternate between Format and Informat fields in the rightmost column of the window.

Display 3.22
Displaying the
Informat Field in
the FSEDIT New
Window

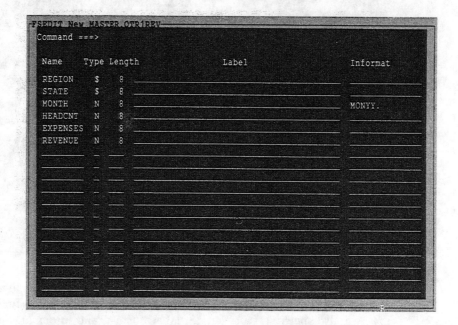

Saving Keystrokes with the SELECT and REPEAT Commands

The SELECT and REPEAT commands can be time-saving features. If you have two or more variables that are similar, these commands save you keystrokes.

Note: The SELECT and REPEAT commands are most effective when they are assigned to function keys. The following example assumes that these key assignments have been made. (To check the current function key definitions, use the KEYS command to open the KEYS window.) To use the commands without function keys, type the command on the command line, position the cursor on the line for the desired variable, and press ENTER.

For example, suppose you are creating a data set with three address lines, ADDR1, ADDR2, and ADDR3. Type in the information required for the variable ADDR1; then position the cursor on ADDR1 and press the SELECT key.

Name	Type	Length	Label	Format
ADDR1	$	30	_____	_____
_____	-	__	_____	_____
_____	-	__	_____	_____
_____	-	__	_____	_____

You have just selected the variable you want repeated. Now position the cursor on the next line and press the REPEAT key.

Name	Type	Length	Label	Format
ADDR1	$	30	_____	_____
ADDR1	$	30	_____	_____
_____	_	__	_____	_____
_____	_	__	_____	_____

Change the name on line 2 to read ADDR2.

Name	Type	Length	Label	Format
ADDR1	$	30	_____	_____
ADDR2	$	30	_____	_____
_____	_	__	_____	_____
_____	_	__	_____	_____

Now position the cursor on the third line and press REPEAT. Change the name to create ADDR3.

Name	Type	Length	Label	Format
ADDR1	$	30	_____	_____
ADDR2	$	30	_____	_____
ADDR3	$	30	_____	_____
_____	_	__	_____	_____

Closing the FSEDIT New Window

Issue the END command to close the FSEDIT New window, create the SAS data set, and open the FSEDIT window so that you can add observations and enter values. Issue the CANCEL command to close the window and terminate the FSEDIT session without creating the new data set.

Note: Once you close the FSEDIT New window, you cannot return to make changes to the structure of an existing data set.

Creating a SAS Data Set Like an Existing One

If you want to create a SAS data set that is identical or similar in structure to an existing one, you can save time by letting the FSEDIT procedure do some of the work. Instead of entering all the variable information, use the LIKE= option in conjunction with the NEW= option to identify an existing SAS data set. When the FSEDIT New window is opened, the variable names and attributes of the data set specified in the LIKE= option are automatically displayed. You have the option of making changes to the variable names and attributes before creating the new data set. To delete a variable entirely, type spaces over its name.

Note: Only the structure of the specified data set is copied, not the contents.

For example, the following PROC FSEDIT statement uses the LIKE= option to display the variable names and attributes of the data set MASTER.QTR1REV defined in the previous example when the FSEDIT New window is opened to define MASTER.QTR2REV:

```
proc fsedit new=master.qtr2rev
     like=master.qtr1rev;
run;
```

Display 3.23 shows the values that appear in the FSEDIT New window when it is opened.

Display 3.23
Using the LIKE=
Option with the
PROC FSEDIT
Statement

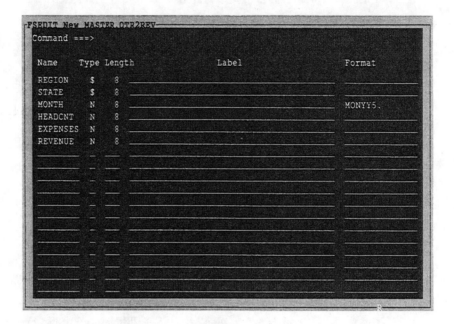

When the variables and their characteristics are displayed, you have three choices:

1. You can create a data set with exactly the same variable attributes as the data set you specified. Issue the END command to create the data set and open the FSEDIT window.

2. You can create a similar data set. Just make any desired changes (such as altering any variable names, lengths, labels, and so on) before you use the END command to create the data set.

3. You can decide not to create the data set. Issue the CANCEL command to close the FSEDIT New window and terminate the FSEDIT session.

Chapter 4 Browsing and Editing SAS® Data Sets Using the FSVIEW Procedure

Introduction

The FSVIEW procedure provides an interactive environment for browsing or editing SAS data sets. The procedure displays data sets as tables with rows of observations and columns of variable values. You can use the procedure to

□ scroll horizontally or vertically through the data set

□ change variable values

□ add new observations to the data set

□ duplicate existing observations to create new ones that are similar

□ delete observations from the data set

□ sort the SAS data set by specified variables

□ create new empty data sets

□ create new data sets containing some or all of the values in the displayed data set.

Once you have invoked the FSVIEW procedure, you can open additional FSVIEW windows within a single FSVIEW session. Concurrent windows allow you to browse or edit other SAS data sets without exiting the procedure.

The FSVIEW procedure also allows you to create new SAS data sets and generate simple reports.

Note: The FSVIEW procedure can be used to browse and edit SAS data views created with SAS/ACCESS software and to browse SAS data views created with the SQL procedure in base SAS software. See SAS/ACCESS documentation for information on using the FSVIEW procedure to browse and edit SAS/ACCESS views. See the *SAS Guide to the SQL Procedure: Usage and Reference, Version 6, First Edition* for more information on browsing PROC SQL views with the FSVIEW procedure.

Browsing SAS Data Sets

When you initiate the FSVIEW procedure, the data set is by default displayed for browsing. This section demonstrates the basic browsing features of the FSVIEW procedure.

A Sample Session: Basic Browsing Features

Suppose the circulation department of a monthly magazine, *The News Monthly*, stores subscriber list information in a SAS data set. Circulation department staff can use the FSVIEW procedure to display names, addresses, and other account information about the subscribers.

The data set used in this example, MASTER.SUBSCRIB, is described in Chapter 1, "Introduction to SAS/FSP Software." To begin viewing the contents of the sample data set, submit the following statements:

```
proc fsview data=master.subscrib;
run;
```

The PROC FSVIEW statement initiates an FSVIEW session and opens the FSVIEW window for browsing. The DATA= option names the data set that is displayed.

You can also initiate an FSVIEW session for this data set by issuing the following command in any SAS System window:

```
fsview master.subscrib
```

Display 4.1 shows the data set MASTER.SUBSCRIB displayed in the default format.

Display 4.1
Displaying a Data Set with the FSVIEW Procedure

The (B) following the window title indicates that the data set is open for browsing only. Observation numbers are displayed in the leftmost column. Because this is a small data set, all observations are displayed. If this data set had more observations, you could scroll forward to view additional observations. However, not all the variables in the data set fit horizontally in the FSVIEW window. You must scroll right to view the remaining variables.

Note: If the data set is compressed, the observation number column is labeled ROW instead of OBS.

Scrolling Variable Columns

To see the additional variable columns, use the RIGHT command to scroll the display. Issue the RIGHT command from the command line, or press the function key to which the RIGHT command has been assigned.

By default, the display moves one variable column to the right each time you issue a RIGHT command. Display 4.2 shows the display after one RIGHT command has been issued.

Display 4.2
Scrolling Variable
Columns to the
Right

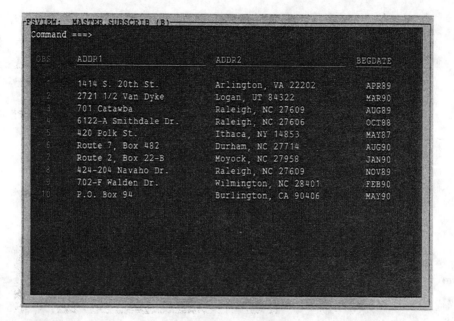

Notice that as you scroll, the observation number column remains at the left side of the display. Use the LEFT command to scroll back to the left.

Ending a Browsing Session

To end an FSVIEW browsing session, issue the END command. This command closes the data set and the FSVIEW window.

Customizing the FSVIEW Display

The FSVIEW procedure allows you to customize the way variable values are presented in the FSVIEW window, both for browsing and for editing. You can

□   reposition a variable in the display

□   remove a variable from the display

□   restore a variable to the display

□   change a variable's format or informat for display and data entry purposes

□   change colors and other highlighting attributes of the display

□   highlight individual lines of the display.

Note: This customization only affects the way variable values are presented in the FSVIEW window. It has no effect on the structure or organization of the data set being displayed.

The following sections demonstrate how to customize the FSVIEW window. The examples use the data set MASTER.SUBSCRIB described in Chapter 1.

Selecting Variables to Display

You can use the VAR and ID statements to specify which variables are displayed, what order the variables are displayed in, and whether or not observation numbers are displayed.

For example, suppose

□ you are only interested in seeing which subscriptions expire soon

□ you do not need the observation numbers displayed but you want each observation identified by the subscriber's name.

Because you do not need to see all the variables in the data set, use the VAR statement to specify which variables you want displayed. Because you do not need observation numbers, use the ID statement to replace the observation number column with a column of variable values. Submit the following statements:

```
proc fsview data=master.subscrib;
   id fullname;
   var begdate yrs;
run;
```

Because an ID variable is specified, observation numbers are not displayed. Values of the ID variable FULLNAME appear in the leftmost column. (The default color for ID variables is red on color display devices.) Because a VAR statement is included, the only other variables displayed are those specified in that statement, BEGDATE and YRS. Display 4.3 shows the modified display.

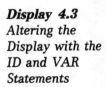

Display 4.3
Altering the
Display with the
ID and VAR
Statements

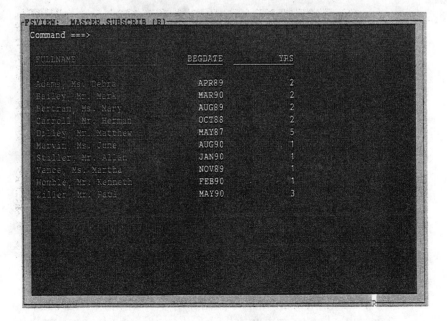

Displaying Additional Variables

If you decide that you need information in variables that are not currently displayed, use the SHOW command to add variables to the display. The SHOW command gives you the choice of displaying the added variable as either an ID or a scrolling variable. An ID variable remains on the left side of the display to identify observations as you scroll. Scrolling variables can be scrolled left and right. When the data set is opened for editing, ID variable values can be edited just like other variable values. Use the ID or VAR argument with the SHOW command to indicate whether the added variable is to be displayed as an ID variable or as a scrolling variable, respectively.

For example, issue the following SHOW command to add the remaining data set variables to the display as scrolling variables:

```
show var addr1 addr2 new
```

Variables are added in the order specified in the SHOW command. For this example, the additions are not immediately obvious when the SHOW command is issued because the ADDR1 variable is too wide to fit in the space available to the right of the YRS variable. Scroll right to see the added variables. Use the LEFT MAX command to return to scroll back to the leftmost variable.

You can use more than one ID variable. For example, issue the following SHOW command to change NEW to an ID variable for the FSVIEW window:

```
show id new
```

As shown in Display 4.4, the new ID variable is added to the right of the current ID variable, FULLNAME.

*Display 4.4
Adding a Second
ID Variable*

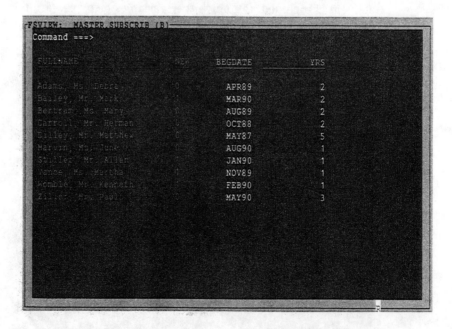

If you have a color display, NEW is now in the ID variable color (red by default). The column for the NEW variable no longer scrolls when you use the LEFT and RIGHT commands.

Note: The FSVIEW procedure limits the combined length of all ID variables to 60 characters. If the first ID variable is greater than 60 characters long, it is truncated in the display (the actual variable values in the data set are not affected). If the first ID variable is less than 60 characters long, additional ID variables are displayed as long as they fit in the allowed space without truncation. Additional ID variables that do not fit are not displayed.

Issue the following SHOW command to change NEW back to a scrolling variable:

```
show var new
```

NEW is once again the rightmost variable in the display.

Moving Variable Columns

If all of the variables you want are displayed but you would prefer a different order, you can move variable columns with the MOVE command. The MOVE command repositions one or more variables to the right of a target variable. Like the other FSVIEW display modification commands, the MOVE command affects only the arrangement of the variables in the display. The order of variables in the data set is unaffected.

For example, issue the following MOVE command to move the BEGDATE and YRS variables following the NEW variable:

```
move begdate-yrs new
```

After this MOVE command is issued, the ADDR1 variable becomes the leftmost variable in the display (after the ID variable, FULLNAME). Scroll right twice to verify that the BEGDATE and YRS variables now appear after the NEW variable. Use the command LEFT MAX to scroll back to the ADDR1 variable column.

Removing Variables from the Display

You can also drop variables from the display using the DROP command. For example, suppose you no longer need to view address information. Issue the following DROP command to remove the ADDR1 and ADDR2 variables from the display:

```
drop addr1 addr2
```

Display 4.5 shows the display after the variables are dropped.

Display 4.5
*Dropping
Variables from the
Display*

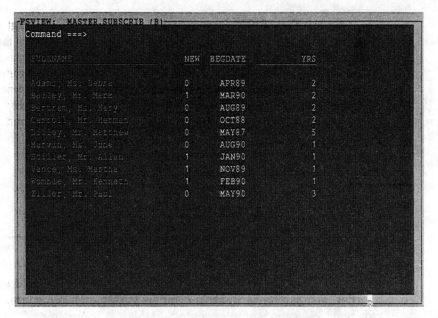

Restoring Observation Numbers

In the example session, observations are identified by the ID variable value rather than by observation number. To find the observation number for a particular observation, use the OBS command. Type OBS on the command line, position the cursor on the line for the desired observation, and press ENTER. A note in the window's message line informs you of the corresponding observation number.

To restore observation numbers, change all the ID variables back to scrolling variables. This example currently has only one ID variable, FULLNAME. Issue the following SHOW command to restore observation numbers:

```
show var fullname
```

Display 4.6 shows the resulting display.

Display 4.6
Displaying
Observation
Numbers

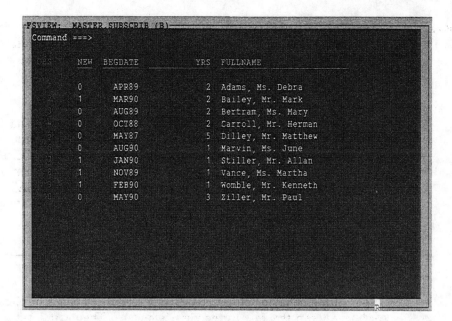

The FULLNAME variable was added to the right of the other variables. Use the MOVE command if you want to reposition it.

Ending the Customized Session

Use the END command to close the FSVIEW window. By default, all customization information is lost when the window is closed. However, it is possible to save this information so that the custom display format is available whenever the data set is viewed. This process is described in Chapter 9, "Creating Data Entry Applications Using the FSVIEW Procedure."

Editing SAS Data Sets

To edit rather than browse a data set with the FSVIEW procedure, you must do one of the following:

□ Use the EDIT option (or the equivalent MODIFY option) in the PROC FSVIEW statement that initiates the procedure.

□ Use the MODIFY command in an FSVIEW window opened for browsing. This changes the current FSVIEW window to editing.

□ Use the EDIT command in an FSVIEW window. Note that this command opens a new FSVIEW window for editing a specified data set. The previous FSVIEW window is not closed.

The following sections demonstrate the basic editing features of the FSVIEW procedure.

▶ *Caution* . . . . *The FSVIEW procedure edits a data set in place.*

The FSVIEW procedure does not leave an unedited copy of the original. If you need to preserve a copy of the original data, be sure to make a copy of the data set before you begin editing the data set. ▲

Note: You can also use the FSVIEW procedure to edit data in tables created by certain database management system (DBMS) software products. You must first create a SAS data view of the table using SAS/ACCESS software; then you can open the view for editing. See SAS/ACCESS documentation for information on creating and editing SAS data views. Only SAS/ACCESS views can be edited. You receive an error message if you attempt to edit a view created with the SQL procedure.

Understanding Control Levels

The editing behavior of the FSVIEW procedure depends on the *control level* selected when the data set or view is opened. The control level is the degree to which the procedure can restrict access to the data set. This section explains the concept of control level; see "Editing Observations" later in this chapter for an explanation of how the control level affects the way you edit observations in the FSVIEW window. The FSVIEW procedure supports two levels of control:

RECORD   locks only the observation currently being edited. With this control level, you can open multiple FSVIEW windows for browsing or editing the same data set. Using SAS/SHARE software, other users can edit the same data set simultaneously.

MEMBER   locks the entire data set. No other window or user can open the data set while this control level is in effect.

By default, the FSVIEW procedure selects a control level of RECORD when it opens a SAS data set.

In the FSVIEW window, you can select the control level with the MODIFY command. If the FSVIEW window is open for browsing, the MODIFY command without arguments opens the data set for editing with a control level of RECORD. The MODIFY RECORD command achieves the same result. Use the MODIFY MEMBER command to open the data set with a control level of MEMBER. If the FSVIEW window is already open for editing, you can use the MODIFY RECORD and MODIFY MEMBER commands to change the current control level of the displayed data set.

The MODIFY command fails if the specified control level would cause a locking conflict. For example, you cannot specify MODIFY MEMBER if the same data set is open with a control level of RECORD in another FSVIEW window.

You can use the CNTLLEV= data set option to select the initial control level when you open an FSVIEW window. The CNTLLEV= data set option can be used

□ with the DATA= option in a PROC FSVIEW statement:

```
proc fsview data=master.subscrib(cntllev=member);
```

□ with the data set name argument in an FSVIEW command:

```
fsview master.subscrib(cntllev=member)
```

□ with the data set name argument in a BROWSE or EDIT command in the FSVIEW window:

```
edit master.subscrib(cntllev=member)
```

Refer to Chapter 15, "SAS Data Set Options," in *SAS Language: Reference, Version 6, First Edition* for more information on the CNTLLEV= option.

A Sample Session: Basic Editing Features

Suppose that the circulation department of a monthly magazine, *The News Monthly*, stores its subscriber list information in a SAS data set. This data set must be updated frequently as new subscribers are added and old subscribers move, renew their subscriptions, cancel their subscriptions, or allow their subscriptions to lapse. The FSVIEW procedure lets you

□ update observations to record renewals and address changes

□ add observations for new subscribers

□ delete observations for canceled or lapsed subscriptions.

The data set used in the following examples, MASTER.SUBSCRIB, is described in Chapter 1. To begin editing the sample data set, submit the following statements:

```
proc fsview data=master.subscrib edit;
run;
```

The PROC FSVIEW statement initiates an FSVIEW session and opens an FSVIEW window. The DATA= option specifies the data set to display. The EDIT option indicates that the data set is displayed for editing rather than the default browsing.

Display 4.7 shows the data set displayed for editing, as indicated by the (E) following the window title.

Display 4.7
*Displaying a Data
Set for Editing*

```
┌FSVIEW: MASTER.SUBSCRIB (E)─────────────────────────────────┐
│Command ===>                                                │
│                                                            │
│  OBS      FULLNAME                    ADDR1                 │
│                                                            │
│    1    Adams, Ms. Debra           1414 S. 20th St.        │
│    2    Bailey, Mr. Mark           2721 1/2 Van Dyke       │
│    3    Bertram, Ms. Mary          701 Catawba             │
│    4    Carroll, Mr. Herman        6122-A Smithdale Dr.    │
│    5    Dilley, Mr. Matthew        420 Polk St.            │
│    6    Marvin, Ms. June           Route 7, Box 482        │
│    7    Stiller, Mr. Allan         Route 2, Box 22-B       │
│    8    Vance, Ms. Martha          424-204 Navaho Dr.      │
│    9    Womble, Mr. Kenneth        702-F Walden Dr.        │
│   10    Ziller, Mr. Paul           P.O. Box 94             │
│                                                            │
│                                                            │
│                                                            │
│                                                            │
└────────────────────────────────────────────────────────────┘
```

Editing Observations

The process of editing observations in the FSVIEW window differs according to
the control level selected for the data set.

When RECORD-Level Control Is Used

When the data set is opened with a control level of RECORD (which is the
default), the FSVIEW window can share control of the data set with other
windows or other users. In this case, the FSVIEW procedure must explicitly
control, or *lock*, an observation before the values in the observation can be
edited.

To lock a particular observation for editing, move the cursor anywhere on
the FSVIEW window line for the desired observation and press ENTER. The line
is highlighted to indicate that it is locked for editing. As long as the observation
is locked, you can change variable values in the observation by typing over the
existing information. If the variables in the observation do not all fit horizontally
in the window, you can scroll right to view additional variables.

Note: You can use the HI command to specify how the line for the locked
observation is highlighted. See Chapter 16, "The FSVIEW Procedure," for
details.

Suppose you want to correct Mary Bertram's street address in the example
data set. Move to her observation (observation 3) and press ENTER; the line is
highlighted, indicating that this FSVIEW window has locked that observation.
Then move to the column for the variable ADDR1 and add *Ave.* after the street
name. Display 4.8 shows the example data set with observation 3 locked for
editing and with the ADDR1 variable value updated.

Display 4.8
Observation
Selected for
Editing

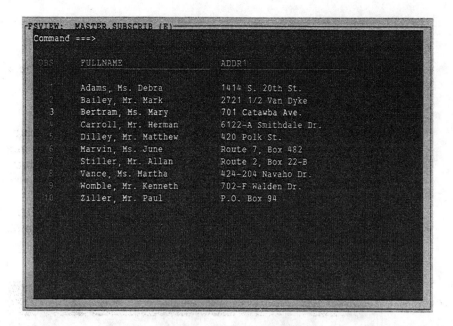

Each FSVIEW window can lock only one observation at a time. When you move to a different observation and press ENTER, the previously locked observation is released. If you attempt to lock an observation that another window or procedure has currently locked for editing, you receive a warning message telling you that the selected observation is unavailable.

The following commands cause the FSVIEW procedure to lose its lock on the current observation if the observation is scrolled out of the window as a result of the command:

FORWARD   *n*
BACKWARD   AUTOADD
TOP   DUP
BOTTOM

The following commands always cause the FSVIEW procedure to lose its lock on the current observation:

DELETE
SORT
WHERE

When MEMBER-Level Control Is Used

The process of editing observations is simpler when the data set is opened with a control level of MEMBER. In that case, the FSVIEW window has exclusive control of the data set, so all observations are available for editing at all times. To change a displayed value, simply type over the existing information. You can use the MODIFY MEMBER command or the CNTLLEV= data set option to select MEMBER-level control for the data set.

Adding Observations

To add observations to the data set, issue the following command:

```
autoadd on
```

When the AUTOADD feature is set on, the FSVIEW procedure automatically displays a new blank observation at the end of the data set and continues to display new observations each time you fill in the current blank one. The observations are not actually added to the data set until you enter values in them.

Display 4.9 shows the FSVIEW window with the AUTOADD feature on. Notice that the new observation is identified by NEW in the observation number column.

Display 4.9
Observation
Added
Automatically

```
┌─FSVIEW:  MASTER SUBSCRIB (E)─────────────────────────────────┐
│ Command ===>                                                  │
│ NOTE: The AUTOADD option has been turned on.                  │
│ OBS      FULLNAME              ADDR1                           │
│                                                               │
│    2     Bailey, Mr. Mark      2721 1/2 Van Dyke              │
│    3     Bertram, Ms. Mary     701 Catawba Ave.              │
│    4     Carroll, Mr. Herman   6122-A Smithdale Dr.          │
│    5     Dilley, Mr. Matthew   420 Polk St.                  │
│    6     Marvin, Ms. June      Route 7, Box 482              │
│    7     Stiller, Mr. Allan    Route 2, Box 22-B             │
│    8     Vance, Ms. Martha     424-204 Navaho Dr.           │
│    9     Womble, Mr. Kenneth   702-F Walden Dr.             │
│   10     Ziller, Mr. Paul      P.O. Box 94                   │
│  NEW                                                          │
└──────────────────────────────────────────────────────────────┘
```

To enter values for the new observation, simply type the values in the fields provided. For example, enter the following information to create an observation for David Freeman, a new subscriber:

FULLNAME	ADDR1	ADDR2	BEGDATE	YRS	NEW
---------	-----	-----	-------	---	---
Freeman, Mr. David	Route 7, Box 483	Durham, NC 27714	AUG90	2	1

You must scroll right to enter all the variables. (Use the RIGHT command to scroll rather than the TAB key. When the cursor is on the rightmost column in the window, the TAB key moves the cursor to the top observation in the window rather than scrolling to the next variable column.) When you have entered values for all the variables, press ENTER to add the new observation to the data set. Because the AUTOADD feature is still on, another blank observation is created after the new one is added, as shown in Display 4.10.

Display 4.10
A New
Observation
Added to the Data
Set

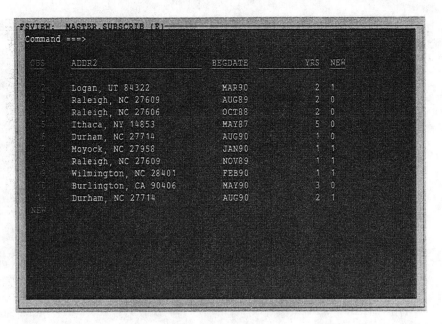

Use the following command to turn off the AUTOADD feature:

`autoadd off`

The NEW observation is removed. Now use the following command to return to the leftmost variables in the window:

`left max`

Duplicating an Existing Observation

If you want to add a new entry that is similar to an existing one, you can use the DUP (duplicate) command to create a new copy of the observation and then type over values that need changing. For example, the values you just entered for David Freeman are very similar to those of June Marvin's (observation 6). You can save typing by duplicating observation 6 and changing the necessary values.

Type DUP on the command line, position the cursor anywhere on June's observation, and press ENTER. (Or position the cursor on the observation and press the function key to which the DUP command has been assigned.) June's observation is duplicated. The new copy is added to the end of the data set. Display 4.11 shows the result.

Display 4.11
Duplicating an
Observation

```
┌─FSVIEW: MASTER.SUBSCRIB (E)──────────────────────────────────┐
│ Command ===>                                                 │
│                                                              │
│  OBS    FULLNAME                ADDR1                         │
│ ──────────────────────────────────────────────────          │
│    3    Bertram, Ms. Mary       701 Catawba Ave.             │
│    4    Carroll, Mr. Herman     6122-A Smithdale Dr.         │
│    5    Dilley, Mr. Matthew     420 Polk St.                 │
│    6    Marvin, Ms. June        Route 7, Box 482             │
│    7    Stiller, Mr. Allan      Route 2, Box 22-B            │
│    8    Vance, Ms. Martha       424-204 Navaho Dr.           │
│    9    Womble, Mr. Kenneth     702-F Walden Dr.             │
│   10    Ziller, Mr. Paul        P.O. Box 94                  │
│   11    Freeman, Mr. David      Route 7, Box 483             │
│   12    Marvin, Ms. June        Route 7, Box 482             │
│                                                              │
│                                                              │
└──────────────────────────────────────────────────────────────┘
```

For practice, edit the values in the duplicate observation to match those in the observation for David Freeman (observation 11). To lock the observation for editing, move the cursor to the line for observation 12 and press ENTER; then you can change the values in that observation.

Deleting an Observation

The DELETE command allows you to mark observations for deletion.

Note: Depending on the access method used, you may not be able to delete observations in the FSVIEW window. For example, you cannot delete observations from Version 5 data sets using this command.

For example, suppose Mary Bertram has canceled her subscription. To delete her observation (observation 3), issue the following DELETE command:

```
delete 3
```

There is another way to use the DELETE command. To delete the duplicate observation for David Freeman (observation 12) created in the example for the DUP command, type DELETE on the command line, position the cursor anywhere on observation 12, and press ENTER. This method is convenient when ID variables are used and observation numbers are not displayed.

Note: The first form of the DELETE command accepts multiple arguments, so you can also delete both observations 3 and 12 with a single command:

```
delete 3 12
```

The updated data set is shown in Display 4.12. (If you have followed the steps of the example, you will need to scroll backward to see all the observations.) Notice that observations 3 and 12 are no longer displayed.

Display 4.12
MASTER.SUBSCRIB
Data Set with
Deleted
Observations

```
┌─FSVIEW: MASTER.SUBSCRIB (E)─────────────────────────────────────────
│Command ===>
│
│ OBS     FULLNAME                   ADDR1
│
│   1     Adams, Ms. Debra           1414 S. 20th St.
│   2     Bailey, Mr. Mark           2721 1/2 Van Dyke
│   4     Carroll, Mr. Herman        6122-A Smithdale Dr.
│   5     Dilley, Mr. Matthew        420 Polk St.
│   6     Marvin, Ms. June           Route 7, Box 482
│   7     Stiller, Mr. Allan         Route 2, Box 22-B
│   8     Vance, Ms. Martha          424-204 Navaho Dr.
│   9     Womble, Mr. Kenneth        702-F Walden Dr.
│  10     Ziller, Mr. Paul           P.O. Box 94
│  11     Freeman, Mr. David         Route 7, Box 483
│
```

Special Topic: Removing Deleted Observations

When you use the DELETE command, the deleted observations
may or may not be physically removed from the data set,
depending on the way the data set is accessed.

For uncompressed Version 6 data sets, the deleted
observation is not physically removed from the data set. For
example, if you delete observation 3 as shown in the previous
example, end the FSVIEW session, and then later edit the data
set again in another FSVIEW session, observation 3 is
inaccessible. Likewise, if you use the PRINT procedure to print
the contents of the data set, nothing is printed for observation 3.

To actually remove the deleted observations, you must create
a new copy of the data set. For example, after ending the
FSVIEW session you can use the following simple DATA step to
eliminate observations marked for deletion in the example data
set:

```
data master.subscrib;
   set master.subscrib;
run;
```

SAS procedures that process data sets to produce other data
sets (the SORT procedure, for example) eliminate deleted
observations. The SORT command described in the following
section also removes deleted observations.

Sorting a SAS Data Set

During this session you have deleted one of the original observations and added one new observation. As a result, the observations are no longer ordered alphabetically by name as they were before. To reorder the data set, issue the following command:

```
sort fullname
```

Display 4.13 shows the result of the SORT command. Freeman's observation, the one that was added, has been moved from the bottom of the display and is now in correct alphabetical position.

Display 4.13
The Sorted Data Set

```
┌─FSVIEW:  MASTER.SUBSCRIB (E)────────────────────────────
│ Command ===>
│
│       FULLNAME                ADDR1
│       ──────────────────────  ──────────────────────
│       Adams, Ms. Debra        1414 S. 20th St.
│       Bailey, Mr. Mark        2721 1/2 Van Dyke
│       Carroll, Mr. Herman     6122-A Smithdale Dr.
│       Dilley, Mr. Matthew     420 Polk St.
│       Freeman, Mr. David      Route 7, Box 483
│       Marvin, Ms. June        Route 7, Box 482
│       Stiller, Mr. Allan      Route 2, Box 22-B
│       Vance, Ms. Martha       424-204 Navaho Dr.
│       Womble, Mr. Kenneth     702-F Walden Dr.
│       Ziller, Mr. Paul        P.O. Box 94
```

The FSVIEW procedure's SORT command actually sorts the data set itself, not just the current display. Therefore, the SORT command is only allowed when editing data sets.

▶ *Caution* . . . . *The FSVIEW procedure sorts a data set in place.*
The FSVIEW procedure does not leave an unsorted copy of the data set. If you need to preserve a copy of the original data, be sure to make a copy of the data set before you issue the SORT command. ▲

Ending the Editing Session

To end the FSVIEW editing session, issue the END command. This saves the
updated data set and closes the FSVIEW window.

Displaying Additional SAS Data Sets

You can browse or edit other SAS data sets without leaving the FSVIEW
procedure or closing the data set currently displayed. Opening multiple FSVIEW
windows from a single FSVIEW session uses fewer resources than using the
FSVIEW command to start additional FSVIEW sessions.

Submit the following statements to create a second example data set named
MASTER.SUBS2 and begin an FSVIEW session for browsing the original
example data set (MASTER.SUBSCRIB):

```
data master.subs2;
   set master.subscrib;
   drop addr1 addr2;
run;

proc fsview data=master.subscrib;
run;
```

Browsing Another Data Set

To browse another data set while the current FSVIEW window is still open, use
the BROWSE command. For example, issue the following BROWSE command in
the current FSVIEW window to open a second FSVIEW window for browsing
the MASTER.SUBS2 data set:

```
browse master.subs2
```

Note: The data set named in the BROWSE command must already exist;
otherwise, an error message appears when you issue the command.

Display 4.14 shows the FSVIEW session with the second FSVIEW window
opened for browsing.

Display 4.14
Displaying
Another SAS Data
Set

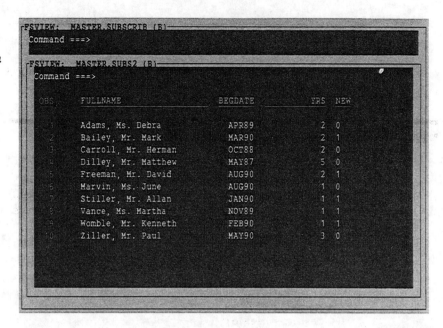

All global commands and FSVIEW window browsing commands are valid in the new window. For example, try the following:

□ Use the SWAP command to return to the first FSVIEW window without closing the new one. Use SWAP again to return to the new window.

□ Use the ZOOM ON command to make the new FSVIEW window occupy the entire display. Use ZOOM OFF to return the window to its original size.

□ Use the MODIFY command to change the added FSVIEW window from browsing to editing.

□ Use the END command to close the second FSVIEW window and return to the first.

Editing Another Data Set

To edit another data set while the current FSVIEW window is open, use the EDIT command. For example, issue the following command in the current FSVIEW window to open a second FSVIEW window that displays the data set MASTER.SUBS2 for editing:

```
edit master.subs2
```

The display is the same as Display 4.14, except for an (E) following the window title to indicate that it is opened for editing. All FSVIEW window commands are valid in the new window. Use the END command to close the new FSVIEW window and return to the original FSVIEW window.

Note: You can also open multiple FSVIEW windows for editing the same data set, as long as all of the windows select a control level of RECORD (the default). If you open multiple FSVIEW sessions for editing a single data set, only one of the windows can lock any given observation at one time.

Using WHERE Clauses

Sometimes you only need to process a subset of the observations in a SAS data set, rather than the entire data set. For such occasions, the SAS System provides WHERE clauses. A WHERE clause is a set of conditions that observations in a data set must meet in order to be processed. Observations that do not satisfy the conditions cannot be viewed or edited. They are effectively excluded from the data set while the WHERE clause is in effect.

Two types of WHERE clauses are available in FSVIEW sessions:

□   those established by WHERE statements when the procedure is started. These are called permanent WHERE clauses because they cannot be modified or canceled while the procedure is executing.

□   those established by WHERE commands during the editing or browsing session. These are called temporary WHERE clauses because they can be modified or canceled while the procedure is executing.

The data set used in the following examples is MASTER.SUBSCRIB as updated in the previous FSVIEW procedure editing examples.

Using Permanent WHERE Clauses

Suppose *The News Monthly* wants to process only observations for first-time subscribers. These subscribers are identified by the value 1 in the variable NEW. Use a WHERE statement to begin an FSVIEW session with a permanent WHERE clause applied that selects the desired subset of the updated MASTER.SUBSCRIB data set:

```
proc fsview data=master.subscrib;
   where new='1';
run;
```

Note that the value 1 in the WHERE statement must be enclosed in quotes to identify it as a character value rather than numeric. NEW is a character variable.

Display 4.15 shows the initial FSVIEW window display after these statements are submitted. The word *Subset* in parentheses following the window title tells you that a permanent WHERE clause is in effect.

Display 4.15
Permanent
WHERE Clause in
Effect

```
┌─FSVIEW:   MASTER.SUBSCRIB (B) (Subset)──────────────────────────────┐
│Command ===>                                                         │
│                                                                     │
│ OBS      FULLNAME                   ADDR1                           │
│ ─────────────────────────────────────────────                      │
│                                                                     │
│   2      Bailey, Mr. Mark           2721 1/2 Van Dyke               │
│   5      Freeman, Mr. David         Route 7, Box 483               │
│   7      Stiller, Mr. Allan         Route 2, Box 22-B              │
│   8      Vance, Ms. Martha          424-204 Navaho Dr.            │
│   9      Womble, Mr. Kenneth        702-F Walden Dr.              │
│                                                                     │
│                                                                     │
└─────────────────────────────────────────────────────────────────────┘
```

Note that the first observation in the display is observation 2. Observation 1 (Debra Adams) is not displayed because the NEW variable value in that observation is 0, not 1. Observations 3, 4, 6, and 10 are also omitted from the display because they do not meet the condition imposed by the WHERE clause.

Using Temporary WHERE Clauses

You can use the WHERE command to create temporary subsets of the input data set. The following examples show the use of the WHERE command in an FSVIEW session that also has a permanent WHERE clause applied by a WHERE statement. However, this is not a requirement; the WHERE command can be used independently of the WHERE statement.

Suppose the FSVIEW session with the permanent WHERE clause initiated in the previous session is still executing and you want to further restrict processing to exclude those subscribers who began their subscriptions before January 1, 1990. The following command establishes a temporary WHERE clause that imposes the desired restriction:

```
where begdate>='01jan90'd
```

Once this command is issued, only observations for those subscribers who began their current subscription on or after the specified date are available for processing. Observation 8 (Martha Vance) is omitted because its BEGDATE value does not meet the WHERE condition. As shown in Display 4.16, the word *Where...* appears in the upper-right corner of the window border to indicate that a temporary WHERE clause is in effect.

Display 4.16
Temporary
WHERE Clause in
Effect

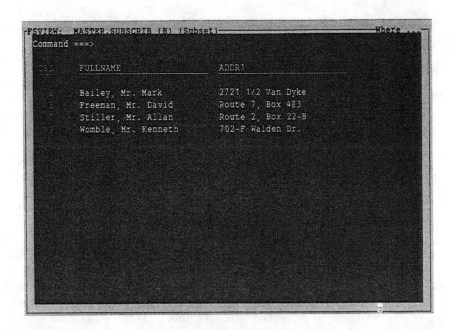

The WHERE command has several additional options. For example, each WHERE command by default replaces the temporary WHERE clause established by the previous one. However, if you use the ALSO option, the specified condition is added to the current clause. To further restrict processing to those observations for new subscribers who began after December 31, 1989 and who subscribed for only one year, issue the following command:

```
where also yrs=1
```

Once this command is executed, observation 2 (Mark Bailey) and observation 5 (David Freeman) are excluded because the YRS variable value for those observations does not satisfy the new WHERE condition.

You can use the UNDO option with a WHERE command to remove the most recently added condition from the current temporary WHERE clause. For example, the following command removes the restriction that limits processing to one-year subscriptions (YRS=1):

```
where undo
```

You can completely cancel the current temporary WHERE clause by entering WHERE alone on the command line, or by using the following command:

```
where clear
```

Canceling the temporary WHERE clause has no effect on the permanent WHERE clause established by the WHERE statement.

Creating New SAS Data Sets

In addition to editing and browsing, you can also use the FSVIEW procedure to

□   create new, empty SAS data sets. Once the data set is created, you can use the FSVIEW procedure to add observations and enter values.

□   create new SAS data sets that duplicate both the structure and contents of the data set currently displayed.

Creating an Empty Data Set

To create a new empty data set, you use the FSVIEW NEW window. You fill in the fields provided to name variables and to specify their characteristics. When you close the FSVIEW NEW window, the data set is created and an FSVIEW window is opened. You can then add observations to the data set and enter variable values for each observation.

The following sections discuss how to create a new SAS data set, including how to create a SAS data set like an existing one without entering all the information yourself. See Chapter 16 for complete descriptions of the commands used in the following examples.

Opening the FSVIEW NEW Window

You can open the FSVIEW NEW window in two different ways:

□   using the NEW= option with the PROC FSVIEW statement when you invoke the procedure

□   using the NEW command after you enter the procedure.

Using the NEW= Option
When you invoke the FSVIEW procedure with the NEW= option rather than with the DATA= option in the PROC FSVIEW statement, the FSVIEW NEW window is opened when the FSVIEW procedure is initiated.

For example, the following statements initiate an FSVIEW session and open the FSVIEW NEW window to create the new data set MASTER.QTR1DAT:

```
proc fsview new=master.qtr1dat;
run;
```

Display 4.17 shows the initial FSVIEW NEW window display.

Display 4.17
The FSVIEW NEW
Window

Using the NEW Command

When you issue a NEW command from an FSVIEW window, the FSVIEW NEW window is opened to define a new data set within an FSVIEW session.

For example, the following command opens the FSVIEW NEW window to define the data set MASTER.QTR2DAT:

```
new master.qtr2dat
```

The display in this case is the same as shown in Display 4.17 (except for the data set name).

Defining the Data Set

Whether you open the FSVIEW NEW window using the NEW= option or the NEW command, the process of defining the data set is the same. You define the structure of the new data set by entering values in the fields of the FSVIEW NEW window. You must specify at least a name for each variable. You can also specify a type, length, label, format, and informat. See Chapter 16 for a summary of the rules for defining variables in the FSVIEW NEW window.

Display 4.18 shows the FSVIEW NEW window from Display 4.17 with six variables defined.

Display 4.18
Defining Variables
for the New Data
Set

```
┌─FSVIEW: NEW.MASTER.QTR1DAT (E)──────────────────────────────────┐
│ Command ===>                                                     │
│                                                                  │
│  Name     Type Length                Label              Format   │
│                                                                  │
│  REGION    $    8   _____  _____  │
│  STATE     $    8   _____  _____  │
│  MONTH     N    8   _____  MONYY5.    │
│  HEADCNT   N    8   _____  _____  │
│  EXPENSES  N    8   _____  _____  │
│  REVENUE   N    8   _____  _____  │
│                                                                  │
│           __   _     _____  _____ │
│           __   _     _____  _____ │
│           __   _     _____  _____ │
│           __   _     _____  _____ │
│           __   _     _____  _____ │
│           __   _     _____  _____ │
│           __   _     _____  _____ │
│           __   _     _____  _____ │
│           __   _     _____  _____ │
│           __   _     _____  _____ │
│           __   _     _____  _____ │
│                                                              R   │
└──────────────────────────────────────────────────────────────┘
```

Displaying the Format and Informat Columns

The Format and Informat columns share the same display area at the far-right
side of the window; only one of these columns is visible at one time. The Format
column is displayed initially. (See Display 4.18.) Use either the RIGHT or the
LEFT command to display the Informat column, as shown in Display 4.19. The
LEFT command and RIGHT commands both alternate between the Format and
Informat fields in the rightmost column of the FSVIEW NEW window.

Display 4.19
Displaying the
Informat Field

```
┌─FSVIEW: NEW.MASTER.QTR1DAT (R)──────────────────────────────────┐
│ Command ===>                                                     │
│                                                                  │
│  Name     Type Length                Label             Informat  │
│                                                                  │
│  REGION    $    8   _____  _____  │
│  STATE     $    8   _____  _____  │
│  MONTH     N    8   _____  MONYY5.    │
│  HEADCNT   N    8   _____  _____  │
│  EXPENSES  N    8   _____  _____  │
│  REVENUE   N    8   _____  _____  │
│                                                                  │
│           __   _     _____  _____ │
│           __   _     _____  _____ │
│           __   _     _____  _____ │
│           __   _     _____  _____ │
│           __   _     _____  _____ │
│           __   _     _____  _____ │
│           __   _     _____  _____ │
│           __   _     _____  _____ │
│           __   _     _____  _____ │
│           __   _     _____  _____ │
│           __   _     _____  _____ │
│                                                              R   │
└──────────────────────────────────────────────────────────────┘
```

Saving Keystrokes with the SELECT and REPEAT Commands

The SELECT and REPEAT commands can be time-saving features. If you have two or more variables that are similar, these commands save you keystrokes.

Note: The SELECT and REPEAT commands are most effective when they are assigned to function keys. The following discussion assumes that these key assignments have been made. (To check the current function key definitions, use the KEYS command to open the KEYS window.) To use the commands without function keys, type the command on the command line, position the cursor on the line for the desired variable, and press ENTER.

For example, type in the information required for the variable ADDR1. Then position the cursor on any of the fields in the definition of ADDR1 and press the SELECT key.

Name	Type	Length	Label	Format
ADDR1	$	30	_____	_____
_____	_	__	_____	_____
_____	_	__	_____	_____
_____	_	__	_____	_____

You have just selected the variable you want repeated. Now move the cursor to the next line and press the REPEAT key.

Name	Type	Length	Label	Format
ADDR1	$	30	_____	_____
ADDR1	$	30	_____	_____
_____	_	__	_____	_____
_____	_	__	_____	_____

Change the name on line 2 to read ADDR2.

Name	Type	Length	Label	Format
ADDR1	$	30	_____	_____
ADDR2	$	30	_____	_____
_____	_	__	_____	_____
_____	_	__	_____	_____

Now position the cursor on the third line and press the REPEAT key again. Change the name to ADDR3.

Name	Type	Length	Label	Format
ADDR1	$	30	_____	_____
ADDR2	$	30	_____	_____
ADDR3	$	30	_____	_____
_____	_	__	_____	_____

Closing the FSVIEW NEW Window

To create the new data set, issue the END command. An FSVIEW window is automatically opened for editing so that you can add observations and enter variable values. If you open the FSVIEW NEW window using the NEW command in an existing FSVIEW window, a new FSVIEW window is opened for the new data set.

Note: After you issue the END command to close the FSVIEW NEW window, you cannot return to that window to make changes to the structure of the data set.

Creating an Empty Data Set Like an Existing One

If you want to create a SAS data set that is identical or similar in structure to an existing one, you can save time by letting the FSVIEW procedure do some of the work. Instead of entering all the variable information, use the LIKE= option to identify an existing SAS data set. When the FSVIEW NEW window is opened, the variable names and attributes of the data set you specify are automatically displayed. (Only the structure of the specified data set is copied, not the contents.)

As discussed earlier, you open the FSVIEW NEW window in one of two ways: either with the NEW= option when you invoke the FSVIEW procedure or with the NEW command when you open an additional FSVIEW window. The LIKE= option can be used with both of these methods.

In the PROC FSVIEW statement, the LIKE= option is used in conjunction with the NEW= option. For example, the following statements initiate an FSVIEW session, open the FSVIEW NEW window to create the data set MASTER.QTR3DAT, and fill in the fields of the FSVIEW NEW window with the names and attributes of the variables in the data set MASTER.QTR1DAT:

```
proc fsview new=master.qtr3dat like=master.qtr1dat;
run;
```

The following command performs the same tasks, but from within an active FSVIEW session:

```
new master.qtr3dat like=master.qtr1dat
```

As shown in Display 4.20, the FSVIEW NEW window is initialized with the attributes of the existing data set.

Display 4.20
Using the LIKE=
Option

```
┌─FSVIEW: NEW MASTER.QTR3DAT (E)──────────────────────────────────────────┐
│Command ===>                                                             │
│                                                                         │
│   Name    Type Length              Label                    Format      │
│                                                                         │
│   REGION   $    8   _____  _____  │
│   STATE    $    8   _____  _____  │
│   MONTH    N    8   _____  MONYY5.     │
│   HEADCNT  N    8   _____  _____  │
│   EXPENSES N    8   _____  _____  │
│   REVENUE  N    8   _____  _____  │
│                                                                         │
│   _____  _    _   _____  _____  │
│                                                                         │
│   _____  _    _   _____  _____  │
│                                                                         │
│   _____  _    _   _____  _____  │
│                                                                         │
│   _____  _    _   _____  _____  │
│                                                                         │
│   _____  _    _   _____  _____  │
│                                                                         │
│   _____  _    _   _____  _____  │
└─────────────────────────────────────────────────────────────────────────┘
```

The display contains all the information necessary to create a SAS data set with exactly the same structure as the one specified. You have three choices:

□ You can create a data set with exactly the same variable attributes as the data set you specified. Just issue the END command to create the data set and open an FSVIEW window for editing the new data set.

□ You can create a similar data set. Just make any necessary changes (such as altering any variable names, lengths, labels, and so on). To delete a variable entirely, simply type spaces over its name. After you have made all the desired changes, issue the END command to create the new data set and open the FSVIEW window.

□ You can decide not to create a data set. Issue the CANCEL command to close the FSVIEW NEW window without creating a new data set. If the FSVIEW NEW window was opened by a NEW command, the procedure returns to the FSVIEW window from which the command was issued. If the window was opened by a NEW= option in a PROC FSVIEW statement, the procedure terminates.

Creating a New Data Set from an Existing One

The FSVIEW procedure allows you to create a new data set that duplicates both the structure and the contents of the one currently displayed in the FSVIEW window. You use the CREATE command to create new data sets. The new data set can incorporate some or all of the variables from the currently displayed data set.

The following example illustrates the use of the CREATE command. The data set used is MASTER.SUBSCRIB, the sample data set described in Chapter 1, updated as described in the FSVIEW procedure editing examples in this chapter.

Suppose you want to create a new data set containing the names and mailing addresses of subscribers who have renewed at least once before. Begin by submitting the following statements to display the subscriber data set in the FSVIEW window:

```
proc fsview data=master.subscrib;
run;
```

Next, issue the following command in the FSVIEW window to view only subscribers who have renewed before:

```
where new='0'
```

You can create a new data set containing the desired variables and observations by issuing the following command in the FSVIEW window:

```
create master.mailing fullname addr1 addr2
```

However, there is also an interactive way to use the CREATE command. Issue the following command instead:

```
create master.mailing
```

The procedure opens the FSVIEW VARLIST window in which you can select which variables you copy into the new data set. Display 4.21 shows the FSVIEW VARLIST window opened by the preceding command.

Display 4.21
Using the FSVIEW
VARLIST Window

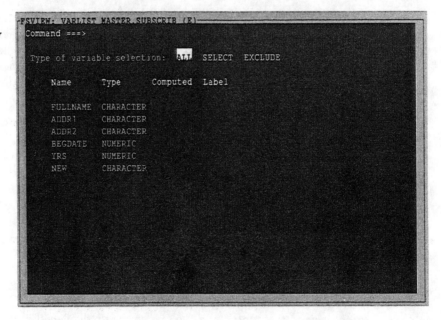

The window includes a list of the variables in the FSVIEW window along with three buttons: ALL, SELECT, and EXCLUDE. The buttons correspond to the three ways to use this window:

□ Select the ALL button to copy all variables.

□ Select the SELECT button; then mark which variables in the list you want to copy. Unmarked variables are not included in the new data set.

□ Select the EXCLUDE button; then mark which variables in the list you want to omit from the new data set. All unmarked variables are included in the new data set.

The selected action is carried out when you use the END command to close the FSVIEW VARLIST window.

For this example, choose the SELECT action by moving the cursor to that button and pressing ENTER. Then select the FULLNAME, ADDR1, and ADDR2 variables by positioning the cursor on the variable names and pressing ENTER. Display 4.22 shows the FSVIEW VARLIST window with these selections.

Display 4.22
Using the FSVIEW
VARLIST Window

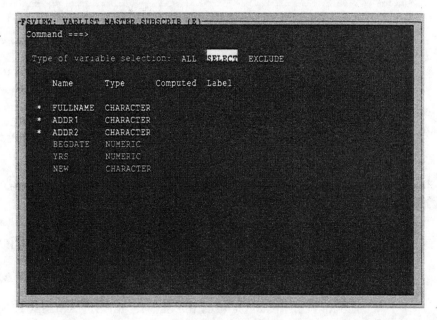

Issue the END command to close the FSVIEW VARLIST window and create the new data set. The new data set is not displayed automatically; you merely receive a message in the current FSVIEW window informing you that the data set has been created. To view the newly created data set, issue the following command:

```
browse master.mailing
```

Display 4.23 shows the new data set. You can also use the EDIT command to open the new data set for editing instead of browsing.

Display 4.23
Newly Created
MASTER.MAILING
Data Set

```
┌─FSVIEW: MASTER.SUBSCRIB (B)─────────────────────────Where────┐
│ Command ===>                                                 │
├─FSVIEW: MASTER.MAILING (B)───────────────────────────────────┤
│ Command ===>                                                 │
│                                                              │
│  OBS      FULLNAME              ADDR1                         │
│                                                              │
│    1      Adams, Ms. Debra      1414 S. 20th St.             │
│    2      Carroll, Mr. Herman   6122-A Smithdale Dr.         │
│    3      Dilley, Mr. Matthew   420 Polk St.                 │
│    4      Marvin, Ms. June      Route 7, Box 482             │
│    5      Ziller, Mr. Paul      P.O. Box 94                  │
│                                                              │
└──────────────────────────────────────────────────────────────┘
```

Notice that the new data set contains only those observations from the
MASTER.SUBSCRIB data set that were displayed when the CREATE command
was issued. The observations excluded from the original FSVIEW window by the
WHERE clause were not copied. Scroll right to verify that the new data set
contains only the specified variables: FULLNAME, ADDR1, and ADDR2.

Use the END command to close the FSVIEW window for the
MASTER.MAILING data set; then issue another END command to close the
FSVIEW window for the MASTER.SUBSCRIB data set.

Generating Simple Reports

Because you have so much control over the display in the FSVIEW procedure,
you can use the procedure as a simple report generator. Use FSVIEW commands
to display the variables you want, in the order and format you want; then use
the global SPRINT command to print the report.

The following example uses the data set MASTER.SUBSCRIB, described in
Chapter 1, as updated in the FSVIEW procedure editing examples in this
chapter.

Suppose you are interested in the new subscribers and you want to see a
report that contains their names and the starting dates and lengths of their
subscriptions. You can customize the FSVIEW display so that it contains the
desired information; then use the global command SPRINT to take a picture of
the display.

Submit the following statements to begin this example:

```
proc fsview data=master.subscrib;
   id fullname;
   var begdate yrs;
   where new='1';
run;
```

The ID and VAR statements select the variables that are displayed. Because FULLNAME is used as an ID variable, no observation numbers are printed. The WHERE statement restricts the procedure to only observations for new subscribers. The resulting display is shown in Display 4.24.

Display 4.24
Customized
Display for
MASTER.SUBSCRIB

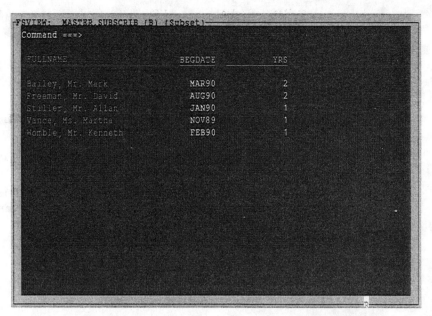

Now use the SPRINT command to take a picture of the display. By default, the SPRINT command captures an image of the entire display (except for the command and message lines), including the window border. Because you are only interested in the data, not in a representation of that data in a window frame, add the NOBORDER option to capture only the text within the FSVIEW window:

```
sprint noborder
```

To send the captured text to a printer or to a file, issue the following command:

```
sprint free
```

Output 4.1 shows the printout of the screen image captured by the SPRINT command. See Chapter 18, "Command Reference," for a complete discussion of the family of commands that make up this print utility.

Output 4.1
Result of the
SPRINT Command

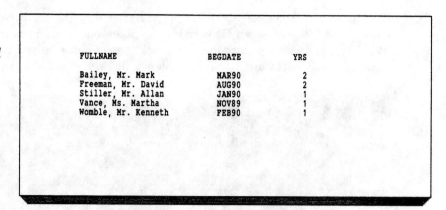

```
     FULLNAME                BEGDATE       YRS

     Bailey, Mr. Mark        MAR90          2
     Freeman, Mr. David      AUG90          2
     Stiller, Mr. Allan      JAN90          1
     Vance, Ms. Martha       NOV89          1
     Womble, Mr. Kenneth     FEB90          1
```

After the display image is captured and printed, issue the END command to close the FSVIEW window for this example.

Note: You can control the appearance of output created using the SPRINT command by modifying information in the form used to provide printing instructions. Refer to Chapter 20, "Forms," for more information.

Chapter 5 Preparing Letters Using the FSLETTER Procedure

Introduction

The FSLETTER procedure provides an interactive environment for composing, formatting, editing, storing, copying, moving, and printing all kinds of text. The procedure also allows you to send your output to an external file rather than to a printer.

You can compose and print a simple letter for one person or personalized versions of a letter for many different recipients. Applications are not limited to letters. You can use the same techniques to create personalized questionnaires, reports, and other documents.

How Text Is Stored

The FSLETTER procedure stores the text you enter in SAS catalog entries having the entry type LETTER. (The type is always LETTER, regardless of whether the text is a letter or some other kind of document.) When you use the FSLETTER procedure, you must specify the name of the catalog in which you want your text stored. You can also specify the name of the SAS data library in which the catalog resides. If you want your text stored beyond the end of the current SAS session, the catalog must reside in a permanent SAS data library. See Chapter 1, "Introduction to SAS/FSP Software," for a discussion of SAS catalogs and SAS data libraries. (Complete details are provided in Chapter 6, "SAS Files," in *SAS Language: Reference, Version 6, First Edition*.)

A complete FSLETTER document name consists of the following four elements:

libref.catalog-name.document-name.LETTER

□ The first element, *libref*, identifies the SAS data library in which the catalog resides. If you omit this element, the FSLETTER procedure assumes the default libref, WORK. Remember that the contents of the WORK library are erased at the end of your SAS session. Use the libref of a permanent SAS data library if you want to store your work beyond the current SAS session.

□ The second element, *catalog-name*, identifies the catalog within the SAS data library in which the catalog entries are stored. The FSLETTER procedure creates a new catalog if you use a catalog name that does not already exist.

□ The third element, *document-name*, identifies the document within the catalog.

□ The fourth element, LETTER, identifies the type of catalog entry. The FSLETTER procedure assumes the default entry type LETTER if you omit this element of the name.

Figure 5.1 illustrates the storage hierarchy for a document named MASTER.LETTERS.RENEWAL.LETTER.

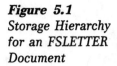

Figure 5.1
Storage Hierarchy for an FSLETTER Document

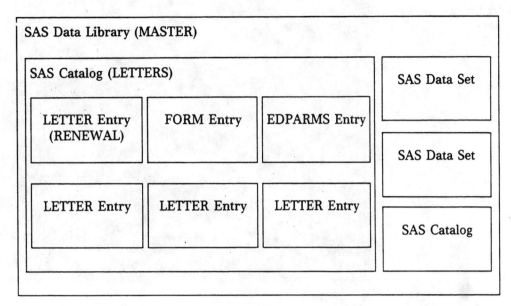

Notice that the catalog LETTERS can hold many different LETTER entries and that the data library MASTER can hold numerous catalogs and data sets. The LETTERS catalog in Figure 5.1 also shows two other catalog entry types used by the FSLETTER procedure: FORM and EDPARMS. These entry types are discussed later in this chapter.

Preparing a Letter for One Person

Suppose you work in the circulation department of *The News Monthly* and you must send a letter replying to a particular concern of one subscriber.

First, use a LIBNAME statement to associate the libref MASTER with the permanent SAS data library in which you want to create your letter catalog. Then use either a PROC FSLETTER statement or an FSLETTER command to initiate the FSLETTER procedure.

For example, submit the following statements to begin an FSLETTER session and create a catalog named LETTERS in the data library to which you assigned the libref MASTER:

```
proc fsletter letter=master.letters;
run;
```

All documents created during this FSLETTER session are stored in the catalog MASTER.LETTERS.

Alternatively, you can initiate the FSLETTER procedure and create the catalog by issuing the following command in any SAS System window:

```
fsletter master.letters
```

Display 5.1 shows the blank catalog directory displayed in the FSLETTER DIRECTORY window when the preceding statements or command are executed.

Display 5.1
An Empty Catalog
Directory

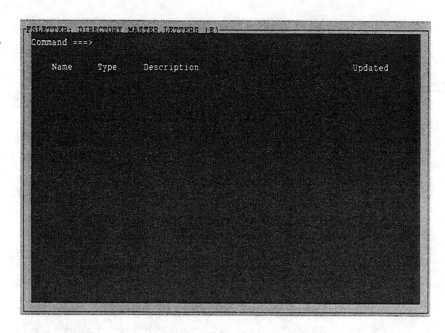

Execute the following command in the FSLETTER DIRECTORY window to begin entering a letter named JONES:

```
edit jones.letter
```

This command opens an FSLETTER window for editing the specified document. Because there is not currently an entry named JONES in the catalog, the FSLETTER window text area is initially blank (see Display 5.2).

Display 5.2
SAS Text Editor
Window for
Entering a New
Letter

The name of the entry appears in the upper-left corner of the window border. In the upper-right corner is the name of the form associated with this entry. The form defines how the text of the document is formatted. As shown, the default form for newly created entries is named FSLETTER. More information on forms is provided in "Enhancing Your Output" later in this chapter. This example uses the default form.

Vertical dashed lines on either side of the window bound the area in which you can enter text. The width of the text area is determined by the line width specified in the associated form. If the form width is greater than the FSLETTER window width, the vertical dashed line for the left margin is omitted and the line for the right margin may not be visible until you scroll to the right.

For practice, enter the text shown in Figure 5.2. Depending on the number of lines available on your device, you may have to scroll down to enter all the text.

Note: The third line of the main paragraph contains a deliberate misuse of the word *effect* and a deliberate misspelling, *subscritpion*. Enter the text exactly as shown.

Figure 5.2
Text for Example
Personal Letter

```
July 27, 1990




Mr. Edgar V. Jones
1066 Camelot Drive
Raleigh, NC  27609


Dear Mr. Jones:

Thank you for your recent letter. It is true that ownership of "The
News Monthly" has changed.  However, please be assured that the change
of ownership will in no way effect your subscritpion. You will continue
to receive your issues on time and for the full remainder of your
subscription term.  We appreciate your readership.



Sincerely,




Margaret E. Ellis
Subscription Department
"The News Monthly"
```

Using the Spelling Checker

Because the FSLETTER window uses the SAS text editor, the editor's spelling checker facility is available for proofing the documents you create. Issue the following command:

```
spell all
```

The spelling checker examines all the words in the document and opens the SPELL Unrecognized Words window to report those not found in its dictionary, as shown in Display 5.3.

Display 5.3
Using the Spelling Checker

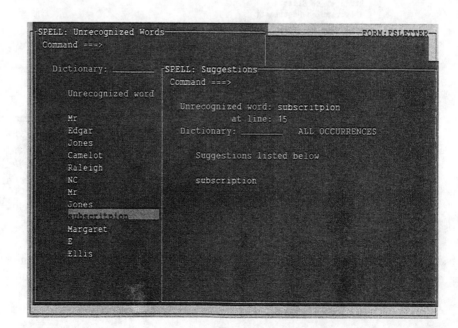

```
┌─SPELL: Unrecognized Words───────────────────────────────FORM:PSLETTER─┐
│  Command ===>                                                         │
│                                                                       │
│   Dictionary: _____                                                │
│                                                                       │
│      Unrecognized word      At line                                   │
│                                                                       │
│      Mr                     6                                         │
│      Edgar                  6                                         │
│      Jones                  6                                         │
│      Camelot                7                                         │
│      Raleigh                8                                         │
│      NC                     8                                         │
│      Mr                     11                                        │
│      Jones                  11                                        │
│      subscritpion           15          e that ownership of "The     │
│      Margaret               25           be assured that the change  │
│      E                      25          scritpion. You will          │
│      Ellis                  25           for the full remainder of   │
│                                          readership.                 │
└───────────────────────────────────────────────────────────────────────┘
```

Most of the words listed in the SPELL Unrecognized Words window are just abbreviations or proper names rather than actual misspellings. However, notice the occurrence of *subscritpion* in line 15 of the letter. This is an incorrect word.

If you want the spelling checker to suggest possible corrections, move the cursor to *subscritpion* in the SPELL Unrecognized Words window and press ENTER. The word is highlighted. Now issue the following command in the SPELL Unrecognized Words window:

suggest

This command opens the SPELL Suggestions window, as shown in Display 5.4.

Display 5.4
Suggested Correction for Misspelled Word

```
┌─SPELL: Unrecognized Words───────────────────────────────FORM:PSLETTER─┐
│  Command ===>                                                         │
│                                                                       │
│   Dictionary: _____ ┌─SPELL: Suggestions───────────────────┐      │
│                        │  Command ===>                         │      │
│      Unrecognized word │                                       │      │
│                        │    Unrecognized word: subscritpion    │      │
│      Mr                │              at line: 15              │      │
│      Edgar             │    Dictionary: _____  ALL OCCURRENCES     │
│      Jones             │                                       │      │
│      Camelot           │       Suggestions listed below        │      │
│      Raleigh           │                                       │      │
│      NC                │       subscription                    │      │
│      Mr                │                                       │      │
│      Jones             │                                       │      │
│      subscritpion      │                                       │      │
│      Margaret          │                                       │      │
│      E                 │                                       │      │
│      Ellis             └───────────────────────────────────────┘      │
└───────────────────────────────────────────────────────────────────────┘
```

The SPELL Suggestions window lists a possible correct spelling, *subscription*. This is the intended word. Move the cursor to the word and press ENTER to highlight it; then issue the following command in the SPELL Suggestions window:

`replace`

When the REPLACE command is executed, the SPELL Suggestions window is closed and you return to the SPELL Unrecognized Words window with a message that *subscritpion* has been replaced. Issue the END command to close the SPELL Unrecognized Words window. When you return to the FSLETTER window, notice that the spelling of *subscription* has been corrected, as shown in Display 5.5.

Display 5.5
Word Corrected
by the Spelling
Checker

For more information about the SPELL command, refer to Chapter 19, "SAS Text Editor Commands," in *SAS Language: Reference.*

Making Corrections

This letter requires a few other minor changes. You can accomplish most small editorial changes by typing over the current text or by using the INSERT or DELETE editing keys on your keyboard. Make the following changes to the example letter:

Note: To help identify the lines to be modified, you can use the NUMS ON command to turn on line numbering. Use the NUMS OFF command to turn line numbering off again.

□ Line 15: The word *effect* is used improperly; the correct verb is *affect*. Simply type an *a* over the *e*. This error was not detected by the spelling checker because *effect* is also a valid word.

□ Line 16: Use the DELETE key to delete the word *full*.

□ Line 17: Use the INSERT key to turn on insert mode; then add the word *loyal* before *readership*.

Printing the Letter

Once you have entered and edited your letter, you are ready to print it. Issue the SEND command, which saves a master copy of the letter in the current catalog and opens the FSLETTER SEND window.

In the FSLETTER SEND window you are given the opportunity to make additional changes to your document before it is printed. Changes that you make in the FSLETTER SEND window appear in the printed copy of the document but are not saved in the master copy. This feature is useful when you want to modify the text of an individual copy of a form letter or other document without having the modifications appear in the master copy.

Issue the END command to close the FSLETTER SEND window. The procedure sends the letter to the printer (or to a file if you issued a PRTFILE command or used the PRINTFILE= option in the PROC FSLETTER statement). For this example, the letter is sent to the default printer at your site because the default form is used and the PRINTFILE= option is not used.

After the letter is sent, you return to the FSLETTER DIRECTORY window.

Ending the FSLETTER Session

To close the FSLETTER DIRECTORY window and end the FSLETTER session, issue the END command.

Preparing Letters for More than One Person

Suppose you work in the circulation department of *The News Monthly* and you want to create a form letter that can be sent to remind magazine subscribers to renew their subscriptions when their expiration date approaches. To begin the FSLETTER session for this task, use the same PROC FSLETTER statement or FSLETTER command as in the previous example:

```
proc fsletter letter=master.letters;
run;
```

or

```
fsletter master.letters
```

This time the FSLETTER DIRECTORY window should show one existing entry, JONES.LETTER, which you created in the previous example.

For this example you want to create a letter that can be used to notify subscribers three months before their subscriptions expire. In the FSLETTER DIRECTORY window, issue the following command to begin entering a letter named RENEWAL:

```
edit renewal.letter
```

This command opens the FSLETTER window for editing the specified document. Because this is a new document, the FSLETTER window text area is initially blank. Enter the text for the example form letter shown in Figure 5.3. You must scroll forward to enter all the text.

The FSLETTER procedure allows you to create generic documents with *fields*, defined areas of the document where you can fill in information that changes from one copy of the document to the next. Where the individual letter in the previous example had the actual name and address of the recipient, this letter has terms beginning with an ampersand (&) and followed by underscore (_) characters. These are fields. Once you create a document with fields, you can produce an unlimited number of personalized copies of the document by filling in the field values for each copy. You can fill in field values in the FSLETTER SEND window when you print the document, or you can have the fields filled in automatically with values from a SAS data set.

Figure 5.3
Text for Example
Form Letter

```
&&DATE_____

&FULLNAME_____
&ADDR1_____
&ADDR2_____

Dear &FULLNAME_____:

We note from our subscription list that your experience with "The News
Monthly" began almost &YRS____ years ago when you received your first
issue in &DATE____. We know that you don't want to miss even one issue
of the latest updates and news from our organization.

You may feel that it's too early to think about renewal with three more
issues to go.  But you can help us keep our costs down by taking
advantage of our early renewal plan.  Let us process your renewal at
current postal rates, and you can avoid any price increase for another
year.

Please make sure that your address information is current.  Attach the
label to the postage-paid renewal card, and return it to us at your
earliest convenience.

Sincerely,


Margaret E. Ellis
Subscription Department
"The News Monthly"


Enclosure
```

Defining Fields

A field in an FSLETTER document is defined with an ampersand, a name for the
field, and, optionally, one or more underscores. The field name must follow
standard SAS naming conventions; see Chapter 4, "Rules of the SAS Language,"
in *SAS Language: Reference* for details.

The ampersand and the field name together define the width of the field. To
extend the field width, you can follow the field name with underscore
characters. The underscores extend the field width but do not become part of
the name. Fields should be wide enough to accept the longest possible valid
value. For example, if one of the values for the field &SEX_ were FEMALE, it
would appear in the document as FEMAL because the total width of the &SEX_
field is only five characters. You need to add another underscore to the field to
avoid this truncation.

Examine the fields in the letter in Figure 5.3. The fields with only one
ampersand at the beginning are those you fill in yourself or arrange to be filled
from a SAS data set. However, the name of the first field, &&DATE, begins with
two ampersands. The first ampersand marks the beginning of the field; the
second is part of the name of the SAS automatic variable &DATE. The value for
this variable is supplied automatically by the SAS System when you send the
letter. The &DATE variable provides today's date in the form *month day, year*.

Using the Text Editor

The following sections explain how to use the basic text editing features available in the FSLETTER window.

Marking Text

You can move blocks of text using the global MARK, STORE, CUT, and PASTE commands. See Chapter 18, "SAS Display Manager Commands," in *SAS Language: Reference* for complete details of these commands. These display manager commands are usually assigned to function keys to make editing faster and easier. Use the KEYS command to review the current function key definitions for your FSLETTER session. If the MARK, STORE, CUT, and PASTE commands are not currently assigned, add function key definitions for these commands in the KEYS window. Refer to Chapter 17, "SAS Display Manager Windows," in *SAS Language: Reference* if you need information about using the KEYS window.

Use the MARK command to indicate the area of text you want to move or duplicate. Place the cursor on the first character of the area you want to mark, and press the MARK function key. Then place the cursor after the last character in the area and use the MARK key again. The marked string is highlighted.

For example, move the cursor to the Y in the sentence that begins with *You may feel*, and issue a MARK command. Then move the cursor to the *w* in the word *with*, and issue another MARK command. The marked phrase is highlighted, as shown in Display 5.6.

Display 5.6
Marking a Text String

```
FSLETTER: RENEWAL.LETTER (E)                              FORM: FSLETTER
Command ===>

  Dear &FULLNAME_____:

  We note from our subscription list that your experience with "The News
  Monthly" began almost &YRS_____ years ago when you received your first
  issue in &DATE_____.
  We know that you don't want to miss even one issue of the latest
  updates and news from our organization.

  You may feel that it's too early to think about renewal with three more
  issues to go.  But you can help us keep our costs down by taking
  advantage of our early renewal plan.  Let us process your renewal at
  current postal rates, and you can avoid any price increase for another
  year.

  Please make sure that your address information is current.  Attach the
  label to the postage-paid renewal card, and return it to us at your
  earliest convenience.


  Sincerely,
```

Notice that the highlighted string begins with the character at which the first MARK command was issued, but it ends with the character that immediately precedes the one at which the second MARK command was issued. The character on which the cursor is positioned when the second MARK command is issued is not included in the marked text.

Storing Text

To remove the marked phrase from the letter and to store it for insertion later, use the CUT command. To leave the marked string in the letter but also store a copy of it for insertion later, use the STORE command.

For this example, issue a CUT command (or press the CUT function key). The marked text is removed from the display, as shown in Display 5.7.

Display 5.7
Using the CUT
Command

Pasting Text

To paste the cut string back into the letter, position the cursor where you want the text string to be inserted, and then issue the PASTE command (or press the PASTE function key).

In the example letter, position the cursor on the period after the word *go* in the line below the one from which the text was cut, and press the PASTE function key. The cut text is inserted at the cursor position, as shown in Display 5.8.

Display 5.8
Inserting Text with
the PASTE
Command

```
┌─FSLETTER:  RENEWAL LETTER (E)──────────────────────────FORM FSLETTER─┐
│Command ===>                                                          │
│                                                                      │
│  Dear &FULLNAME_____:                                     │
│                                                                      │
│  We note from our subscription list that your experience with "The News
│  Monthly" began almost &YRS_____ years ago when you received your first
│  issue in &DATE_____.                                                │
│  We know that you don't want to miss even one issue of the latest    │
│  updates and news from our organization.                            │
│                                                                      │
│  with three more                                                     │
│  issues to goYou may feel that it's too early to think about renewal .
│    But you can help us keep our costs down by taking                 │
│  advantage of our early renewal plan.  Let us process your renewal at│
│  current postal rates, and you can avoid any price increase for another
│  year.                                                               │
│                                                                      │
│  Please make sure that your address information is current.  Attach the
│  label to the postage-paid renewal card, and return it to us at your │
│  earliest convenience.                                               │
│                                                                      │
└──────────────────────────────────────────────────────────────────────┘
```

Flowing Text Lines

You have cut text from the letter and pasted it where you want it, but this disrupted the spacing in the paragraph. The TF (text flow) line command allows you to flow paragraphs and to delete unwanted spaces between words. Type the following command on the command line, position the cursor on the *w* in the phrase *with three more,* and press ENTER* :

`:tf`

Note: The TF command is easier to use if you assign it to a function key. Then you can just position the cursor and press the corresponding key. When making the function key assignment, remember to add a colon before the command name.

Display 5.9 shows the result. The TF command only affects text from the cursor position to the first blank line.

---

* You can execute SAS text editor line commands from the command line if you precede the command name with a colon (:).

Display 5.9
Using the TF (Text Flow) Line Command

```
┌─FSLETTER:  RENEWAL LETTER (E)────────────────────────FORM:FSLETTER─┐
│ Command ===>                                                        │
│                                                                     │
│  Dear &FULLNAME                  :                                  │
│                                                                     │
│  We note from our subscription list that your experience with "The News │
│  Monthly" began almost &YRS         years ago when you received your first │
│  issue in &DATE     .                                               │
│  We know that you don't want to miss even one issue of the latest   │
│  updates and news from our organization.                           │
│                                                                     │
│  with three more issues to goYou may feel that it's too early to think │
│  about renewal .  But you can help us keep our costs down by taking │
│  advantage of our early renewal plan.  Let us process your renewal at │
│  current postal rates, and you can avoid any price increase for another │
│  year.                                                              │
│                                                                     │
│  Please make sure that your address information is current.  Attach the │
│  label to the postage-paid renewal card, and return it to us at your │
│  earliest convenience.                                             │
│                                                                     │
│                                                                     │
│  Sincerely,                                                        │
└─────────────────────────────────────────────────────────────────┘
```

Using Keyboard Features

Not all changes require you to move and to reposition large amounts of text. Remember from the first example that small changes can be made by typing over the current text or by using the INSERT or DELETE editing keys on your keyboard.

Follow these steps to correct the example letter:

□ Type an uppercase W over the *w* in the phrase *with three more*.

□ Position the cursor on the Y in *goYou*, press the INSERT key, and insert a comma and a blank space (with the space bar) after the word *go*. Then press whatever key or key combination turns off insert mode on your device.

□ Type a lowercase *y* over the Y in *go, You may feel*.

□ Use the DELETE key to remove the space before the period following the word *renewal*.

Splitting Text Lines

To insert new text, you may need to first create space within the existing text. Use the TS (text split) line command to create the needed space. Type the following command in the FSLETTER window command line, position the cursor on the *i* in *is current. Attach*, and press ENTER:

    :ts2

The text line is split as shown in Display 5.10.

Display 5.10
Inserting Space
with the TS Line
Command

```
┌FSLETTER:  RENEWAL LETTER (E)─────────────────────────FORM:FSLETTER─┐
│Command ===>                                                         │
│                                                                     │
│ Dear &FULLNAME_____:                                     │
│                                                                     │
│ We note from our subscription list that your experience with "The News │
│ Monthly" began almost &YRS_____ years ago when you received your first │
│ issue in &DATE_____.                                               │
│ We know that you don't want to miss even one issue of the latest    │
│ updates and news from our organization.                             │
│                                                                     │
│ With three more issues to go, you may feel that it's too early to think │
│ about renewal.  But you can help us keep our costs down by taking   │
│ advantage of our early renewal plan.  Let us process your renewal at │
│ current postal rates, and you can avoid any price increase for another │
│ year.                                                               │
│                                                                     │
│ Please make sure that your address information                      │
│                                                                     │
│ is current.  Attach the                                             │
│ label to the postage-paid renewal card, and return it to us at your │
│ earliest convenience.                                               │
│                                                                     │
└─────────────────────────────────────────────────────────────────────┘
```

Note: Like the TF command, the TS command is easier to use if it is assigned to a function key.

Now you can enter additional text, as shown in Display 5.11.

Display 5.11
Entering
Additional Text

```
┌FSLETTER:  RENEWAL LETTER (E)─────────────────────────FORM:FSLETTER─┐
│Command ===>                                                         │
│                                                                     │
│ Dear &FULLNAME_____:                                     │
│                                                                     │
│ We note from our subscription list that your experience with "The News │
│ Monthly" began almost &YRS_____ years ago when you received your first │
│ issue in &DATE_____.                                               │
│ We know that you don't want to miss even one issue of the latest    │
│ updates and news from our organization.                             │
│                                                                     │
│ With three more issues to go, you may feel that it's too early to think │
│ about renewal.  But you can help us keep our costs down by taking   │
│ advantage of our early renewal plan.  Let us process your renewal at │
│ current postal rates, and you can avoid any price increase for another │
│ year.                                                               │
│                                                                     │
│ Please make sure that your address information on the enclosed mailing │
│ label                                                               │
│ is current.  Attach the                                             │
│ label to the postage-paid renewal card, and return it to us at your │
│ earliest convenience.                                               │
└─────────────────────────────────────────────────────────────────────┘
```

Once again, unused spaces remain after text has been added. Position the cursor on the P in *Please make sure;* then issue the TF command (or press the TF function key) to delete unused and unwanted spaces. Display 5.12 shows the completed letter.

Display 5.12
Revised Text for
Form Letter
Example

```
┌FSLETTER: RENEWAL LETTER (E)─────────────────────FORM.FSLETTER─┐
│                                                                │
│  Dear &FULLNAME_____:                               │
│                                                                │
│  We note from our subscription list that your experience with "The News
│  Monthly" began almost &YRS_____ years ago when you received your first
│  issue in &DATE_____.                                          │
│  We know that you don't want to miss even one issue of the latest
│  updates and news from our organization.                       │
│                                                                │
│  With three more issues to go, you may feel that it's too early to think
│  about renewal.  But you can help us keep our costs down by taking
│  advantage of our early renewal plan.  Let us process your renewal at
│  current postal rates, and you can avoid any price increase for another
│  year.                                                         │
│                                                                │
│  Please make sure that your address information on the enclosed mailing
│  label is current.  Attach the label to the postage-paid renewal card,
│  and return it to us at your earliest convenience.             │
│                                                                │
│  Sincerely,                                                    │
│                                                                │
└────────────────────────────────────────────────────────────────┘
```

Assigning Field Attributes

By default, the FSLETTER procedure adds the text you enter in fields to your document exactly as you provide it. However, you can assign field attributes to modify the way values entered in fields are handled.

Field attributes are assigned in the FSLETTER ATTR window. Once you have created your letter and defined fields, you can use the FSLETTER ATTR window to view and modify the attributes of each field in the document. For complete descriptions of the attributes you can assign in the FSLETTER ATTR window, refer to Chapter 14, "The FSLETTER Procedure."

Using the FSLETTER ATTR Window

To open the FSLETTER ATTR window, issue the ATTR command in the FSLETTER window. The FSLETTER ATTR window has a separate frame for each field in the document. The attribute frames are displayed in the same order that the fields appear in the document.

Display 5.13 shows the first attribute frame for the RENEWAL example letter. This frame shows the attributes of the first field in the letter, &DATE.

Display 5.13
Attribute Frame
for the &DATE
Field

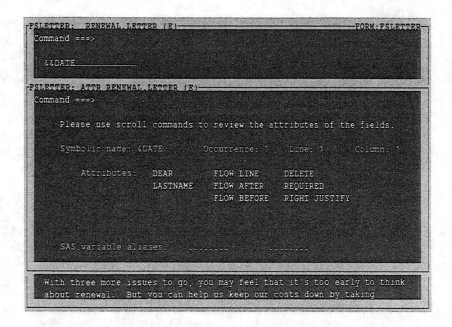

The attributes for the &DATE field require no changes, so use the FORWARD command to view the attribute frame for the next field, FULLNAME (the first of two occurrences of this field).

To assign an attribute in the FSLETTER ATTR window, move the cursor to the name of the desired attribute and press ENTER. The attribute name is highlighted to indicate that it is selected. Use the TAB key to move among the attributes. To turn off a currently selected attribute, position the cursor on the highlighted attribute name and press ENTER. The attribute name then appears without highlighting to indicate that the corresponding attribute is no longer assigned to the current field.

In the subscriber data set used by *The News Monthly*, names are stored last name first. However, names in the letter need to be printed in the normal order. The LASTNAME attribute causes the procedure to rearrange field values (whether typed or from a SAS data set) with the form *lastname, firstname middle* to *firstname middle lastname*. Thus, you need to assign the LASTNAME attribute for the first FULLNAME field.

Move the cursor to LASTNAME in the FSLETTER ATTR frame for the first FULLNAME field, and press ENTER. The attribute name is highlighted, indicating that it is selected for the indicated variable. Display 5.14 shows the FSLETTER ATTR frame for the FULLNAME field with the LASTNAME attribute selected.

Display 5.14
Attribute Frame
for the First
FULLNAME Field

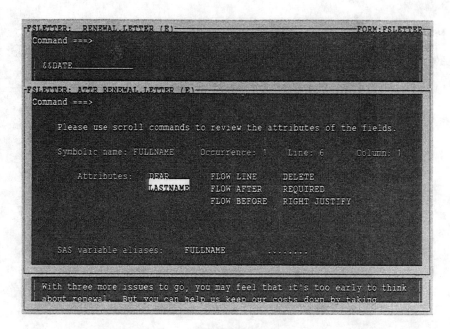

Notice that the frame for FULLNAME also has a value in the SAS variable aliases: field. This field determines the name of the variable used to fill the field when copies are generated automatically for observations in a SAS data set. By default, the corresponding variable name is the same as the field name. (The first field does not have a variable alias because &DATE is an automatic variable.)

Continue to use the FORWARD command to view the attribute frames for the other fields. (Because the letter includes two FULLNAME fields, there are two separate attribute frames for FULLNAME.) Assign the following attributes:

□ For the second occurrence of the FULLNAME field, select both the LASTNAME and DEAR attributes. The DEAR attribute takes names in the form *title firstname lastname* and makes them *title lastname*.

□ For the YRS field, select the FLOW BEFORE attribute. This attribute flows text (deletes extra space) before and after the field value up to the first blank line after the field. Flowing is described in the following section.

□ For the DATE field (which, unlike &DATE, is not an automatic field because its name does not include a second ampersand), change the value in the SAS variable aliases: field to BEGDATE. This links the DATE field to the variable BEGDATE so that values for that variable in a data set can be used to fill the field. (This is described in "Printing Documents Using Information from SAS Data Sets" later in this chapter.)

Flowing Fields

The FSLETTER procedure reserves the full field width for each field in the document, regardless of the width of the value entered in the field. For example, suppose your document contains the following sentence:

```
Your subscription has &REMAIN months remaining.
```

After the field is filled, the sentence looks like this:

```
Your subscription has       3 months remaining.
```

The FSLETTER procedure does not automatically remove the extra spaces before the 3. However, you can assign an attribute to the field that causes the procedure to remove the extra spaces when the document is printed. The process of deleting extra spaces is called flowing the text.

The following flow attributes are available:

FLOW AFTER   deletes extra spaces following the field, flowing text for the remainder of the paragraph (until a blank line is encountered).

FLOW BEFORE   deletes extra spaces before and following the field, flowing text for the remainder of the paragraph (until a blank line is encountered).

A third attribute, FLOW LINE, flows text for a single line of the document rather than to the end of the current paragraph.

In each paragraph of text, you only need to specify a text flow attribute (FLOW BEFORE or FLOW AFTER) for the first field within the paragraph. The attribute for the first field causes text to be flowed for the remainder of the paragraph. For example, it is not necessary to select a text flow attribute for the DATE field in the example form letter because the YRS field earlier in the same paragraph of the letter is assigned the FLOW BEFORE attribute.

Flowing is performed at the beginning of the second step of printing the document. See "Printing the Document" later in this chapter for details.

Using the \NOFLOW and \FLOW Control Lines

When you use the FLOW AFTER or FLOW BEFORE attributes, the FSLETTER procedure by default flows all text from the field position to the next blank line in the document. However, if the paragraph contains a table or other text in which you want to maintain the spacing as entered, you can use \NOFLOW and \FLOW control lines to override this default behavior. Place \NOFLOW at the beginning of a line by itself before the text to be protected. Similarly, follow the last line in the protected text with a \FLOW line. These lines are not included in the printed copy of the document.

For example, suppose your document contains the following text and the field REMAIN is assigned the FLOW BEFORE attribute:

```
With &REMAIN more issues to go, you may feel that it's too early to
think about renewal. But you can help us keep our costs down by taking
advantage of our early renewal plan
at the following rates:
\NOFLOW
      1 year     $12.50
      2 years    $22.00    (a savings of $3.00)
      3 years    $30.00    (a savings of $7.50)
\FLOW
Let us process your renewal at
current postal rates, and you can avoid any price increase for another
year.
```

When you print the document, the text is flowed as follows:

```
With 3 more issues to go, you may feel that it's too early to think
about renewal. But you can help us keep our costs down by taking
advantage of our early renewal plan at the following rates:
    1 year     $12.50
    2 years    $22.00   (a savings of $3.00)
    3 years    $30.00   (a savings of $7.50)
Let us process your renewal at current postal rates, and you can
avoid any price increase for another year.
```

Note: You can also use \NOFLOW and \FLOW control lines to control text flowing when you use the TF line command in the FSLETTER window.

Closing the FSLETTER ATTR Window

Use the END command to close the FSLETTER ATTR window and return to the FSLETTER window.

Saving a Master Copy of Your Document

Once you have entered your letter, defined fields, and assigned field attributes, you can store the letter in the catalog as a master copy. By storing the letter with the fields defined but not filled in, you can use it many times.

You can store a master copy in one of three ways, depending on whether or not you are ready to print a copy of the document:

□ If you want to store the current contents of the document but want to continue working in the FSLETTER window, issue the SAVE command.

□ If you want to store the document and close the FSLETTER window, issue the END command. The document is stored in your catalog, and you return to the FSLETTER DIRECTORY window.

□ If you are ready to fill in the fields and to print a copy of the document, execute the SEND command. The SEND command stores a master copy of the document in your catalog before opening the FSLETTER SEND window.

Because you have completed work on the example letter, issue a SEND command to store the letter and move to the printing step.

Printing the Document

When you execute the SEND command, the FSLETTER SEND window is opened. When the document to be printed contains fields, printing is a two-step process, and the FSLETTER window behaves differently in each of the steps. The following sections explain the steps involved in printing a document that contains fields.

Step 1: Filling Fields

In the first step of the process, only the contents of the fields in the document can be changed; the rest of the text is protected. Display 5.15 shows the initial FSLETTER SEND window for the form letter example:

Display 5.15
The FSLETTER
SEND Window:
Step 1

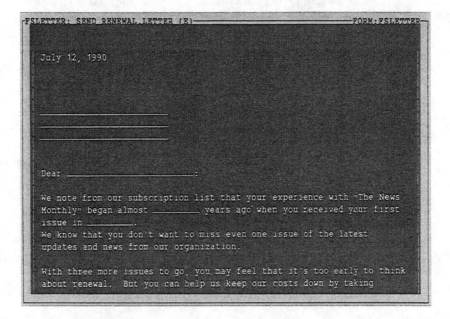

Underscores are displayed for all the fields in which you can enter field values. (Notice that the &DATE field is automatically filled in.) You can use your keyboard's TAB editing key to move the cursor from one field to the next. Scroll forward to view fields not currently displayed.

To test the example letter you created, enter the field values shown in Display 5.16.

Display 5.16
Filling In the
Fields

You do not need to enter a value in the second FULLNAME field. When a field appears in a document more than once (as is the case for FULLNAME), you need to fill in only the first field; the FSLETTER procedure automatically fills in the other fields of the same name when you press ENTER after filling in the first field.

Issue the END command to complete the first step of the SEND process. The FSLETTER procedure processes any other field attributes, flows the text (if any of the fields have been assigned flow attributes), and then enters the second step.

Note: Because you selected the LASTNAME attribute for the FULLNAME fields, you could also enter the name in the FULLNAME field in the form

```
Doe, Mr. John
```

The FSLETTER procedure rearranges the name in the proper order when you press END to begin the second step of the SEND process.

The LASTNAME attribute has no effect when the value entered in the field does not include a comma.

Step 2: Final Editing

Once all fields have been processed, the FSLETTER procedure displays the letter for final editing, as shown in Display 5.17. You then have a chance to make final changes to the document. In this step, all text can be modified, not just the fields. The changes you make in this step are not recorded in the master copy of the document.

Display 5.17
The FSLETTER
SEND Window:
Step 2

```
FSLETTER: SEND RENEWAL.LETTER (E)                              FORM:FSLETTER
Command ===>
NOTE: Please make any final changes needed to this letter.
  July 12, 1990



  Mr. John Doe
  222 W. Vermont Ave.
  Springfield, IL 61720


  Dear Mr. Doe:

  We note from our subscription list that your experience with "The News
  Monthly" began almost 3 years ago when you received your first issue in
  NOV87.  We know that you don't want to miss even one issue of the latest
  updates and news from our organization.


  With three more issues to go, you may feel that it's too early to think
  about renewal.  But you can help us keep our costs down by taking
  advantage of our early renewal plan.  Let us process your renewal at
```

Issue the END command to send a copy of the letter to the printer (or to the specified print file), to close the FSLETTER SEND window, and to return to the FSLETTER DIRECTORY window. Issue the END command again to close the FSLETTER DIRECTORY window and end the FSLETTER session.

Sending Documents to an External File

By default, the FSLETTER procedure sends documents to the destination specified in the form entry for the document. To send a document to an external file rather than to a printer, you can use

□   the PRINTFILE= option in the PROC FSLETTER statement

□   the PRTFILE command in the FSLETTER window

□   the FILE= option in the SEND command in the FSLETTER window.

For example, the following SAS statements begin an FSLETTER session and designate an external file (rather than the printer) as the destination for output:

```
proc fsletter letter=master.letters
    printfile='filename';
run;
```

You can accomplish the same result within an FSLETTER session by issuing the following command:

```
prtfile 'filename'
```

The PRINTFILE= option and the PRTFILE command affect all subsequent SEND commands. You can cancel the print file assignment by using the PRTFILE CLEAR command.

Alternatively, you can use the following form of the SEND command when you are ready to send the document:

```
send file='filename'
```

Use this method to send a single document to a file or to send an individual document to a file other than the current print file.

Notice in the preceding examples that the filename is enclosed in quotes. If you use a FILENAME statement to associate a SAS fileref with that external file before you begin the FSLETTER session, you can use the fileref instead of the complete filename in the PRINTFILE= option, the PRTFILE command, or the FILE= option. If you use a fileref, do not enclose it in quotes.

When you execute the second END command in the FSLETTER SEND window, the document with its fields filled in is sent to the external file. After exiting from the SAS System, you can print the file contents using your operating system's file printing command.

Sending More than One Document to a Single File

When you use the FSLETTER SEND window to send letters, each new document you send to the file by default replaces any text currently in the file. However, you can have the text for each new document you send appended to the current contents of the file. Simply add the APPEND option when you issue the PRTFILE command. (The APPEND option is not valid with the PRINTFILE= option of the PROC FSLETTER statement.) The general form of the command is

```
prtfile 'filename' append
```

Once you issue this command, you can continue to append finished documents to the external file during your FSLETTER session and then print the entire contents of the file after you end the SAS session.

To restore the print file to its default behavior, use the REPLACE option in the PRTFILE command:

```
prtfile 'filename' replace
```

To append an individual document to the print file, add the APPEND option following the FILE= option in the SEND command:

```
send file='filename' append
```

Using Multiple FSLETTER Windows

If you want to view or edit another document without closing the current FSLETTER window, you can open another FSLETTER window. Use the EDIT command to open the additional FSLETTER window for editing or the BROWSE command to open it for browsing only. You can use this feature when you need to consult information in another document or when you want to copy information from an existing document into a new document.

Opening additional FSLETTER windows using the EDIT or BROWSE commands in the current FSLETTER window consumes fewer resources than starting additional FSLETTER sessions using the FSLETTER command.

You can use both display manager global commands and SAS/FSP global commands to change the size, position, and other characteristics of the additional FSLETTER windows. (See Chapter 18 for details.)

For example, submit the following statements to begin entering a new letter named SUBSCRIB.LETTER:

```
proc fsletter letter=master.letters.subscrib.letter;
run;
```

When the FSLETTER window is opened, issue the following command to open a second FSLETTER window for browsing the RENEWAL letter created in the previous example:

```
browse renewal.letter
```

Display 5.18 shows the result.

Display 5.18
Opening a Second
FSLETTER
Window

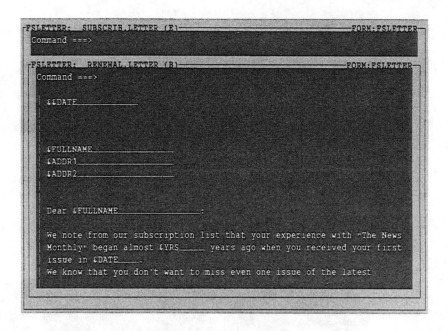

After the second FSLETTER window is opened, it becomes the active window. You can use all valid FSLETTER window browsing commands in the second FSLETTER window.

Copying Text between Windows

You can use the global MARK, STORE, CUT, and PASTE commands to copy text between concurrent FSLETTER windows. The following steps are required:

1. In the window from which you want to copy the text, use the MARK command to highlight the block to be copied.

2. Use the CUT or STORE commands to copy the text into a paste buffer. (The CUT command also removes the text from the displayed document; it is not valid if the document is opened for browsing only.)

3. Use the SWAP command to move to the window that displays the document into which you want to paste the text. (Or, if no more text is to be copied, use the END command to close the window from which the text was cut or stored and return to the previous window.)

4. Use the PASTE command to paste the text into the target window.

The following sections discuss these steps.

Marking the Text to Copy

Suppose you want to copy the heading from the existing document into the new document. Begin by marking the text to copy in the second FSLETTER window (the one that displays RENEWAL.LETTER).

Position the cursor on the first ampersand in the &&DATE field at the top of the window; then issue a MARK command (or press the MARK function key). Move the cursor to the W in *We note from our*; then issue another MARK command.

The selected block of text is highlighted, as shown in Display 5.19.

Display 5.19
Marking Text in
the Second
FSLETTER
Window

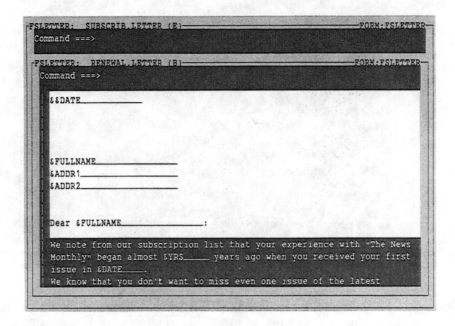

Storing the Highlighted Text

To store a copy of the highlighted text in a paste buffer, issue a STORE command (or press the STORE function key). The highlighting is turned off when the text is stored.

Note: Because the FSLETTER window in which the RENEWAL letter is displayed is opened for browsing only, the CUT command cannot be used in this case.

Now use the END command to close the second FSLETTER window and return to the original FSLETTER window opened for the SUBSCRIB letter.

Copying Text to the New Document

To copy text from a paste buffer into an FSLETTER document, use the PASTE command.

Position the cursor in the upper-left corner of the FSLETTER window, and issue a PASTE command (or press the PASTE function key). The heading from the existing letter is copied into the new letter, as shown in Display 5.20.

Display 5.20
*Copying Text to
the First
FSLETTER
Window*

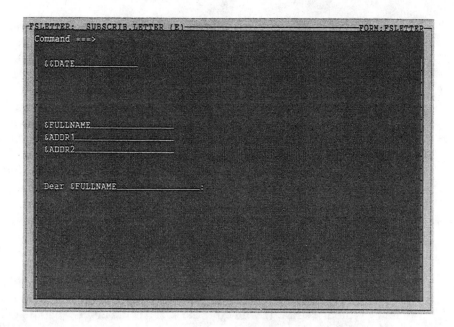

Use the END command to close the FSLETTER window and end the example
FSLETTER session.

Enhancing Your Output

The FSLETTER procedure provides default printing specifications that should be
satisfactory in many cases. However, the procedure also provides features that
allow you to take advantage of any special printer capabilities that may be
available at your site. The following sections discuss ways you can exercise
greater control over your printed output.

Defining Your Own Forms

A *form* is a catalog entry that contains specifications for formatting text and
printing a document. Every document you create with the FSLETTER procedure
has an associated form; many documents can share the same form. The name of
the associated form is stored in the letter entry for the document. The
FSLETTER procedure uses a default form, FSLETTER.FORM, unless you use a
FORM command to specify another form.

You can define your own forms by filling in information in a series of form
definition frames in the FORM window. The FORM window is a component of
base SAS software. Chapter 20, "Forms," provides an introduction to forms.
Refer to Chapter 17 in *SAS Language: Reference* for complete details about using
the FORM window.

Storing Forms

Before you begin defining your own forms, you need to understand how the
FSLETTER procedure locates forms. Whenever a document is displayed, the
FSLETTER procedure looks for the specified form first in the current catalog
(the one specified in the LETTER= argument of the PROC FSLETTER statement

or the *letter-name* argument of the FSLETTER command). If the entry is not found in that catalog, the FSLETTER procedure next looks in your personal PROFILE catalog (SASUSER.PROFILE, or WORK.PROFILE if the SASUSER library is not allocated). Finally, the procedure looks in the SASHELP.FSP system catalog. If the specified form is not found, the procedure looks for the default form, FSLETTER.FORM, in the same sequence of catalogs.

If you want to use the form you create only with documents in a particular catalog, store the form in the catalog with the letter entries. If you want to use the same form with any catalog of letter entries, store it in your SASUSER.PROFILE catalog. (Generally, individual users do not have the authority to alter entries in the SASHELP.FSP system catalog.) If you want your form to replace the Institute-supplied default, name your form FSLETTER.FORM.

Using the FORM Window

You can open the FORM window by executing an EDIT command from the FSLETTER DIRECTORY window or the FSLETTER window and specifying an entry type of FORM. (By default, the EDIT command opens an additional FSLETTER window.) However, when you specify an entry type of FORM, the EDIT command opens the FORM window instead. You can also open the FORM window by issuing the FSFORM command in any SAS System window.

Suppose you decide not to use the default form for printing the renewal letter RENEWAL.LETTER from the earlier example in this chapter. Instead, you want to create your own form so that you can take advantage of special printer features when you print the renewal letter. First, submit the following statements to begin an FSLETTER session:

```
proc fsletter letter=master.letters.renewal.letter;
run;
```

After the FSLETTER window is opened, execute the following command to open the FORM window:

```
edit formlet1.form
```

The first frame of the FORM window is the Printer Selection frame. In this frame you must specify the type of printer you use to print the document. The choice of printer determines the default values of a number of other form parameters. Display 5.21 shows an example of the Printer Selection frame.

Display 5.21
FORM Window:
Printer Selection
Frame

```
┌─FORM: FORMLET1.FORM (E)──────────────────────────────┐
│ Command ===>                                         │
│                                                      │
│                    Printer Selection                 │
│                                                      │
│                                                      │
│        Form description:   FORMLET1.FORM             │
│                                                      │
│                                                      │
│  To select printer, position cursor on selection and press ENTER. │
│                                                      │
│                    IBM 3800                          │
│                    IBM 3820                          │
│                    IBM 6670                          │
│                    Xerox 2700                        │
│                    Xerox 5700                        │
│                    Xerox 9700                        │
│                    Other                             │
│                                                      │
│                                                      │
│                                                      │
└──────────────────────────────────────────────────────┘
```

Note: The example display is for the MVS operating system. The list of available printers is different in other environments.

To select a printer, move the cursor to the desired printer name; then press ENTER. You may have to scroll forward to view the entire list of available printers. Once you choose a printer type for a form, you cannot change your selection. (To change printer types, you must create a new form.)

After you choose a printer type, the first of a series of form definition frames is displayed, as shown in Display 5.22.

Display 5.22
FORM Window:
Text Body and
Margin
Information Frame

```
┌─FORM: FORMLET1.FORM (E)──────────────────────────────┐
│ Command ===>                                         │
│                                                      │
│                                                      │
│              Text Body and Margin Information        │
│                                                      │
│  Text Body:                                          │
│                                                      │
│        Characters per line:   72                     │
│        Lines on first page:   54                     │
│        Lines on following:    54                     │
│                                                      │
│  Margins:                                            │
│                                                      │
│      First page        Left:  0      Top:  0      Bottom:  0 │
│      Following pages   Left:  0      Top:  0      Bottom:  0 │
│                                                      │
│                                                      │
└──────────────────────────────────────────────────────┘
```

The Characters per line: parameter in the Text Body and Margin Information frame is particularly important because it controls the width of the text area in the FSLETTER window as well as the width of the printed output.

Use the NEXTSCR command to proceed through the form definition frames, entering the information necessary for defining the form. Refer to Chapter 20 in this book or to Chapter 17 in *SAS Language: Reference* if you need more information on any parameters. Use the END command to close the window and to save the form.

You can now issue the following command in the FSLETTER window to assign the new form to RENEWAL.LETTER:

```
form formlet1
```

The form name in the upper-right corner of the window border shows that the new form FORMLET1 has replaced the default form FSLETTER. See Display 5.23.

Display 5.23
New Form
Assigned to
FSLETTER
Document

Using Color and Highlighting Attributes

Color and highlighting have both aesthetic and practical applications in FSLETTER documents. You can use these attributes to change both the way your text looks and the way it is printed. Even if the device you are using does not support color, read this section for a general introduction to the way the FSLETTER procedure handles printing instructions. All the features described here can be used without a color display.

Using Color to Enhance Data Entry

If your device supports extended color and highlighting features, you can change the color and highlighting of text in a document as you type or overtype characters. These changes are stored with the document. You can also set color and highlighting attributes using the COLOR command or the color parameters in the EDPARMS window.

You can use color and highlighting in any part of your document, but these attributes are particularly useful for drawing attention to fields in which users must enter values. As an example, press the key or key combination that produces cyan on your device; then overtype the characters for the fields that the user must fill in RENEWAL.LETTER: the first occurrence of the FULLNAME field and ADDR1, ADDR2, YRS, and DATE. (See Display 5.24.)

Display 5.24
Assigning Colors
to Fields

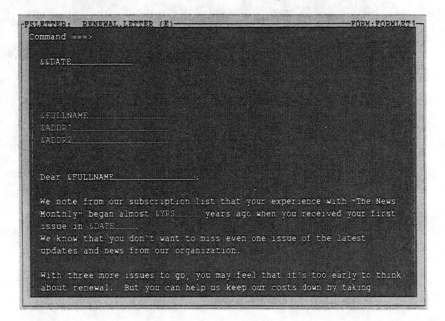

The color difference makes the fields easier to locate when the document is displayed in the FSLETTER SEND window.

Using Highlighting to Enhance Data Entry

You can draw attention to fields with highlighting attributes as well as with color attributes. As an example, press the key or key combination that produces reverse video on your device; then overtype the fields that are filled automatically when the letter is printed: &DATE and the second FULLNAME field. These fields are now displayed in reverse video. (See Display 5.25.)

Display 5.25
Assigning
Highlighting to
Fields

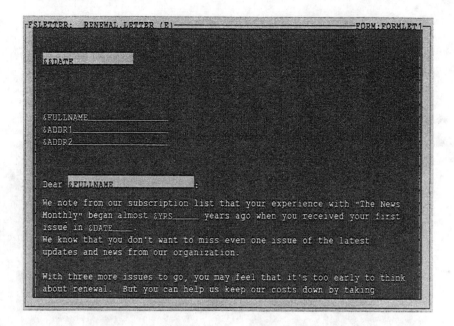

Highlighting attributes are especially appropriate when users of your document do not have color devices.

Using Color and Highlighting to Signal Printing Instructions

You can also use color and highlighting to signal special printing instructions. As an example, consider the underlining feature of some printers. If your printer has commands to turn underlining on and off, you can dictate that all text appearing in a particular color or highlight in the document is underlined in the printed output. If your printer has multiple typefaces (also called fonts), you can specify that each different text color corresponds to a different font in printed output. You can signal printing instructions with color only, with highlighting only, or with combinations of color and highlighting.

These printing instructions are defined in the form entry for the document. (When creating or editing forms, printing instructions are entered in the Font Control Information frame of the FORM window.) When a document is printed, the information in the form is used to determine what commands to send to the printer when the defined colors are encountered.

You can use the global FONT command in the FSLETTER window to check which color and highlighting attributes signal printing instructions for the current form. If no font control information has been defined, a message to that effect is printed. Otherwise, the FSLETTER FONT window is opened showing which colors and highlighting attributes are currently defined as printing instructions.

Defining Printing Instructions

Look at the reference to the magazine title *The News Monthly* in the opening sentence of the example letter RENEWAL.LETTER. Book and magazine titles are usually italicized in printed material and underlined in typed material. Suppose that you decide to use the combination of red and reverse video to mark text that should be underlined in printed output. Move the cursor to the title, and press whatever keys or key combinations select red and reverse video on your device; then overtype the title in red and reverse video. Use the DELETE key to delete the quotation marks around the title. Display 5.26 shows the modified letter.

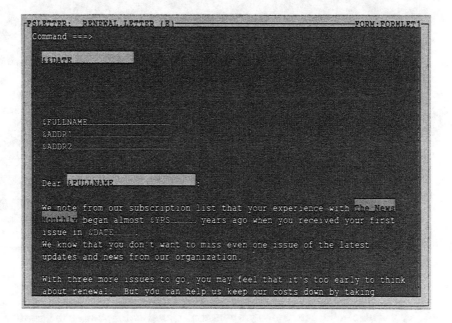

Now change the second occurrence of the magazine title, following the sender's name at the bottom of the letter.

You now need to edit the form entry for this letter so that text entered in red and reverse video comes out underlined when printed. Issue the following command:

```
edit formlet1.form
```

The FORM window is opened. Because you have already created the form FORMLET1 in a previous example, the Text Body and Margin Information frame is displayed initially instead of the Printer Selection frame. Issue the following command in the FORM window to move to the Font Control Information frame:

```
=4
```

Display 5.27 shows a Font Control Information frame with no printing instructions currently defined. Each form can include multiple printing instruction definitions. Scroll forward to view additional slots for defining printing instructions.

Display 5.27
Font Control
Information Frame

```
┌─FORM:  FORMLET1.FORM (E)──────────────────────────────────────────┐
│ Command ===>                                                       │
│                                                                    │
│                                                                    │
│                        Font Control Information                    │
│                                                                    │
│                                                                    │
│      Character   Number  Description      Character  Number  Description │
│         ~          27    Escape              ]        ___    Control │
│         _         ___    _____          _        ___    _____ │
│         _         ___    _____          _        ___    _____ │
│         _         ___    _____          _        ___    _____ │
│                                                                    │
│                                                    Scroll down for more │
│      Color       Attribute                                         │
│                                                                    │
│      _____    _____      Start: _____ │
│                                Stop:  _____ │
│                                Desc:  _____ │
│                                                                    │
│                                                                    │
└────────────────────────────────────────────────────────────────────┘
```

To define the printing instruction, type RED in the Color column and REVERSE in the Attribute column. Then, in the Start and Stop fields, enter the control characters or symbols that signal your printer to produce underlined text.

For example, the code sequence to start underlining on a Hewlett-Packard® LaserJet™ printer is an escape character (ASCII 27) followed by the characters &dD. The code sequence to stop underlining is escape followed by &d@. Notice in the top portion of the Font Control Information frame that the tilde (~) character is defined as a substitute for the nonprintable escape character. Enter the following value in the Start field to define the command that starts underlining:

~&dD

Enter the following value in the Stop field:

~&d@

▶ *Caution* .... **Printer commands are highly device-specific.**
The codes shown above work only for the specified printer. Consult the technical documentation for your printer for a listing of the codes that control printing features on that device. If you need further assistance, see your system administrator. ▲

Enter the word *Underlining* in the Desc (description) field to remind you what feature this color and highlighting combination is used to signal. Display 5.28 shows the completed definition.

Hewlett-Packard is a registered trademark and LaserJet is a trademark of Hewlett-Packard Company.

Display 5.28
*Specifying Color
and Attribute for
Underlining Text*

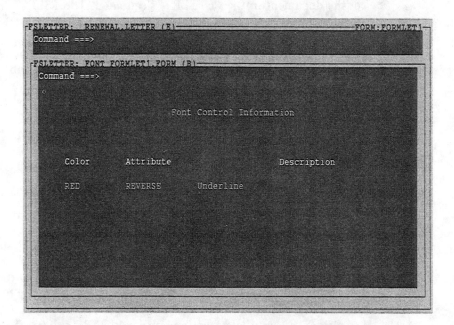

```
┌─FORM:  FORMLET1.FORM (E)────────────────────────────────────────┐
│ Command ===>                                                    │
│                                                                 │
│                                                                 │
│                      Font Control Information                   │
│                                                                 │
│                                                                 │
│   Character   Number  Description      Character  Number  Description │
│       ~         27    Escape               ]        ___   Control     │
│      ___       ___    _____           ___      ___    _____   │
│      ___       ___    _____           ___      ___    _____   │
│      ___       ___    _____           ___      ___    _____   │
│                                                                 │
│                                              Scroll down for more │
│                                                                 │
│      Color       Attribute                                      │
│                                                                 │
│      RED         REVERSE       Start: ~&dD                      │
│                                Stop:  ~&də                      │
│                                Desc:  Underline                 │
│                                                                 │
└─────────────────────────────────────────────────────────────────┘
```

Now execute the END command to store the new version of
FORMLET1.FORM, to close the FORM window, and to return to the FSLETTER
window. To check your font control definition, enter the following command
from the FSLETTER window:

    font

The FONT command opens the FSLETTER FONT window, as shown in
Display 5.29.

Display 5.29
*Checking Current
Font Control
Definitions*

```
┌─FSLETTER:  RENEWAL LETTER (E)──────────────────────FORM:FORMLET1─┐
│ Command ===>                                                    │
│                                                                 │
│ ┌─FSLETTER: FONT FORMLET1.FORM (B)─────────────────────────────┐ │
│ │ Command ===>                                                 │ │
│ │                                                              │ │
│ │                                                              │ │
│ │                    Font Control Information                  │ │
│ │                                                              │ │
│ │                                                              │ │
│ │      Color       Attribute            Description            │ │
│ │                                                              │ │
│ │      RED         REVERSE       Underline                     │ │
│ │                                                              │ │
│ │                                                              │ │
│ └──────────────────────────────────────────────────────────────┘ │
└──────────────────────────────────────────────────────────────────┘
```

Now when you use this form to print a document, all text displayed in red
and reverse video is underlined. See Output 5.1 at the end of this chapter for
the resulting letter with underlined text.

Use the END command to close the FSLETTER FONT window and return to the FSLETTER window. Execute the END command again in the FSLETTER window to store the altered version of the RENEWAL letter.

Printing Documents Using Information from SAS Data Sets

SAS/FSP software provides several ways to print copies of FSLETTER documents with fields filled from observations in a SAS data set or a SAS data view. You can initiate printing from the FSBROWSE and FSEDIT procedures as well as from the FSLETTER procedure. The following sections explain the available methods.

Using the FSLETTER Procedure

There are two different ways to produce copies of documents for observations in a SAS data set using the FSLETTER procedure. You can produce the letters noninteractively without opening an FSLETTER window, or interactively from an open FSLETTER or FSLETTER DIRECTORY window. The following sections explain both methods.

Producing Copies Noninteractively

Use the DATA= option in the PROC FSLETTER statement to specify the SAS data set containing the values you want to use to fill in the fields of the document. To use the DATA= option, you must also specify the complete name of the document in the LETTER= argument. (The FSLETTER procedure terminates with an error message if you specify only a catalog name.)

All fields in the document with names or aliases that match the names of variables in the data set are filled automatically with values from observations in the data set. Any field that has no matching data set variable is left blank. A separate copy of the document is printed for each observation. The process is noninteractive; no FSLETTER window is opened. There is a pause while the letters are generated; then the procedure terminates.

For example, the following statements create a copy of the renewal reminder letter for each observation in the subscriber data set:

```
proc fsletter letter=master.letters.renewal.letter
     data=master.subscrib;
run;
```

Use the PRINTFILE= option in the PROC FSLETTER statement to send the text of the copies to an external file rather than to the printer specified in the form associated with the document. All copies are sent to the same file.

By default, the FSLETTER procedure produces a copy of the document for every observation in the specified SAS data set. To produce copies for only a particular subset of observations, use a WHERE statement with the PROC FSLETTER statement to specify criteria that observations must meet for letters to be produced.

For example, the following statements create a copy of the renewal reminder letter for only those observations in the subscriber data set where the BEGDATE variable value is NOV89 and the YRS variable value is 1:

```
proc fsletter letter=master.letters.renewal.letter
    data=master.subscrib;
  where begdate='01nov89'd and yrs=1;
run;
```

Producing Copies from FSLETTER Windows

You can print copies of a document for values in a SAS data set from an open FSLETTER or FSLETTER DIRECTORY window. The first step is to identify the data set using the DATA command. For example, the following command identifies the subscriber data set used in previous examples as the source of field information for subsequent printing:

```
data master.subscrib
```

Once you have issued a DATA command, the FSLETTER procedure attempts to fill fields with values from the specified data set whenever a SEND command is executed. To print a copy of the renewal letter for all observations in the subscriber data set, issue the following command from the FSLETTER DIRECTORY window:

```
send renewal all
```

If the RENEWAL.LETTER entry is already displayed in the FSLETTER window, use the following command:

```
send all
```

Copies of the document are created for each observation in the data set. The FSLETTER SEND window is not opened; after a pause, a message appears telling you that copies have been sent.

Note: If you omit the ALL option, the SEND command produces a copy of the document for only the first observation in the data set. The FSLETTER SEND window is opened with fields filled from that observation.

By default, the SEND command with the ALL option generates a copy of the document for every observation in the data set. To produce copies for only a particular subset of observations, use a WHERE command before using the SEND command.

For example, the following command restricts processing to only those observations in the subscriber data set where the BEGDATE variable value is NOV89 and the YRS variable value is 1:

```
where begdate='01nov89'd and yrs=1
```

With the WHERE clause in effect, the SEND ALL command produces copies for all observations that meet the WHERE conditions, not for all observations in the data set.

When you are through printing copies for a given data set, use the CLOSE command to close the data set. After a CLOSE command is executed, the FSLETTER procedure no longer uses the data set to fill fields.

Using the SEND Command's DATA= Option

You can also print copies of a document for all observations in a data set by using the DATA= option in the SEND command. For example, the following command prints a copy of the renewal reminder letter for all observations in the subscriber data set:

```
send renewal data=master.subscrib
```

The ALL option is not required when the DATA= option is used. Copies are produced for all observations by default.

This form of the SEND command is also valid when a DATA command is used. The data set specified in the DATA= option takes precedence over the one specified in the DATA command.

Using the FSBROWSE or FSEDIT Procedures

SAS/FSP software provides several ways to access the FSLETTER procedure from the FSBROWSE and FSEDIT procedures to generate copies of a document for observations in a data set. All of these methods require that you initiate the FSBROWSE or FSEDIT session with a PROC FSBROWSE or PROC FSEDIT statement and include the LETTER= option with the PROC statement.

Producing Copies for All Observations

You can specify the complete three- or four-level name of the letter entry in the LETTER= option to print a copy of the document for each observation in the data set specified in the DATA= option. All fields in the document with names or aliases that match the names of variables in the data set are filled automatically with values from observations in the data set. Any field that has no matching data set variable is left blank. A separate copy of the document is printed for each observation. The process is noninteractive; no FSBROWSE or FSEDIT window is opened. There is a pause while the letters are generated; then the procedure terminates.

For example, the following statements print a copy of the renewal reminder letter for all observations in the subscriber data set:

```
proc fsbrowse data=master.subscrib
    letter=master.letters.renewal.letter;
run;
```

The results are the same if you specify only a catalog name in the LETTER= option but also include the SEND= option giving a letter entry name. The following statements also print a copy of the renewal reminder letter for all observations in the subscriber data set:

```
proc fsbrowse data=master.subscrib
    letter=master.letters
    send=renewal;
run;
```

Use the PRINTFILE= option in the PROC FSBROWSE or PROC FSEDIT statement to send the text of the copies to an external file rather than to the printer specified in the form associated with the document. All copies of the document are sent to the same file.

By default, the FSBROWSE and FSEDIT procedures produce a copy of the document for every observation in the specified SAS data set. To produce copies for only a particular subset of observations, use a WHERE statement with the PROC FSBROWSE or PROC FSEDIT statement to specify criteria that observations must meet for letters to be produced.

For example, the following statements create a copy of the renewal reminder letter for only those observations in the data set where the BEGDATE variable value is NOV89 and the YRS variable value is 1:

```
proc fsbrowse data=master.subscrib
    letter=master.letters.renewal.letter;
  where begdate='01nov89'd and yrs=1;
run;
```

Producing Copies for Individual Observations

It is also possible to print copies of a document for individual observations rather than for all observations. If you specify only a catalog name in the LETTER= option, no document is printed automatically. The FSBROWSE or FSEDIT procedure displays an observation for browsing or editing in the usual manner. However, when you use this form or the option, three additional commands are available in the FSBROWSE or FSEDIT window:

LETTER

> opens the FSLETTER DIRECTORY window showing the contents of the catalog specified in the LETTER= option. From the FSLETTER DIRECTORY window you can create, edit, browse, and print documents just as if you had opened the window with a PROC FSLETTER statement, with one important exception: when you print the document, any fields with names or aliases that match variable names in the data set are filled with corresponding variable values from the observation displayed when you issued the LETTER command.
>
> When you close the FSLETTER DIRECTORY window, you return to the FSBROWSE or FSEDIT window with the same observation still displayed.

EDIT *letter-entry*

    opens the FSLETTER window for entering or editing the specified document. The FSLETTER window behaves just as if you had opened it with a PROC FSLETTER statement, with one important exception: if you issue a SEND command to print the document, any fields with names or aliases that match variable names in the data set are filled automatically with the corresponding values from the observation displayed when you issued the EDIT command.

    When you close the FSLETTER window, you return to the FSBROWSE or FSEDIT window with the same observation still displayed.

SEND *letter-entry*

    opens the FSLETTER SEND window for printing the specified document. The FSLETTER SEND window behaves just as if you had opened it with a PROC FSLETTER statement, with one important exception: any fields with names or aliases that match variable names in the data set are filled automatically with the corresponding values from the observation displayed when you issued the SEND command.

    When you close the FSLETTER SEND window, you return to the FSBROWSE or FSEDIT window with the same observation still displayed.

For example, submit the following statements to initiate an FSEDIT session and identify a catalog containing letter entries:

```
proc fsedit data=master.subscrib
     letter=master.letters;
run;
```

The FSEDIT window initially displays the first observation in the MASTER.SUBSCRIB data set. You can use the FSEDIT procedure's search commands to locate the individuals in the data set who should receive the renewal reminder.

The renewal letter is designed to be sent three months before a subscriber's last issue is mailed. Thus, the search command argument depends on the current date. For example, in July 1990 you need to identify those individuals whose last issue will be mailed in October 1990. Because subscriptions are sold for varying terms, several searches may be necessary to locate all possible recipients. For example, a one-year subscription that began in November 1989 expires in October 1990, as does a two-year subscription that began in November 1988 or a three-year subscription that began in November 1987.

Issue the following command to locate any one-year subscribers who need to receive the renewal reminder letter in July 1990:

```
find begdate=NOV89 yrs=1
```

The command locates one subscriber, Martha Vance, as shown in Display 5.30.

Display 5.30
An FSEDIT
Observation
Display

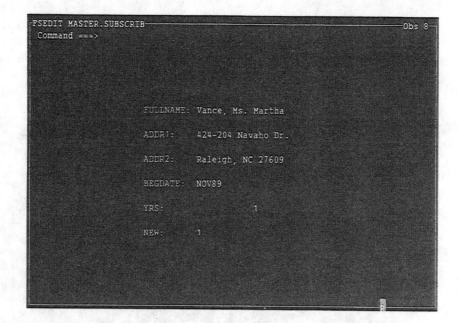

You can use the SEND command to print a copy of the renewal reminder letter for this subscriber. Issue the following command in the FSEDIT window:

```
send renewal
```

This opens the FSLETTER SEND window in the first step of the printing process.

The variables in MASTER.SUBSCRIB have the same names as the fields in the RENEWAL document, except for BEGDATE. However, remember that BEGDATE was assigned as an alias for the DATE field in the field's FSLETTER ATTR window frame. Thus, the procedure fills all the letter's fields automatically, as shown in Display 5.31.

Display 5.31
Document with
Fields Filled from
a SAS Data Set

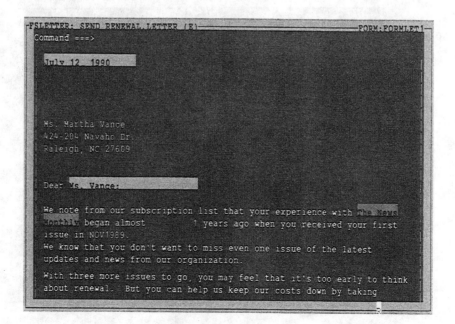

Issue the END command to enter the second printing step. The text is flowed, and the document is presented for final editing. In this step you can make any changes necessary for this particular letter. For example, delete the *s* from the word *years* so that the text reads *1 year ago.* Display 5.32 shows the edited letter ready for printing.

Display 5.32
Final Editing of Document Containing Data Set Values

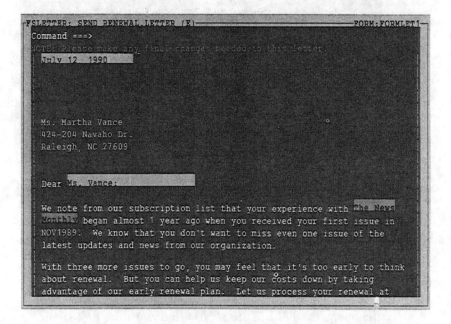

Issue the END command to close the FSLETTER SEND window and print the letter. After the FSLETTER SEND window is closed, you return to the FSEDIT window. The observation for which the letter was sent is still displayed. A message appears in the message line informing you that a copy of the letter has been sent for this observation, as shown in Display 5.33.

Display 5.33
Observation after Printing

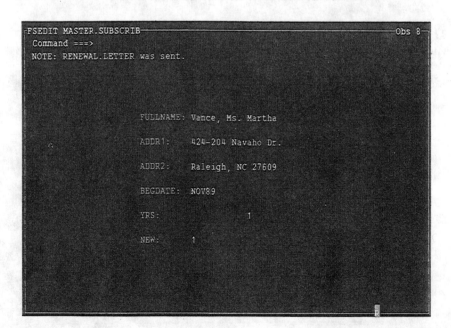

The printed letter is shown in Output 5.1.

Output 5.1
Printed Letter

```
July 12, 1990



Ms. Martha Vance
424-204 Navaho Dr.
Raleigh, NC 27609


Dear Ms. Vance:

We note from our subscription list that your experience with The News
Monthly began almost 1 year ago when you received your first issue in
NOV1989.  We know that you don't want to miss even one issue of the
latest updates and news from our organization.

With three more issues to go, you may feel that it's too early to think
about renewal. But you can help us keep our costs down by taking
advantage of our early renewal plan. Let us process your renewal at
current postal rates, and you can avoid any price increase for another
year.

Please make sure that your address information on the enclosed mailing
label is current. Attach the label to the postage-paid renewal card,
and return it to us at your earliest convenience.


Sincerely,




Margaret E. Ellis
Subscription Department
The News Monthly


Enclosure
```

Chapter 6 Browsing External Files Using the FSLIST Procedure

Introduction

The FSLIST procedure provides an interactive environment for browsing external files during a SAS session. External (non-SAS) files are files that use your operating system's file structure. Types of information stored in external files include

☐ raw data

☐ text, possibly including carriage-control information

☐ SAS source statements

☐ output from previous SAS sessions.

Refer to Chapter 1, "Introduction to SAS/FSP Software," for a discussion of external files.

Browsing External Files

The FSLIST procedure does more than simply list the contents of the external file. It displays the file in an FSLIST window that provides commands to

☐ scroll freely through the file

☐ select colors for various areas of the display

☐ display line and column numbers

□ view the file in hexadecimal format

□ search for specific strings within the file

□ copy text from the file to other SAS windows.

The remainder of this chapter illustrates these features.

Opening the FSLIST Window

You can invoke the FSLIST procedure and open the FSLIST window using either
the PROC FSLIST statement or the FSLIST command. You can identify the file to
be browsed in either of two ways:

□ by specifying the physical name of the file

□ by specifying a *fileref*, a SAS nickname associated with the file.

The following sections illustrate both of these methods.

Identifying the File by Filename

You can specify the actual name of the file in the FILEREF= argument of the
PROC FSLIST statement or following the FSLIST command. The filename must
be enclosed in quotes. The form of the filename depends on the file and on the
directory naming conventions of the operating system under which you are
running the SAS System.

To initiate the FSLIST procedure and open the FSLIST window, submit the
following statements:

```
proc fslist fileref='actual-filename';
run;
```

where *actual-filename* is the complete file specification, called the fully qualified
pathname under some operating systems, for the external file.

Alternatively, you can use the following command from the command line of
any SAS System window:

```
fslist 'actual-filename'
```

Identifying the File by Fileref

You can specify a fileref for the file in the FILEREF= argument of the PROC
FSLIST statement or following the FSLIST command. A fileref is a nickname that
identifies the file to the SAS System.

The FILENAME statement is used to assign a fileref to an external file. For
example, the following FILENAME statement assigns the fileref MEMO to the
specified file:

```
filename memo 'actual-filename';
```

The form of the *actual-filename* value depends on the naming conventions of the
operating system under which you are running the SAS System. Supply the
complete file specification, called the fully qualified pathname under some
operating systems, for the external file. The filename must be enclosed in quotes.

Once the fileref is assigned, initiate the FSLIST procedure and open the FSLIST window by submitting the following statements:

```
proc fslist fileref=memo;
run;
```

Do not enclose the fileref in quotes; if you do, it is treated as a filename.

Alternatively, you can issue the following command from any SAS System window:

```
fslist memo
```

A Sample Session

Although you can use the FSLIST procedure to browse almost any type of external file, the following examples use a simple text file. This file is available in the SAS/FSP sample library as member FU06N01. See "Using This Book" at the beginning of this book for information on accessing the sample library at your site.

Use either of the methods described in the preceding section to invoke the FSLIST procedure for browsing the example file. Display 6.1 shows the file displayed in the FSLIST window.

Display 6.1
External File
Displayed in the
FSLIST Window

```
-FSLIST: SAS SAMPLES V606(FU06N01)
Command ===>

  TO: Budget Advisory Committee
FROM: Susan Hall
SUBJ: Meeting
DATE: March 26, 1990

There will be a meeting of the budget advisory committee on Tuesday,
March 27, at 4:00 p.m. in the first floor conference room. Please
be prepared to discuss the second and third quarter projections.

Below are the most recent figures for calculated profit before taxes.
Information for the years 1984 through 1989 is included.

      YEAR         SALES         COST         PROFIT

      1984         12132         11021         1111
      1985         19823         12928         6895
      1986         16982         14002         2980
      1987         18432         14590         3842
      1988         19937         15378         4559
      1989         23435         17867         5568
```

Note: The window title in the upper-left corner of the window border reflects the physical name of the file. This example is from the MVS environment. The format of the name is different under other operating systems.

Scrolling

The FSLIST procedure provides the familiar scrolling commands found in other SAS/FSP procedures. You use commands such as BACKWARD and FORWARD,

LEFT and RIGHT, and TOP and BOTTOM to view different sections of the file. The HSCROLL and VSCROLL commands enable you to set default horizontal and vertical scrolling increments.

Customizing the Display

You can change features of the FSLIST window to suit your needs and tastes. The following sections show some of the commands you can use to customize the FSLIST environment.

Changing Colors and Highlighting Attributes

If your device supports color, the COLOR command allows you to change the color and highlighting attributes of various areas of the window. For example, issue the following command to change the text color to yellow:

```
color text yellow
```

You can also change the color of the window's border, banner, command line, and message line. Note that your color selections are retained only for the duration of the current FSLIST session.

Adding Line Numbers

Long files are easier to browse when the data lines are numbered. The FSLIST procedure provides sequential line numbers in a column on the left side of the window. Issue the following command to turn on line numbers:

```
nums on
```

If your device supports color, you can assign the number column a different color from the text area. For example, issue the following command:

```
color numbers green
```

Issue the following command to turn off line numbers:

```
nums off
```

You can also use the NUMS command without an argument. Issued alone, the NUMS command acts as a toggle, turning line numbers on if they are currently off or off if they are currently on.

Adding a Column Ruler

If you need a reference to determine what column of the display a character occupies, the FSLIST procedure provides a column ruler at the top of the FSLIST window. Issue the following command:

```
column on
```

Display 6.2 shows the FSLIST window with the column ruler on.

Display 6.2
FSLIST Window
with Column Ruler

```
FSLIST: SAS.SAMPLES.V606(FU06N01)─────────────────────────────────
Command ===>

----|----10---|----20---|----30---|----40---|----50---|----60---|----70---|--
     TO:  Budget Advisory Committee
FROM:  Susan Hall
SUBJ:  Meeting
DATE:  March 26, 1990

There will be a meeting of the budget advisory committee on Tuesday,
March 27, at 4:00 p.m. in the first floor conference room. Please
be prepared to discuss the second and third quarter projections.

Below are the most recent figures for calculated profit before taxes.
Information for the years 1984 through 1989 is included.

        YEAR         SALES         COST         PROFIT

        1984         12132         11021         1111
        1985         19823         12928         6895
        1986         16982         14002         2980
        1987         18432         14590         3842
        1988         19937         15378         4559
```

To turn the ruler off, issue the following command:

```
column off
```

You can also use the COLUMN command without an argument. Issued alone, the COLUMN command acts as a toggle, turning the column ruler on if it is currently off or off if it is currently on.

Displaying Hexadecimal Values

If you need to know the hexadecimal character code values for the displayed text, the FSLIST procedure provides a hexadecimal display format. In this format, each line from the file occupies three lines in the FSLIST window. The first line is the standard display of the line from the file. The next two lines give the hexadecimal character code values for each character in the line above. The hexadecimal values are displayed vertically, with the most significant byte on top.

Issue the following command to turn on the hexadecimal display:

```
hex on
```

Display 6.3 shows the FSLIST window with the hexadecimal format turned on.

Display 6.3
Displaying
Hexadecimal
Values

Note: The relationship between text characters and hexadecimal codes depends on the character coding system used by your operating system. The example display is from the MVS environment, which uses the EBCDIC character coding system. The hexadecimal values you see will be different if your operating system uses a different character coding system (for example, ASCII).

To turn off the hexadecimal format, issue the following command:

```
hex off
```

You can also use the HEX command without an argument. Issued alone, the HEX command acts as a toggle, turning hexadecimal format on if it is currently off or off if it is currently on.

Searching the Text

Searching line by line through a long or unfamiliar file can be time-consuming. The FSLIST procedure's FIND, RFIND, and BFIND commands allow you to go directly to a particular text string rather than scrolling randomly through the file.

For example, issue the following command:

```
find 'profit'
```

The cursor moves to the word *profit* in the second paragraph of the text.

Use the RFIND command to repeat the search beginning just beyond the current cursor position and proceeding toward the end of the file. Use the BFIND command to repeat the search in the opposite direction, toward the top of the file. The RFIND and BFIND commands are most useful when assigned to function keys so that you can move from one occurrence of the string to another simply by pressing a single key.

Issue the RFIND command to repeat the search specified in the preceding FIND command. You will get a message that no additional occurrences of *profit* were found, despite the fact that the column heading PROFIT appears later in the text. The FIND command is case-sensitive. The previous FIND command locates occurrences of the string *profit*, but not *PROFIT* or *Profit*. Be sure to use the correct case for your search string in the FIND command.

If you have a particularly large file, you may want to be more restrictive in your searches. The FIND command allows you to specify options that designate the occurrence of the string (NEXT, FIRST, LAST, PREV, or ALL) for which to search. For example, the following command reports (in the window's message line) how many times the specified string appears in the file and moves the cursor to the first occurrence:

```
find '1984' all
```

The following command moves the cursor to the last occurrence of the string in the file:

```
find '1984' last
```

The default qualifier for the FIND command is NEXT, which moves to the next occurrence of the specified string.

By default, the FIND command locates any occurrence of the string. For example, the following command would find the *for* embedded in the words *before* and *information*:

```
find 'for'
```

You can make the search more restrictive by adding options to the FIND command that specify the context in which the string must appear to constitute a match. The available options are PREFIX, SUFFIX, or WORD. For example, the following command locates only those occurrences where *for* appears as a distinct word and ignores embedded occurrences of the string (as in the word *before*):

```
find 'for' word
```

Searching Sections of a File

When a file is long, you can save time by limiting the search to smaller sections of the file. Use the global MARK command to identify the portion of the file to be searched. To mark a section of a file, type MARK on the command line, position the cursor at the beginning of the desired section, and press ENTER (or position the cursor and press the function key to which the MARK command is assigned). Then type MARK on the command line again, move to the end of the section, and press ENTER (or move to the end of the section and press the MARK key). The portion of the file between the marks will be highlighted. When you execute a FIND command while the cursor is positioned in the marked section of the file, the search is restricted to that section.

Use the global command UNMARK to turn off the mark highlighting.

Copying Text from the File

The FSLIST procedure makes the text of the displayed file available for copying into any window that uses the SAS text editor and allows editing.

Use the global MARK command to define the portion of the file to be copied; then issue a STORE command to copy the highlighted text into a buffer. You can then open any window that uses the SAS text editor for editing and use the global PASTE command to copy the buffer contents into the new window.

Suppose you want to use some of the information from the current external file in a report created with the FSLETTER procedure. Display 6.4 shows the FSLIST window with the desired text marked.

Display 6.4
FSLIST Window
with Marked Text
Block

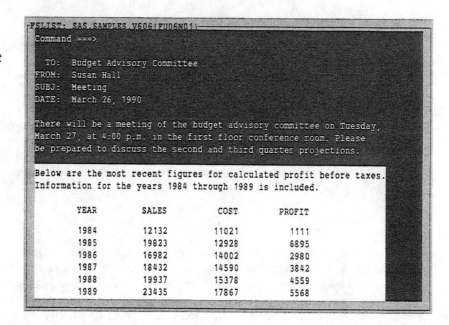

Follow these steps to mark and store this text:

1. Mark the upper-left corner of the block of text to be copied.

    Type MARK BLOCK on the command line, place the cursor on the B in the word *Below*, and press ENTER. (The MARK BLOCK form of the command is used to ensure that the marked area of text is not wider than the window into which it will be pasted.)

2. Mark the lower-right corner of the block of text.

    Type MARK on the command line, move the cursor to the bottom of the file and far enough to the right to include all of the text in the top sentence of the marked area, and then press ENTER. Or position the cursor and press the MARK function key.

    When you execute the second MARK command, the marked area of the text is highlighted as shown in Display 6.4. If you do not position the marks properly to include all the desired text in the highlighted area, issue the UNMARK command to remove the highlighting and then try again.

3. Store a copy of the text in the paste buffer.

Execute a STORE command from the command line (or press the function key to which the STORE command is assigned). The mark highlighting is removed, and the block you marked is stored in a paste buffer, waiting for you to use a PASTE command to insert it elsewhere.

Now execute the following command from the FSLIST window to open an FSLETTER window and create a blank document:

```
fsletter master.letters.report.letter
```

Note: This command assumes that you have defined the libref MASTER in your current SAS session. If you have not defined this libref, use the default libref WORK instead.

In the FSLETTER window, type PASTE on the command line, position the cursor where you want the stored text to be pasted, and press the ENTER key. Or position the cursor and press the function key to which the PASTE command is assigned. The text from the buffer is pasted into the FSLETTER document, as shown in Display 6.5.

Display 6.5
Text Pasted into an FSLETTER Window

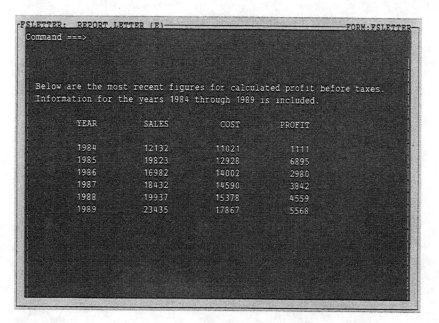

If you want, you can now edit the text you pasted into the window or add whatever additional text you need to create your report. When you use the END command to close the FSLETTER window, you return to the FSLIST window.

Displaying Another File

You can display another external file without exiting the FSLIST procedure. Use the BROWSE command in the FSLIST window and specify the filename or fileref of the file you want displayed. The procedure does not open a second FSLIST window. Instead, the current file is closed and the new file is displayed. Any custom FSLIST window characteristics you have selected (color changes or a column ruler, for example) remain in effect for the new file.

Closing the FSLIST Window

Use the END command to close the FSLIST window and exit the FSLIST procedure.

Part 3
Usage: Developers' Tools

Chapter 7 Overview: Part 3

Introduction

SAS/FSP software provides valuable data set manipulation capabilities for all SAS System users, but applications developers can also use the FSBROWSE, FSEDIT, and FSVIEW procedures as the basis for sophisticated data presentation and data entry systems. These procedures simplify the chore of developing such systems by providing an interactive environment for browsing, entering, and editing data. Furthermore, the procedures provide tools for customizing the appearance of the data display or data entry window and for validating or otherwise processing entered values.

Chapters 8 through 10 show how to use the FSBROWSE, FSEDIT, and FSVIEW procedures to create data entry applications. These chapters assume familiarity with the basic features of the FSBROWSE, FSEDIT, and FSVIEW procedures. Refer to Chapter 3 if you need to review the fundamentals of the FSBROWSE and FSEDIT procedures, and to Chapter 4 if you need to review the fundamentals of the FSVIEW procedure.

For detailed reference information on SAS/FSP software, turn to Parts 4 and 5, Chapters 11 through 20.

Selecting the Proper SAS/FSP Procedure

Table 7.1 tells you which SAS/FSP procedure to select to accomplish a given applications development task. It also directs you to the chapter that illustrates the use of the procedure in a sample application.

Task	Solutions
Create a simple data entry application	If you want your application to allow entering or editing values in one observation at a time, use the FSEDIT procedure. Tools are provided for customizing FSEDIT window characteristics and for defining many characteristics of the data entry fields. See Chapter 8 for details.

Table 7.1 Procedure Selection Guidelines: Developers' Tools

(continued)

Table 7.1 (continued)	Task	Solutions
		If you want your application to allow entering or editing values in a tabular format, use the FSVIEW procedure. Tools are provided for customizing FSVIEW window characteristics and for defining some characteristics of the data entry fields. See Chapter 9 for details.
	Create a simple data presentation application	If you want your application to allow browsing values in one observation at a time without allowing changes to the displayed values, use the FSBROWSE procedure. Tools are provided for customizing FSBROWSE window characteristics. The information about FSEDIT applications in Chapter 8 also applies to FSBROWSE applications.
		If you want your application to allow browsing values in a tabular format, use the FSVIEW procedure. Tools are provided for customizing FSVIEW window characteristics. See Chapter 9 for details.
	Create a data entry application that includes cross-validation of field values and other data manipulations	If you want your application to perform calculations involving data set variables with results displayed in a tabular format, use the formula facility in an FSVIEW application. The results can be displayed in special computed variables, or they can be used to automatically update variables in the data set. See Chapter 9 for details.
		For more sophisticated manipulations, you can include Screen Control Language functions in your formula definitions. See Chapter 10 for details.

(continued)

Table 7.1 *(continued)*	**Task**	**Solutions**
		If you want your application to perform advanced data manipulations with results displayed one observation at a time, use a Screen Control Language (SCL) program in an FSEDIT application. SCL programs can □ perform calculations involving data set variables or temporary window variables □ cross-validate field values with values from other SAS data sets □ display and manipulate values from other SAS data sets □ manipulate external files. See Chapter 10 for details.
	Create a data presentation application that includes computed values and other data manipulations	If you want your application to perform calculations involving data set variables with the results displayed in a tabular format, use the formula facility in an FSVIEW application. The results can be displayed in special fields or in the fields for data set variables. (When the FSVIEW window is opened for browsing, computed values displayed in data set variable fields do not update the corresponding data set variables.) See Chapter 9 for details.
		If you want your application to perform advanced data manipulations with results displayed for one observation at a time, use a Screen Control Language (SCL) program in an FSBROWSE application. The information about SCL programs with FSEDIT applications in Chapter 10 also applies to FSBROWSE applications. **Note:** You cannot enter values in computational fields in FSBROWSE applications.

Chapter 8 Creating Data Entry Applications Using the FSEDIT Procedure

Introduction

If you design data entry applications, whether for yourself or for other users, you can take advantage of the tools the FSEDIT procedure provides for customizing your applications. For example, you can

□   redesign the display to suit the needs of a specific application

□   assign field attributes to enhance data entry

□   assign parameters to be in effect during an FSEDIT session

□   write a Screen Control Language program that manipulates variables and calculates values.

This chapter describes the first three of these features, followed by a sample session that walks you through applying these features to the subscription application described in Chapter 3, "Browsing and Editing SAS Data Sets Using the FSBROWSE and FSEDIT Procedures." The FSEDIT procedure's programming capabilities are discussed in Chapter 10, "Enhancing Data Entry Applications Using Screen Control Language."

Note: All of the features described in this chapter for creating data entry and editing applications using the FSEDIT procedure are also available for creating data presentation applications using the FSBROWSE procedure. FSBROWSE applications can only show the contents of a data set; observations cannot be added, deleted, or modified.

Creating a Data Entry Application

Creating a custom application involves the following steps:

1. Invoke the FSEDIT procedure, specifying the SCREEN= option in the PROC FSEDIT statement or the *screen-name* argument with the FSEDIT command to identify a screen entry in which customized features are saved.

2. Open the FSEDIT Menu window to select customization tasks.

3. Customize the display to suit your application.

4. Assign attributes to the variable fields.

5. Modify general parameters to enhance your application.

Getting Started

To begin creating the example application, initiate the FSEDIT procedure using the SCREEN= option in the PROC FSEDIT statement:

```
proc fsedit data=master.subscrib
    screen=master.display.scrsub.screen;
 run;
```

You should have previously assigned the libref MASTER to a permanent SAS data library. The example data set, MASTER.SUBSCRIB, is described in Chapter 1, "Introduction to SAS/FSP Software."

Notice that a SCREEN= option appears here in addition to the DATA= option specifying the data set. The SCREEN= option specifies the catalog and catalog entry in which information about the FSEDIT application is stored. The catalog, MASTER.DISPLAY, is created if it does not already exist. The catalog entry is not created until you open the FSEDIT Menu window to begin building the application.

Alternatively, you can use an FSEDIT command in any SAS System window to achieve the same results:

```
fsedit master.subscrib master.display.scrsub.screen
```

Note: You can omit the screen entry name in the SCREEN= option or *screen-name* argument in the preceding examples. In that case, customization information for the application is stored with the default entry name, FSEDIT.SCREEN.

Opening the FSEDIT Menu Window

When you invoke the FSEDIT procedure, the FSEDIT window is opened by default. To open the FSEDIT Menu window, issue the MODIFY command from the command line of any observation.

Alternatively, you can invoke the procedure and go directly to the FSEDIT Menu window by adding the MODIFY option to the PROC FSEDIT statement:

```
proc fsedit data=master.subscrib
    screen=master.display.scrsub.screen
    modify;
 run;
```

Display 8.1 shows the FSEDIT Menu window. From this window you can perform all of the tasks required to create a customized application. To select an option, type the corresponding option number on the command line and press ENTER, or move the cursor to the desired option number in the menu and press ENTER or the mouse button.

Display 8.1
The FSEDIT Menu
Window

```
┌─FSEDIT Menu─────────────────────────────────────────┐
│ Select Option ===>                                   │
│                                                      │
│                                                      │
│             1 Information about screen modification  │
│             2 Screen Modification and Field Identification │
│             3 Edit Program Statements and Compile    │
│             4 Assign Special Attributes to Fields    │
│             5 Modification of General Parameters     │
│             6 Browse Program Statements              │
│                                                      │
│                                                      │
│                                                      │
│                                                      │
│                                                      │
│                                                      │
└──────────────────────────────────────────────────────┘
```

This chapter describes the tasks performed using options 2, 4, and 5. Option 1 provides information about the process of creating a customized application and about the commands available during this process. (This option opens the same HELP window as executing the HELP command in the FSEDIT menu window.) Options 3 and 6 are used to create, edit, or browse a Screen Control Language program for the application. Those options are discussed in Chapter 10.

Menu Option 2: Creating a Customized Display

You can make data entry easier for users by enhancing the FSEDIT window display with

□ comments

□ additional information and instructions

□ field labels that are more informative than simple variable names

□ color and highlighting.

How to Start

Select option 2, "Screen Modification and Field Identification," from the FSEDIT Menu window to begin the process of designing a customized display for your application. This option opens the FSEDIT Modify window, in which you can modify the content and appearance of the FSEDIT window display.

Using the FSEDIT Modify Window

Display 8.2 shows the initial FSEDIT Modify window for the example data set. Variable names and fields are displayed using the default format because this is a new screen entry with no existing customization information.

Display 8.2
The FSEDIT
Modify Window

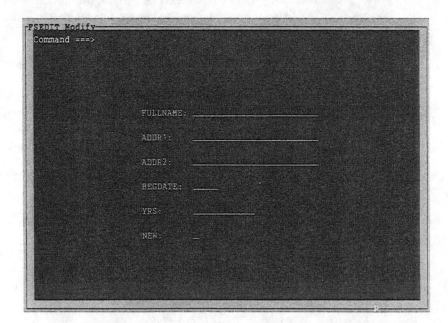

The FSEDIT Modify window uses the SAS text editor. Use any of the standard text editor commands to modify the display to suit your application. (SAS text editor commands are described in Chapter 19, "SAS Text Editor Commands," in *SAS Language: Reference, Version 6, First Edition.*) You can write over any part of the display, including variable names and the underscores that indicate variable fields.

Selecting Text Colors

If your terminal or workstation supports color, any text you enter in the FSEDIT Modify window is displayed in yellow by default. You can change the color and highlighting characteristics of the text as you enter it. Simply use the special keys on your device that control text color and highlighting as you enter or modify information. The colors and highlighting characteristics you use in the FSEDIT Modify window are recorded and used in the customized display for your application.

Special Topic: Systems without Special Color Keys

For operating systems where terminals do not provide special keys to set text color and highlighting characteristics, the SAS System recognizes combinations of the ESC key and a letter or number key as commands to change text color or highlighting.

The following list shows the key sequences that select the color attribute for subsequent text:

ESC A	gray	ESC K	black	ESC P	pink
ESC B	blue	ESC M	magenta	ESC R	red
ESC C	cyan	ESC N	brown	ESC W	white
ESC G	green	ESC O	orange	ESC Y	yellow

For example, to type text in cyan, press the ESC and then the C key. The next characters entered are displayed in cyan.

The following list shows the key sequences that select the highlighting attribute for subsequent text:

ESC 0　　turns off all highlighting attributes and returns to
　　　　　base color
ESC 1　　turns on high intensity
ESC 2　　turns on underlining
ESC 3　　turns on reverse video
ESC 4　　turns on blinking.

Note: Some operating systems may require a different prefix key rather than ESC. If ESC does not work on your system, consult the companion or other documentation for the SAS System on your operating system for the correct prefix.

Defining Variable Fields

Use underscores (_) to identify the variable fields. The underscores for each field must be preceded and followed by at least one blank.

Note: In the FSEDIT Modify window, you must use underscores to identify fields to the procedure. The way the field is actually displayed to users is determined by the assigned pad character. See "Menu Option 4: Assigning Special Field Attributes" later in this chapter.

Be sure to type enough underscores for each field so that users of your application have room to enter any valid value for that field. Remember to consider any assigned informats and formats when you are determining the number of underscores needed for the field. Default field widths are as follows:

character variables　　equal to the variable's length, the variable's format width, or the variable's informat width, whichever is longer.

numeric variables　　equal to the longer of the variable's format width or informat width. If the variable has no assigned format, the default field width is 12 underscores since the default numeric format is BEST12.

For character variables, the underscores for a field do not all have to be contiguous. You can use an asterisk (*) at the end of a series of underscores to indicate that the character field continues in the next set of underscores encountered to the right of or below the current field. (The asterisks count toward the field width.) For example, the underscores after Phone number: in the following are treated as one 10-character field, not three separate fields:

```
Phone number: ( __* ) __* - ____
```

Notice that the requirement that each group of underscores must be preceded and followed by a blank space still applies.

The positions marked with asterisks show up as underscores (or pad characters) in the FSEDIT window display.

Modifying the Display

Display 8.3 shows a redesigned display for the example data set MASTER.SUBSCRIB.

Display 8.3
Redesigned
Display for
MASTER.SUBSCRIB

```
┌─FSEDIT Modify───────────────────────────────────────────────┐
│ Command ===>                                                 │
│                                                              │
│                                                              │
│                                                              │
│        Subscriber: _____                 │
│                                                              │
│    Street Address: _____                 │
│                                                              │
│     City/State/ZIP: _____                │
│                                                              │
│                 Is this a new subscription? _               │
│                 (enter 1 if yes, 0 if no)                    │
│                                                              │
│  Date of first issue: _____    Length of subscription: __  │
│                                                              │
└──────────────────────────────────────────────────────────────┘
```

Follow these steps to produce the new display. If you need more information on the text editor commands used in these steps, refer to Chapter 19 in *SAS Language: Reference*.

1. Use the NUMS ON command to turn on line numbers.

2. Use the line commands M and B to move the line containing the NEW variable field above the one containing the BEGDATE variable field.

3. Use the line command I2 on the line containing the NEW variable to insert two blank lines between NEW and BEGDATE.

4. Use the line command D to delete the blank line between the BEGDATE and YRS fields.

5. Move to the underscores for the YRS field; then use the DELETE key to delete all but two. (The 12 underscores that are provided by default are much more than necessary to hold the valid values for this variable.)

6. Starting in the first column of each line, type the new labels for the field (shown in Display 8.3). Then use the DELETE key to eliminate the extra space and old labels between the new labels and the underscores for the fields. If your device supports color, type the new labels for the FULLNAME, ADDR1, and ADDR2 fields in yellow, the new label for the NEW field in cyan, and the new labels for the BEGDATE and YRS fields in white.

7. Add the extra line of descriptive text beneath the label "Is this a new subscription?" (in cyan if your device supports color).

8. Use the TF line command on the line containing the Date of first issue: field to pull the Length of subscription: field onto the same line.

9. Use the NUMS OFF command to turn off line numbers.

10. Use the INSERT key to turn on insert mode; then move the cursor to each line and insert spaces as necessary to align the fields as shown in Display 8.3.

When you are satisfied with the results, issue the END command. You will be asked the following question:

```
Have you added any computational or repeated fields (Y or N)? _
```

For this example, type N in the field provided because you have not created any special fields. (Special fields are discussed in Chapter 10.) The FSEDIT Modify window is closed, and the FSEDIT Identify window is opened.

Using the FSEDIT Identify Window

The FSEDIT Identify window is where you tell the FSEDIT procedure where each variable field is located on the display. The procedure knows the original location of all variable fields. However, if you edit any part of a line that contains variable fields, the procedure loses track of the positions of all variable fields in that line. Changes involving entire lines, such as deleting blank lines or moving lines containing fields, do not cause the procedure to lose track of the fields.

In the FSEDIT Identify window, you are prompted to identify the location of each variable field that the procedure is unable to identify in the modified display. Display 8.4 shows the prompt for the FULLNAME variable. Regardless of how you have changed the label that identifies variable fields to users, the FSEDIT procedure always refers to variable fields by the actual variable names as defined in the SAS data set. When you receive a prompt, position the cursor on any underscore in that variable field, and press ENTER.

Display 8.4
Prompt for
Identifying
Variable Field

```
┌FSEDIT Identify──────────────────────────────────────
Command ===>
Please put cursor on field: FULLNAME and press ENTER ... or UNWANTED




        Subscriber: _____

    Street Address: _____

    City/State/ZIP: _____

              Is this a new subscription? _
              (enter 1 if yes, 0 if no)

Date of first issue: _____      Length of subscription: __




                                                              R
```

Continue identifying variable fields until you receive the following message:

NOTE: All fields are identified.

Now issue the END command to return to the FSEDIT Menu window. The customized display you have created is saved in the screen entry for your application.

Menu Option 4: Assigning Special Field Attributes

You can use the FSEDIT procedure's special field attributes to help users of your application avoid errors during data entry and editing. The attributes give you control over how the fields are presented and what values can be entered in the fields.

How to Start

Select option 4, "Assign Special Attributes to Fields," from the FSEDIT Menu window to begin the process of assigning attributes. This option opens the FSEDIT Attribute window. The FSEDIT Attribute window is partitioned into a series of frames. Each frame is used to assign a different attribute. The following list shows the frames and their corresponding attributes:

INITIAL   sets the initial value for the field when a new observation is
                   added.

MAXIMUM   sets the largest value that can be entered in the field.

MINIMUM   sets the smallest value that can be entered in the field.

REQUIRED	indicates that a value must be entered in the field when a new observation is added.
CAPS	indicates that values entered in the field are to be automatically capitalized.
FCOLOR	specifies the color for the field.
ECOLOR	specifies the color for flagging erroneous values in the field.
FATTR	specifies the highlighting attribute of the field.
EATTR	specifies the highlighting attribute for flagging erroneous values in the field.
PAD	specifies the pad character for the field when the value for the field is missing.
PROTECT	indicates fields that cannot be edited.
JUSTIFY	specifies how values are aligned in the field (left, right, or centered).
NONDISPLAY	indicates fields that are not visible in the display.
NOAUTOSKIP	identifies fields on which the cursor remains after a value is entered until the cursor is explicitly moved.

Using the FSEDIT Attribute Window

The FSEDIT Attribute frames appear in the sequence shown in the preceding list. Use the BACKWARD and FORWARD commands or scroll keys to move from one frame in the series to another.

You can also move directly to a particular frame by typing the name of the attribute (CAPS, FCOLOR, and so forth) on the command line and pressing ENTER.

When all the variables for a single observation cannot be displayed at one time, as in multiscreen applications, use the LEFT and RIGHT commands to display the additional screens, as indicated in Figure 8.1.

Figure 8.1   *Scrolling Field Attribute Frames*

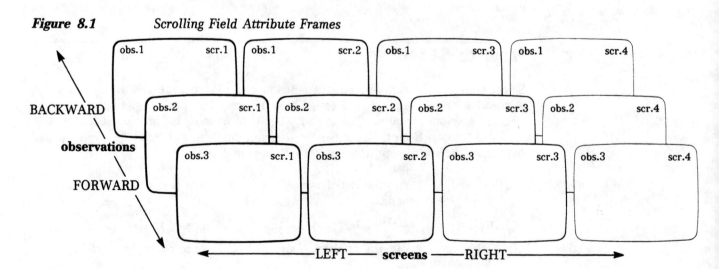

Assigning Initial Values: INITIAL

The INITIAL attribute allows you to specify initial values for fields. For fields that are assigned this attribute, the initial value is displayed instead of pad characters when a new observation is added using the ADD command.

In the data set containing the *The News Monthly* mailing list, the value of the variable NEW is 1 when a subscription is new, 0 if not. Because all observations added to the mailing list represent new subscriptions, you can initialize the value of the NEW variable to 1 by entering a 1 in the blank beside the field for NEW, as shown in Display 8.5. (Note that in the customized display the field for the NEW variable is identified by a descriptive label, "Is this a new subscription?," rather than by the variable name.)

Display 8.5
Initial Value
Attributes
(INITIAL)

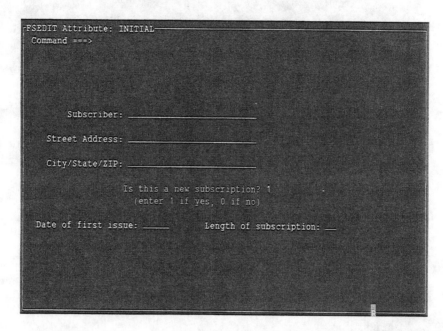

When a user issues the ADD command to add a new observation, a 1 automatically appears in the NEW field to indicate that a new subscriber is being added to the data set.

Assigning Maximum Values: MAXIMUM

The MAXIMUM attribute allows you to specify maximum values for the fields. If a user attempts to enter a value greater than the maximum for a field, an error message is displayed and the cursor is positioned on the field.

For example, suppose you want to limit subscriptions to *The News Monthly* to five years. To specify this maximum value for the YRS variable, type 5 in the field for the YRS variable, as shown in Display 8.6. (Note that in the customized display the field for the YRS variable is identified by a descriptive label, Length of subscription:, rather than by the variable name.)

You can also use the MAXIMUM attribute with character variables. In this case, the "greater than" comparison is based on the character collating sequence for your operating system. In the example application, the only valid values for the character variable NEW are the characters (not the numbers) 0 and 1. The 1 character appears later in the collating sequence than the 0 character, so assign 1 as the maximum value for the NEW field (labeled "Is this a new subscription?"), as shown in Display 8.6.

Display 8.6
Maximum Value
Attributes
(MAXIMUM)

If a value greater than 5 is entered in the YRS field or if a character higher in the collating sequence than 1 is entered in the NEW field, the FSEDIT procedure recognizes that an invalid value has been entered and displays an error message.

Note: By default, users can issue the OVERRIDE command to cancel the error message and move to another observation even if fields contain invalid values. See "Menu Option 5: Assigning General Parameters" later in this chapter for information on how you can block the OVERRIDE command in your application.

Assigning Minimum Values: MINIMUM

The MINIMUM attribute allows you to specify minimum values allowed for the fields. If a user attempts to enter a value less than the minimum for a field, an error message is displayed and the cursor is positioned on the field.

For example, suppose that *The News Monthly* offers no subscriptions for less than one year. Enter a 1 in the YRS field to specify that the minimum value allowed for the YRS variable is one year, as shown in Display 8.7. (Note that in the customized display the field for the YRS variable is identified by a descriptive label, Length of subscription:, rather than by the variable name.)

You can also use the MINIMUM attribute with character variables. In this case, the "less than" comparison is based on the character collating sequence for your operating system. In the example application, the only valid values for the character variable NEW are the characters (not the numbers) 0 and 1. The 0 character appears earlier in the collating sequence than the 1 character, so assign 0 as the maximum value for the NEW field (labeled "Is this a new subscription?"), as shown in Display 8.7.

Display 8.7
Minimum Value
Attributes
(MINIMUM)

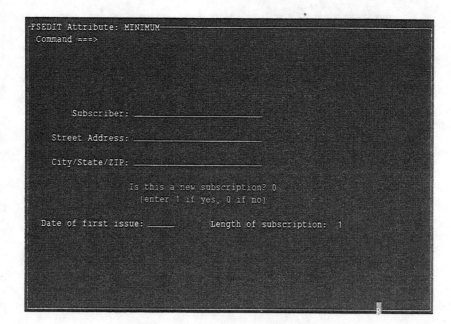

If a value less than 1 is entered in the YRS field or if a character earlier in the collating sequence than 0 is entered in the NEW field, the FSEDIT procedure recognizes that an invalid value has been entered and displays an error message.

Note: By default, users can issue the OVERRIDE command to cancel the error message and move to another observation even if fields contain invalid values. See "Menu Option 5: Assigning General Parameters" later in this chapter for information on how you can block the OVERRIDE command in your application.

Indicating Required Fields: REQUIRED

The REQUIRED attribute allows you to require users to supply values in certain fields when a new observation is added. If a user tries to move to another observation before filling in all required fields, an error message is displayed and the cursor is positioned on the first required field that remains unfilled.

The status of this attribute is determined by the character in the first position of each field in the REQUIRED frame. The letter R indicates that the corresponding variable field is required. Type an R in the first position to mark a field as required. To change a required field to unrequired, type a space over the R.

In the example application, all fields except the one for the NEW variable (labeled "Is this a new subscription?") must be given a value each time an observation is added. Type R in each required field, as shown in Display 8.8.

Display 8.8
Required Field
Attributes
(REQUIRED)

```
┌─FSEDIT Attribute: REQUIRED───────────────────────────────────────────
│ Command ===>
│ NOTE: The letter R indicates which fields are required.



        Subscriber: R_____

   Street Address: R_____

    City/State/ZIP: R_____

                      Is this a new subscription? _
                        (enter 1 if yes, 0 if no)

  Date of first issue: R____        Length of subscription: R_
```

Note: By default, users can issue the OVERRIDE command to cancel the error message and move to another observation even if required fields are left unfilled. See "Menu Option 5: Assigning General Parameters" later in this chapter for information on how you can block the OVERRIDE command in your application.

Indicating Fields to be Capitalized: CAPS

The CAPS attribute allows you to indicate fields that are capitalized automatically when a value is entered. This attribute affects only character fields.

The status of this attribute is determined by the character in the first position of each field in the CAPS frame. The letter C indicates that values entered in the field are converted to all uppercase characters. Type a C in the first position to turn on automatic capitalization for a field. To turn off automatic capitalization, type a space over the C.

Note: Some fields may be assigned this attribute by default. The FSEDIT procedure determines the initial status of this attribute for each field by looking at the values of the corresponding variables in the first observation of the data set. If a variable's value in the first observation contains lowercase characters, then capitalization is turned off for that variable's field; otherwise, capitalization is left on. By default, the CAPS attribute is on for the fields of all numeric variables. However, this attribute has no effect on numeric variables.

Display 8.9 shows the default CAPS field attribute assignments for the example application.

Display 8.9
Capitalized Value
Attributes (CAPS)

```
┌FSEDIT Attribute: CAPS──────────────────────────────────────────────┐
│ Command ===>                                                        │
│ NOTE: The letter C indicates which fields are to be capitalized.    │
│                                                                     │
│                                                                     │
│        Subscriber: _____                         │
│                                                                     │
│     Street Address: _____                        │
│                                                                     │
│      City/State/ZIP: _____                       │
│                                                                     │
│                   Is this a new subscription? C                     │
│                   (enter 1 if yes, 0 if no)                         │
│                                                                     │
│    Date of first issue: C____     Length of subscription: C_        │
│                                                                     │
└─────────────────────────────────────────────────────────────────────┘
```

Because observation 1 of the example data set MASTER.SUBSCRIB has mixed-case values for the FULLNAME, ADDR1, and ADDR2 variables, the CAPS attribute is off for the corresponding fields (labeled Subscriber:, Street Address:, and City/State/ZIP:, respectively). The attribute is on for the NEW field (labeled "Is this a new subscription?") because the value for that variable in observation 1 of the data set is not an alphabetic character. The attribute is also on by default for the two numeric fields, BEGDATE and YRS (labeled Date of first issue: and Length of subscription:, respectively), but the attribute has no effect on numeric fields.

For the example application, no changes to the default settings are required.

Assigning Field Colors: FCOLOR

The FCOLOR (field color) attribute allows you to specify colors for the fields. You can assign different colors to fields to draw the user's attention to particular data values or to visually group values of related variables.

This attribute only controls the colors of the fields in the customized display. The color of descriptive text, including field labels, is defined when you create the customized display. See "Menu Option 2: Creating a Customized Display" earlier in this chapter for details. The colors of window features such as the border, command line, and message line are defined in the FSEDIT Parms window. See "Menu Option 5: Assigning General Parameters" later in this chapter for details.

Note: You can specify colors in the FCOLOR frame even if your device does not support color. The colors are not visible to you, but users of your application who have color devices see the specified colors. If a specified color is not available on the user's device, the FSEDIT procedure substitutes the available color that most nearly matches the specified color. Color attributes are ignored if the user's device does not support color.

The color for each field is indicated by the character in the first position of the corresponding field in the FCOLOR frame. The frame provides a legend showing what character is used for each color. To change the color of a field, type the letter for the new color over the current character. The field then changes to the specified color.

When the frame is displayed, the fields in the FCOLOR frame show the current field colors in the customized display. (Unless you change the field colors when you customize the display, all fields are initially yellow.) For the example application, change the field colors to match the label colors used in the customized display, as shown in Display 8.10.

Display 8.10
Field Color
Attributes
(FCOLOR)

```
┌─FSEDIT Attribute: FCOLOR─────────────────────────────────────────
│  Command ===>
│  B=Blue R=Red P=Pink G=Green C=Cyan Y=Yellow W=White K=Black M=Magenta
│
│
│
│
│         Subscriber: Y_____
│
│     Street Address: Y_____
│
│      City/State/ZIP: Y_____
│
│              Is this a new subscription? C
│              (enter 1 if yes, 0 if no)
│
│   Date of first issue: W____      Length of subscription: W_
│
│
│
│
```

Note: The Unprotected and Protected parameters in the FSEDIT Parms window can override the colors specified in this frame. See "Menu Option 5: Assigning General Parameters" later in this chapter for details.

Assigning Error Field Colors: ECOLOR

The ECOLOR (error color) attribute allows you to specify the colors used to indicate that fields contain erroneous values.

Note: You can specify colors in the ECOLOR frame even if your device does not support color. The colors are not visible to you, but users of your application who have color devices see the specified colors. If a specified color is not available on the user's device, the FSEDIT procedure substitutes the available color that most nearly matches the specified color. Color attributes are ignored if the user's device does not support color. (If most users of your application do not have color monitors, the highlighting attribute discussed later in "Highlighting Error Fields: EATTR" may be more useful.)

The error color for each field is indicated by the character in the first position of the corresponding field in the ECOLOR frame. The frame provides a legend showing what character is used for each color. The default error color for all fields is red (indicated by R in the ECOLOR frame). To change the color of a field, type the letter for the new color over the current character.

In the example application, date values are most likely to be entered in error. Change the error color for these fields to yellow. Type a Y over the R in the BEGDATE (Date of first issue:) and YRS (Length of subscription:) fields, as shown in Display 8.11.

Display 8.11
Field Error Color
Attributes
(ECOLOR)

```
┌─FSEDIT Attribute: ECOLOR──────────────────────────────────────────────
  Command ===>
  B=Blue R=Red P=Pink G=Green C=Cyan Y=Yellow W=White K=Black M=Magenta



          Subscriber: R_____

      Street Address: R_____

      City/State/ZIP: R_____

                      Is this a new subscription? R_
                      (enter 1 if yes, 0 if no)

  Date of first issue: Y_____      Length of subscription: Y_
```

YRS values that are outside the range of valid values (as determined by the MIN and MAX attributes) and BEGDATE values that are incorrectly entered are displayed in yellow.

Indicating Special Emphasis: FATTR

The FATTR (field attribute) attribute allows you to define highlighting characteristics for the fields. This attribute is useful for emphasizing important fields. The available highlighting characteristics are high intensity, underlined, reverse video, and blinking. If a user's device does not support the specified type of highlighting, the attribute is ignored.

The highlighting characteristic for each field is indicated by the character in the first position of the corresponding field in the FATTR frame. The frame provides a legend showing what character is used for each type of highlighting. To change the highlighting for a field, type the letter for the new highlighting over the current character. The field then changes to the new highlighting.

When the frame is displayed, the fields in the FATTR frame show the current field highlighting from the customized display. (Unless you change the field highlighting when you customize the display, all fields initially have no highlighting.) For the example application, change the highlighting attribute of the NEW field (labeled "Is this a new subscription?") to reverse video, as shown in Display 8.12.

Display 8.12
Field Highlighting
Attributes
(FATTR)

```
┌─FSEDIT Attribute: FATTR──────────────────────────────────────┐
│  Command ===>                                                 │
│  NOTE: H=Highlight   U=Underline   R=Reverse video   B=Blink  │
│                                                               │
│                                                               │
│                                                               │
│           Subscriber: _____                │
│                                                               │
│        Street Address: _____               │
│                                                               │
│         City/State/ZIP: _____              │
│                                                               │
│                    Is this a new subscription? H              │
│                      (enter 1 if yes, 0 if no)                │
│                                                               │
│     Date of first issue: _____    Length of subscription: __ │
│                                                               │
│                                                               │
│                                                               │
│                                                               │
│                                                               │
└───────────────────────────────────────────────────────────────┘
```

Highlighting Error Fields: EATTR

The EATTR (error attribute) attribute allows you to define highlighting characteristics for fields containing erroneous values. The available highlighting characteristics are high intensity, underlined, reverse video, and blinking. If a user's device does not support the specified type of highlighting, the attribute is ignored.

The error highlighting characteristic for each field is indicated by the character in the first position of the corresponding field in the EATTR frame. The frame provides a legend showing what character is used for each type of highlighting. The default error attribute for all fields is high intensity. To change the highlighting for a field, type the letter for the new highlighting over the current character.

In the example application, date values are most likely to be entered in error. To draw the user's attention to errors in these fields, change the highlighting for these fields to reverse video. Type an R over the H in the BEGDATE (Date of first issue:) and YRS (Length of subscription:) fields, as shown in Display 8.13.

Display 8.13
Field Error
Highlighting
Attributes
(EATTR)

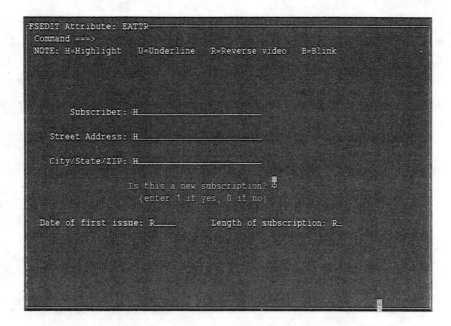

YRS values that are outside the range of valid values (as determined by the MIN and MAX attributes) and BEGDATE values that are incorrectly formatted are displayed in reverse video.

Indicating the Pad Character for Fields: PAD

The PAD attribute allows you to specify the character used to fill fields in which no value has been entered. The default pad character for all fields is the underscore. You can specify a different pad character to draw users' attention to fields that have not yet been given a value.

The pad character for each field is determined by the character in the first position of corresponding fields in the the PAD frame. To change the current pad character, type the new character in the first position of the desired field and press ENTER. The field is filled with the new pad character.

For the example application, change the pad character for the YRS variable (labeled Length of subscription:) to a question mark. Type a question mark in the first position of the YRS field; then press ENTER. The field is filled with question marks, as shown in Display 8.14.

Display 8.14
Pad Character
Attributes (PAD)

```
┌FSEDIT Attribute: PAD─────────────────────────────────────────────
│ Command ===>
│ NOTE: The first character of each field is the Pad character.
│
│
│
│
│
│        Subscriber: _____
│
│    Street Address: _____
│
│     City/State/ZIP: _____
│
│                Is this a new subscription? ▮
│                 (enter 1 if yes, 0 if no)
│
│    Date of first issue: _____      Length of subscription: ??
│
│
│
│
│
│                                                              ▮
```

Note: You can use a blank as the pad character, but then it is difficult to know where the values for the variable should be entered unless you frame the field with brackets or other characters or assign the reverse video attribute in the FATTR frame.

Indicating Protected Fields: PROTECT

The PROTECT field attribute allows you to protect fields from being edited. Values for fields marked as protected are displayed but cannot be edited. When a new observation is created, values cannot be entered in protected fields. This attribute is useful when you want to display values for the users' information only.

The status of this attribute for each field is determined by the character in the first position of the corresponding field in the PROTECT frame. Type a P in the first position to mark a field as protected. Type a space over the P to change a protected field to unprotected.

As shown in Display 8.15, no fields are protected by default. In the example application users need to be able to enter values in all fields, so you do not want to protect any fields.

Display 8.15
Protection
Attributes
(PROTECT)

```
┌─FSEDIT Attribute: PROTECT──────────────────────────────────────────
│ Command ===>
│ NOTE: The letter P indicates which fields are protected.
│
│
│
│
│       Subscriber: _____
│
│   Street Address: _____
│
│    City/State/ZIP: _____
│
│               Is this a new subscription? █
│              (enter 1 if yes, 0 if no)
│
│  Date of first issue: _____      Length of subscription: ??
│
│
│
│
│                                                              █
└────────────────────────────────────────────────────────────────────
```

Note: Be sure that you do not assign both the PROTECT and REQUIRED attributes to the same field.

Indicating the Alignment of Values in Fields: JUSTIFY

The JUSTIFY attribute allows you to specify how values are aligned in the fields. By default, numeric values align on the right side of the field, and character values align on the left. You can use the JUSTIFY attribute to change this default alignment.

The justification for each field is determined by the character in the first position of the corresponding field in the JUSTIFY frame. If the first position is blank (that is, if it contains the field pad character), the default field alignment is used. Type an L to left-align field values, a C to center values, or an R to right-align values.

In the example application, realign the display of the YRS value (labeled Length of subscription:). The value is never larger than one digit, so align the numeric value on the left of the field to simplify editing. Enter L in the YRS field, as shown in Display 8.16.

Display 8.16
Value Alignment
Attributes
(JUSTIFY)

```
┌─FSEDIT Attribute: JUSTIFY──────────────────────────────────────────┐
│  Command ===>                                                        │
│  NOTE: L=left justify   C=center   R=right justify   blank=default   │
│                                                                      │
│                                                                      │
│                                                                      │
│                                                                      │
│        Subscriber: _____                           │
│                                                                      │
│    Street Address: _____                           │
│                                                                      │
│     City/State/ZIP: _____                          │
│                                                                      │
│              Is this a new subscription? ▌                           │
│                   (enter 1 if yes, 0 if no)                          │
│                                                                      │
│   Date of first issue: _____      Length of subscription: L?        │
│                                                                      │
└──────────────────────────────────────────────────────────────────┘
```

Preventing the Display of Data: NONDISPLAY

The NONDISPLAY attribute allows you to prevent fields from being displayed to users. This attribute does not protect the field from editing. Users can still move the cursor to nondisplay fields and enter values, even though the values they enter are invisible.

The status of this attribute for each field is determined by the character in the first position of the corresponding field in the NONDISPLAY frame. Type an N in the first position of each field you do not want displayed. Type a space over the N to change a nondisplay field to a displayed field.

No fields are assigned this attribute by default, as shown in Display 8.17. In the example application, users need to see all the variable values, so do not assign this attribute to any fields.

You can use this attribute to hide sensitive values. For example, if your application requires users to enter a password to perform certain actions, you can assign this attribute to the password field so that the password a user enters is not displayed for others to see.

Display 8.17
Nondisplay
Attributes
(NONDISPLAY)

```
┌─FSEDIT Attribute: NONDISPLAY─────────────────────────────────────────
  Command ===>
  NOTE: The letter N indicates which fields are non-display fields.



        Subscriber: _____

    Street Address: _____

    City/State/ZIP: _____

                    Is this a new subscription? █
                    (enter 1 if yes, 0 if no)

  Date of first issue: _____      Length of subscription: ??
```

Screen Control Language programs (described in Chapter 10) can only use data set variables identified as wanted in the customized display. All wanted variables must have a field in the display, so if you want variables to be available to an SCL program but not to users, assign both the NONDISPLAY and PROTECT attributes to the fields for the variables (and don't give the variables labels). In that case, users have no clue that the variables are present, since the fields do not appear in the display and the cursor does not move to the fields.

Holding the Cursor: NOAUTOSKIP

The NOAUTOSKIP attribute allows you to hold the cursor on fields until it is explicitly moved with cursor keys or commands. By default, the cursor automatically skips ahead to the first position of the next field when you type a character in the last position of a field. When you use the NOAUTOSKIP attribute, the cursor is held just beyond the end of the field after the last position is filled.

The status of this attribute for each field is determined by the character in the first position of the corresponding field in the NOAUTOSKIP frame. Type an N in the first position to mark fields on which you want the cursor held. Type a space over the N to allow the cursor to automatically skip to the next field.

No fields are assigned this attribute by default. For the example application, the NEW field (labeled "Is this a new subscription?") is only one character wide, so the cursor automatically jumps to the next field whenever you enter a value. To hold the cursor on this field so that you can verify your entry before moving to the next field, assign this field the NOAUTOSKIP attribute. Type an N in the field, as shown in Display 8.18.

Display 8.18
Noautoskip
Attributes
(NOAUTOSKIP)

```
┌─FSEDIT Attribute: NOAUTOSKIP──────────────────────────────────────────┐
│ Command ===>                                                          │
│ NOTE: The letter N indicates which fields are noautoskip fields.      │
│                                                                       │
│                                                                       │
│                                                                       │
│          Subscriber: _____                │
│                                                                       │
│      Street Address: _____                │
│                                                                       │
│      City/State/ZIP: _____                │
│                                                                       │
│                    Is this a new subscription? N                     │
│                      (enter 1 if yes, 0 if no)                       │
│                                                                       │
│    Date of first issue: _____       Length of subscription: ??       │
│                                                                       │
│                                                                       │
│                                                                      N │
└───────────────────────────────────────────────────────────────────────┘
```

Closing the FSEDIT Attribute Window

When you have finished assigning field attributes, issue the END command to
close the FSEDIT Attribute window and return to the FSEDIT Menu window. The
field attributes you have defined are stored in the screen entry for your
application.

Menu Option 5: Assigning General Parameters

The FSEDIT procedure automatically assigns values to parameters that control the
appearance and behavior of the FSEDIT window, including

□ the colors of window features such as the background, border, banner,
  command line, and message line

□ the size and position of the window within the display

□ the KEYS entry containing function key definitions for the application

□ the number of changes for the AUTOSAVE parameter

□ the status of the OVERRIDE command.

You can take greater control over the use of your FSEDIT application by altering
the default settings for these parameters. You can also make searches more
convenient for users by assigning default values for some frequently used
searching commands. And you can assign a password to protect your application
from unauthorized modification. All this information is recorded in the screen
entry and becomes part of your application.

How to Start

Select option 5, "Modification of General Parameters," from the FSEDIT Menu window to review and edit general parameters for the FSEDIT application. This option opens the FSEDIT Parms window.

Display 8.19 shows the initial FSEDIT Parms window for the example application.

Display 8.19
The FSEDIT
Parms Window

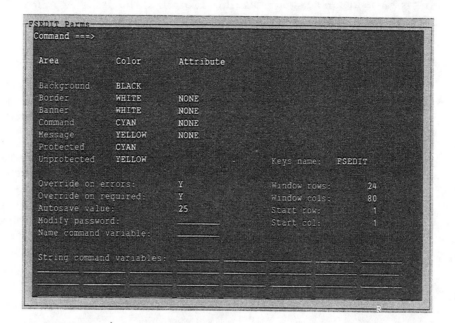

Using the FSEDIT Parms Window

To change parameter settings, simply move the cursor to the desired field in the FSEDIT Parms window and type new values over the current contents of the field. For example, customize the example application as follows:

□ Block the use of the OVERRIDE command for invalid value errors. Type an N over the Y in the Override on errors: field. Leave the Y in the Override on required: field.

These parameters control whether users can issue the OVERRIDE command to store observations even if they contain invalid values or do not have all required fields filled. You can prevent the use of OVERRIDE in either or both cases.

□ Add a password for application modification. Type RACHEL in the Modify password: field.

This parameter allows you to assign a password to protect the customized features of your application from alteration by users. Once this password is in effect, the following command must be used to open the FSEDIT Menu window for the application:

```
modify rachel
```

The password has no effect on the users' ability to use the application, but only those users who know the password can change the application. A password-protected application is secure as long as you keep the password secret.

□ Add a default variable for LOCATE and LOCATE: searches. Type FULLNAME in the Name command variable: field.

This parameter provides a default value for the NAME command. In the sample application, observations are located most often by the subscriber's name. When you assign FULLNAME as the default search variable, a user can issue a LOCATE or LOCATE: command, such as

```
locate: Dilley
```

without having to issue a NAME command beforehand. This is particularly useful in applications with customized displays, where the actual variable names are not shown. (The user must know the variable name to issue a NAME command.)

□ Add a list of default variables for SEARCH and SEARCH@ searches. Type FULLNAME, ADDR1, and ADDR2 in the first three String command variables: fields.

This parameter provides default values for the STRING command. In the sample application, observations are located most often by the subscriber's name and address. When you assign FULLNAME, ADDR1, and ADDR2 as the default search variables, a user can issue a SEARCH or SEARCH@ command, such as

```
search@ Dilley 'Polk St.' NY
```

without having to issue a STRING command beforehand.

Display 8.20 shows the modified FSEDIT Parms window.

Display 8.20
Customized Parameters Settings

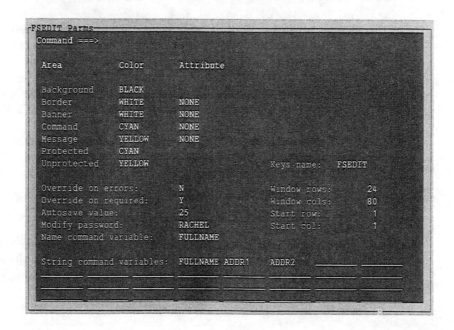

Other FSEDIT Parameters

Other parameters in the FSEDIT Parms window allow you to control the following FSEDIT window features:

□ the colors of the window background, border, banner, command line, and message line. (Note that some devices do not allow you to change the background color.)

□ the highlighting characteristics of the window border, banner, command line, and message line.

□ the colors for protected and unprotected areas of the window. However, you should use these fields only if you have not otherwise defined colors for your application. If you change the color in the Protected field, you override the current colors of all descriptive text in the customized display. If you change the value in the Unprotected field in this window, you override the current colors of all fields in the customized display, regardless of where the fields have been assigned the PROTECT attribute in the FSEDIT Attributes window.

□ the KEYS entry that contains function key assignments for the application. If you change the entry name in this parameter, the system looks for the new keys entry first in the catalog containing the screen entry for the application, then in the user's PROFILE catalog, then in the SASHELP.FSP catalog.

□ the size of the FSEDIT window and the position of the window on the user's monitor. By default, the FSEDIT window occupies the full width and height of the display. You can indicate the number of rows and columns and the row and column in which the window should begin.

Closing the FSEDIT Parms Window

Issue the END command to close the FSEDIT Parms window and return to the FSEDIT Menu window. The parameter settings you have defined are stored in the screen entry for your application.

This completes the development of the sample application. Issue the END command in the FSEDIT Menu window to return to the FSEDIT window with all the newly defined features in force. At this point, if you want to begin using the sample application immediately you can skip ahead to "Adding Observations" later in this chapter. Otherwise, issue an END command in the FSEDIT window to end the FSEDIT application.

Using a Custom Application: A Sample Session

If you followed the steps outlined in the previous sections, you created a screen entry that defines a customized FSEDIT application. The following section shows how using this customized application simplifies the data entry process. The previous sections of this chapter look at the application from the developer's perspective. This section approaches the application from the user's perspective.

Starting the Application

To begin using the FSEDIT application you created, submit the following
statements:

```
proc fsedit data=master.subscrib
     screen=master.display.scrsub.screen;
run;
```

This assumes that the libref MASTER was previously assigned to the permanent
SAS data library that contains the data set SUBSCRIB and the catalog DISPLAY
in which the screen entry for the application is stored. It also assumes that you
used the name SCRSUB.SCREEN for your screen entry. If you used any other
name for the screen entry, be sure to add the correct entry name following the
catalog name in the SCREEN= option.

When the FSEDIT window is opened, the first observation in the data set is
displayed, as shown in Display 8.21

Display 8.21
Customized
Display with Field
Attributes

```
┌─FSEDIT MASTER.SUBSCRIB──────────────────────────────────────Obs 1─┐
│ Command ===>                                                       │
│                                                                    │
│                                                                    │
│          Subscriber: Adams, Ms. Debra                              │
│                                                                    │
│       Street Address: 1414 S. 20th St.                             │
│                                                                    │
│       City/State/ZIP: Arlington, VA 22202                          │
│                                                                    │
│                      Is this a new subscription? 0                 │
│                        (enter 1 if yes, 0 if no)                   │
│                                                                    │
│   Date of first issue: APR89        Length of subscription: 2      │
│                                                                    │
└────────────────────────────────────────────────────────────────────┘
```

Adding Observations

Suppose you want to add a new subscriber, Nathan Thomas, to the data set.
Issue the ADD command to create a new observation. Display 8.22 shows the
new blank observation. Note that the field "Is this a new subscription?" already
contains a 1 because the initial value attribute automatically assigns that value to
the variable NEW in new observations. Also, the YRS field (Length of
subscription:) is filled with question marks, the pad character assigned to that
field.

Display 8.22
*Customized
Display for a New
Observation*

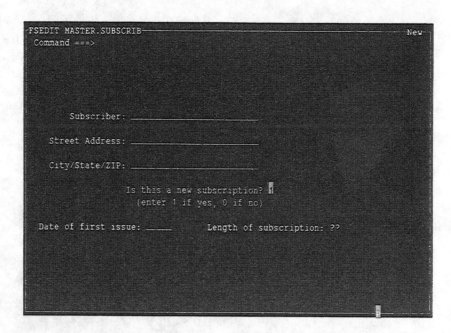

```
┌─FSEDIT MASTER.SUBSCRIB─────────────────────────────────────────New─┐
│ Command ===>                                                       │
│                                                                    │
│                                                                    │
│                                                                    │
│                                                                    │
│          Subscriber: _____                     │
│                                                                    │
│      Street Address: _____                     │
│                                                                    │
│      City/State/ZIP: _____                     │
│                                                                    │
│                    Is this a new subscription? █                  │
│                    (enter 1 if yes, 0 if no)                       │
│                                                                    │
│   Date of first issue: _____      Length of subscription: ??       │
│                                                                    │
│                                                                    │
│                                                                    │
└────────────────────────────────────────────────────────────────█──┘
```

Entering Values

Enter the name and address information shown in Display 8.23 in the fields of
the new observation; then try to enter the value 7 for the YRS variable (Length
of subscription:). This is an invalid value for this field because the maximum
value for YRS, specified in the MAXIMUM attribute, is 5. You receive the error
message shown in Display 8.23 when you press ENTER or issue another
command.

Display 8.23
*Entering a Value
Out of Range*

```
┌─FSEDIT MASTER.SUBSCRIB─────────────────────────────────────────New─┐
│ Command ===>                                                       │
│ ERROR: Data value is greater than maximum.  Please reenter.        │
│                                                                    │
│                                                                    │
│                                                                    │
│          Subscriber: Thomas, Mr. Nathan                           │
│                                                                    │
│      Street Address: 2704 Powers St.                              │
│                                                                    │
│      City/State/ZIP: Birmingham, AL 35206                         │
│                                                                    │
│                    Is this a new subscription? █                  │
│                    (enter 1 if yes, 0 if no)                       │
│                                                                    │
│   Date of first issue: _____      Length of subscription: █        │
│                                                                    │
│                                                                    │
│                                                                    │
└────────────────────────────────────────────────────────────────█──┘
```

The field with the incorrect value is displayed using the color and highlighting attribute specified by the ECOLOR and EATTR field attributes. The error message displayed just below the command line helps you identify the problem.

Correct the error in the Length of subscription: field by changing the field value from 7 to 5. Then try to use any of the commands that scroll to another observation: BACKWARD, for example. When you do, an additional error is indicated. Display 8.24 shows the error message.

Display 8.24
*Leaving a
Required Field
Blank*

```
┌FSEDIT MASTER.SUBSCRIB──────────────────────────────────────New─┐
│ Command ===>                                                    │
│ NOTE: A value is required at the cursor location.               │
│                                                                 │
│                                                                 │
│                                                                 │
│        Subscriber: Thomas, Mr. Nathan                           │
│                                                                 │
│    Street Address: 2704 Powers St.                              │
│                                                                 │
│    City/State/ZIP: Birmingham, AL 35206                         │
│                                                                 │
│              Is this a new subscription? █                      │
│                (enter 1 if yes, 0 if no)                        │
│                                                                 │
│  Date of first issue: _____     Length of subscription: 5       │
│                                                                 │
└─────────────────────────────────────────────────────────────────┘
```

The BEGDATE field (Date of first issue:) is a required field because you have assigned it the REQUIRED field attribute. You must provide a value before you leave the observation. If you are unsure of the format required for the field value, type HELP on the command line, position the cursor on the field, and press ENTER. (Or position the cursor on the field and press the function key to which the HELP command has been assigned.)

You can bypass the error condition by issuing the OVERRIDE command. The Override on required parameter for the application is set to allow overriding of errors caused by missing required values, even though invalid value errors cannot be canceled. Thus, you can use the OVERRIDE command to force the application to accept the observation without a value entered.

After you issue the OVERRIDE command, the application accepts commands that allow you to leave the observation. You can leave this observation for now and return later when you have the necessary information.

Locating Observations

To update subscription information for a subscriber named Stiller, you must first display that observation. You can use the LOCATE: command to search the subscriber names in the data set for the one that begins with Stiller. Because the variable FULLNAME is defined as the default NAME command variable in the general parameters of the application, any LOCATE: command you issue searches the FULLNAME variable. Use the following command:

```
locate: Stiller
```

If the command reaches the end of the data set without locating a match, issue the following command to resume the search from the beginning:

```
rfind
```

Display 8.25 shows the observation located by this command.

Display 8.25
Observation Found
by the LOCATE:
Command

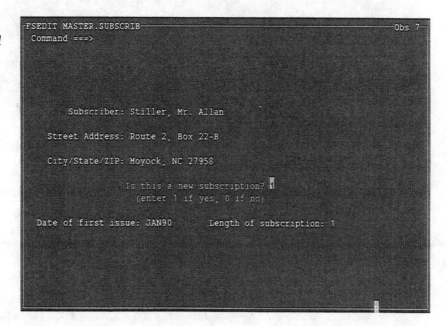

```
┌─FSEDIT MASTER.SUBSCRIB─────────────────────────────────────Obs 7─┐
│ Command ===>                                                      │
│                                                                   │
│                                                                   │
│                                                                   │
│            Subscriber: Stiller, Mr. Allan                         │
│                                                                   │
│         Street Address: Route 2, Box 22-B                         │
│                                                                   │
│         City/State/ZIP: Moyock, NC 27958                          │
│                                                                   │
│                     Is this a new subscription? ▪                 │
│                      (enter 1 if yes, 0 if no)                    │
│                                                                   │
│     Date of first issue: JAN90      Length of subscription: 1     │
│                                                                   │
└───────────────────────────────────────────────────────────────────┘
```

You can also use the SEARCH and SEARCH@ commands without having to specify what fields you want to search. Because ADDR1 and ADDR2 were specified as the default STRING command variables in the general parameters for the application, any SEARCH@ command you issue looks for the specified strings in the FULLNAME, ADDR1, and ADDR2 fields.

For example, to locate the observation of a subscriber whose address is Box 94, Burlington, issue the following command:

```
search@ 'Box 94' Burlington
```

Display 8.26 shows the observation located by this command.

Display 8.26
Observation Found
by the SEARCH@
Command

```
┌─FSEDIT MASTER.SUBSCRIB────────────────────────────────────Obs 10─┐
│ Command ===>                                                      │
│                                                                   │
│                                                                   │
│                                                                   │
│          Subscriber: Ziller, Mr. Paul                             │
│                                                                   │
│      Street Address: P.O. Box 94                                  │
│                                                                   │
│    City/State/ZIP: Burlington, CA 90406                           │
│                                                                   │
│                     Is this a new subscription? 0                 │
│                        (enter 1 if yes, 0 if no)                  │
│                                                                   │
│  Date of first issue: MAY90       Length of subscription: 3       │
│                                                                   │
│                                                                   │
│                                                                   │
└───────────────────────────────────────────────────────────────────┘
```

Ending the Application

When you have finished editing the data set, use the END command to end the
FSEDIT application.

Adding Variables to the Application

You may discover once your application is in use that you need to include
additional variables. The variables must be added to both the data set and the
customized display. This section shows how to accomplish this task.

Suppose that *The News Monthly* decides to make its subscriber mailing list
available to advertisers. However, to avoid annoying those readers who object to
receiving unsolicited advertisements, the management gives each subscriber the
right to withhold his or her address from the distributed mailing list. To
implement this, you need to add a variable for each observation in the
subscriber data set to indicate whether the subscriber's address can be
distributed. You also need to add this variable to the customized display for your
application.

Adding the Variable to the Data Set

Use a DATA step to add the new variable to the data set. Submit the following
statements:

```
data master.subscr2;
   length share $ 1;
   set master.subscrib;
run;
```

These statements add a new variable, SHARE, to the data set. (To preserve the original example data set, these statements create a new data set named MASTER.SUBSCR2.) The new variable initially contains a missing value in all observations, and you receive a note in the SAS log informing you that the variable is uninitialized.

SHARE is a character variable of length 1 like the existing NEW variable. It is used like NEW, to hold a one-character value representing either yes or no.

Adding the Variable to the Display

Submit the following statements to start the existing subscriber application with the new data set:

```
proc fsedit data=master.subscr2
    screen=master.display.scrsub.screen;
run;
```

When the FSEDIT window is opened, notice that the new SHARE variable does not appear in the display. Because it does not have a field in the customized display, the application treats it as an unwanted variable.

Creating the Field

To create a field for the new variable, enter the FSEDIT Modify window by issuing the following command:

```
modify rachel;2
```

(By combining commands with the semicolon, you skip having to view the FSEDIT Menu window.)

Now type the text for the new field label and the underscore for the single-character field, as shown in Display 8.27. Also add the text explaining what values are valid. If your device supports color, enter the text in cyan.

Display 8.27
Creating an
Additional Field

```
┌─FSEDIT Modify────────────────────────────────────────────┐
│ Command ===>                                              │
│                                                           │
│                                                           │
│                                                           │
│                                                           │
│          Subscriber: _____         │
│                                                           │
│      Street Address: _____         │
│                                                           │
│      City/State/ZIP: _____         │
│                                                           │
│               Is this a new subscription? █               │
│                  (enter 1 if yes, 0 if no)                │
│                                                           │
│  Date of first issue: _____     Length of subscription: __│
│                                                           │
│                Share mailing list info? _                 │
│                  (enter 1 if yes, 0 if no)                │
│                                                           │
└───────────────────────────────────────────────────────────┘
```

When you are satisfied with the display, issue the END command. Answer N to the "Did you create any computed or repeated fields?" question. The new field you created is for a data set variable, not a special variable. The FSEDIT Identify window is then opened.

Identifying the New Field

In the FSEDIT Identify window, issue the following command to indicate that SHARE is now a wanted variable:

```
wanted share
```

You receive a prompt to position the cursor on the field for the SHARE variable, as shown in Display 8.28.

Display 8.28
Identifying the
SHARE Field

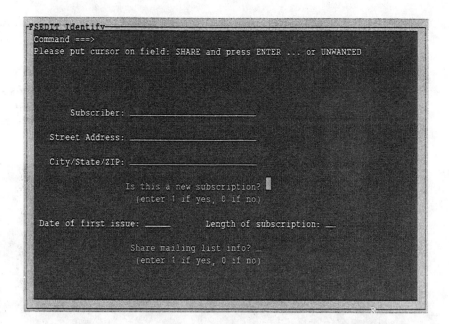

Note: If you add more than one variable, you can use the WANTED command without any following variable names to have the FSEDIT procedure prompt you for the positions of all unidentified variables.

Move the cursor to the underscore for the new field you created; then press ENTER. The field is identified, and you receive the following message:

```
NOTE: All fields are identified.
```

The SHARE variable is now included in both the data set and the application display. Issue the END command to close the FSEDIT Identify window and return to the FSEDIT Menu window.

Assigning Attributes to the New Field

To define the attributes of the new field, select option 4 from the FSEDIT Menu window. The SHARE variable field is identified in the FSEDIT Attribute window frames with the label "Share mailing list info?". Assign the following attributes for the field:

INITIAL	1
MAXIMUM	1
MINIMUM	0
FCOLOR	C
FATTR	R
NOAUTOSKIP	N

Issue the END command to close the FSEDIT Attribute window and return to the FSEDIT Menu window; then issue the END command again to close the FSEDIT Menu window and open the FSEDIT window for your application.

Using the Modified Application

When you return to the FSEDIT window, the field for the new variable has no value. (Remember that the INITIAL attribute affects only newly added observations.) You must manually enter values for the variable in all existing observations. Display 8.29 shows the first observation with the SHARE field filled:

Display 8.29
Application with
Added Field

```
┌FSEDIT MASTER.SUBSCR2─────────────────────────────────────────────Obs 1─┐
│ Command ===>                                                           │
│                                                                        │
│                                                                        │
│                                                                        │
│          Subscriber: Adams, Ms. Debra                                  │
│                                                                        │
│      Street Address: 1414 S. 20th St.                                  │
│                                                                        │
│      City/State/ZIP: Arlington, VA 22202                               │
│                                                                        │
│                      Is this a new subscription? 0                     │
│                         (enter 1 if yes, 0 if no)                      │
│                                                                        │
│ Date of first issue: APR89       Length of subscription: 2             │
│                                                                        │
│                      Share mailing list info? 1                        │
│                         (enter 1 if yes, 0 if no)                      │
│                                                                        │
└────────────────────────────────────────────────────────────────────────┘
```

Use the END command to end the FSEDIT session for the modified example application.

Chapter **9** Creating Data Entry Applications Using the FSVIEW Procedure

Introduction

If you design data entry or data browsing applications, whether for yourself or for other users, you can use the FSVIEW procedure as the basis for your applications. To customize an FSVIEW session for use as a data entry application, you can

□ modify the order and appearance of variable columns to suit the needs of your application

□ create computed variables calculated from the values of other variables in the display

□ define general parameters for the FSVIEW session.

This chapter explains the process of creating applications using the FSVIEW procedure.

Note: All of the features described in this chapter for creating data entry and editing applications are also available for creating data browsing applications. The FSVIEW procedure can be used as a browse-only tool as well as an entry and editing tool.

Creating a Data Entry Application

Chapter 4, "Browsing and Editing SAS Data Sets Using the FSVIEW Procedure," shows how to customize the FSVIEW window by adding, dropping, and moving variables. However, Chapter 4 does not show how to save the custom features beyond the current FSVIEW session. To create applications with the FSVIEW procedure, you must be able to save the custom features you design. The facility provided in the FSVIEW procedure for storing information about the FSVIEW environment is the *formula entry*. A formula entry is a SAS catalog entry of type FORMULA. Formula entries store the following information for FSVIEW applications:

□   the current size, position, and colors of the FSVIEW window

□   the order in which variables are displayed

□   general parameters of the FSVIEW window, such as the current HSCROLL and VSCROLL settings

□   the formulas for any computed variables defined for the application.

Creating a custom application involves the following steps:

1. Invoke the FSVIEW procedure, specifying the FORMULA= option in the PROC FSVIEW statement or the *formula-name* argument in the FSVIEW command to identify the formula entry in which custom features are saved.

2. Create computed variables to perform calculations based on other variable values.

3. Drop, add, and move variables to customize the display to suit your needs.

4. Change the formats and informats for variables.

5. Assign attributes to variables.

6. Modify colors and general parameters to enhance your session.

Getting Started

To begin creating the example application, initiate the FSVIEW procedure using the FORMULA= option in the PROC FSVIEW statement to specify where the information about your custom FSVIEW session will be stored. Submit the following statements:

```
proc fsview data=master.subscrib
     formula=master.display.subdate.formula;
run;
```

You should have previously assigned the libref MASTER to a permanent SAS data library. The example data set, MASTER.SUBSCRIB, is described in Chapter 1, "Introduction to SAS/FSP Software."

Notice that a FORMULA= option appears here in addition to the DATA= option specifying the data set. The specified catalog, MASTER.DISPLAY, is created if it does not already exist. The specified catalog entry, SUBDATE.FORMULA, is used to hold the custom features of your application.

Alternatively, you can issue the following command in any SAS System window to achieve the same results:

```
fsview master.subscrib master.display.subdate.formula
```

Display 9.1 shows the window opened when the preceding statements or command are executed. The warning message in the display simply means that the formula entry did not previously exist. It is created when you define custom features for your application.

Display 9.1
Initial Display for
the FSVIEW
Session

```
┌─FSVIEW:  MASTER.SUBSCRIB (B)──────────────────────────────────────┐
│Command ===>                                                       │
│NOTE: Unable to find MASTER.DISPLAY.SUBDATE.FORMULA.               │
│ OBS      FULLNAME                    ADDR1                         │
│                                                                   │
│   1      Adams, Ms. Debra            1414 S. 20th St.             │
│   2      Bailey, Mr. Mark            2721 1/2 Van Dyke            │
│   3      Bertram, Ms. Mary           701 Catawba                  │
│   4      Carroll, Mr. Herman         6122-A Smithdale Dr.         │
│   5      Dilley, Mr. Matthew         420 Polk St.                 │
│   6      Marvin, Ms. June            Route 7, Box 482             │
│   7      Stiller, Mr. Allan          Route 2, Box 22-B            │
│   8      Vance, Ms. Martha           424-204 Navaho Dr.           │
│   9      Womble, Mr. Kenneth         702-F Walden Dr.             │
│  10      Ziller, Mr. Paul            P.O. Box 94                  │
│                                                                   │
└───────────────────────────────────────────────────────────────────┘
```

Note: The FORMULA= option in the preceding PROC FSVIEW statement and the *formula-name* argument in the preceding FSVIEW command include an explicit formula entry name. Customization information for this application is stored in the specified entry, SUBDATE.FORMULA. If you omit the entry name and specify only the catalog name, the FSVIEW procedure by default uses the data set name for the formula entry name. For the preceding examples, the default formula entry name is SUBSCRIB.FORMULA.

Adding Computed Variables

In addition to the data set variables, you can define *computed variables* in the FSVIEW window. These computed variables are not added to the displayed data set; they exist only in the FSVIEW window. However, within an FSVIEW application computed variables can be manipulated just like data set variables, with one exception: you cannot use computed variables with the SORT command. (That is, you cannot sort the data set according to the values of a computed variable.)

Note: If you want to change computed variables to data set variables, use the CREATE command to create a new data set containing all the variables and variable values in the displayed data set. Data set variables are created in the new data set for the computed variables in the displayed data set.

Use the DEFINE command to create computed variables. The command can include the complete definition for the variable, or it can open an interactive window for defining the variable. The following sections explain both methods.

You can also use the DEFINE command to assign formulas to data set variables. When a data set variable is assigned a formula, the specified calculations are performed on the current variable values and the results are displayed in the variable column. If the data set is opened for browsing, the stored values in the data set are not changed. If the data set is opened for editing, the computed values replace the stored values.

Using the FSVIEW Define Window

The subscriber information application currently has variables that give the starting date of the subscription and the length of the subscription. Suppose you want to add a new computed variable, ENDDATE, that gives the ending date of the subscription. Issue the following command in the FSVIEW window:

```
define enddate
```

The FSVIEW Define window is opened, as shown in Display 9.2.

Display 9.2
FSVIEW Define
Window for the
ENDDATE
Variable

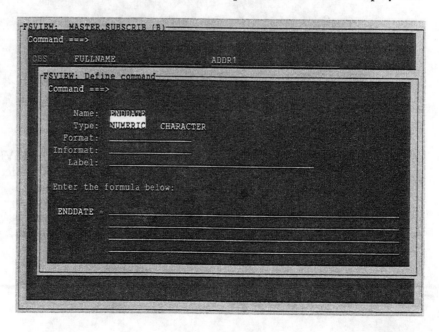

The FSVIEW Define window shows the variable name ENDDATE and the default type NUMERIC, which is correct for this variable. Since this variable will hold date values, assign it the format MONYY5. in the Format field. Add the descriptive label "Month of last issue" in the Label field to help you remember the purpose of the variable. (The FSVIEW procedure does not display variable labels.) Then enter the formula to calculate the month of the last issue, as shown in Display 9.3.

Display 9.3
Defining the
Formula for the
ENDDATE
Variable

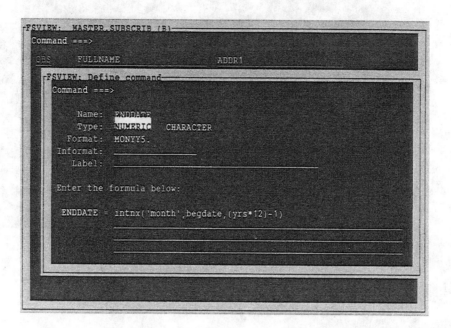

INTNX is a SAS function that advances a SAS date value by a specified interval—in this case, the number of months (YRS*12) since the subscription began. (Refer to Chapter 11, "SAS Functions," in *SAS Language: Reference, Version 6, First Edition* for more information on the INTNX function.) The ending month should be one month earlier than the beginning month, hence the −1 in the formula.

After you enter the formula, issue an END command in the FSVIEW Define window. If the formula contains errors, an error message is printed in the FSVIEW Define window's message line and the window remains open. If the formula is a valid SAS expression, it is added to the formula entry for the application; then the FSVIEW Define window is closed and you return to the FSVIEW window.

When you return to the FSVIEW window, the new variable is displayed to the right of the existing variables, as shown in Display 9.4.

Display 9.4
FSVIEW Window
with a Computed
Variable Added

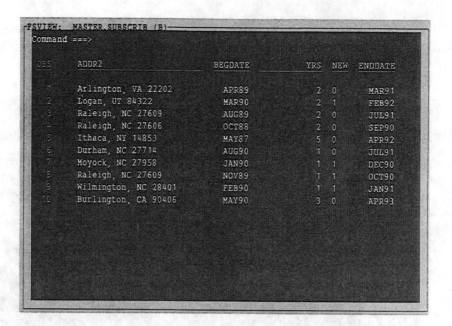

Using the DEFINE Command Noninteractively

You can also use the DEFINE command without opening the FSVIEW Define window. Simply follow the variable name in the command argument with an equal sign (=) and the formula for the variable. For example, suppose you want to add the computed variable REMAIN that gives the number of issues remaining for a subscription. Issue the following command from the FSVIEW window:

```
define remain=int((enddate-date())/30)
```

DATE() is a SAS function that returns the current date, so this formula calculates the number of months from the current date to the ending date of the subscription. Notice that the formula for the REMAIN variable involves another computed variable, ENDDATE.

When the command is executed, the new variable is added to the right of the existing variables, as shown in Display 9.5.

Display 9.5
Adding a Second
Computed
Variable to the
FSVIEW Window

```
┌─FSVIEW:  MASTER.SUBSCRIB (B)────────────────────────────────┐
│Command ===>                                                 │
│                                                             │
│ OBS       BEGDATE        YRS  NEW  ENDDATE      REMAIN       │
│                                                             │
│   1         APR89         2    0    MAR91         19         │
│   2         MAR90         2    1    FEB92         30         │
│   3         AUG89         2    0    JUL91         23         │
│   4         OCT88         2    0    SEP90         13         │
│   5         MAY87         5    0    APR92         32         │
│   6         AUG90         1    0    JUL91         23         │
│   7         JAN90         1    1    DEC90         16         │
│   8         NOV89         1    1    OCT90         14         │
│   9         FEB90         1    1    JAN91         17         │
│  10         MAY90         3    0    APR93         45         │
│                                                             │
└─────────────────────────────────────────────────────────────┘
```

Note: The actual values displayed in the REMAIN column depend on the date on which you issue the command.

Defining Formats, Informats, and Labels

You can also define a format, informat, and label for the variable in the DEFINE command. Include the values between the variable name and the equal sign in the following form:

(*format,informat,label*)

You can omit any of the values as long as you include all necessary commas.

You can also use this feature to add attributes to existing computed variables. For example, issue the following command to add a format and a label to the REMAIN variable:

```
define remain (6.,,'Number of issues remaining')
```

Two commas follow the format argument (6.) because no value is being supplied for the informat argument.

When this command is executed, the variable changes to the specified format, as shown in Display 9.6.

Display 9.6
Assigning a
Format with the
DEFINE Command

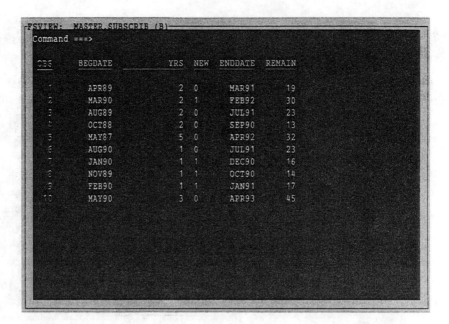

Assigning a Formula to a Data Set Variable

Formulas can also be assigned to data set variables. Suppose you decide that you want the application to display the length of subscriptions in months rather than years. Issue the following command:

```
define yrs=yrs*12
```

The values in the YRS column change to reflect the specified calculation, as shown in Display 9.7.

Display 9.7
Using a Formula
with a Data Set
Variable

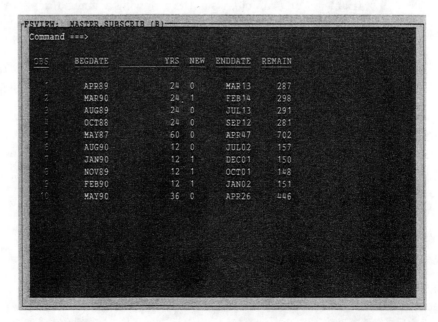

Removing Formulas

To delete computed variables or remove formulas from data set variables, use the RESET command. For example, assigning the formula to the YRS variable has an undesired consequence; because the YRS value is used in the calculation of the computed variables ENDDATE and REMAIN, changing the YRS value also affects these variables, leading to invalid ending dates and remaining issue totals.

To eliminate the formula for the YRS variable, issue the following command:

```
reset yrs
```

Since the data set is currently opened for browsing only, the stored values were not changed when the formula was assigned. The original years values reappear in the YRS column when the formula is removed.

Note: Computed variables have no meaning without their associated formulas. Thus, the RESET command deletes computed variables.

Reviewing Current Formulas

To see the formula entries you have currently defined, issue the following command:

```
review
```

This command opens the FSVIEW REVIEW window, in which all current formulas are listed, as shown in Display 9.8.

Display 9.8
Viewing Formulas in the FSVIEW REVIEW Window

```
┌─FSVIEW· REVIEW MASTER.SUBSCRIB (B)─────────────────────┐
│ Command ===>                                           │
│                                                        │
│ ENDDATE= intnx('month',begdate,(yrs*12)-1)             │
│                                                        │
│ REMAIN=int((enddate-date())/30)                        │
│                                                        │
│ *** END OF TEXT ***                                    │
│                                                        │
│                                                        │
│                                                        │
│                                                        │
│                                                        │
│                                                        │
│                                                        │
│                                                        │
└────────────────────────────────────────────────────────┘
```

The FSVIEW REVIEW window displays the formulas for browsing only. You cannot make changes to the formulas in this window. The formula definitions are listed in the order in which they are entered. Use the END command to close the FSVIEW REVIEW window and return to the FSVIEW window.

Saving Formula Definitions

All defined formulas are saved automatically whenever you end the application or load a different formula entry. You can also save the formula definitions at any time using the SAVE FORMULA command. For example, issue the following command to save the current contents of the formula entry:

```
save formula
```

A message is displayed informing you that the formula entry MASTER.DISPLAY.SUBDATE.FORMULA has been saved. (The formula entry name is the one you specified when you started the application.) You can also use this command to create another copy of the formula entry. Simply follow the command with the name of the new entry. For example, issue the following command to create a backup copy of the current formula definitions:

```
save formula master.display.backup.formula
```

Changing Formula Entries

The FSVIEW procedure allows you to change formula entries during an FSVIEW session. Use the FORMULA command to load the new formula entry. For example, issue the following command to remove all computed variables and load the backup copy of the formula entry you created in the previous example:

```
formula master.display.backup.formula
```

The computed variables from the new formula entry are displayed. (Since this is a copy of the original entry, the computed variables are the same as before, but this does not have to be the case.)

To resume development of the sample application, issue the following command to restore the original formula entry:

```
formula master.display.subdate.formula
```

Note: You can use the FORMULA command to load a formula entry for your FSVIEW session even if you do not use the FORMULA= option in the PROC FSVIEW statement that invokes the procedure (or the *formula-name* argument in the FSVIEW command). You can use this command to add custom features at any time.

Using Screen Control Language in FSVIEW Formulas

The previous examples show formulas consisting of simple SAS expressions. However, formula definitions can also include any of the functions and statements in SAS Screen Control Language (except those that are valid only in SAS/AF software). Using SCL in FSVIEW applications, you can perform sophisticated validation of entered values, invoke additional applications, and manipulate the contents of other data sets or external files.

For more information and an example of using SCL in an FSVIEW application, see Chapter 10, "Enhancing Data Entry Applications Using Screen Control Language."

You can also use the Screen Control Language source-level debugger as an aid in debugging FSVIEW formulas. See *SAS Screen Control Language: Reference, Version 6, First Edition* for a complete description of the debugger.

Creating a Custom Display

Formula entries store more than just formula definitions. They also record information about the appearance of the FSVIEW window and the way variable values are presented in the window. When a formula entry is read in, the FSVIEW window is customized according to the information in the entry. Thus, formula entries allow you to design custom displays for your application.

You can enhance the FSVIEW window display by

□ reordering variables

□ assigning formats and informats for entry and display purposes

□ selecting colors and highlighting attributes.

Use the LEFT MAX command to return to the initial FSVIEW window display shown in Display 9.1. Then follow these steps to design a new display for the sample application. If you need more information about any of the commands used in the following steps, refer to Chapter 16, "The FSVIEW Procedure."

1. Eliminate observation numbers by making FULLNAME an ID variable:

   ```
   show id fullname
   ```

2. Move the address variables to the far right of the display so that all the date and duration information is displayed without having to scroll:

   ```
   move addr1-addr2 remain
   ```

3. Reduce the width of the YRS column by assigning a new format:

   ```
   format yrs '3.'
   ```

Display 9.9 shows the customized FSVIEW display after these steps are performed.

Display 9.9
Customized
Display for the
FSVIEW
Application

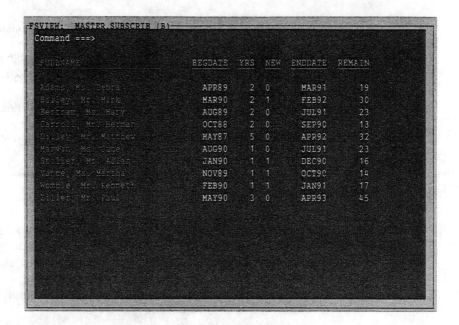

The display features you define are recorded in the formula entry when it is next saved. (Use the SAVE FORMULA command to record the modifications at this time.)

How Variable Order Affects Formula Evaluation

When you use the MOVE command to rearrange variables in the display, you should keep in mind that the order in which variables are displayed affects the way formulas are evaluated. The FSVIEW procedure looks at the variable columns from left to right for associated formulas. Formulas for ID variables are evaluated first, followed by formulas for VAR variables, and finally by formulas for dropped variables. (It is the order in which the variables are displayed, not the order in which the formulas are defined, that determines the evaluation sequence.)

For example, the formula for the computed variable REMAIN in the example application involves the computed variable ENDDATE. Thus, it is important that the REMAIN column appear to the right of the ENDDATE column so that the ENDDATE value is calculated before the REMAIN value. To illustrate this, issue the following command:

```
move enddate-enddate remain
```

This MOVE command reorders the variables so that the REMAIN column appears to the left of the ENDDATE column. Notice that all the values in the REMAIN column change to missing. The REMAIN value cannot be calculated without the ENDDATE value.

To restore the FSVIEW window to its previous arrangement, issue the following command:

```
move remain-remain enddate
```

Assigning General Parameters

The FSVIEW procedure also records various general parameters of the FSVIEW window in the formula entry. These parameters can be browsed or edited in the FSVIEW Parameters window. You can take greater control over the use of your FSVIEW application by altering the default settings for general parameters of the FSVIEW session.

How to Start

Issue the PARMS command in the FSVIEW window to review and edit general parameters for the FSVIEW application. This command opens the FSVIEW Parameters window.

Display 9.10 shows the initial FSVIEW Parameters window for the example application.

Display 9.10
The FSVIEW
Parameters
Window

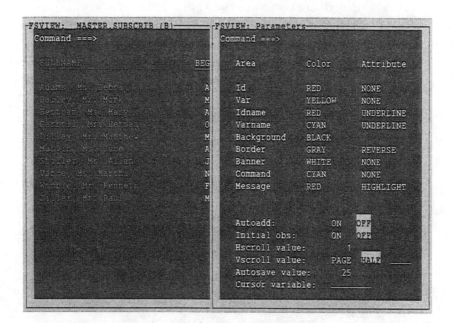

Using the FSVIEW Parameters Window

To change parameter settings, simply move the cursor to the desired field in the FSVIEW Parameters window and type new values over the current contents of the field. (To select a setting for the Autoadd: and Vscroll value: parameters, move the cursor to the button (highlighted term) corresponding to the desired status and press ENTER. The Initial obs: parameter is displayed for information only; it cannot be changed in the FSVIEW Parameters window.)

Customize the sample application as follows:

1. Change the color for the ID column to white by typing WHITE over the current value (RED) in the Id Color field. Change the color for the ID column heading to cyan, matching the other column headings, by typing CYAN over the current value in the Idname Color field.

   The Color fields in the FSVIEW Parameters window reflect the colors currently used by the application. You can also set these colors using the global COLOR command in the FSVIEW window.

   Note: You can enter a question mark (?) in lieu of a color value in these fields to open a HELP window showing a list of available colors. To select a color from the list, move the cursor to the bar of the desired color and press ENTER.

2. Change the highlighting attributes for the column headings to reverse video by changing UNDERLINE to REVERSE in the Idname Attribute and Varname Attribute fields.

   The Attribute fields in the FSVIEW Parameters window reflect the highlighting attributes currently used by the application. You can also set these attributes using the global COLOR command in the FSVIEW window.

3. Change the HSCROLL value to five columns by typing a 5 in the Hscroll value: field. With this setting, users can scroll directly over the five columns in the initial display to the first address variable with a single RIGHT command.

   The Hscroll value: and Vscroll value: fields in the FSVIEW Parameters window reflect the current scrolling defaults for the application. You can also set these attributes using the HSCROLL and VSCROLL commands in the FSVIEW window.

Display 9.11 shows the FSVIEW Parameters window after these steps are performed.

Display 9.11
Customized
Parameters
Settings

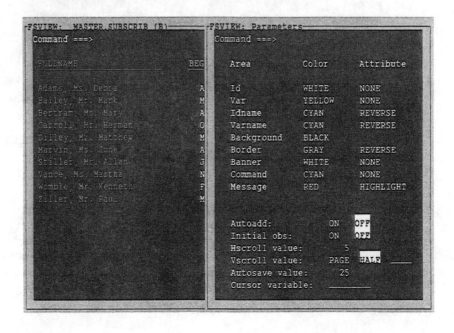

Notice that the FSVIEW window is not yet affected by the parameters specified in the FSVIEW Parameters window. Your selections do not take effect until you close the FSVIEW Parameters window.

Other FSVIEW Parameters

Other parameters in the FSVIEW Parameters window allow you to control the following FSVIEW window features:

Autoadd
: controls whether new observations are automatically added to the displayed data set. This parameter reflects the current status of the autoadd feature, which can also be controlled using an AUTOADD command in the FSVIEW window.

Autosave value
: controls how frequently the data set is automatically saved. An automatic save is performed whenever the number of observations specified in this parameter have been modified since the last save. The default value is 25. If you use an AUTOSAVE command in the FSVIEW window, the value you specify in that command is shown in this parameter.

Cursor variable
: controls which variable the cursor is positioned on when an observation is selected for editing. If you use a CURSOR command in the FSVIEW window, the variable you specify in that command is shown in this parameter.

One parameter in the FSVIEW Parameters window is displayed for information only; its value cannot be changed:

Initial obs
: indicates whether an observation has been selected to fill added observations. This parameter is set on when you use an INITIAL command in the FSVIEW window. The INITIAL command selects an observation whose values are copied into new observations added by the autoadd feature.

Closing the FSVIEW Parameters Window

Execute the END command to close the FSVIEW Parameters window and return to the FSVIEW window. The parameter settings you have defined are stored in the formula entry for your application.

This completes development of the sample application. Issue the END command to close the FSVIEW window and exit the FSVIEW procedure. All the customized features you have defined are recorded in the formula entry.

Using a Custom Application: a Sample Session

If you followed the steps outlined in the previous sections, you created a formula entry that defines a customized FSVIEW application. The remainder of this chapter shows how using this customized application simplifies the data entry process. The previous sections of this chapter look at the application from the developer's perspective. The remainder of this chapter approaches the application from the user's perspective.

Starting the Application

To begin using the FSVIEW application you created, submit the following statements:

```
proc fsview data=master.subscrib
     formula=master.display.subdate.formula
     edit;
run;
```

This assumes that you have previously assigned the libref MASTER to the permanent SAS data library that contains the data set SUBSCRIB and the catalog DISPLAY in which the formula entry for your application, SUBDATE.FORMULA, is stored.

Note: For data browsing applications, you can substitute the BROWSEONLY option for the EDIT option in the preceding code. This prevents editing of the displayed data set.

Display 9.12 shows the initial display for the application.

Display 9.12
Customized
Display

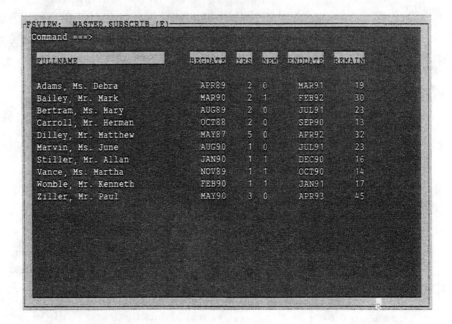

Notice that the data set is opened for editing because you added the EDIT option to the PROC FSVIEW statement.

Adding Observations

Suppose you want to add a new subscriber, Nathan Thomas, to the data set. Execute the AUTOADD command to create a new observation. Display 9.13 shows the display for a new blank observation.

Display 9.13
Blank Observation
Added

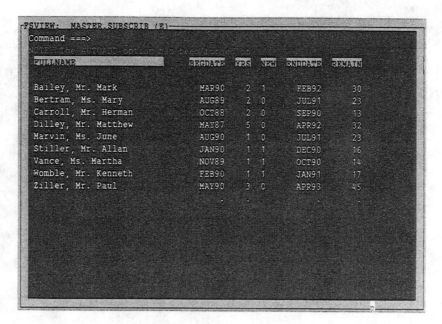

```
┌─FSVIEW:  MASTER.SUBSCRIB (E)────────────────────────────────────┐
│ Command ===>                                                    │
│ Note: The AUTOADD option is in effect...                        │
│  FULLNAME                      BEGDATE  YRS  NEW  ENDDATE  REMAIN │
│                                                                  │
│  Bailey, Mr. Mark              MAR90    2    1    FEB92    30     │
│  Bertram, Ms. Mary             AUG89    2    0    JUL91    23     │
│  Carroll, Mr. Herman           OCT88    2    0    SEP90    13     │
│  Dilley, Mr. Matthew           MAY87    5    0    APR92    32     │
│  Marvin, Ms. June              AUG90    1    0    JUL91    23     │
│  Stiller, Mr. Allan            JAN90    1    1    DEC90    16     │
│  Vance, Ms. Martha             NOV89    1    1    OCT90    14     │
│  Womble, Mr. Kenneth           FEB90    1    1    JAN91    17     │
│  Ziller, Mr. Paul              MAY90    3    0    APR93    45     │
│                                  .      .    .      .      .     │
│                                                                  │
│                                                                  │
│                                                                  │
│                                                                  │
└──────────────────────────────────────────────────────────────────┘
```

Entering Values

Enter the following information in the new observation:

FULLNAME	BEGDATE	YRS	NEW	ADDR1	ADDR2
Thomas, Mr. Nathan	MAY90	2	1	2704 Powers St.	Birmingham, AL 35206

You must scroll right to enter the address values. Notice that you cannot enter values in the computed fields (ENDDATE and REMAIN).

When you press ENTER, the new observation is added to the data set. Values for the ENDDATE and REMAIN variables are calculated and displayed, as shown in Display 9.14. (Scroll left to view these variable columns.)

Display 9.14
Blank Observation
Filled

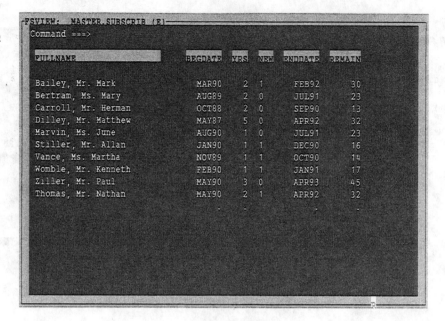

```
┌─FSVIEW: MASTER.SUBSCRIB (E)──────────────────────────────────┐
│ Command ===>                                                 │
│                                                              │
│                                                              │
│  FULLNAME                     BEGDATE  YRS  NEW  ENDDATE  REMAIN │
│                                                              │
│  Bailey, Mr. Mark              MAR90    2    1   FEB92    30  │
│  Bertram, Ms. Mary             AUG89    2    0   JUL91    23  │
│  Carroll, Mr. Herman           OCT88    2    0   SEP90    13  │
│  Dilley, Mr. Matthew           MAY87    5    0   APR92    32  │
│  Marvin, Ms. June              AUG90    1    0   JUL91    23  │
│  Stiller, Mr. Allan            JAN90    1    1   DEC90    16  │
│  Vance, Ms. Martha             NOV89    1    1   OCT90    14  │
│  Womble, Mr. Kenneth           FEB90    1    1   JAN91    17  │
│  Ziller, Mr. Paul              MAY90    3    0   APR93    45  │
│  Thomas, Mr. Nathan            MAY90    2    1   APR92    32  │
│                                  .      .    .     .      .   │
│                                                              │
│                                                              │
│                                                              │
│                                                              │
└──────────────────────────────────────────────────────────────┘
```

Ending the Application

When you have finished editing the data set, use the END command to close the
FSVIEW window and end the FSVIEW application.

Chapter **10** Enhancing Data Entry Applications Using Screen Control Language

Introduction

Screen Control Language (SCL) is a programming language that provides functions and routines to manipulate data and control windows in FSBROWSE, FSEDIT, and FSVIEW applications. SCL provides the power and flexibility to build all types of applications, from programs that perform simple calculations to sophisticated systems that integrate several procedures and products. Although SCL programs can include many of the same statements that you use in the SAS DATA step, SCL provides special statements and functions to control program flow and interaction with all interactive elements of windows.

This chapter provides an overview of SCL features as well as examples that demonstrate how to use some of the basic SCL statements and functions. See *SAS Screen Control Language: Usage, Version 6, First Edition* for more detailed examples of SCL in FSBROWSE, FSEDIT, and FSVIEW applications. See *SAS Screen Control Language: Reference, Version 6, First Edition* for complete details of SCL functions, statements, and routines.

Overview of SCL Features

SCL includes variables, statements, and functions that allow you to control every aspect of your application. Basic statements and functions enable you to start building applications immediately and, depending on the complexity of the tasks, may be all you need. You can use SCL statements and functions to

□ control the application environment

□ control interaction between the user and the application

□ control communication between windows in an application

□ obtain information from SAS data sets and external files

□ modify the contents of SAS data sets and external files

□ control error handling and provide messages specific to your application.

Writing an SCL Program

SCL programs consist of Screen Control Language statements and functions that control applications. Like all languages, SCL requires you to follow syntax rules for combining the statements and functions into programs. These rules are described in *SAS Screen Control Language: Reference.*

The SAS/FSP procedures that support SCL have different systems for entering SCL programs, as described in the following sections.

Programming in the FSBROWSE and FSEDIT Procedures

In the FSBROWSE and FSEDIT procedures, you compose SCL programs in a Program window (the FSBROWSE Program window or the FSEDIT Program window, respectively). To open these windows for entering and editing SCL programs, you must first open the FSBROWSE Menu window or the FSEDIT Menu window by issuing the MODIFY command in the FSBROWSE window or FSEDIT window. Select option 3 from the respective Menu window to open the corresponding Program window for editing.

The programs you create are automatically compiled and stored in the application's screen entry when you close the window. Refer to Chapter 13, "The FSEDIT Procedure," for information on creating screen entries.

Programming in the FSVIEW Procedure

When using SCL with the FSVIEW procedure, you do not create programs in the same sense as in the FSBROWSE and FSEDIT procedures. Each formula you define in the FSVIEW window is treated as a block of SCL code. You define formulas with the DEFINE command in the FSVIEW window. You can either supply the SCL code in the argument for the DEFINE command or, more conveniently, use the DEFINE command to open the FSVIEW Define window and enter the SCL code in that window.

The SCL code segments are compiled individually when the formulas are defined and are stored with the application's formula entry. Refer to Chapter 16,

"The FSVIEW Procedure," for information on how to create and store formula entries.

Controlling Program Execution

Unlike SAS programs, SCL programs require the applications developer to specify when statements in the program will be executed. The mechanisms for controlling program execution vary according to the procedure used.

Controlling Execution in FSBROWSE and FSEDIT Applications

Program execution in FSBROWSE and FSEDIT applications is controlled by grouping statements into sections. Each section of the program begins with a reserved SCL label and ends with a RETURN statement. FSBROWSE or FSEDIT application programs can include the following five execution sections:

1. FSEINIT: an initialization phase before any observations are displayed, marked by the label FSEINIT. This section is invoked only once during an FSBROWSE or FSEDIT session. The tasks in this phase are completed before the FSBROWSE or FSEDIT window is opened.
    Typical uses of the statements following the FSEINIT label are to

    □   import values through macro variables

    □   display initial messages on the message line (once for the application)

    □   open auxiliary data sets or external files used or referenced by the application.

    Note: The section following the FSEINIT label is also executed when the FSBROWSE or FSEDIT window is reopened after an SCL program is compiled in the Program window.
    You cannot assign initial values to window variables (variables with fields in the FSBROWSE or FSEDIT window) in the FSEINIT section. Only nonwindow variables can be initialized in this section because no observation is open during the processing for this block.

2. INIT: an initialization phase before each observation is displayed, marked by the label INIT. This section is executed once per observation, just before the observation is displayed in the FSBROWSE or FSEDIT window.
    Typical uses of the statements following the INIT label are to

    □   initialize variables for the observation

    □   initialize computed fields

    □   display initial messages on the message line (once for each observation).

3. MAIN: a main processing phase marked by the label MAIN. This section is repeated each time the user modifies a field in the window and presses the ENTER key or a function key. When a field is modified, the FSEDIT procedure

□ checks the input values for validity. The FSEDIT procedure uses any field attributes assigned when the application was created.

□ executes the SCL statements following the MAIN label only if the input values are valid. If errors are detected, the statements are not executed and the procedure issues an error message. When the user corrects the error, the MAIN section is executed. The CONTROL statement can be used to override this default behavior.

Note: Field values are checked for validity only before the SCL program is entered, not after. No error is detected if manipulations in the SCL program produce a field value that is outside the range specified in the MIN and MAX field attributes.

During the main processing phase, the user interacts directly with the application to accomplish specific tasks. The SCL program can prompt the user for information, verify values, check data sets, and call other programs that prompt the user for information.

4. TERM: a termination phase before moving to another observation, marked by the label TERM. This section is executed once for each observation, just before the next observation is displayed.

A typical use of the TERM section is to update an auxiliary data set.

5. FSETERM: a termination phase before the FSBROWSE or FSEDIT session ends, marked by the label FSETERM. This section is executed when the user issues the END command to terminate the session.

Typical uses of the statements following the FSEINIT label are to

□ close data sets or external files used or referenced by the application

□ export values through macro variables.

Note: The section following the FSETERM label is also executed when you select option 3 from the FSBROWSE Menu window or the FSEDIT Menu window to open the corresponding Program window for editing.

As you write your program, think about how each statement or group of statements interacts with the user and with other windows so that you can group the SCL statements correctly based on when they should be executed. If your application includes an SCL program, the program must include at least one of the SCL reserved labels; otherwise, the program will compile but no code will be executed when the application is displayed.

Be sure to use a RETURN statement to indicate the end of each labeled section of your program.

Controlling Execution in FSVIEW Applications

Unlike FSBROWSE and FSEDIT applications, no reserved labels are used in SCL programming in FSVIEW applications. When you define a formula, the FSVIEW procedure internally adds a label for the formula and a RETURN statement so that each formula can be treated as a separate SCL block. (The label is the same as the variable name.)

For example, suppose you define a computed variable named ENDDATE with the following formula:

```
enddate=intnx('month',begdate,(yrs*12)-1)
```

The SCL block for the ENDDATE variable would be stored as follows:

```
ENDDATE:enddate=intnx('month',begdate,(yrs*12)-1);RETURN;
```

These blocks are executed in the order that the variables appear in the FSVIEW window. (Formulas are also executed for variables that are dropped from the FSVIEW window.) It is the order of the variables, not the order in which the formulas are defined, that determines the execution order. When the FSVIEW window is displayed or redrawn, the blocks are executed for all displayed observations. When an observation is edited, the blocks are executed for the edited observation only.

SCL Variables

You can use three types of variables in SCL programs:

window variables
> variables that have fields in the application window, including variables from the SAS data set as well as variables for computational fields.
>
> Each field in the FSBROWSE or FSEDIT application window (or each column in an FSVIEW application window) has a corresponding window variable in SCL. When a user modifies the values in the fields or columns of the application window, the values of the corresponding SCL variables are automatically updated. Similarly, when the SCL program modifies the value of a window variable, the value of the corresponding field in the application window is updated. If the field is for a data set variable, the variable in the data set is updated also.

nonwindow variables
> variables that do not correspond to fields in the application window. These include temporary variables used in the program, such as variables used to hold the return codes of SCL functions. These variables can be used in calculations and are treated by SCL in the same manner as window variables.
>
> **Note:** Variables identified as unwanted in an FSBROWSE or FSEDIT application are not available for use by SCL programs. Refer to Chapter 13 for a discussion of unwanted variables.
>
> Nonwindow variables are initialized to missing values or to initial values given in declarative statements (such as ARRAY statements) before SCL is executed. Nonwindow variables retain their current values until the display is terminated.

system variables
> reserved variables such as _MSG_ provided by SCL to check information set by the system or to set information displayed or used by the system.

Using SCL in FSEDIT Applications

The following section illustrates a Screen Control Language program in a very simple FSEDIT application. You should already know how to customize an FSEDIT display and create a screen entry to store the SCL program before using this example. Refer to Chapter 8, "Creating Data Entry Applications Using the FSEDIT Procedure," if you need more information.

Note: Much of the following information is also applicable to creating data browsing applications with the FSBROWSE procedure. However, FSBROWSE applications do not allow data entry, even in computational fields.

Writing a Sample Application

Suppose you want to design an FSEDIT application to display values in each observation of a SAS data set, to sum the values, and to return a total. Follow the steps outlined in this section.

Step 1: Creating the Data Set

Begin by submitting the following statements:

```
proc fsedit new=master.sum
     screen=master.display.sumscr.screen;
run;
```

Note: You must have previously assigned the libref MASTER to a permanent SAS data library.

Because the PROC FSEDIT statement includes the NEW= option, the FSEDIT procedure begins by opening the FSEDIT New window. In the FSEDIT New window, define the following two variables:

Name	Type	Length	Label	Format
A	N	8	_____	_____
B	N	8	_____	_____

Use the END command to close the FSEDIT New window, to create the data set MASTER.SUM, and to open the FSEDIT window for editing the data set. Display 10.1 shows the initial FSEDIT window.

Display 10.1
Default FSEDIT Window for MASTER.SUM

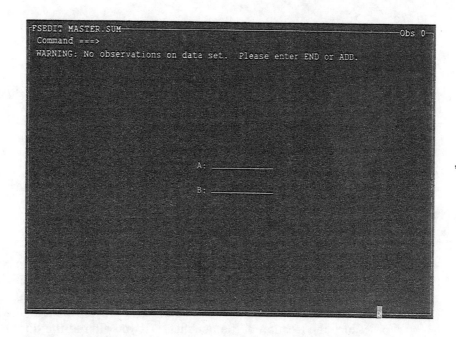

For now, ignore the message telling you to enter END or ADD.

Step 2: Customizing the Display

Issue the MODIFY command in the FSEDIT window. This opens the FSEDIT Menu window, from which you create custom applications.

Select option 2, "Screen Modification and Field Identification." This opens the FSEDIT Modify window.

Using the commands available in the FSEDIT Modify window, alter the display so that it looks like Display 10.2. Refer to Chapter 13 if you need more information on the commands available in the FSEDIT Modify window.

Display 10.2
Custom FSEDIT Display for MASTER.SUM

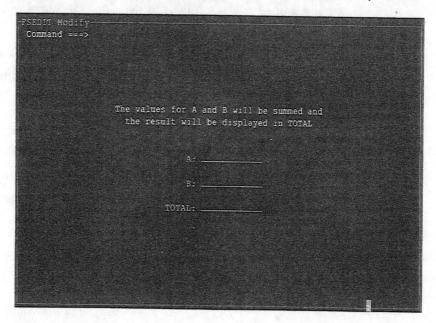

When you have completed modifying the display, execute the END command. The procedure displays the following question:

```
Did you create any computational or repeated fields (Y or N)? _
```

Answer Y, because you created the computational field TOTAL. Press ENTER to continue.

The FSEDIT Names window is then opened. In this window you tell the FSEDIT procedure the name and type of the new field:

```
Name    Type    Format   Informat


TOTAL__  N      _____  _____
```

Once you have entered this information, execute the END command to close the FSEDIT Names window and to open the FSEDIT Identify window.

In the FSEDIT Identify window, you are prompted to place the cursor on the underscores for the TOTAL field and press ENTER. This tells the FSEDIT procedure the location of the new field. (If you altered the lines containing the variables A or B, you may be asked to identify those fields also.) Once all fields are identified, execute the END command to return to the FSEDIT Menu window.

Step 3: Writing the Program

From the FSEDIT Menu window, select option 3, "Edit Program Statements and Compile." This opens the FSEDIT Program window, in which you enter your SCL program.

In this example, you want the SCL program to accomplish the following tasks:

□ add the values of A and B (obtained from the data set) and display the result in the TOTAL variable

□ show the updated total as the user changes the values of A and B.

Display 10.3 shows an SCL program that performs the desired tasks. Enter these statements in the FSEDIT Program window.

Display 10.3
SCL Program for
the Application

```
 FSEDIT Program
 Command ===>

   /* This section executes when each */
   /* observation is displayed.       */
 INIT:
    total = A + B;
    _msg_ = 'This is the INIT section.';
 return;

   /* This section executes each time the user modifies */
   /* a field and presses ENTER or a function key.       */
 MAIN:
    total = A + B;
    _msg_ = 'This is the MAIN section.';
 return;

   /* This section executes each time the */
   /* user moves to a new observation.    */
 TERM:
 return;

 *** END OF TEXT ***
```

Notice that the INIT and MAIN sections have the same statements. Remember that the statements in the INIT block are executed before the observation is displayed, so this block ensures that the TOTAL field contains the proper sum when the observation is displayed. The MAIN block is executed each time a field value is modified, so this block ensures that the TOTAL field contains the proper sum after each modification.

After typing in the program, issue the END command to automatically compile the program and save it in the screen entry for the application, to close the FSEDIT Program window, and to return to the FSEDIT Menu window. You receive one of the three following messages, depending on the success of the compilation:

□ `Compile successful. Program size = ` *nnnnn* ` bytes.`

□ `Compile was successful, but see LOG for warning`
  `messages.`

□ `ERROR: See LOG for compile error listing.`

Assuming your program compiled successfully, execute the END command from the FSEDIT Menu window to save the screen entry containing the newly created application and to return to the FSEDIT window. The application is now ready for use.

Note: If you use the PMENU facility, the action bar item for exiting the FSEDIT Menu window is Goback rather than End.

Add an initial observation to the data set by issuing an ADD command. Enter the value 1 in the A field and the value 3 in the B field. The TOTAL field should show the result, 4, as shown in Display 10.4.

Display 10.4
Adding an Initial Observation

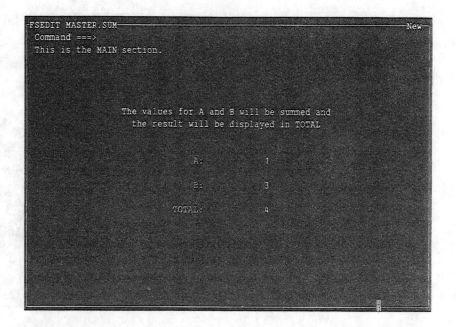

To end development of the application, issue the END command to close the FSEDIT window and end the FSEDIT session.

Using the FSEDIT Application

A user accesses your stored application by submitting the following statements:

```
proc fsedit data=master.sum
     screen=master.display.sumscr.screen;
run;
```

In these statements, MASTER is a previously defined libref, SUM is the SAS data set name, DISPLAY is the SAS catalog containing your application, and SUMSCR.SCREEN is the name of the screen entry in which the SCL program is stored.

When the FSEDIT procedure is initiated, the statements in the INIT section of the program are executed. In the initial observation you created, the variable A contains the value 1, and the variable B contains the value 3. The SCL program calculates the total of the A and B fields and displays the result, 4 in this case, in the TOTAL field.

If the user enters a value in a field, the procedure first verifies that the value entered is a valid numeric value (because A and B were defined as numeric variables when the data set was created). Then, the statements in the MAIN section of the program are executed. Each time the user enters a value and presses the ENTER key, the total is calculated and displayed in the variable TOTAL.

For example, enter the value 7 in the field for A and 12 in the field for B. When you press ENTER, a total is calculated and displayed, as shown in Display 10.5.

Display 10.5
Total Calculated
from User Input

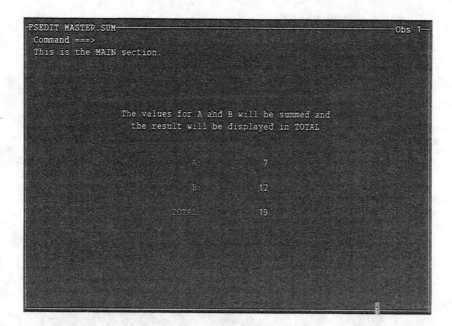

To end the application, issue the END command. The FSEDIT window is closed, and control is returned to the calling task.

Additional FSEDIT Examples

The following examples illustrate some of the SCL features that are particularly useful in FSEDIT applications. Once you become familiar with some of the basic SCL features used in these examples, you can refer to the statement and function descriptions in *SAS Screen Control Language: Reference* to build SCL programs that meet your particular needs.

Cross-Validating Data Set Values

The following example shows how to validate a user-entered value based on other values in the data set.

Submit the following statements to begin developing the application:

```
proc fsedit data=master.sum
            screen=master.display.vertot.screen;
run;
```

This example uses the data set created in the previous example.

When the FSEDIT window opens, issue the following command to move to the FSEDIT Modify window:

```
modify;2
```

Using the same process described in the previous example, create the modified display shown in Display 10.6:

Display 10.6
Custom Display
for Cross-Field
Validation
Example

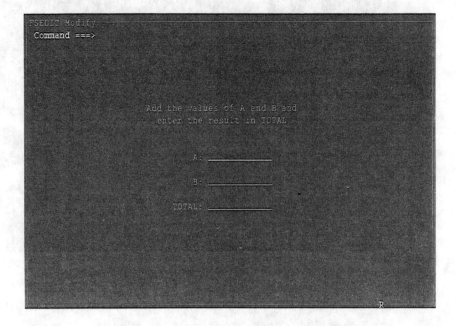

Once you have modified the display and defined and identified the fields, return to the FSEDIT Menu window and open the FSEDIT Program window by choosing option 3.

Enter the following SCL program:

```
        /* A and B are protected fields containing values in the data */
        /* set not to be modified by the user. TOTAL will be validated */
        /* and ERROR turned on or off depending on whether the user    */
        /* gives a correct answer.                                     */
INIT:
return;

MAIN:
   check=a + b;

      /* Check answer; if incorrect, then display warning */
   if total ne check then
      do;
         erroron total;
         _msg_='Your answer is not correct. Try again.';
      end;

      /* If answer correct, then display this message   */
   else _msg_='Very good.';
return;

TERM:
return;
```

The MAIN section calculates the sum of the values in the variables A and B and then compares that total against the value entered in the TOTAL field. If the entered total does not match the calculated sum, the ERRORON statement causes an error condition for the TOTAL field.

To use the application, a user fills in the TOTAL field with the sum of the values in the A and B fields. The application then displays a message indicating whether or not the entered value is correct. Display 10.7 shows the FSEDIT display after the user has entered an incorrect value for TOTAL.

Display 10.7
Validating User Input

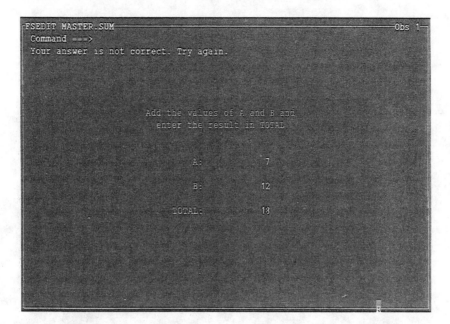

Cross-Checking Data Sets

This example illustrates an order entry system that uses two data sets (MASTER.ORDER and MASTER.PRICE) to collect and process orders. Submit the following statements to create the data sets and begin developing the application:

Note: The source code for this example is available in member FU10N03 of the SAS/FSP sample library. See "Using This Book" for information on accessing the SAS/FSP sample library at your site.

```
data master.order;
   length unit1-unit10 8;
run;

data master.price;
   length desc $8 cost 8;
   input desc cost;
   cards;
Socks     1.75
Belt      4.50
Loafers  21.25
Tie       6.20
Wallet    5.75
T-shirt   3.95
Purse    12.35
```

```
    Sweater  42.50
    Dress    29.90
    Coat     59.00
    ;

proc fsedit data=master.order
     screen=master.display.orderscr
     mod;
run;
```

The MOD option in the PROC FSEDIT statement opens the FSEDIT Menu window when the procedure begins. Choose option 2 to open the FSEDIT Modify window; then create the display shown in Display 10.8.

Display 10.8
Customized
Display for
MASTER.ORDER

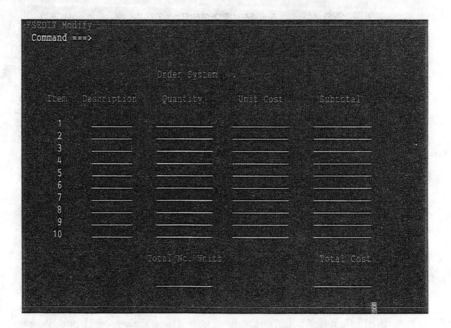

The display consists of 42 fields and descriptive text.

In the FSEDIT Names window, define variables DESC1 through DESC10 as character variables, COST1 through COST10 as numeric variables with the format DOLLAR10.2, STOT1 through STOT10 as numeric variables with the format DOLLAR10.2, TOTUNIT as a numeric variable, and TOTCOST as a numeric variable with the format DOLLAR10.2.

In the FSEDIT Identify window, identify the fields in the Quantity column as UNIT1 through UNIT10 (the 10 variables in the MASTER.ORDER data set). The other fields are computational fields. Identify DESC1 through DESC10 as the fields in the Description column, COST1 through COST10 as the fields in the Unit Cost column, STOT1 through STOT10 as the fields in the Subtotal column, TOTUNIT as the Total No. Units field, and TOTCOST as the Total Cost field.

After you identify all the fields, return to the FSEDIT Menu window and select option 4 to open the FSEDIT Attributes window. All the fields except those in the Quantity column display values calculated by the program, not values of variables in the data set, so you should assign the PROTECT attribute to all fields except those in the Quantity column.

Return to the FSEDIT Menu window and select option 3 to enter the following SCL program:

```
array item{10} $;
array price{10};
array desc{10}desc1-desc10;
array unit{10}unit1-unit10;
array cost{10}cost1-cost10;
array stot{10}stot1-stot10;

FSEINIT:
   dsid=open('master.price','i');
   if (dsid=0) then _msg_=sysmsg();
   d=varnum(dsid,'desc');
   c=varnum(dsid,'cost');
   do i=1 to 10;
      rc=fetchobs(dsid,i);
      item{i}=getvarc(dsid,d);
      price{i}=getvarn(dsid,c);
   end;
return;

INIT:
   do i=1 to 10;
      desc{i}=item{i};
      cost{i}=price{i};
   end;

MAIN:
   do i=1 to 10;
      stot{i}=cost{i}*unit{i};
   end;
   totunit=sum(of unit1--unit10);
   totcost=sum(of stot1--stot10);
return;

TERM:
return;

FSETERM:
   call close(dsid);
return;
```

Note: This program does not have a RETURN statement at the end of the INIT section. This technique allows the INIT section to perform the tasks in the MAIN section without having to repeat the code.

Notice that the DESC1 through DESC10 and COST1 through COST10 variables cannot be initialized in the FSEINIT section because they are window variables. Only nonwindow variables like ITEM and PRICE can be initialized in the FSEINIT section.

To use the application, a user fills in the number of units of each item ordered, supplying up to 10 variable values in the Quantity column. The other fields display variable values that are read from the MASTER.PRICE data set or calculated by the program. Because you assigned the PROTECT field attribute to these fields, the user cannot modify these calculated values.

When the user enters the number of units ordered and presses ENTER, the program calculates the subtotal and total values and displays them immediately. These calculations are based on information from two sources:

□ Price information is supplied by the data set MASTER.PRICE.

□ The actual number of units ordered is supplied by the user.

Display 10.9 shows the display after the user has entered the number of units ordered for three items and after the values for STOT1 through STOT10, TOTUNIT, and TOTCOST have been calculated. The variables DESC1 through DESC10 and COST1 through COST10 are read from the MASTER.PRICE data set.

Display 10.9
Display with
Entered and
Calculated Values

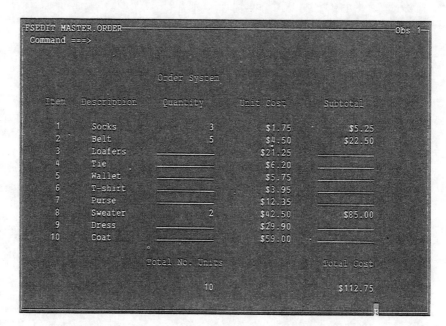

Using SCL in FSVIEW Applications

SCL is used somewhat differently in FSVIEW applications than in FSBROWSE and FSEDIT applications. Instead of writing a distinct program, each formula that you define for a variable in the FSVIEW window is treated as a separate SCL routine. When the FSVIEW window is redrawn or when an observation is modified, the routines are executed in the order that the corresponding variables appear in the FSVIEW window. (When the FSVIEW window is redrawn, the routines are executed for all observations; when an observation is modified, the routines are evaluated only for the edited observation.)

The following sections illustrate how you can use Screen Control Language to enhance an FSVIEW application. You should already know how to define formulas and create formula entries to store the formula definitions before you attempt to use the example in this section. Refer to Chapter 9, "Creating Data Entry Applications Using the FSVIEW Procedure," if you need more information on the basics of creating FSVIEW applications.

Creating a Sample Application

Chapter 9 shows how to use the FSVIEW procedure to create a data entry application for updating magazine subscriber information. Display 10.10 shows the custom display for that application.

Display 10.10
Custom Display
for SUBDATE
Application

```
┌─FSVIEW:  MASTER.SUBSCRIB (B)──────────────────────────────────────┐
│ Command ===>                                                      │
│ NOTE: MASTER.DISPLAY.SUBDATE.FORMAT has been OPENED.              │
│ FULLNAME                         BEGDATE NRS NEW ENDDATE REMAIN    │
│                                                                   │
│  Adams, Ms. Debra                APR89   2   0   MAR91   19        │
│  Bailey, Mr. Mark                MAR90   2   1   FEB92   30        │
│  Bertram, Ms. Mary               AUG89   2   0   JUL91   23        │
│  Carroll, Mr. Herman             OCT88   2   0   SEP90   13        │
│  Dilley, Mr. Matthew             MAY87   5   0   APR92   32        │
│  Marvin, Ms. June                AUG90   1   0   JUL91   23        │
│  Stiller, Mr. Allan              JAN90   1   1   DEC90   16        │
│  Vance, Ms. Martha               NOV89   1   1   OCT90   14        │
│  Womble, Mr. Kenneth             FEB90   1   1   JAN91   17        │
│  Ziller, Mr. Paul                MAY90   3   0   APR93   44        │
│                                                                   │
│                                                                   │
│                                                                   │
└───────────────────────────────────────────────────────────────────┘
```

The original application is useful for updating starting dates and subscription lengths because that information appears in the FSVIEW window by default. It is less convenient for updating address information because you must scroll to the right to view the address columns. Suppose you want to enhance the FSVIEW application by having it open a data entry window requesting verification of the subscriber's current address information whenever the subscriber name, starting date, or subscription length is changed. The following example shows how you can use SCL to provide this enhancement.

Creating the Application Window

The additional data entry window for the enhanced application is a program entry created with SAS/AF software. (SAS/AF software must be licensed at your site for you to create this entry.) This example uses only the most basic features of SAS/AF software, so no previous experience with that product is required.

To begin, submit the following statements to open the DISPLAY window for creating a new program entry:

```
proc build catalog=master.display.veraddr.program;
run;
```

Because this entry did not previously exist, the DISPLAY window is initially blank, as shown in Display 10.11.

Display 10.11
*Initial DISPLAY
Window for the
VERADDR
Program Entry*

The DISPLAY window is where you design the display for SAS/AF
application windows. Because the DISPLAY window uses the SAS text editor, all
standard text editor commands are valid. The process of designing a display in
this window is the same as the process of designing a custom display for the
FSEDIT window in the FSEDIT Modify window.

To create the data entry window for this example, enter the text shown in
Display 10.12.

Display 10.12
*Designing the
Application
Window*

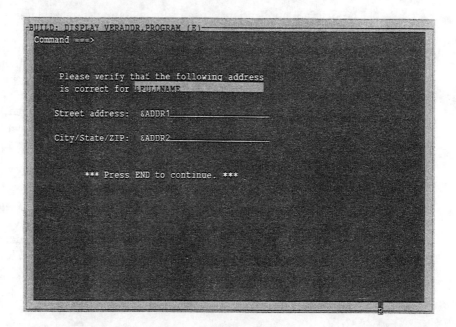

The terms in the application window that begin with ampersands (&) and are
followed by underscores are the data entry fields. The next step is to assign
attributes for these fields.

Assigning Field Attributes

Issue the following command in the DISPLAY window:

    attr

This command opens the ATTR window, in which the attributes of the fields in the data entry window are defined. This window is partitioned into a series of frames, one frame for each field in the window. Display 10.13 shows the frame for the first field, FULLNAME.

Display 10.13
ATTR Window for
Defining Field
Attributes

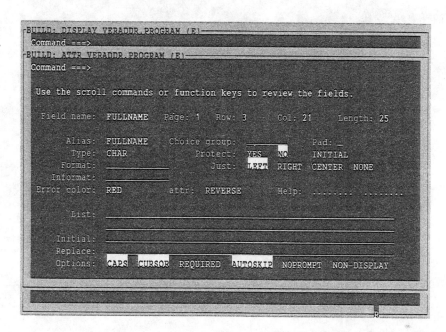

In the frame for the FULLNAME field, move the cursor to the YES following the label Protect and press ENTER. The YES is highlighted to indicate that this field is now protected from editing. Next move the cursor to the highlighted term CAPS in the Options line and press ENTER to turn off the CAPS attribute. (You don't want this field automatically changed to uppercase.) Finally, move the cursor to the highlighted term CURSOR in the Options line and press ENTER to turn off the CURSOR attribute. (Since this is now a protected field, you don't want the cursor positioned on it by default.)

Use the FORWARD command to scroll to the frame for the next field, ADDR1. In this frame, turn off the CAPS attribute and turn on the CURSOR attribute. You want users to be able to enter values in this field, so leave the Protect attribute set to NO.

Scroll forward again to reach the frame for the ADDR2 field. The only change required in this frame is to turn off the CAPS attribute.

This completes the process of assigning field attributes. Use the END command to close the ATTR window and return to the DISPLAY window.

Assigning General Parameters

The BUILD procedure also allows you to set general parameters for the application window. Issue the following command from the DISPLAY window:

    gattr

This command opens the GATTR window.

One of the general features you can define in this window is the title used in the upper-left corner of the application window border. Enter **Address Verification** in the Name field at the top of this window, as shown in Display 10.14.

Display 10.14
GATTR Window
for Defining
General Attributes

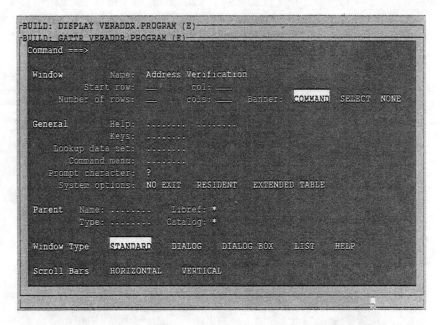

No other general parameters need to be changed, so issue the END command to close the GATTR window and return to the DISPLAY window.

Entering a Program

The only remaining step is to enter the SCL code for the application window. For SAS/AF program entries, the associated SCL program is entered in the SOURCE window. Issue the following command to open the SOURCE window:

```
source
```

The SOURCE window uses the SAS text editor, so all standard text editor commands are available. Enter the following statements in the SOURCE window:

```
entry fullname addr1 addr2 $25;


INIT:
MAIN:
TERM:
return;
```

The ENTRY statement defines a list of variables whose values are passed to this SCL program from a calling program and whose values are passed back to the calling program when this program ends. Because the application window is used only to display and collect variable values, no processing of the entered values is required. Thus, the INIT, MAIN, and TERM blocks consist simply of a single RETURN statement.

Unlike the FSEDIT Program window, program code in the SOURCE window is not compiled automatically when you close the window. Issue the following command to compile the statements in the SOURCE window:

```
compile
```

If you entered the code without typing errors, you will receive a message that the program was successfully compiled.

This completes development of the application window. Issue an END command to close the SOURCE window and return to the DISPLAY window. Issue another END command to close the DISPLAY window. When the DISPLAY window is closed, the BUILD procedure's DIRECTORY window is opened. Issue an additional END command to close this window and end the BUILD procedure.

Updating the FSVIEW Application

The remaining step is to add SCL code to the FSVIEW application to call the SAS/AF program entry you just designed. Submit the following statements to initiate the FSVIEW procedure with the SUBDATE formula entry created in Chapter 9:

```
proc fsview data=master.subscrib
     formula=master.display.subdate.formula;
run;
```

Once the FSVIEW window is opened, issue the following command to change the default formula entry name so that a different formula entry is created for the enhanced application:

```
formula master.display.veraddr.formula
```

Because the VERADDR formula entry did not previously exist, a message appears informing you that the formula entry was not found. However, an entry with the specified name is now created when you close the FSVIEW window.

To define the formula, issue the following command to open the FSVIEW Define window to create a computed variable named CHANGED:

```
define changed
```

Once the FSVIEW Define window is open, enter the formula shown in Display 10.15.

Display 10.15
Formula
Definition
Containing SCL

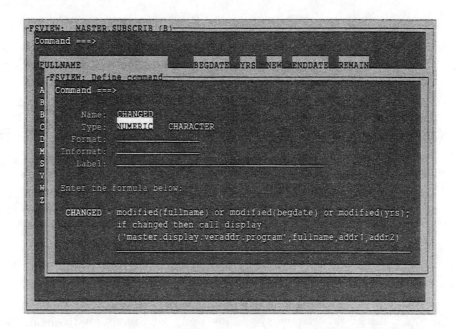

The example formula consists of two statements. The first (or only) statement in any formula must always provide a value for the variable shown to the left of the equal sign. The value provided should match the type (numeric or character) selected for the formula.

In the first statement of the example formula, the SCL function MODIFIED returns the value 1 if the specified variable has been modified, and 0 if it has not been changed. Thus, the first statement in the formula sets the value of the CHANGED variable to 1 if any of the three window variables were changed, and to 0 if none of the variables were changed.

The second statement executes the SCL statement CALL DISPLAY if the value of the CHANGED variable is anything other than 0. This test ensures that the CALL DISPLAY statement is executed only when the observation has been changed. Without this test, the statement is executed for every observation when the FSVIEW window is redrawn. The CALL DISPLAY statement calls the specified entry: in this case, the application window you created in the previous steps. The CALL DISPLAY arguments also identify three variables (FULLNAME, ADDR1, and ADDR2) whose values are passed to the called program, and which will be updated with values returned from the called program.

After you enter the formula definition, issue an END command to compile the formula. If no errors are detected, the FSVIEW Define window is closed and you return to the FSVIEW window. The computed variable CHANGED is now displayed as the rightmost variable in the window, as shown in Display 10.16.

Display 10.16
CHANGED
Variable Added to
the FSVIEW
Window

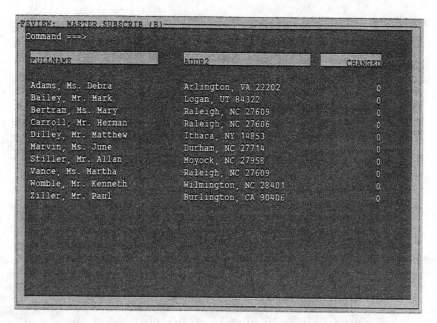

Because you do not need to see the value of the CHANGED variable, issue the following command to exclude it from the FSVIEW window:

```
drop changed
```

Formulas are still executed for dropped variables. In the execution sequence, formulas for dropped variables are evaluated after all displayed variables have been evaluated.

This completes development of the example application. Because the FSVIEW procedure records which observations and variables are being displayed when the FSVIEW window is closed, you should issue the following command to return to the initial display:

```
left max
```

Now issue the END command to close the FSVIEW window, to store the VERADDR formula entry, and to end the FSVIEW procedure.

Using the FSVIEW Application

A user invokes your stored application by submitting the following statements:

```
proc fsview data=master.subscrib
     formula=master.display.veraddr.formula
     edit;
run;
```

In these statements, MASTER is a previously defined libref, SUBSCRIB is the SAS data set to be displayed, DISPLAY is the SAS catalog containing the application, and VERADDR.FORMULA is the formula entry in which the formula and other information about the FSVIEW window is stored.

When the FSVIEW procedure is initiated, the initial display in the FSVIEW window is the same as in the original application (see Display 10.10). However, if the user changes the values in the FULLNAME, BEGDATE, or YRS columns of an observation, the formula for the CHANGED variable is executed.

For example, move the cursor to the observation for Herman Carroll and press ENTER to lock the observation for editing. Then change the value in the BEGDATE column of that observation to OCT90 and the value in the YRS column to 1. When you press ENTER to record these changes, the formula for the CHANGED variable is executed, which opens the VERADDR application window, as shown in Display 10.17.

Display 10.17
Address
Verification
Window Opened
by the Formula

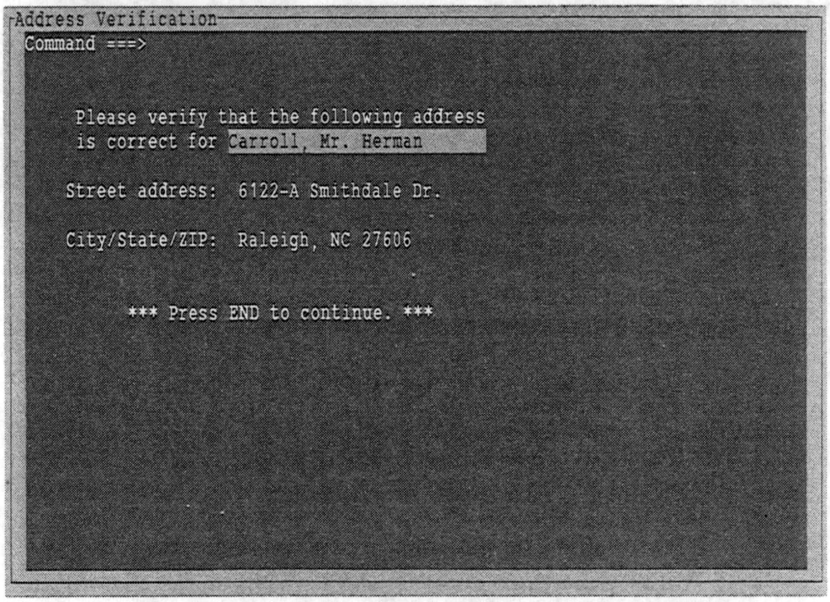

For Herman Carroll's observation, update his street address by entering `1402 Braxton Ct`. in the Street address field of the Address Verification window; then issue an END command to close the Address Verification window and to return to the FSVIEW window.

When you return to the FSVIEW window, scroll right to view the column for the ADDR1 variable. Verify that the address in the data set has been updated, as shown in Display 10.18.

Display 10.18
ADDR1 Variable
Updated in the
Displayed Data
Set

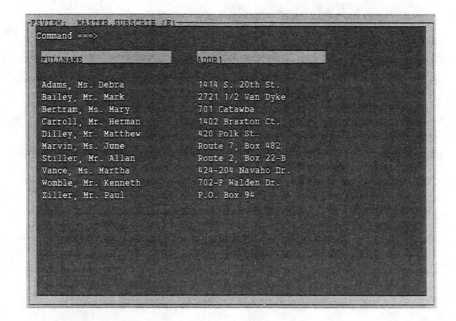

Issue the END command in the FSVIEW window to close the FSVIEW window and to end the enhanced application.

Part 4

Reference: SAS/FSP®
Software Procedures

Chapter 11 Overview: Part 4

Introduction 221

Guide to SAS/FSP Procedures 221

Introduction

Chapters 12 through 16 provide a description and the complete syntax for all SAS/FSP procedures and for the commands specific to each procedure.

These chapters do not provide examples of how the procedures are used. Refer to Parts 2 and 3, Chapters 2 through 10, for more information on using SAS/FSP procedures to accomplish specific tasks.

Refer to Chapters 17 through 20 for a summary of global commands, information on the PMENU facility, and details of forms for printing.

Guide to SAS/FSP Procedures

Table 11.1 tells you which tasks each SAS/FSP procedure performs and what special features it provides. It also directs you to the chapter that documents each procedure.

Table 11.1
Guide to SAS/FSP
Procedures

Procedure	Chapter	Uses and Features
FSBROWSE	12	**Uses** Browsing existing SAS data sets Creating data presentation applications **Features** Displays one observation at a time. Window characteristics can be customized. Application-specific key definitions can be assigned. Associated Screen Control Language programs can display computed variables and values from other SAS data sets. The FSLETTER procedure can be called to create letters or reports customized with information from the data set.

(continued)

	Procedure	Chapter	Uses and Features
Table 11.1 *(continued)*	FSEDIT	13	**Uses** Browsing existing SAS data sets Editing and updating existing SAS data sets Creating new SAS data sets Creating data entry and editing applications **Features** Displays one observation at a time. Window characteristics can be customized. Application-specific key definitions can be assigned. Associated Screen Control Language programs can display computed variables, validate field values, and manipulate other data sets. The FSLETTER procedure can be called to create letters or reports customized with information from the data set.
	FSLETTER	14	**Uses** Creating individual letters and reports Creating personalized form letters and reports incorporating values from a SAS data set **Features** Customized forms can be used to define printer characteristics. Text field highlighting can be used to take advantage of all available printer capabilities. The text editor's spelling checker can be used to verify words in the entered text.

(continued)

Procedure	Chapter	Uses and Features
Table 11.1 *(continued)* FSLIST	15	**Uses** Browsing external (non-SAS) files, including files containing output from SAS procedures **Features** Text in the FSLIST window can be copied into windows that use the SAS text editor. The hexadecimal representation of the file contents can be displayed.
FSVIEW	16	**Uses** Browsing existing SAS data sets Editing and updating existing SAS data sets Creating new SAS data sets **Features** Displays observations in tabular format. Window characteristics can be customized. Associated formulas can display computed variables and validate or otherwise manipulate field values.

Chapter **12** The FSBROWSE Procedure

Overview

The FSBROWSE procedure allows you to browse the contents of a SAS data set or SAS data view one observation at a time.

The procedure provides the tools for building end-user data presentation applications. An FSBROWSE application provides a custom display in which you can specify how values are presented and also add descriptive text. The application can also include a Screen Control Language program that

☐ displays computed values in special fields

☐ manipulates values in other SAS data sets.

The FSBROWSE procedure also allows you to call the FSLETTER procedure from within an FSBROWSE session to create form letters or reports personalized with information from the observations displayed by the FSBROWSE procedure.

Terminology

You will encounter the following special terms in the discussion of the FSBROWSE procedure. Refer to the Glossary at the end of this book if you are unsure of the meaning of these terms:

field
field attributes
format
FSBROWSE application
screen
screen entry

FSBROWSE Procedure Syntax

You can use the following statements to invoke the FSBROWSE procedure:

□ The PROC FSBROWSE statement is required.

> **PROC FSBROWSE** ⟨DATA=*data-set*⟩
> ⟨KEYS=*keys-entry*⟩
> ⟨SCREEN=*SAS-catalog*⟨*.screen-entry*⟩⟩ | ⟨*display-options*⟩
> ⟨*procedure-options*⟩
> ⟨*letter-options*⟩;

where

□ *display-options* can be one or more of the following:

LABEL
NC=*n*
NR=*n*
STCOL=*n*
STROW=*n*
TAB=*n*

□ *procedure-options* can be one or more of the following:

DEBUG
MODIFY | MOD
OBS=*n*
PRINTALL

□ *letter-options* can be one or more of the following:

LETTER=*SAS-catalog*⟨*.letter-entry*⟩ ⟨SEND=*letter-entry*⟩
PRINTFILE=*fileref*

□ The following statements are optional.

   FORMAT *variable-list format* ⟨. . . *variable-list-n format-n*⟩;

   LABEL *variable*='label' ⟨. . . *variable-n*='label-n' ⟩;

   VAR *variable* ⟨. . . *variable-n*⟩;

   WHERE *expression*;

Statement Descriptions

The following is a brief description of each of the FSBROWSE procedure statements:

PROC FSBROWSE   initiates the FSBROWSE procedure.

FORMAT   associates formats with variables in the input data set.

LABEL   assigns labels that can be used in place of variable names to identify fields in the display.

VAR   selects which variables are available to the procedure.

WHERE   specifies a condition or set of conditions that observations in the input data set must meet in order to be processed.

Requirements

The FSBROWSE procedure must have an input data set. By default, the procedure uses the most recently created data set (the data set identified by the _LAST_= system variable) as its input data set. If you do not specify a data set name with the PROC FSBROWSE statement or with the FSBROWSE command and no data set has previously been created in the current SAS session, an error occurs and the procedure terminates.

FSBROWSE Command

The FSBROWSE procedure can also be initiated by entering the following command on the command line of any SAS System window:

   FSBROWSE ⟨? | *data-set* ⟨*screen-name*⟩⟩

where

□ *data-set* is the input data set to be processed

□ *screen-name* is the associated screen entry.

PROC FSBROWSE Statement

The PROC FSBROWSE statement initiates the FSBROWSE procedure. It allows you to specify the data set to view and allows you to identify a screen entry containing information used to customize the FSBROWSE session. Additional statement options allow you to modify the display, change the default behavior of the procedure, and generate letters using the FSLETTER procedure within the FSBROWSE session.

Refer to "FSBROWSE Procedure Syntax" earlier in this chapter for a complete list of the options that can be used with the PROC FSBROWSE statement.

PROC FSBROWSE Statement Options

Some of the options that you can use with the PROC FSBROWSE statement fall into one of two special categories: *display options* and *letter options*.

display options
: provide control over the appearance of the FSBROWSE window. These options are ignored if an existing screen entry is specified with the SCREEN= option. The options are

  LABEL
  NC=*n*
  NR=*n*
  STCOL=*n*
  STROW=*n*
  TAB=*n*

letter options
: allow you to generate letters and reports during an FSBROWSE session, things that you can also do independently with the FSLETTER procedure. The options are

  LETTER=*SAS-catalog⟨.letter-entry⟩*
  PRINTFILE=*fileref*
  SEND=*letter-entry*

These options are marked as such in the option descriptions that follow.

The following options can be used with the PROC FSBROWSE statement:

DATA=*data-set⟨(data-set-options)⟩*
: names an existing SAS data set to be browsed. By default, the FSBROWSE procedure uses the data set most recently created.

  You can add a list of data set options following the data set name. The list must be enclosed in parentheses. Refer to Chapter 15, "SAS Data Set Options," in *SAS Language: Reference, Version 6, First Edition* for a listing and descriptions of data set options.

  Note: The FSBROWSE procedure ignores the data set options FIRSTOBS= and OBS=. All other data set options are valid.

DEBUG
: turns on the Screen Control Language (SCL) source-level debugger, which provides step-by-step assistance in resolving errors in SCL programs. This option is useful when you are creating or modifying an application that includes a SCL program.

  See *SAS Screen Control Language: Reference, Version 6, First Edition* for information on the SCL debugger.

KEYS=*keys-entry*

names the keys entry to be associated with the FSBROWSE session. The keys entry contains function key assignments for the FSBROWSE window.

Note: The KEYS= option is ignored when the SCREEN= option is also used in the PROC FSBROWSE statement, unless a new screen entry is being created. If you specify an existing screen entry with the SCREEN= option, the keys entry name recorded in the screen entry takes precedence over the one specified in the KEYS= option.

The *keys-entry* value should be a one-level name. The search sequence for the specified entry is as follows:

1. If you also supply the SCREEN= option with the PROC FSBROWSE statement, the procedure looks in the catalog named in that option for an entry with the specified name and the type KEYS.

2. If the keys entry is not found in the catalog containing the screen entry, or if the SCREEN= option is not supplied, the procedure looks for an entry with the specified name and the type KEYS in the SASUSER.PROFILE catalog (or in WORK.PROFILE if the SASUSER library is not allocated).

3. If the keys entry is not found in your personal PROFILE catalog, the procedure looks for an entry with the specified name and the type KEYS in the SASHELP.FSP catalog.

4. If the keys entry is not found in the SASHELP.FSP catalog, the procedure searches the same sequence of catalogs for the default keys entry, FSEDIT.KEYS.

See "Creating Application-Specific Key Definitions" in Chapter 13, "The FSEDIT Procedure," for more information on this topic.

LABEL

(display option; ignored when an existing screen entry is specified with the SCREEN= option)

specifies that variable labels, rather than variable names, are used to identify variable fields. If a variable has no associated label, the variable name is used to identify that variable's field.

LETTER=*SAS-catalog⟨.letter-entry⟩*

(letter option)

names a SAS catalog containing letters or produces letters for observations in the data set. If the specified catalog does not exist, it is created.

The behavior of the FSBROWSE procedure depends on which form of the option you use:

□   If you specify only the catalog, the procedure does not automatically produce letters (unless the SEND= option is also used). This form of the option enables the EDIT, LETTER, and SEND commands during the FSBROWSE session; these commands allow you to create and print letters for individual observations.

(LETTER= continued)

The general form of the *SAS-catalog* value is

⟨*libref.*⟩*catalog-name*

If you specify only a one-level name, it is treated as a catalog name in the default library, WORK. You must specify a two-level catalog name if you want to specify a letter name.

□ If you specify a letter name in addition to the catalog name, a copy of the specified letter is produced for each observation in the input data set. (If a WHERE statement is used in conjunction with the PROC FSBROWSE statement, letters are produced only for those observations that satisfy the specified criteria.) In this case, the procedure does not open an FSBROWSE window. A pause occurs while the letters are produced; then the procedure terminates.

The general form of the *letter-entry* value is

entry-name⟨*.LETTER*⟩

If you specify a two-level letter name with anything other than LETTER as the second level (entry type), the specified type is ignored; LETTER is used instead.

You must specify an existing letter entry. The procedure terminates with an error message if the specified letter entry does not exist.

MODIFY
MOD
opens the FSBROWSE Menu window before opening the FSBROWSE window. From the FSBROWSE Menu window, you can perform tasks that modify the appearance and behavior of the FSBROWSE window. For details, see "Creating an FSBROWSE Application" later in this chapter.

The MODIFY option is ignored (and a warning message is generated) if the PROC FSBROWSE statement also includes the SCREEN= option specifying an existing screen entry that is protected by a password.

NC=*n*
(display option)
specifies the width in columns of the FSBROWSE window. By default, the FSBROWSE window occupies the maximum number of columns allowed by the output device. The value of *n* must be at least 35. If you specify a value that exceeds the maximum number of columns available on your device, the procedure sets the window width to the maximum available width; no warning message is generated.

NR=*n*
(display option; ignored when an existing screen entry is specified with the SCREEN= option)
specifies the height in rows of the FSBROWSE window. By default, the FSBROWSE window occupies the maximum number of rows allowed by the output device. The value of *n* must be at least 10. If you specify a

value that exceeds the maximum number of rows available on your
device, the procedure sets the window height to the maximum available
height; no warning message is generated.

OBS=*n*

specifies the number of the observation displayed when the FSBROWSE
window is opened. By default, the initial observation displayed is the
first observation in the data set (observation 1). If the *n* value is greater
than the number of observations in the input data set, the last
observation in the data set is displayed when the FSBROWSE window is
opened.

This option is not valid if a WHERE statement is used with the
PROC FSBROWSE statement.

PRINTALL

prints a copy of the FSBROWSE display for each observation in the data
set. (If a WHERE statement is used in conjunction with the PROC
FSBROWSE statement, only those observations that meet the specified
criteria are printed.) If the SCREEN= option is also specified, the
custom display format is used.

The procedure output is written to the location designated for SAS
System output. If you are using the SAS Display Manager System, the
output is written to the OUTPUT window.

When you use the PRINTALL option, the procedure does not open
an FSBROWSE window. A pause occurs while the output is created;
then the procedure terminates.

PRINTFILE=*fileref*
PRTFILE=*fileref*
PRINT=*fileref*
DDNAME=*fileref*

(letter option)

names an external file to which letters produced during the
FSBROWSE session are written. By default, letters are sent to the output
destination specified in the form entry associated with the letter entry.
When this option is used, letters are instead written to the specified file.

You must use a FILENAME statement to assign the fileref to an
external file before submitting a PROC FSBROWSE statement containing
this option.

SCREEN=*SAS-catalog⟨.screen-entry⟩*

names a catalog or a specific screen entry containing information for a
custom FSBROWSE application, or where the procedure can store
features defined during the current session. If the specified catalog does
not already exist, it is created.

The general form of the *SAS-catalog* value is

⟨*libref.*⟩*catalog-name*

If you specify only a one-level name, it is treated as a catalog name in
the default library, WORK. You must use a two-level catalog name if you
want to specify a screen entry name.

(SCREEN= continued)

The general form of the *screen-entry* value is

entry-name⟨.SCREEN⟩

If you specify a two-level screen name with anything other than SCREEN as the second level (entry type), the specified entry type is ignored; SCREEN is used instead.

When the SCREEN= option is used, the procedure attempts to load a screen entry when the FSBROWSE session is initiated:

□ If only the catalog name is provided, the procedure attempts to load an entry named FSEDIT.SCREEN.

□ If both catalog and entry name are provided, the procedure attempts to load the specified entry.

If the entry is not found, the FSBROWSE session is initiated with default FSBROWSE window characteristics.

If you do not supply the SCREEN= option, any changes made to the display format are available only during the current FSBROWSE session.

SEND=*letter-entry*
(letter option)

generates a copy of the specified letter for each observation in the input data set. (If a WHERE statement is used in conjunction with the PROC FSBROWSE statement, letters are generated for only those observations that meet the specified criteria.) This option is valid only when the LETTER= option is also used.

The *letter-entry* value must be the name of an existing letter entry in the catalog identified in the LETTER= option. The value should be a one-level name; the entry type LETTER is assumed. The procedure terminates with an error message if the specified entry does not exist.

When you specify the SEND= option, the procedure does not open an FSBROWSE window. A pause occurs while the letters are produced; then the procedure terminates.

STCOL=*n*
(display option; ignored when an existing screen entry is specified with the SCREEN= option)

specifies the display column in which the leftmost column of the FSBROWSE window is positioned. By default, the FSBROWSE window begins at the leftmost column of the display (STCOL=1).

STROW=*n*
(display option; ignored when an existing screen entry is specified with the SCREEN= option)

specifies the display row in which the top row of the FSBROWSE window is positioned. By default, the window begins at the top row of the display (STROW=1).

TAB=*n*
> (display option; ignored when an existing screen entry is specified with the SCREEN= option)
>> specifies the interval used for column spacing when more than one column is necessary to display variables in the default screen format.

FORMAT Statement

The FORMAT statement associates formats with variables in the input data set. *Formats* are patterns the SAS System uses to determine how variable values are displayed. The formats can be either SAS formats or custom formats you have defined with the FORMAT procedure.

FORMAT Statement Syntax

The general form of the FORMAT statement is

> **FORMAT** *variable-list format* ⟨. . . *variable-list-n format-n*⟩;

where *variable-list* consists of one or more variable names from the input data set.

Using the FORMAT Statement

You can use a single FORMAT statement to assign the same format to several variables or to assign different formats to different variables. You can use any number of FORMAT statements with each PROC FSBROWSE statement.

Variable formats specified in a FORMAT statement take precedence over formats defined in the data set itself. Formats assigned in a FORMAT statement remain in effect only for the duration of the procedure; the FORMAT statement does not affect any variable format assignments stored in the data set.

If you are creating a new application or if you do not use a custom FSBROWSE display, the format widths you specify may affect the field widths for the associated variables. If you are using an existing application, the assigned formats determine how variable values are displayed, but they do not affect field widths.

Refer to *SAS Language: Reference* for more detailed information on formats and on the FORMAT statement. See the *SAS Procedures Guide, Version 6, Third Edition* for information on defining your own formats with the FORMAT procedure.

LABEL Statement

The LABEL statement associates descriptive labels with variables in the input data set. By default, the FSBROWSE procedure identifies each variable field in the FSBROWSE window with the corresponding variable name. Labels can be more informative than variable names.

LABEL Statement Syntax

The general form of the LABEL statement is

    LABEL *variable*='*label*' ⟨. . . *variable-n*='*label-n*'⟩;

where *label* is a string up to 40 characters long.

Using the LABEL Statement

Labels defined by a LABEL statement are not used by default. To identify fields
with labels rather than with variable names, you must specify the LABEL option
in the PROC FSBROWSE statement. Thus, the LABEL statement is useful only in
conjunction with the LABEL option. (Remember that the LABEL option is
ignored if you specify an existing screen entry in the SCREEN= option.)

    Variable labels specified in a LABEL statement take precedence over labels
stored in the data set itself. The LABEL statement does not affect any variable
labels stored in the data set.

VAR Statement

The VAR statement selects which variables you want displayed and in what
order. By default, the FSBROWSE procedure displays all the variables in the
data set and arranges the variables in the order in which they appear in the data
set.

VAR Statement Syntax

The general form of the VAR statement is

    VAR *variable* ⟨. . . *variable-n*⟩;

When more than one variable name is supplied, any valid form of variable list
can be used. See Chapter 4, "Rules of the SAS Language," in *SAS Language:
Reference* for details of variable lists.

Using the VAR Statement

Variables are arranged in the FSBROWSE window in the order specified in the
VAR statement. The maximum number of variable fields visible at any given
time depends on the width and height of the FSBROWSE window.

    During an FSBROWSE session, you can modify the display to add or remove
variable fields. See "Creating an FSBROWSE Application" later in this chapter
for details.

    The VAR statement is ignored if a screen entry is specified in the SCREEN=
option of the PROC FSBROWSE statement.

WHERE Statement

The WHERE statement defines criteria that observations must meet in order to be displayed. By default, the FSBROWSE procedure displays all the observations in the data set.

WHERE Statement Syntax

The general form of the WHERE statement is

WHERE *expression*;

where *expression* is any valid WHERE expression involving one or more of the variables in the input data set. Refer to the description of the WHERE statement in Chapter 9 of *SAS Language: Reference* for details of the operators and operands that are valid in WHERE expressions.

Using the WHERE Statement

The WHERE statement is useful when you want to display only a subset of the observations in a SAS data set. For example, to display only observations for which the variable YEAR has a value less than 5, follow the PROC FSBROWSE statement with the following statement:

```
where year<5;
```

In this case, the FSBROWSE procedure displays only those observations that meet the specified criterion. Observations that do not satisfy the condition are not shown and cannot be displayed.

Conditions imposed by a WHERE statement (or, equivalently, by a WHERE= data set option) are called permanent WHERE clauses because they remain in effect for the duration of the FSBROWSE session and cannot be canceled or modified while the procedure is active.

When you use a WHERE statement in conjunction with the PROC FSBROWSE statement, the behavior of the FSBROWSE procedure is affected in the following ways:

□ The word *Subset* appears in parentheses following the FSBROWSE window title to indicate that a permanent WHERE clause is in effect.

□ Observation numbers may not be sequential because some observations may be excluded.

□ You cannot scroll directly to a particular observation by typing the corresponding observation number on the command line.

FSBROWSE Command

The FSBROWSE command provides a handy way to initiate an FSBROWSE session from any SAS System window. The command allows you to specify the data set to be browsed or to select the desired data set from a list of all available data sets. It also provides the option of specifying a screen entry containing custom field attributes and window characteristics for the FSBROWSE session.

FSBROWSE Command Syntax

The general form of the FSBROWSE command is

FSBROWSE ⟨? | *data-set* ⟨*screen-name*⟩⟩

FSBROWSE Command Arguments

You can specify the following arguments with the FSBROWSE command:

?

opens a selection window from which you can choose the data set to be processed by the FSBROWSE procedure. The selection list in the window includes all data sets in all SAS data libraries identified in the current SAS session (all data libraries with defined librefs).

To select a data set, position the cursor on the desired data set name and press ENTER.

data-set

specifies the data set to be processed by the FSBROWSE procedure. The general form of the argument is

⟨*libref.*⟩*data-set-name*⟨(*data-set-options*)⟩

If you omit the libref, the default library, WORK, is assumed.

If you specify a data set that does not exist, a selection window is opened showing all available data sets. An error message in the selection window indicates that the specified data set does not exist.

If you omit this argument altogether and do not specify ? for a selection window, the data set most recently created (the one identified in the _LAST_= system variable) is selected. If no data set has previously been created in the current SAS session, a selection window is opened showing all available data sets. An error message in the selection window indicates that no default data set is available.

You can add a list of data set options following the data set name. The list must be enclosed in parentheses. The FIRSTOBS= and OBS= options are ignored; all other data set options are valid. Refer to Chapter 15 in *SAS Language: Reference* for a listing and descriptions of data set options.

screen-name

specifies a screen entry containing custom field attributes and window characteristics for the FSBROWSE session. The general form of the argument is

⟨*libref.*⟩*catalog-name*⟨*.entry-name*⟨*.SCREEN* ⟩⟩

You can specify a one-, two-, three-, or four-level name:

□ If a one-level name is specified, it is treated as a catalog name in the default library, WORK. If the specified catalog does not already exist in the WORK library, it is created. The procedure attempts to load the default screen entry FSEDIT.SCREEN from the catalog when the FSBROWSE session is initiated. If that entry does not already exist, it is created when the MODIFY command is used for the first time.

Remember that all catalogs in the WORK library are erased when you terminate your SAS session.

□ If a two-level name is specified, it is treated as *libref.catalog-name*. If the specified catalog does not already exist in the specified library, it is created. The procedure attempts to load the default screen entry FSEDIT.SCREEN from the catalog when the FSBROWSE session is initiated. If that entry does not already exist, it is created when the MODIFY command is used for the first time.

□ If a three-level name is specified, it is treated as *libref.catalog-name.entry-name*. The entry type is assumed to be SCREEN. The procedure attempts to load the specified screen entry when the FSBROWSE session is initiated.

If the specified screen entry is not found, the FSBROWSE session is initiated with the default display format. However, if the MODIFY command is used during the FSBROWSE session, a screen entry with the specified name is created to store customization information.

□ If a four-level name is specified, the fourth level should be SCREEN. Any other value is ignored; SCREEN is used instead. The procedure attempts to load the specified screen entry when the FSBROWSE session is initiated.

If the specified screen entry is not found, the FSBROWSE session is initiated with the default display format. However, if the MODIFY command is used during the FSBROWSE session, a screen entry with the specified name is created to store customization information.

Using the FSBROWSE Command

The advantage of the FSBROWSE command over the PROC FSBROWSE statement is that the command can be issued in any SAS System window, while the statement must be submitted from the PROGRAM EDITOR window. When you end an FSBROWSE session initiated with the FSBROWSE command, you return to whatever window was active when the command was issued. Thus, the command is particularly useful when you want to view the contents of a data set while another interactive windowing procedure is executing.

The disadvantage of the FSBROWSE command compared to the PROC FSBROWSE statement is that the command does not allow you to specify any of the procedure options or display options. You must use a PROC FSBROWSE statement rather than the FSBROWSE command to initiate the procedure with these options. You must use the PROC FSBROWSE statement to produce letters from the FSBROWSE session because the FSBROWSE command does not provide a substitute for the statement's LETTER= option. You must also use the PROC FSBROWSE statement if you want to modify procedure behavior with the FORMAT, LABEL, VAR, or WHERE statements.

Using the FSBROWSE Procedure

In the FSBROWSE procedure, observations are browsed in the FSBROWSE window. By default, this window is opened when you begin an FSBROWSE session. Figure 12.1 identifies important features of the FSBROWSE window.

Figure 12.1
FSBROWSE
Window Features

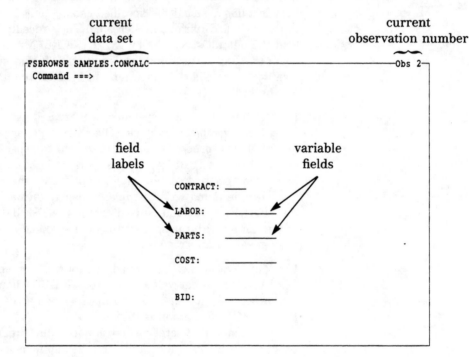

Scrolling

When the FSBROWSE window is opened, an initial observation is displayed for browsing. Scroll forward or backward to view other observations. The current observation number is displayed in the upper-right corner of the window border.

Note: The observation number is not displayed when the access method used to read the data set does not support access by observation number. For example, no observation number is displayed if the data set is compressed.

If an observation contains more variables than can be displayed in the FSBROWSE window at one time, the information in each observation is divided into discrete units called *screens*. Each screen contains as many variable fields as will fit in the FSBROWSE window. Scroll right or left to move among the screens to view the additional variables. Figure 12.2 illustrates the scrolling process for a multiscreen application.

Figure 12.2   *Scrolling in Multiscreen Applications*

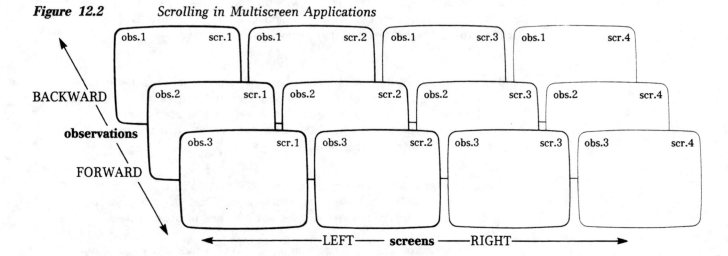

FSBROWSE Window Commands

In addition to the global commands listed in Chapter 18, "Command Reference," you can use the following commands while browsing observations:

Scrolling

n
=*n*
=*variable*
BACKWARD
FORWARD
LEFT
RIGHT

Searching

FIND *search-criterion* ⟨. . . *search-criterion-n*⟩
FIND@ *search-criterion* ⟨. . . *search-criterion-n*⟩
LOCATE | LOC *search-value*
LOCATE: | LOC: *search-string*
NAME ⟨*variable*⟩
RFIND
SEARCH *search-string*
SEARCH@ *search-string* ⟨. . . *search-string-n*⟩
STRING ⟨*variable* ⟨. . . *variable-n*⟩⟩

Creating Letters and Reports
(These commands are valid only if the LETTER= option is used in the PROC FSBROWSE statement that initiates the procedure.)

EDIT *letter-name*
LETTER
SEND *letter-name*

Other

CURSOR
END
HELP
KEYS
MODIFY ⟨*password*⟩
WHERE ⟨⟨ALSO⟩ *expression*⟩ | ⟨UNDO | CLEAR⟩

Command Descriptions

Descriptions of the special FSBROWSE window commands follow. Refer to
Chapter 3, "Browsing and Editing SAS Data Sets Using the FSBROWSE and
FSEDIT Procedures," for examples of using these commands.

n

> displays the specified observation. If the *n* value is greater than the number of
> observations in the data set, the last observation in the data set is displayed.
>
> This command is not valid when the access method used to read the data
> set does not support access by observation number or when a permanent or
> temporary WHERE clause is in effect.

=*n*

> displays the specified screen of the current observation in a multiscreen
> application. If the =*n* value is greater than the number of screens in the
> application, the highest-numbered screen of the current observation is
> displayed.
>
> This command has no effect if the FSBROWSE window does not use
> multiple screens.

=*variable*

> positions the cursor on the display field for the specified variable.
>
> This command is particularly useful in multiscreen applications and
> custom displays.

BACKWARD

> displays the previous observation.

CURSOR

> selects the position on the display (usually in a variable field) where the
> cursor is positioned each time an observation is displayed. To specify the
> position, type CURSOR on the command line, move the cursor to the desired
> position, and press ENTER.
>
> Although editing is not permitted, the CURSOR command can be used in
> the FSBROWSE procedure to call attention to a particular field or location in
> the window.

EDIT *letter-name*

> initiates the FSLETTER procedure and displays the specified letter for editing
> in the FSLETTER window. The *letter-name* value is the one-level name of a
> letter entry in the SAS catalog specified in the LETTER= option of the PROC
> FSBROWSE statement that initiates the FSBROWSE session. (The EDIT
> command is valid only when the LETTER= option is used in the PROC
> FSBROWSE statement.) If the letter does not already exist, it is created.
>
> If you use the SEND command in the FSLETTER window, fields in the
> letter are filled with corresponding variable values from the current
> FSBROWSE observation during the FSLETTER send step. When you end the
> FSLETTER session, the FSBROWSE session resumes.
>
> For more information on creating letters, refer to Chapter 14, "The
> FSLETTER Procedure." See also the LETTER and SEND commands in this
> chapter.

END

closes the FSBROWSE window and ends the FSBROWSE session.

FIND *search-criterion* ⟨. . . *search-criterion-n*⟩

locates and displays the next observation that meets the specified criteria. The general form of the *search-criterion* values is

> *variable-name comparison-operator search-value*

where

- □ *variable-name* is the name of a variable in the data set

- □ *comparison-operator* is one of the following:

=	^= or ¬=	>	>=	<	<=
EQ	NE	GT	GE	LT	LE

- □ *search-value* is a valid value for the variable.

The following restrictions apply to the *search-value* value:

- □ Character values must be enclosed in quotes if they contain embedded blanks or special characters.

- □ Character values must match the case of the variable values, unless the variable field being searched is assigned the CAPS attribute. For example, the command

  ```
  find city=raleigh
  ```

  will not locate observations in which the CITY variable value is stored as `Raleigh`. You must instead use

  ```
  find city=Raleigh
  ```

  When the variable field being searched is assigned the CAPS attribute, the value is converted to uppercase for purposes of the search, regardless of the case in which it is entered.

- □ Numeric values must be entered using the standard notation for numeric constants, regardless of the format or informat associated with the variable. For example, if a variable named COST has the informat COMMA8.2 and the format DOLLAR10.2, you must specify

  ```
  find cost=573.04
  ```

  to locate an observation in which the COST field value is displayed as $573.04.

  If a list of criteria is specified, all those criteria must be met in order for an observation to be selected. For example, the command

  ```
  find yrs=3 state=NC
  ```

locates only those observations for which the YRS variable contains the value 3 and the STATE variable contains NC. The command will not

(FIND continued)

locate observations that meet only one of the criteria. Use the FIND@ command to locate observations that meet some but not all of the conditions in the list.

After you issue a FIND command, you can use the RFIND command to repeat the search for the next matching observation.

See also the FIND@ and RFIND commands.

FIND@ *search-criterion* ⟨. . . *search-criterion-n*⟩

locates and displays the next observation that meets at least one criterion in a list of criteria. For example, use the command

```
finda yrs>1 state=NC
```

to locate an observation that has either a value greater than 1 for the variable YRS or the value NC for the variable STATE.

See the discussion of the FIND command for an explanation of the format for *search-criterion* values.

After you issue a FIND@ command, you can use the RFIND command to repeat the search for the next matching observation.

FORWARD

displays the next observation.

HELP

displays information about browsing observations with the FSBROWSE procedure.

You can also use this command to request information about a specific variable in an FSBROWSE window. Type HELP on the command line, position the cursor anywhere in the desired variable field, and press ENTER. The name and type of the variable are displayed on the window's message line. If the variable has an assigned format or informat, these are shown also.

Note: You can replace the SAS System's help information with custom information for your FSBROWSE application. Use the SETHELP command to assign a catalog containing custom help information to the FSBROWSE window. See Chapter 18 for details.

KEYS

opens the KEYS window for browsing and editing function key definitions for the FSBROWSE window. Function key definitions are stored in catalog entries of type KEYS.

The default key definitions for the FSBROWSE window are stored in the FSEDIT.KEYS entry in the SASHELP.FSP catalog. If you are using this default set of key definitions when you issue the KEYS command and you change any key definitions in the KEYS window, a new copy of the FSEDIT.KEYS entry is created in your personal PROFILE catalog (SASUSER.PROFILE, or WORK.PROFILE if the SASUSER library is not allocated). The changes you make are recorded in your personal copy of the keys entry.

Note: The FSBROWSE and FSEDIT procedures use the same default keys entry. Changes you make in the FSBROWSE window affect the default key definitions for the FSEDIT window also.

If your FSBROWSE session does not use an existing screen entry, you can specify a keys entry for your FSBROWSE session using the KEYS= option with the PROC FSBROWSE statement. If you do use an existing screen entry, the keys entry name recorded in the screen entry is used. If you issue a KEYS command when a particular keys entry has been specified, the FSBROWSE procedure looks for that entry first in the catalog containing the screen entry (if a screen entry is used), then in your personal PROFILE catalog. The first keys entry found with the specified name is opened for editing.

If the specified keys entry is not found in either catalog, all function key definitions are blank when the KEYS window is opened. If you then enter key definitions, the specified entry is created when the KEYS window is closed. The new entry is created in the catalog containing the current screen entry if one was used; otherwise, it is created in your personal PROFILE catalog.

LEFT

scrolls to the previous screen of the current observation. This command is valid only in multiscreen applications.

LETTER

initiates the FSLETTER procedure and opens the FSLETTER DIRECTORY window to display the directory of the SAS catalog specified in the LETTER= option. This command is valid only if you specify the LETTER= option in the PROC FSBROWSE statement that initiates the FSBROWSE session.

From the FSLETTER DIRECTORY window, you can create new letters or select existing letters for editing or printing. If you issue a SEND command in the FSLETTER window, fields in the letter are filled with corresponding variable values from the current FSBROWSE observation. When you end the FSLETTER session, the FSBROWSE session resumes.

Note: The LETTER command replaces the CATALOG command in Version 5 SAS/FSP software.

LOCATE *search-value*
LOC *search-value*

locates and displays the next observation that contains a variable value that exactly matches the specified numeric or character value. The FSBROWSE procedure searches for the matching value in the variable field identified in the most recent NAME command.

The following restrictions apply to the *search-value* value:

□ Character values must be enclosed in quotes if they contain embedded blanks or special characters.

□ Character values must match the case of the variable values, unless the variable field being searched is assigned the CAPS attribute. For example, the command

```
locate raleigh
```

(LOCATE continued)

will not locate observations in which the CITY variable value is stored as `Raleigh`. You must instead use

```
locate Raleigh
```

When the variable field being searched is assigned the CAPS attribute, the value is converted to uppercase for purposes of the search, regardless of the case in which it is entered.

□ Numeric values must be entered using the standard notation for numeric constants, regardless of the format or informat associated with the variable. For example, if a variable named COST has the informat COMMA8.2 and the format DOLLAR10.2, you must specify

```
locate 573.04
```

to locate an observation in which the COST field value is displayed as $573.04.

The LOCATE command only finds observations for which the specified search value exactly matches the variable value. Use the LOCATE: or SEARCH command to find partial matches.

After you issue a LOCATE command, you can use the RFIND command to repeat the search for the next observation containing the specified value.

See also the LOCATE:, NAME, and RFIND commands.

LOCATE: *search-string*
LOC: *search-string*
locates and displays the next observation that contains a variable value for which the beginning characters match the specified character value. The FSBROWSE procedure searches for the matching value in the variable field specified in the most recent NAME command. See the description of the LOCATE command for a list of restrictions on the search value.

The LOCATE: command only finds observations for which the specified search value matches the beginning characters of the variable value. For example, the command

```
locate: Bur
```

finds occurrences of both Burlington and Burnsville.

Use the SEARCH command to find matches anywhere in the variable value rather than just at the beginning.

After you issue a LOCATE: command, you can use the RFIND command to repeat the search for the next observation containing the specified value.

See also the LOCATE, NAME, and RFIND commands.

MODIFY ⟨*password*⟩

> opens the FSBROWSE Menu window, from which you can customize the appearance and behavior of the FSBROWSE environment. See "Creating an FSBROWSE Application" later in this chapter for details of the tasks you can perform from this window.
>
> If the application you are using is password-protected, you must specify the assigned password with the MODIFY command before you can modify the screen entry. See "Option 5: Modification of General Parameters" in Chapter 13 for information on how to assign passwords.

NAME ⟨*variable*⟩

> specifies the variable searched by the LOCATE or LOCATE: commands. Execute the NAME command alone to display the current NAME variable.
>
> For example, to find observations that contain particular values of a variable named DISTRICT, execute the command

    name district

> Then specify the desired district value in a LOCATE command to find observations belonging to a specific district.
>
> In a custom application, you can specify a default search variable in the FSBROWSE Parms window. See "Creating an FSBROWSE Application" later in this chapter for details.
>
> See also the LOCATE and LOCATE: commands.

RFIND

> repeats the most recent FIND, FIND@, LOCATE, LOCATE:, SEARCH, or SEARCH@ command.

RIGHT

> scrolls to the next screen of the current observation. This command is valid only in multiscreen applications.

SEARCH *search-string*

> locates and displays the next observation that contains a variable value that includes the specified character value. (The SEARCH command is only valid for character variables.) The FSBROWSE procedure searches for the value in the variable fields identified in the most recent STRING command.
>
> The following restrictions apply to the *search-string* value:

> □ Values must be enclosed in quotes if they contain embedded blanks or special characters.

> □ Values must match the case of the variable values, unless the variable fields being searched are assigned the CAPS attribute. For example, the command

    search raleigh

> will not locate observations in which the CITY variable value is stored as `Raleigh`. You must instead use

    search Raleigh

When the variable field being searched is assigned the CAPS attribute, the value is converted to uppercase for purposes of the search, regardless of the case in which it is entered.

If a list of values is specified, all the strings must occur in an observation for it to be located. For example, the following command locates only those observations for which the specified variables include both the strings Smith and NC:

```
search Smith NC
```

The strings can occur in two different variable values (if more than one variable is named in the STRING command) or both in the same variable value.

To find observations that contain some but not necessarily all of the values in the list, use the SEARCH@ command.

After you issue a SEARCH command, you can use the RFIND command to repeat the search for the next observation containing the specified value.

See also the SEARCH@, STRING, and RFIND commands.

SEARCH@ *search-string* ⟨*. . . search-string-n*⟩

locates and displays the next observation that contains variable values that include one or more of the specified character values. (The SEARCH@ command is only valid for character values.) The FSBROWSE procedure searches for the values in the variables identified in the most recent STRING command. See the description of the SEARCH command for restrictions that apply to the *character-string* value.

For example, the command

```
search@ Cary Raleigh 'Chapel Hill'
```

displays the next observation containing either Cary, Raleigh, or Chapel Hill in one of the variables identified in the STRING command.

After you issue a SEARCH@ command, you can use the RFIND command to repeat the search for the next observation containing the specified value.

See also the SEARCH, STRING, and RFIND commands.

SEND *letter-name*

initiates the FSLETTER procedure in its send step, displays the specified letter, and fills any entry fields in the letter with corresponding variable values from the current observation. The SEND command is valid only when the LETTER= option is used in the PROC FSBROWSE statement that initiated the FSBROWSE session.

The *letter-name* value is the one-level name of an existing letter entry in the SAS catalog specified in the LETTER= option of the PROC FSBROWSE statement. An error message is printed if the specified letter does not exist.

Use the END command to enter the second stage of the send step or the CANCEL command to cancel the letter. When you end the FSLETTER session, the FSBROWSE session resumes.

The SEND command provides a method for producing one letter for one observation. See Chapter 14 for information about producing a letter for each observation in a data set.

STRING ⟨*variable* ⟨. . . *variable-n*⟩⟩

identifies the variable or variables searched by the SEARCH and SEARCH@ commands. The variables specified with this command must be character variables.

For example, the following command causes the next SEARCH or SEARCH@ command to search the two specified variables:

```
string address1 address2
```

If you forget which variables are currently identified, execute the STRING command with no following values to display the current variable list on the window's message line.

In a custom application, you can specify default search variables in the FSBROWSE Parms window. See "Creating an FSBROWSE Application" later in this chapter for details.

WHERE ⟨⟨ALSO⟩ *expression*⟩ | ⟨UNDO | CLEAR⟩

imposes one or more sets of conditions that observations in the data set must meet in order to be processed. *Expression* is any valid WHERE expression involving one or more of the variables in the input data set. (Refer to the description of the WHERE statement in Chapter 9 of *SAS Language: Reference* for details of the operators and operands that are valid in WHERE expressions.) Observations that do not satisfy the specified conditions cannot be displayed.

The complete set of conditions imposed by a WHERE command is called a temporary WHERE clause. These conditions can be modified or canceled during the FSBROWSE session. In contrast, a WHERE statement, submitted with the PROC FSBROWSE statement, defines a permanent WHERE clause that cannot be changed or canceled during the FSBROWSE session and which is not affected by WHERE commands. See "WHERE Statement" earlier in this chapter for details.

The word *Where...* appears in the upper-right corner of the window border whenever a temporary WHERE clause is in effect.

The WHERE command has the following forms:

WHERE *expression*   applies the conditions specified in *expression* as the new temporary WHERE clause, replacing any clause previously in effect.

WHERE ALSO *expression*   adds the conditions specified in *expression* to any existing temporary WHERE clause.

WHERE UNDO   deletes the most recently added set of conditions from the temporary WHERE clause.

WHERE
WHERE CLEAR   cancels the current temporary WHERE clause.

Whenever you change the temporary WHERE clause, the procedure scrolls to the first observation in the data set that meets the specified conditions. When you cancel the temporary WHERE clause, the procedure displays the first observation in the data set.

Creating an FSBROWSE Application

If you are an applications developer, you can use the FSBROWSE procedure as the basis for data presentation applications. The FSBROWSE procedure allows you to tailor your application environment to suit the needs of your users. Customization can include

□ redesigning the FSBROWSE window display

□ creating special fields.

□ writing a Screen Control Language program to drive the application

□ assigning field attributes to determine how variable values are presented

□ setting the general parameters that control the FSBROWSE session.

Note: FSBROWSE applications can be used for data presentation only. No data entry or editing is allowed, even in fields for computed variables.

Because the process of creating an FSBROWSE application is the same as the process of creating an FSEDIT application, it is not described in this chapter. Refer to "Creating an FSEDIT Application" in Chapter 13 for details. Each of the auxiliary FSEDIT windows described in Chapter 13 has a corresponding FSBROWSE window that behaves in an identical manner. The following table lists the auxiliary FSBROWSE windows and their uses:

Task	Window
Customizing the FSBROWSE session	FSBROWSE Menu
Redesigning the display	FSBROWSE Modify
Defining special fields	FSBROWSE Names
Identifying field locations	FSBROWSE Identify
Writing an SCL program	FSBROWSE Program
Assigning field attributes	FSBROWSE Attributes
Setting session parameters	FSBROWSE Parms

Chapter **13** The FSEDIT Procedure

Overview

The FSEDIT procedure allows you to edit a SAS data set or SAS data view one observation at a time. You can also use it to create a new SAS data set.

The procedure provides the tools for building end-user data entry and editing applications. An FSEDIT application provides a custom display in which each data entry field has a set of attributes that can

□ assign an initial value to the field

□ restrict the range of values that can be entered in the field

□ protect the field from editing

□ require that a value be entered in the field.

The application can also include a Screen Control Language program that

□ performs sophisticated error-checking and validation of values entered in the variable fields

□ displays computed values in special fields

□ manipulates values in other SAS data sets.

The FSEDIT procedure also allows you to call the FSLETTER procedure from within an FSEDIT session to create form letters or reports personalized with information from the observations displayed by the FSEDIT procedure.

Terminology

You will encounter the following special terms in the discussion of the FSEDIT procedure. Refer to the Glossary at the end of this book if you are unsure of the meaning of these terms:

field	informat
field attributes	screen
format	screen entry
FSEDIT application	

FSEDIT Procedure Syntax

You can use the following statements to invoke the FSEDIT procedure:

□ The PROC FSEDIT statement is required.

PROC FSEDIT ⟨DATA=*data-set*⟩ | ⟨NEW=*data-set* ⟨LIKE=*data-set*⟩⟩
⟨KEYS=*keys-entry*⟩
⟨SCREEN=*SAS-catalog*⟨*.screen-entry*⟩⟩ | ⟨*display-options*⟩
⟨*procedure-options*⟩
⟨*letter-options*⟩;

where

□ *display-options* can be one or more of the following:

LABEL
NC=*n*
NR=*n*
STCOL=*n*
STROW=*n*
TAB=*n*

□ *procedure-options* can be one or more of the following:

ADD
DEBUG
MODIFY | MOD
OBS=*n*
PRINTALL

□ *letter-options* can be one or more of the following:

LETTER=*SAS-catalog*⟨*.letter-entry*⟩ ⟨SEND=*letter-entry*⟩
PRINTFILE=*fileref*

□ The following statements are optional.

FORMAT *variable-list format* ⟨. . . *variable-list-n format-n*⟩;

INFORMAT *variable-list informat* ⟨. . . *variable-list-n informat-n*⟩;

LABEL *variable*='*label*' ⟨. . . *variable-n*='*label-n*'⟩;

VAR *variable* ⟨. . . *variable-n*⟩;

WHERE *expression;*

Statement Descriptions

The following is a brief description of each of the FSEDIT procedure statements:

PROC FSEDIT	initiates the FSEDIT procedure.
FORMAT	associates formats with variables in the input data set.
INFORMAT	associates informats with variables in the input data set.

LABEL   assigns labels that can be used in place of variable names to identify fields in the display.

VAR   selects which variables are available to the procedure.

WHERE   specifies a condition or set of conditions that observations in the input data set must meet in order to be processed.

Requirements

Unless you are using the FSEDIT procedure to create a new SAS data set, it must have an input data set. By default, the procedure uses the most recently created data set (the data set identified by the _LAST_= system option) as its input data set. You can use the DATA= option in the PROC FSEDIT statement to select a particular data set. If you do not specify a data set and none has previously been created in the current SAS session, the procedure terminates with an error message.

FSEDIT Command

The FSEDIT procedure can also be initiated by entering the following command on the command line of any SAS System window:

FSEDIT ⟨? | *data-set* ⟨*screen-name*⟩⟩

where

□ *data-set* is the input data set to be processed.

□ *screen-name* is the associated screen entry.

PROC FSEDIT Statement

The PROC FSEDIT statement initiates the FSEDIT procedure. It allows you to specify the data set to edit and allows you to identify a screen entry containing information used to customize the FSEDIT session. Additional statement options allow you to modify the display, change the default behavior of the procedure, and generate letters and other documents using the FSLETTER procedure within the FSEDIT session.

▶ *Caution* . . . . *The FSEDIT procedure edits a data set in place.*
The FSEDIT procedure does not leave an unedited copy of the original. If you need to preserve a copy of the original data, be sure to make a copy of the data set before you begin editing. ▲

Refer to "FSEDIT Procedure Syntax" earlier in this chapter for a complete list of the options that can be used with the PROC FSEDIT statement.

PROC FSEDIT Statement Options

Some of the options that you can use with the PROC FSEDIT statement fall into one of two special categories: *display options* and *letter options*.

display options provide control over the appearance of the FSEDIT window. These options are ignored if an existing screen entry is specified with the SCREEN= option. The options are

> LABEL
> NC=*n*
> NR=*n*
> STCOL=*n*
> STROW=*n*
> TAB=*n*

letter options allow you to generate letters, reports, and other documents during an FSEDIT session, things that you can also do independently with the FSLETTER procedure. The options are

> LETTER=*SAS-catalog⟨.letter-entry⟩*
> PRINTFILE=*fileref*
> SEND=*letter-entry*

These options are marked as such in the option descriptions that follow.

The following options can be used with the PROC FSEDIT statement:

ADD
> creates a new blank observation when the procedure is initiated. The new observation is displayed for editing when the FSEDIT window is opened.

DATA=*data-set⟨(data-set-options)⟩*
> names an existing SAS data set to be edited. By default, the FSEDIT procedure uses the data set most recently created.
>
> If you specify both the DATA= option and the NEW= option in the same PROC FSEDIT statement, the DATA= option is ignored.
>
> You can add a list of data set options following the data set name. The list must be enclosed in parentheses. Refer to Chapter 15, "Data Set Options," in *SAS Language: Reference, Version 6, First Edition* for a listing and descriptions of data set options.
>
> **Note:** The FSEDIT procedure ignores the data set options FIRSTOBS= and OBS=. All other data set options are valid.

DEBUG
> turns on the Screen Control Language (SCL) source-level debugger, which provides step-by-step assistance in resolving errors in SCL programs. This option is useful when you are creating or modifying an application that includes a SCL program.
>
> See *SAS Screen Control Language: Reference, Version 6, First Edition* for information on the SCL debugger.

KEYS=*keys-entry*
>   names the keys entry to be associated with the FSEDIT session. The keys
>   entry contains function key assignments for the FSEDIT window.
>   **Note:** The KEYS= option is ignored when the SCREEN= option is
>   also used in the PROC FSEDIT statement, unless a new screen entry is
>   being created. If you specify an existing screen entry with the
>   SCREEN= option, the keys entry name recorded in the screen entry
>   takes precedence over the one specified in the KEYS= option.
>   The *keys-entry* value should be a one-level name. The search
>   sequence for the specified entry is as follows:
>
>   1. If you also supply the SCREEN= option with the PROC FSEDIT
>   statement, the procedure looks in the catalog named in that option
>   for an entry with the specified name and the type KEYS.
>
>   2. If the keys entry is not found in the catalog containing the screen
>   entry, or if the SCREEN= option is not supplied, the procedure
>   looks for an entry with the specified name and the type KEYS in
>   the SASUSER.PROFILE catalog (or in WORK.PROFILE if the
>   SASUSER library is not allocated).
>
>   3. If the keys entry is not found in your personal PROFILE catalog,
>   the procedure looks for an entry with the specified name and the
>   type KEYS in the SASHELP.FSP catalog.
>
>   4. If the keys entry is not found in the SASHELP.FSP catalog, the
>   procedure searches the same sequence of catalogs for the default
>   keys entry, FSEDIT.KEYS.
>
>   See "Creating Application-Specific Key Definitions" later in this
>   chapter for more information on this topic.

LABEL
>   (display option; ignored when an existing screen entry is specified with
>   the SCREEN= option)
>   specifies that variable labels, rather than variable names, are used to
>   identify variable fields. If a variable has no associated label, the variable
>   name is used to identify that variable's field.

LETTER=*SAS-catalog⟨.letter-entry⟩*
>   (letter option)
>   names a SAS catalog containing letter entries, or produces copies of
>   a specified document for all observations in the data set. If the specified
>   catalog does not exist, it is created.
>   The behavior of the FSEDIT procedure depends on which form of
>   the option you use:
>
>   □   If you specify only the catalog, the procedure does not
>   automatically produce copies of a document (unless the SEND=
>   option is also used). This form of the option enables the EDIT,
>   LETTER, and SEND commands during the FSEDIT session; these
>   commands allow you to create and print copies of a document
>   for individual observations.
>   The general form of the *SAS-catalog* value is
>
>   *⟨libref.⟩catalog-name*

If you specify only a one-level name, it is treated as a catalog name in the default library, WORK. You must specify a two-level catalog name if you want to specify a letter name.

□ If you specify a letter name in addition to the catalog name, a copy of the specified document is produced for each observation in the input data set. (If a WHERE statement is used in conjunction with the PROC FSEDIT statement, copies are produced only for those observations that satisfy the specified criteria.) In this case, the procedure does not open an FSEDIT window. A pause occurs while the copies are produced; then the procedure terminates.

The general form of the *letter-entry* value is

entry-name⟨.LETTER⟩

If you specify a two-level letter name with anything other than LETTER as the second level, the specified entry type is ignored; LETTER is used instead.

You must specify an existing letter entry. The procedure terminates with an error message if the specified letter entry does not exist.

LIKE=*data-set*⟨(*data-set-options*)⟩
names an existing SAS data set whose structure is copied when a new SAS data set is created. (This option must be used in conjunction with the NEW= option.) When the FSEDIT New window is opened, the variable names and attributes of the data set specified in this option are displayed.

You can add a list of data set options following the data set name. The list must be enclosed in parentheses. Refer to Chapter 15 in *SAS Language: Reference* for a list and descriptions of data set options.

MODIFY
MOD
opens the FSEDIT Menu window before opening the FSEDIT window. From the FSEDIT Menu window, you can perform tasks that modify the appearance and behavior of the FSEDIT window. For details, see "Creating an FSEDIT Application" later in this chapter.

The MODIFY option is ignored (and a warning message is generated) if the PROC FSEDIT statement also includes the SCREEN= option specifying an existing screen entry that is protected by a password.

NC=*n*
(display option; ignored when an existing screen entry is specified with the SCREEN= option)
specifies the width in columns of the FSEDIT window. By default, the FSEDIT window occupies the maximum number of columns allowed by the output device. The value of *n* must be at least 35. If you specify a value that exceeds the maximum number of columns available on your device, the procedure sets the window width to the maximum available width; no warning message is generated.

NEW=*data-set⟨(data-set-options)⟩*

    creates a new SAS data set. The procedure terminates with an error message if a data set with the specified name already exists.

    When this option is used, the FSEDIT procedure begins by opening the FSEDIT New window, in which the names and attributes of the variables in the new data set are defined. Use the LIKE= option in conjunction with the NEW= option to initialize the FSEDIT New window with the variable names and attributes of an existing data set. After the structure of the new data set is defined, the FSEDIT window is opened so that observations can be added. For details, see "Creating a New Data Set" later in this chapter.

    You can add a list of data set options following the data set name. The list must be enclosed in parentheses. Refer to Chapter 15 in *SAS Language: Reference* for a list and descriptions of data set options.

NR=*n*

(display option)

    specifies the height in rows of the FSEDIT window. By default, the FSEDIT window occupies the maximum number of rows allowed by the output device. The value of *n* must be at least 10. If you specify a value that exceeds the maximum number of rows available on your device, the procedure sets the window height to the maximum available height; no warning message is generated.

OBS=*n*

specifies the number of the observation displayed when the FSEDIT window is opened. By default, the initial observation displayed is the first observation in the data set (observation 1). If the *n* value is greater than the number of observations in the input data set, the last observation in the data set is displayed when the FSEDIT window is opened.

    This option is not valid if a WHERE statement is used with the PROC FSEDIT statement.

PRINTALL

prints a copy of the FSEDIT display for each observation in the data set. (If a WHERE statement is used in conjunction with the PROC FSEDIT statement, only those observations that meet the specified criteria are printed.) If the SCREEN= option is also specified, the custom display format is used.

    The procedure output is written to the location designated for SAS System output. If you are using the SAS Display Manager System, the output is written to the OUTPUT window.

    When you use the PRINTALL option, the procedure does not open an FSEDIT window. A pause occurs while the output is created; then the procedure terminates.

PRINTFILE=*fileref*
PRTFILE=*fileref*
PRINT=*fileref*
DDNAME=*fileref*

(letter option)

    names an external file to which documents produced during the FSEDIT session are written. By default, output is sent to the output destination specified in the form entry associated with the letter entry. When this option is used, output is instead written to the specified file.

You must use a FILENAME statement to assign the fileref to an external file before submitting a PROC FSEDIT statement containing this option.

SCREEN=*SAS-catalog⟨.screen-entry⟩*

names a catalog or a specific screen entry containing information for a custom FSEDIT application, or where the procedure can store custom features defined during the current session. If the specified catalog does not already exist, it is created.

The general form of the *SAS-catalog* value is

⟨*libref.*⟩*catalog-name*

If you specify only a one-level name, it is treated as a catalog name in the default library, WORK. You must use a two-level catalog name if you want to specify a screen entry name.

The general form of the *screen-entry* value is

entry-name⟨.SCREEN⟩

If you specify a two-level screen name with anything other than SCREEN as the second level (entry type), the specified entry type is ignored; SCREEN is used instead.

When the SCREEN= option is used, the procedure attempts to load a screen entry when the FSEDIT session is initiated:

□ If only the catalog name is provided, the procedure attempts to load an entry named FSEDIT.SCREEN.

□ If both catalog and entry name are provided, the procedure attempts to load the specified entry.

If the entry is not found, the FSEDIT session is initiated with default FSEDIT window characteristics.

See "Storing Customization Information" later in this chapter for details of saving screen entries. If you do not supply the SCREEN= option, any changes made to the display format are available only during the current FSEDIT session.

SEND=*letter-entry*
(letter option)

generates a copy of the specified document for each observation in the input data set. (If a WHERE statement is used in conjunction with the PROC FSEDIT statement, copies are generated for only those observations that meet the specified criteria.) This option is valid only when the LETTER= option is also used.

The *letter-entry* value must be the name of an existing letter entry in the catalog identified in the LETTER= option. The value should be a one-level name; the entry type LETTER is assumed. The procedure terminates with an error message if the specified entry does not exist.

When you specify the SEND= option, the procedure does not open an FSEDIT window. A pause occurs while the copies of the document are produced; then the procedure terminates.

STCOL=*n*

(display option; ignored when an existing screen entry is specified with the SCREEN= option)

specifies the display column in which the leftmost column of the FSEDIT window is positioned. By default, the FSEDIT window begins at the leftmost column of the display (STCOL=1).

STROW=*n*

(display option; ignored when an existing screen entry is specified with the SCREEN= option)

specifies the display row in which the top row of the FSEDIT window is positioned. By default, the window begins at the top row of the display (STROW=1).

TAB=*n*

(display option; ignored when an existing screen entry is specified with the SCREEN= option)

specifies the interval used for column spacing when more than one column is necessary to display variables in the default screen format.

FORMAT Statement

The FORMAT statement associates formats with variables in the input data set. *Formats* are patterns the SAS System uses to determine how variable values are displayed. The formats can be either SAS formats or custom formats you have defined with the FORMAT procedure.

FORMAT Statement Syntax

The general form of the FORMAT statement is

FORMAT *variable-list format* ⟨. . . *variable-list-n format-n*⟩;

where *variable-list* consists of one or more variable names from the input data set.

Using the FORMAT Statement

You can use a single FORMAT statement to assign the same format to several variables or to assign different formats to different variables. You can use any number of FORMAT statements with each PROC FSEDIT statement.

Variable formats specified in a FORMAT statement take precedence over formats defined in the data set itself. Formats assigned in a FORMAT statement remain in effect only for the duration of the procedure; the FORMAT statement does not affect any variable format assignments stored in the data set.

If you are creating a new application or if you do not use a custom FSEDIT display, the format widths you specifiy may affect the widths of the fields for the associated variables. If you are using an existing application, the assigned formats determine how variable values are displayed, but they do not affect field widths.

FORMAT statements are ignored if you use them in conjunction with a PROC FSEDIT statement that includes the NEW= option.

Refer to *SAS Language: Reference* for more detailed information on formats and on the FORMAT statement. See the *SAS Procedures Guide, Version 6, Third Edition* for information on defining your own formats with the FORMAT procedure.

INFORMAT Statement

The INFORMAT statement associates informats with variables in the input data set. *Informats* are patterns the SAS System uses to determine how values entered in variable fields should be interpreted. The informats can be either SAS informats or custom informats you have defined with the FORMAT procedure.

INFORMAT Statement Syntax

The general form of the INFORMAT statement is

INFORMAT *variable-list informat* ⟨. . . *variable-list-n informat-n*⟩;

where *variable-list* consists of one or more variable names from the input data set.

Using the INFORMAT Statement

You can use a single INFORMAT statement to assign the same informat to several variables or to assign different informats to different variables. You can use any number of INFORMAT statements with each PROC FSEDIT statement.

Variable informats specified in an INFORMAT statement take precedence over informats defined in the data set itself. Informats assigned in an INFORMAT statement remain in effect only for the duration of the procedure; the INFORMAT statement does not affect any variable informat assignments stored in the data set.

When using INFORMAT statements with the FSEDIT procedure, you should take care that the informats you assign to variables are compatible with the formats for those variables. Otherwise, you will complicate the process of editing variable values. For example, suppose the data set displayed by the FSEDIT procedure contains a variable AMOUNT that is assigned the informat 10.2 and the format DOLLAR10.2. Because of the format, values in the field for the variable AMOUNT are displayed with commas and a leading dollar sign:

```
AMOUNT:   $1,250.00
```

However, if you edit this field value (for example, changing it to $1,150.00) and press ENTER, an error condition occurs. The 10.2 informat does not allow the $ or , characters in entered values. An appropriate informat for this variable would be COMMA., which does allow these characters.

INFORMAT statements are ignored if you use them in conjunction with a PROC FSEDIT statement that includes the NEW= option.

Refer to *SAS Language: Reference* for more detailed information on informats and on the INFORMAT statement. See the *SAS Procedures Guide* for information on defining your own informats with the FORMAT procedure.

LABEL Statement

The LABEL statement associates descriptive labels with variables in the input data set. By default, the FSEDIT procedure identifies each variable field in the FSEDIT window with the corresponding variable name. Labels can be more informative than variable names.

LABEL Statement Syntax

The general form of the LABEL statement is

 LABEL *variable*='*label*' ⟨. . . *variable-n*='*label-n*'⟩;

where *label* is a string up to 40 characters long.

Using the LABEL Statement

Labels defined by a LABEL statement are not used by default. To identify fields with labels rather than with variable names, you must specify the LABEL option in the PROC FSEDIT statement. Thus, the LABEL statement is useful only in conjunction with the LABEL option. (Remember that the LABEL option is ignored if you specify an existing screen entry in the SCREEN= option.)

 Variable labels specified in a LABEL statement take precedence over labels stored in the data set itself. The LABEL statement does not affect any variable labels stored in the data set.

VAR Statement

The VAR statement selects which variables you want displayed and in what order. By default, the FSEDIT procedure displays all the variables in the data set and arranges the variables in the order in which they appear in the data set.

VAR Statement Syntax

The general form of the VAR statement is

 VAR *variable* ⟨. . . *variable-n*⟩;

When more than one variable name is supplied, any valid form of variable list can be used. See Chapter 4, "Rules of the SAS Language," in *SAS Language: Reference* for details of variable lists.

Using the VAR Statement

Variables are arranged in the FSEDIT window in the order specified in the VAR statement. The maximum number of variable fields visible at any given time depends on the width and height of the FSEDIT window.

During an FSEDIT session, you can modify the display to add or remove variable fields. See "Creating an FSEDIT Application" later in this chapter for details.

The VAR statement is ignored if a screen entry is specified in the SCREEN= option of the PROC FSEDIT statement. The VAR statement causes an error if it is used in conjunction with a PROC FSEDIT statement that includes·the NEW= option.

WHERE Statement

The WHERE statement defines criteria that observations must meet in order to be displayed for editing. By default, the FSEDIT procedure displays all the observations in the data set.

WHERE Statement Syntax

The general form of the WHERE statement is

WHERE *expression*;

where *expression* is any valid WHERE expression involving one or more of the variables in the input data set. Refer to the description of the WHERE statement in Chapter 9 of the *SAS Language: Reference* for details of the operators and operands that are valid in WHERE expressions.

Using the WHERE Statement

The WHERE statement is useful when you want to process only a subset of the observations in a SAS data set. For example, to process only observations for which the variable YEAR has a value less than 5, follow the PROC FSEDIT statement with the following statement:

```
where year<5;
```

In this case, the FSEDIT procedure displays only those observations that meet the specified criterion. Observations that do not satisfy the condition are not shown and cannot be edited.

Conditions imposed by a WHERE statement (or, equivalently, by a WHERE= data set option) are called permanent WHERE clauses because they remain in effect for the duration of the FSEDIT session and cannot be canceled or modified while the procedure is active.

When you use a WHERE statement in conjunction with the PROC FSEDIT statement, the behavior of the FSEDIT procedure is affected in the following ways:

□ The word *Subset* appears in parentheses following the FSEDIT window title to indicate that a permanent WHERE clause is in effect.

□ Observation numbers may not be sequential because some observations may be excluded.

□ You cannot scroll directly to a particular observation by typing the corresponding observation number on the command line.

The WHERE statement causes an error if it is used in conjunction with a PROC FSEDIT statement that includes the NEW= option.

FSEDIT Command

The FSEDIT command provides a handy way to initiate an FSEDIT session from any SAS System window. The command allows you to specify the data set to be edited or to select the desired data set from a list of all available data sets. It also provides the option of specifying a screen entry containing custom field attributes and window characteristics for the FSEDIT session.

FSEDIT Command Syntax

The general form of the FSEDIT command is

FSEDIT ⟨? | *data-set* ⟨*screen-name*⟩⟩

FSEDIT Command Arguments

You can specify the following arguments with the FSEDIT command:

?

opens a selection window from which you can choose the data set to be processed by the FSEDIT procedure. The selection list in the window includes all data sets in all SAS data libraries identified in the current SAS session (all data libraries with defined librefs).

To select a data set, position the cursor on the desired data set name and press ENTER.

data-set

specifies the data set to be processed by the FSEDIT procedure. The general form of the argument is

⟨*libref.*⟩*data-set-name*⟨(*data-set-options*)⟩

If you omit the libref, the default library, WORK, is assumed.

If you specify a data set that does not exist, a selection window is opened showing all available data sets. An error message in the selection window indicates that the specified data set does not exist.

If you omit this argument altogether and do not specify ? for a selection window, the data set most recently created (the one identified in the _LAST_= system variable) is selected. If no data set has previously been created in the current SAS session, a selection window is opened showing all available data sets. An error message in the selection window indicates that no default data set is available.

You can add a list of data set options following the data set name. The list must be enclosed in parentheses. The FIRSTOBS= and OBS= options are ignored; all other data set options are valid. Refer to Chapter 15 in *SAS Language: Reference* for a list and descriptions of data set options.

screen-name

specifies a screen entry containing custom field attributes and window characteristics for the FSEDIT session. The general form of the argument is

⟨*libref.*⟩*catalog-name*⟨*.entry-name*⟨*.SCREEN* ⟩⟩

You can specify a one-, two-, three-, or four-level name:

□ If a one-level name is specified, it is treated as a catalog name in the default library, WORK. If the specified catalog does not already exist in the WORK library, it is created. The procedure attempts to load the default screen entry FSEDIT.SCREEN from the catalog when the FSEDIT session is initiated. If the default entry does not exist, it is created when a MODIFY command is used during the FSEDIT session.

Remember that all catalogs in the WORK library are erased when you terminate your SAS session.

□ If a two-level name is specified, it is treated as *libref.catalog-name*. If the specified catalog does not already exist in the specified library, it is created. The procedure attempts to load the default screen entry FSEDIT.SCREEN from the catalog when the FSEDIT session is initiated. If the default entry does not exist, it is created when a MODIFY command is used during the FSEDIT session.

□ If a three-level name is specified, it is treated as *libref.catalog-name.entry-name*. The entry type is assumed to be SCREEN. The procedure attempts to load the specified screen entry when the FSEDIT session is initiated.

If the specified screen entry is not found, the FSEDIT session is initiated with the default display format. However, if the MODIFY command is used during the FSEDIT session, a screen entry with the specified name is created to store customization information.

□ If a four-level name is specified, the fourth level (entry type) should be SCREEN. Any other value for the type is ignored; SCREEN is used instead. The procedure attempts to load the specified screen entry when the FSEDIT session is initiated.

If the specified screen entry is not found, the FSEDIT session is initiated with the default display format. However, if the

MODIFY command is used during the FSEDIT session, a screen
entry with the specified name is created to store customization
information.

Using the FSEDIT Command

The FSEDIT command can be issued in any SAS System window. When you end
an FSEDIT session initiated with the FSEDIT command, you return to whatever
window was active when the command was issued. Thus, the command is
particularly useful when you want to view the contents of a data set while
another interactive windowing procedure is executing.

The FSEDIT command does not allow you to specify procedure options such
as KEYS= and ADD. You must use a PROC FSEDIT statement rather than the
FSEDIT command to initiate the procedure with these options. You must use the
PROC FSEDIT statement to produce letters or other documents from the FSEDIT
session because the FSEDIT command does not provide a substitute for the
statement's LETTER= option. You must also use the PROC FSEDIT statement if
you want to modify the procedure's behavior using the FORMAT, INFORMAT,
LABEL, VAR, or WHERE statements.

Using the FSEDIT Procedure

You can use the FSEDIT procedure to perform a variety of tasks. Each task has
its own associated window, as shown in the following table:

Task	Window
Editing observations	FSEDIT
Creating a new SAS data set	FSEDIT New
Customizing the FSEDIT session	FSEDIT Menu
□ redesigning the display	FSEDIT Modify
□ defining special fields	FSEDIT Names
□ identifying field locations	FSEDIT Identify
□ writing an SCL program	FSEDIT Program
□ assigning field attributes	FSEDIT Attribute
□ setting session parameters	FSEDIT Parms

The remainder of this chapter explains

□ how these tasks are performed with the FSEDIT procedure

□ how the associated windows are used

□ what commands are valid in each window.

Editing Observations

In the FSEDIT procedure, observations are edited in the FSEDIT window. By default, this window is opened when you begin an FSEDIT session. If you use the procedure to create a new data set, the FSEDIT window is opened after the structure of the new data set has been defined in the FSEDIT New window.

▶ *Caution* . . . . *The FSEDIT procedure edits a data set in place.*
The FSEDIT procedure does not leave an unedited copy of the original. If you need to preserve a copy of the original data, be sure to make a copy of the data set before you begin editing. ▲

Figure 13.1 identifies important features of the FSEDIT window.

Figure 13.1
FSEDIT Window
Features

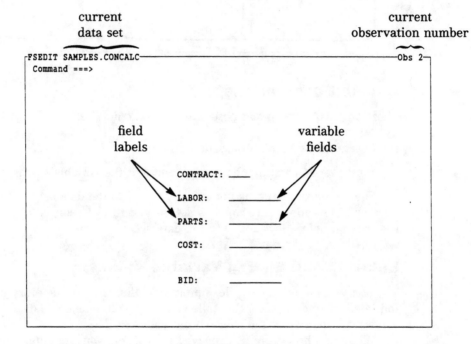

No observation number is displayed in the upper-right corner of the window border when the access method used to read the data set does not support access by observation number. For example, observation numbers are not displayed when the data set is compressed.

Scrolling

When the FSEDIT window is opened, an initial observation is displayed for editing. Scroll forward or backward to view other observations.

If an observation contains more variables than can be displayed in the FSEDIT window at one time, the information in each observation is divided into discrete units called *screens*. Each screen contains as many variable fields as will fit in the FSEDIT window. Scroll right or left to move among the screens to view the additional variables. Figure 13.2 illustrates the scrolling process for a multiscreen application.

Figure 13.2　　　*Scrolling in Multiscreen Applications*

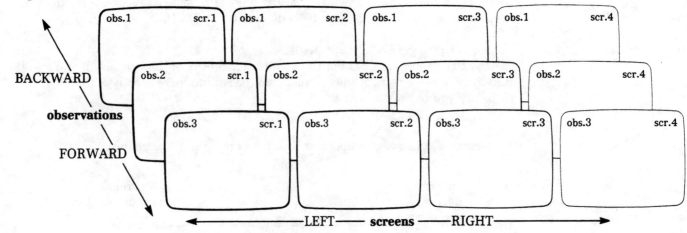

Adding Observations

There are two ways to add observations to the data set:

□　Create a new blank observation and enter variable values.

□　Duplicate an existing observation and edit the variable values.

　　The new observation is not actually added to the data set until you move to another observation, save the data set, or end the procedure. You can cancel the observation before it is added to the data set.

Entering and Editing Variable Values

To enter a value for a variable, simply type the value in the entry field (usually indicated by underscores) that follows the variable name or label. To edit a value, type the new value over the old value.

　　When an observation is displayed for editing, you can enter values only on the command line and in entry fields. All other areas of the window are protected.

FSEDIT Window Commands

In addition to the global commands listed in Chapter 18, "Command Reference," you can use the following commands while editing observations:

Scrolling

n
=*n*
=*variable*
BACKWARD
FORWARD
LEFT
RIGHT

Searching

FIND *search-criterion* ⟨.... *search-criterion-n*⟩
FIND@ *search-criterion* ⟨... *search-criterion-n*⟩
LOCATE | LOC *search-value*
LOCATE: | LOC: *search-string*
NAME ⟨*variable*⟩
RFIND
SEARCH *search-string*
SEARCH@ *search-string* ⟨... *search-string-n*⟩
STRING ⟨*variable* ⟨... *variable-n*⟩⟩

Editing Observations

ADD
CANCEL
CURSOR
DELETE
DUP
OVERRIDE

Saving Data

AUTOSAVE ⟨*n*⟩
END
SAVE

Creating Letters and Reports
(These commands are valid only if the LETTER= option is used in the PROC FSEDIT statement.)

EDIT *letter-name*
LETTER
SEND *letter-name*

Other

HELP
KEYS
MODIFY ⟨*password*⟩
WHERE ⟨⟨ALSO⟩ *expression*⟩ | ⟨UNDO | CLEAR⟩

Command Descriptions

Descriptions of the special FSEDIT window commands follow. Refer to Chapter 3, "Browsing and Editing SAS Data Sets Using the FSBROWSE and FSEDIT Procedures," and Chapter 8, "Creating Data Entry Applications Using the FSEDIT Procedure," for examples of using these commands.

n

> displays the specified observation. If the *n* value is greater than the number of observations in the data set, the last observation in the data set is displayed.
>
> This command is not valid when the access method used to read the data set does not support access by observation number or when a permanent or temporary WHERE clause is in effect.

=*n*

> displays the specified screen of the current observation in a multiscreen application. If the =*n* value is greater than the number of screens in the application, the highest-numbered screen of the current observation is displayed.
>
> This command has no effect if the FSEDIT window does not use multiple screens.

=*variable*

> positions the cursor on the entry field for the specified variable.
>
> This command is particularly useful in multiscreen applications and custom displays.

ADD

> creates a new blank observation for the data set and displays it so that you can enter values.
>
> The new observation is not actually added to the data set until you scroll to another observation, issue a SAVE command, or end the FSEDIT session. You can use the CANCEL or DELETE commands to cancel the new observation before it is added to the data set.

AUTOSAVE ⟨*n*⟩

> specifies how frequently the procedure automatically saves the data set. The *n* value determines the number of observations that must be modified (changed, added, or deleted) before an automatic save is performed. By default, the FSEDIT procedure saves the data set automatically whenever 25 observations have been modified since the last save.
>
> To check the current AUTOSAVE parameter value, issue the AUTOSAVE command without specifying an *n* value.
>
> When creating a FSEDIT application, you can change the default AUTOSAVE value by changing the Autosave value: field in the FSEDIT Parms window.
>
> Regardless of the AUTOSAVE value, you can save the data set at any time using the SAVE command.

BACKWARD

> displays the previous observation.

CANCEL

cancels all changes made to the current observation. You can only cancel changes while the observation is displayed. Once you scroll to another observation or issue a SAVE command, the changes cannot be canceled.

CURSOR

selects the position on the display (usually in a variable field) where the cursor is positioned each time an observation is displayed. To specify the position, type CURSOR on the command line, move the cursor to the desired position, and press ENTER.

DELETE

marks the displayed observation for deletion. After you move to another observation, you cannot return to a deleted one.

Depending on the access method used, deleted observations may not be physically removed from the data set, even though they are no longer accessible. To remove deleted observations, use a DATA step or any other process, such as the SORT procedure, that re-creates the data set.

DUP

creates a duplicate of the displayed observation and displays the newly created observation for editing. Duplicating an observation is useful when you are adding an observation with values similar to an existing observation.

The duplicate observation is not actually added to the data set until you scroll to another observation, issue a SAVE command, or end the FSEDIT procedure. You can use the CANCEL or DELETE commands to cancel the new observation before it is added to the data set.

EDIT *letter-name*

initiates the FSLETTER procedure and displays the specified document for editing in the FSLETTER window. The *letter-name* value is the one-level name of a letter entry in the SAS catalog specified in the LETTER= option of the PROC FSEDIT statement that initiates the FSEDIT session. (The EDIT command is valid only when the LETTER= option is used in the PROC FSEDIT statement.) If the letter entry does not already exist, it is created.

If you use the SEND command in the FSLETTER window, fields in the document are filled with corresponding variable values from the current FSEDIT observation during the FSLETTER send step. When you end the FSLETTER session, the FSEDIT session resumes.

For more information on creating letters and other documents, refer to Chapter 14, "The FSLETTER Procedure." See also the LETTER and SEND commands in this chapter.

END

saves the data set, closes the FSEDIT window, and ends the FSEDIT session.

FIND *search-criterion* ⟨. . . *search-criterion-n*⟩
> locates and displays the next observation that meets the specified criteria. The general form of the *search-criterion* value is

> *variable-name comparison-operator search-value*

where

□ *variable-name* is the name of a variable in the data set

□ *comparison-operator* is one of the following:

$$= \quad \hat{\ }= \; or \; \neg = \quad > \quad >= \quad < \quad <=$$
$$\text{EQ} \quad \text{NE} \quad \quad \text{GT} \quad \text{GE} \quad \text{LT} \quad \text{LE}$$

□ *search-value* is a valid value for the variable.

The following restrictions apply to the *search-value* value:

□ Character values must be enclosed in quotes if they contain embedded blanks or special characters.

□ Character values must match the case of the variable values, unless the variable field being searched is assigned the CAPS attribute. For example, the command

```
find city=raleigh
```

will not locate observations in which the CITY variable value is stored as `Raleigh`. You must instead use

```
find city=Raleigh
```

When the variable field being searched is assigned the CAPS attribute, the value is converted to uppercase for purposes of the search, regardless of the case in which it is entered.

□ Numeric values must be entered using the standard notation for numeric constants, regardless of the format or informat associated with the variable. For example, if a variable named COST has the informat COMMA8.2 and the format DOLLAR10.2, you must specify

```
find cost=573.04
```

to locate an observation in which the COST field value is displayed as $573.04.

□ Date values must be enclosed in quotes.

If a list of criteria is specified, all those criteria must be met in order for an observation to be selected. For example, the command

```
find yrs=3 state=NC
```

locates only those observations for which the YRS variable contains the value 3 and the STATE variable contains NC. The command will not locate observations that meet only one of the criteria. Use the FIND@

command to locate observations that meet some but not all of the conditions in the list.

After you issue a FIND command, you can use the RFIND command to repeat the search for the next matching observation.

See also the FIND@ and RFIND commands.

FIND@ *search-criterion* ⟨. . . *search-criterion-n*⟩

locates and displays the next observation that meets at least one criterion in a list of criteria. For example, use the command

```
find@ yrs>1 state=NC
```

to locate an observation that has either a value greater than 1 for the variable YRS or the value NC for the variable STATE.

See the discussion of the FIND command for an explanation of the format for *search-criterion* values.

After you issue a FIND@ command, you can use the RFIND command to repeat the search for the next matching observation.

FORWARD

displays the next observation.

HELP

displays information about editing observations with the FSEDIT procedure.

You can also use this command to request information about a specific variable in an FSEDIT window. Type HELP on the command line, position the cursor anywhere in the desired variable field, and press ENTER. The name and type of the variable are displayed on the window's message line. If the variable has an assigned format or informat, these are also shown.

Note: You can replace the SAS System's help information with custom information for an FSEDIT application. Use the SETHELP command to assign a catalog containing custom help information to the FSEDIT window. See Chapter 18 for details.

KEYS

opens the KEYS window for browsing and editing function key definitions for the FSEDIT window. Function key definitions are stored in catalog entries of type KEYS.

The default key definitions for the FSEDIT window are stored in the FSEDIT.KEYS entry in the SASHELP.FSP catalog. If you are using this default set of key definitions when you issue the KEYS command and you change any key definitions in the KEYS window, a new copy of the FSEDIT.KEYS entry is created in your personal PROFILE catalog (SASUSER.PROFILE, or WORK.PROFILE if the SASUSER library is not allocated). The changes you make are recorded in your personal copy of the keys entry.

Note: The FSEDIT and FSBROWSE procedures use the same default keys entry. Changes you make in the FSEDIT window affect the default key definitions for the FSBROWSE window also.

If your FSEDIT session does not use an existing screen entry, you can specify a keys entry for your FSEDIT session using the KEYS= option with the PROC FSEDIT statement. If you do use an existing screen entry, the keys entry name recorded in the screen entry is used.

If you issue a KEYS command when a keys entry has been specified, the FSEDIT procedure looks for that entry first in the catalog containing the screen entry (if a screen entry is used), then in your personal PROFILE catalog. The first keys entry found with the specified name is opened for editing.

If the specified keys entry is not found in either catalog, all function key definitions are blank when the KEYS window is opened. If you then enter key definitions, the specified entry is created when the KEYS window is closed. The new entry is created in the catalog containing the current screen entry if one is used; otherwise, it is created in your personal PROFILE catalog.

LEFT

scrolls to the previous screen of the current observation. This command is valid only in multiscreen applications.

LETTER

initiates the FSLETTER procedure and opens the FSLETTER DIRECTORY window to display the directory of the SAS catalog specified in the LETTER= option. This command is valid only if you specify the LETTER= option in the PROC FSEDIT statement that initiates the FSEDIT session.

From the FSLETTER DIRECTORY window, you can create new documents or select existing documents for editing or printing. If you issue a SEND command in the FSLETTER window, fields in the document are filled with corresponding variable values from the current FSEDIT observation. When you end the FSLETTER session, the FSEDIT session resumes.

Note: The LETTER command replaces the CATALOG command in Version 5 SAS/FSP software.

LOCATE *search-value*
LOC *search-value*

locates and displays the next observation that contains a variable value that exactly matches the specified numeric or character value. The FSEDIT procedure searches for the matching value in the variable field identified in the most recent NAME command.

The following restrictions apply to the *search-value* value:

□ Character values must be enclosed in quotes if they contain embedded blanks or special characters.

□ Character values must match the case of the variable values, unless the variable field being searched is assigned the CAPS attribute. For example, the command

```
locate raleigh
```

will not locate observations in which the CITY variable value is stored as `Raleigh`. You must instead use

```
locate Raleigh
```

When the variable field being searched is assigned the CAPS attribute, the value is converted to uppercase for purposes of the search, regardless of the case in which it is entered.

□ Numeric values must be entered using the standard notation for numeric constants, regardless of the format or informat associated with the variable. For example, if a variable named COST has the informat COMMA8.2 and the format DOLLAR10.2, you must specify

```
locate 573.04
```

to locate an observation in which the COST field value is displayed as $573.04.

□ Date values must be enclosed in quotes.

The LOCATE command only finds observations for which the specified search value exactly matches the variable value. Use the LOCATE: or SEARCH command to find partial matches.

After you issue a LOCATE command, you can use the RFIND command to repeat the search for the next observation containing the specified value.

See also the LOCATE:, NAME, and RFIND commands.

LOCATE: *search-string*
LOC: *search-string*

locates and displays the next observation that contains a variable value for which the beginning characters match the specified character value. The FSEDIT procedure searches for the matching value in the variable field specified in the most recent NAME command. See the description of the LOCATE command for a list of restrictions on the search value.

The LOCATE: command only finds observations for which the specified search value matches the beginning characters of the variable value. For example, the command

```
locate: Bur
```

finds occurrences of both Burlington and Burnsville.

Use the SEARCH command to find matches anywhere in the variable value rather than just at the beginning.

After you issue a LOCATE: command, you can use the RFIND command to repeat the search for the next observation containing the specified value.

See also the LOCATE, NAME, and RFIND commands.

MODIFY ⟨*password*⟩

opens the FSEDIT Menu window, from which you can customize the appearance and behavior of the FSEDIT environment. See "Creating an FSEDIT Application" later in this chapter for details of the tasks you can perform from this window.

If the application you are using is password-protected, you must specify the assigned password with the MODIFY command before you can modify the screen entry. See "Option 5: Modification of General Parameters" later in this chapter for information on how to assign passwords.

NAME ⟨*variable*⟩

specifies the variable searched by the LOCATE or LOCATE: commands. Execute the NAME command alone to display the current NAME variable.

For example, to find observations that contain particular values of a variable named DISTRICT, execute the command

```
name district
```

Then specify the desired district value in a LOCATE command to find observations belonging to a specific district.

In an application, you can specify a default search variable in the FSEDIT Parms window. See "Creating an FSEDIT Application" later in this chapter for details.

See also the LOCATE and LOCATE: commands.

OVERRIDE

cancels all outstanding error conditions, permitting you to exit an observation even though you have entered values outside of the acceptable range or have left some required fields empty. Values flagged as outside the acceptable range are recorded in the data set as entered. Values for fields in which nothing was entered are recorded as missing values.

Note: When you are using an FSEDIT application, the OVERRIDE command is valid only if the application permits overriding. Applications developers can block overriding of error conditions caused by blank required fields, values outside the acceptable range, or both. For details, see "Option 5: Modification of General Parameters" later in this chapter.

RFIND

repeats the most recent FIND, FIND@, LOCATE, LOCATE:, SEARCH, or SEARCH@ command.

RIGHT

scrolls to the next screen of the current observation. This command is valid only in multiscreen applications.

SAVE

saves the SAS data set you are editing without ending the FSEDIT session. You can issue a SAVE command at any time while you are editing observations.

See also the AUTOSAVE command.

SEARCH *search-string*

locates and displays the next observation that contains a variable value that includes the specified character value. (The SEARCH command is only valid for character variables.) The FSEDIT procedure searches for the value in the variable fields identified in the most recent STRING command.

The following restrictions apply to the *search-string* value:

□ Values must be enclosed in quotes if they contain embedded blanks or special characters.

□ Values must match the case of the variable values, unless the variable fields being searched are assigned the CAPS attribute. For example, the command

```
search raleigh
```

will not locate observations in which the CITY variable value is stored as `Raleigh`. You must instead use

```
search Raleigh
```

When the variable field being searched is assigned the CAPS attribute, the value is converted to uppercase for purposes of the search, regardless of the case in which it is entered.

If a list of values is specified, all the strings must occur in an observation for it to be located. For example, the following command locates only those observations for which the specified variables include both the strings Smith and NC:

```
search Smith NC
```

The strings can occur in two different variable values (if more than one variable is named in the STRING command) or both in the same variable value.

To find observations that contain some but not necessarily all of the values in the list, use the SEARCH@ command.

After you issue a SEARCH command, you can use the RFIND command to repeat the search for the next observation containing the specified value.

See also the SEARCH@, STRING, and RFIND commands.

SEARCH@ *search-string* ⟨ . . . *search-string-n*⟩
locates and displays the next observation that contains variable values that include one or more of the specified character values. (The SEARCH@ command is only valid for character values.) The FSEDIT procedure searches for the values in the variables identified in the most recent STRING command. See the description of the SEARCH command for restrictions that apply to the *character-string* value.

For example, the command

```
search@ Cary Raleigh 'Chapel Hill'
```

displays the next observation containing either Cary, Raleigh, or Chapel Hill in one of the variables identified in the STRING command.

After you issue a SEARCH@ command, you can use the RFIND command to repeat the search for the next observation containing the specified value.

See also the SEARCH, STRING, and RFIND commands.

SEND *letter-name*
> initiates the FSLETTER procedure in its send step, displays the specified document, and fills any entry fields in the document with corresponding variable values from the current observation. The SEND command is valid only when the LETTER= option is used in the PROC FSEDIT statement that initiates the FSEDIT session.
>
> The *letter-name* value is the one-level name of an existing letter entry in the SAS catalog specified in the LETTER= option of the PROC FSEDIT statement. An error message is printed if the specified letter entry does not exist.
>
> Use the END command to enter the second stage of the send step, or use the CANCEL command to cancel the FSLETTER session. When you end the FSLETTER session, the FSEDIT session resumes.
>
> The SEND command provides a method for producing one copy of a document for one observation. See Chapter 14 for information about producing copies of a document for each observation in a data set.

STRING ⟨*variable* ⟨. . . *variable-n*⟩⟩
> identifies the variable or variables searched by the SEARCH and SEARCH@ commands. The variables specified with the command must be character variables.
>
> For example, the following command causes the next SEARCH or SEARCH@ command to search the two specified variables:

```
string address1 address2
```

> If you forget which variables are currently identified, execute the STRING command with no following values to display the current variable list on the window's message line.
>
> In a custom application, you can specify default search variables in the FSEDIT Parms window. See "Creating an FSEDIT Application" later in this chapter for details.

WHERE ⟨⟨ALSO⟩ *expression*⟩ | ⟨UNDO | CLEAR⟩
> imposes one or more sets of conditions that observations in the data set must meet in order to be processed. *Expression* is any valid WHERE expression involving one or more of the variables in the input data set. (Refer to the description of the WHERE statement in Chapter 9 of *SAS Language: Reference* for details of the operators and operands that are valid in WHERE expressions.) Observations that do not satisfy the specified conditions cannot be displayed or edited.
>
> The complete set of conditions imposed by a WHERE command is called a temporary WHERE clause. These conditions can be modified or canceled during the FSEDIT session. In contrast, a WHERE statement, submitted with the PROC FSEDIT statement, defines a permanent WHERE clause that cannot be changed or canceled during the FSEDIT session and which is not affected by WHERE commands. See "WHERE Statement" earlier in this chapter for details.
>
> The word *Where* appears in the upper-right corner of the window border whenever a temporary WHERE clause is in effect.

The WHERE command has the following forms:

WHERE *expression*	applies the conditions specified in *expression* as the new temporary WHERE clause, replacing any clause previously in effect.
WHERE ALSO *expression*	adds the conditions specified in *expression* to any existing temporary WHERE clause.
WHERE UNDO	deletes the most recently added set of conditions from the temporary WHERE clause.
WHERE WHERE CLEAR	cancels the current temporary WHERE clause.

Whenever you change the temporary WHERE clause, the procedure scrolls to the first observation in the data set that meets the specified conditions. When you cancel the temporary WHERE clause, the procedure displays the first observation in the data set.

If you edit values in an observation so that it no longer meets the conditions of the WHERE clause, that observation can still be displayed and edited. However, a warning message is printed whenever the observation is displayed indicating that the observation no longer meets the WHERE conditions.

When you use the ADD or DUP commands to add a new observation, you can enter values that do not meet the WHERE conditions. However, once you scroll to another observation, that observation cannot be displayed or edited again while the WHERE clause is in effect.

Creating a New Data Set

You can use the FSEDIT procedure to create a SAS data set. You name the variables and specify their attributes in fields in the FSEDIT New window. After you exit the FSEDIT New window, the data set is created and the FSEDIT window is opened so that you can enter values in the new data set.

See Chapter 3 for a detailed example of using this feature.

Opening the FSEDIT New Window

To open the FSEDIT New window, invoke the FSEDIT procedure using the NEW= option in the PROC FSEDIT statement. For example, to create a data set named QTR2REV in the SAS data library with the libref MASTER, submit the following statements:

```
proc fsedit new=master.qtr2rev;
run;
```

Display 13.1 shows the FSEDIT New window opened when these statements are executed.

Display 13.1
The FSEDIT New
Window

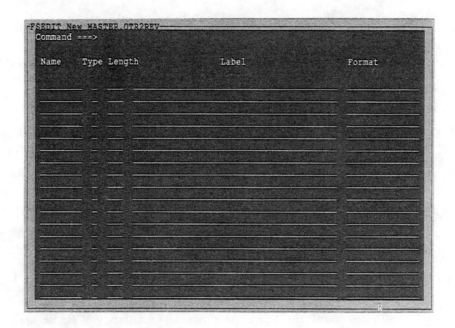

Defining Variables

The following rules apply when defining variables in the FSEDIT New window:

□ You must give each variable a name. The name must follow SAS naming conventions. See Chapter 4 in *SAS Language: Reference* for details.

□ You can identify the type for each variable. Use N for numeric or $ (or C) for character. If you leave the Type field blank, the default type is numeric.

□ You can specify the length of each variable. If you leave the Length field blank, the default length is 8.

□ You can assign a label, a format, and an informat for each variable. See Chapter 4 in *SAS Language: Reference* for a complete discussion of SAS variable attributes.

If you want to create a data set with variable names and attributes that are identical or similar to those of an existing data set, use the LIKE= option in conjunction with the NEW= option. The LIKE= option initializes the fields of the FSEDIT New window with the names and attributes of the variables in the specified data set. You can edit any of the variable names and attributes and define additional variables before creating the data set.

Closing the FSEDIT New Window

Use the END command to close the FSEDIT New window, create the data set, and open the FSEDIT window for adding observations to the newly created data set. After you execute the END command to create the data set, you cannot return to the FSEDIT New window to make structural changes to the data set.

FSEDIT New Window Commands

In addition to the global commands listed in Chapter 18 you can use the following commands in the FSEDIT New window to scroll information, to duplicate selected lines, or to exit with the choice of creating a data set or canceling it.

Scrolling

BACKWARD ⟨HALF | PAGE | MAX | n⟩
BOTTOM
FORWARD ⟨HALF | PAGE | MAX | n⟩
LEFT
RIGHT
TOP

Duplicating

REPEAT
SELECT

Other

CANCEL
END
HELP
KEYS

Command Descriptions

A description of each of the special FSEDIT New window commands follows. Refer to Chapter 3 for examples of using these commands.

BACKWARD ⟨HALF | PAGE | MAX | n⟩

scrolls vertically toward the top of the window. The following scroll amounts can be specified:

HALF   scrolls upward by half the number of lines in the window.

PAGE   scrolls upward by the number of lines in the window.

MAX   scrolls upward until the first line is displayed.

n   scrolls upward the specified number of lines.

The default scroll amount is HALF.

BOTTOM

scrolls downward until the last line containing a variable definition is displayed.

CANCEL

closes the FSEDIT New window and ends the FSEDIT session. The new data set is not created.

END

closes the FSEDIT New window, creates the SAS data set defined in the window, and opens an FSEDIT window for adding observations to the newly created data set.

FORWARD ⟨HALF | PAGE | MAX | n⟩

scrolls vertically toward the bottom of the window.
     Note: You can scroll forward only if you have filled the last blank variable definition line currently displayed, or if there are more variables to be displayed.

(FORWARD continued)

The following scroll amounts can be specified:

HALF   scrolls downward by half the number of lines in the window.

PAGE   scrolls downward by the number of lines in the window.

MAX   scrolls downward until the last line containing a variable definition is displayed.

n   scrolls downward the specified number of lines.

The default scroll amount is HALF.

HELP

displays information about creating new data sets in the FSEDIT New window.

KEYS

opens the KEYS window for browsing and editing function key definitions.

The default set of key definitions for FSEDIT windows is stored in the FSEDIT.KEYS entry in the SASHELP.FSP catalog. If you use this default set of key definitions when you issue the KEYS command and you change any key definitions in the KEYS window, a new copy of the FSEDIT.KEYS entry is created in your personal PROFILE catalog (SASUSER.PROFILE, or WORK.PROFILE if the SASUSER library is not allocated). The changes you make are recorded in your personal copy of the keys entry.

Note: All FSEDIT and FSBROWSE procedure windows use the same default keys entry. Changes you make from the FSEDIT New window affect the default key definitions for the other windows also.

Unlike the other FSEDIT windows, the FSEDIT New window ignores the keys entry name recorded in the screen entry if an existing screen entry is specified. The FSEDIT New window always uses the default keys entry or the one specified in the KEYS= option if that option is used with the PROC FSEDIT statement.

LEFT

displays the FORMAT column when the INFORMAT column is displayed or vice versa. The RIGHT command has the same effect.

REPEAT

indicates the target line on which you want a selected line to be repeated. After executing the SELECT command, type REPEAT on the command line, position the cursor on the desired line, and press ENTER. The selected line is then copied to the indicated target line.

RIGHT

displays the FORMAT column when the INFORMAT column is displayed or vice versa. The LEFT command has the same effect.

SELECT

indicates a line whose contents you want to be repeated on another line. Type SELECT on the command line, position the cursor on the line you want to repeat, and press ENTER. (Or position the cursor on the line you want to repeat and press the function key to which the SELECT command has been assigned.) The selected line is remembered; any REPEAT command issued subsequently copies the selected line to the indicated target line.

TOP

scrolls upward until the first variable definition line is displayed.

Creating an FSEDIT Application

If you are an applications developer, you can use the FSEDIT procedure as the basis for data entry and editing applications. The FSEDIT procedure allows you to tailor the application environment to suit the needs of your users. Customization can include

□ redesigning the display

□ creating special fields

□ creating a Screen Control Language program to drive the application

□ assigning field attributes to determine how variable values are presented

□ setting general parameters that control behavior of the FSEDIT session.

Note: All the following information about creating FSEDIT applications is equally applicable to creating data presentation applications using the FSBROWSE procedure.

Storing Customization Information

To create a custom FSEDIT application, you must perform the following steps:

1. Identify the SAS catalog in which information about the customized features is to be stored. Use the SCREEN= option in the PROC FSEDIT statement or the *screen-name* argument in the FSEDIT command to identify the catalog. The procedure can supply a default name for the screen entry, or you can specify a name.

2. Execute the MODIFY command in the FSEDIT window (or use the MODIFY option in a PROC FSEDIT statement) to open the FSEDIT Menu window. From there you can choose from several tasks involved in creating a customized application.

Information about the features of an FSEDIT application is stored in a *screen entry*, a SAS catalog entry of type SCREEN. All the customization information for an application is stored in a single screen entry.

Use the SCREEN= option in the PROC FSEDIT statement or the *screen-name* argument in the FSEDIT command to identify the catalog and, optionally, the entry name. When the FSEDIT procedure is initiated, the procedure looks in the specified catalog for a screen entry. If the catalog does not exist, it is created. If you do not specify an entry name, the procedure looks for an entry with the default name FSEDIT.SCREEN. If a screen entry with the designated name is found, an FSEDIT session with customized features is initiated. If the screen entry does not exist, the FSEDIT session is initiated without customized features. (The screen entry is not created until the MODIFY command is used.)

For example, if you submit the following statements, the procedure looks for an entry named FSEDIT.SCREEN in the MASTER.SCRSUB catalog:

```
proc fsedit data=master.subscrib
     screen=master.scrsub;
run;
```

If the MASTER.SCRSUB catalog does not exist, it is created. If the FSEDIT.SCREEN entry does not exist in the catalog, it is created when the MODIFY command is used for the first time.

If you submit the following statements, the procedure looks for an entry named BASIC.SCREEN in the MASTER.SCRSUB catalog:

```
proc fsedit data=master.subscrib
     screen=master.scrsub.basic.screen;
run;
```

If the MASTER.SCRSUB catalog does not exist, it is created. If the BASIC.SCREEN entry does not exist in the catalog, it is created when the MODIFY command is used for the first time. To use the customized application in a future session, users must specify the complete three- or four-level name of the catalog entry. (The fourth level, the entry type, can be omitted because the type for screen entries is always SCREEN.)

Creating or Modifying a Screen Entry

The screen entry for an FSEDIT application can hold a variety of information, including

□   the customized display format

□   a Screen Control Language program

□   attribute information for all the fields

□   the general parameters of the FSEDIT session.

Each of these elements is defined or modified in a separate FSEDIT auxiliary window. You must use the FSEDIT Menu window to gain access to any of the auxiliary windows.

Opening the FSEDIT Menu Window

Execute the MODIFY command in the FSEDIT window to open the FSEDIT Menu window. You can also open the FSEDIT Menu window at the beginning of an FSEDIT session, before the FSEDIT window is opened, by using the MODIFY option with the PROC FSEDIT statement. Display 13.2 shows the FSEDIT Menu window.

Display 13.2
FSEDIT Menu
Window

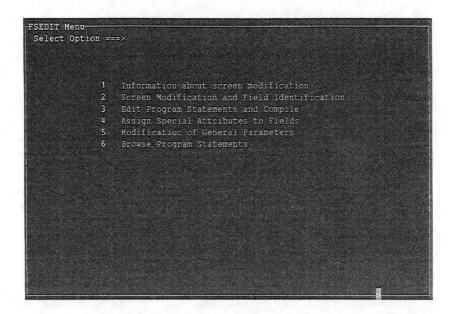

```
FSEDIT Menu
 Select Option ===>



            1   Information about screen modification
            2   Screen Modification and Field Identification
            3   Edit Program Statements and Compile
            4   Assign Special Attributes to Fields
            5   Modification of General Parameters
            6   Browse Program Statements
```

To select an option from the main menu, type the option number on the command line and press ENTER. Alternatively, you can move the cursor to the desired item number and press ENTER.

The following is a brief explanation of the available options:

Option 1   provides information about the tasks involved in customizing the FSEDIT application. This option opens a Help window; the effect is the same as using the HELP command in the FSEDIT Menu window.

Option 2   allows you to redesign the display, define special fields, and identify the variable associated with each field. This option opens the FSEDIT Modify window.

Option 3   allows you to create and compile a Screen Control Language (SCL) program. This option opens the FSEDIT Program window.

Option 4   allows you to define or change the attributes of variable fields. This option opens the FSEDIT Attribute window.

Option 5   allows you to define or change the general parameters of your FSEDIT application. This option opens the FSEDIT Parms window.

Option 6   allows you to browse an SCL program without compiling it. This option opens the FSEDIT Program window.

Later sections describe each option and its associated window in greater detail.

Closing the FSEDIT Menu Window

Use the END command to close the FSEDIT Menu window, update the screen entry, and return to the FSEDIT window. Any customized features you define using the options in the FSEDIT Menu window take effect immediately.

Note: Customization information is not saved after the current FSEDIT session unless you specify the SCREEN= option in the PROC FSEDIT statement or the *screen-name* argument in the FSEDIT command.

Protecting Your Application

You can protect the integrity of your FSEDIT application by assigning a password to the screen entry. Once the password is assigned, a user of the application must specify it with the MODIFY command in order to change customized features. Others can use your application to edit a SAS data set, but the application itself is protected from unwanted changes to the display, SCL program, field attributes, or FSEDIT general parameter settings.

Passwords are assigned in the Modify password: field of the FSEDIT Parms window. For details, see "Option 5: Modification of General Parameters" later in this chapter.

Option 1: Information about Screen Modification

Select option 1 from the FSEDIT Menu window for access to information about creating customized applications. This option opens a HELP window from which you can select topics related to the customization process. To view information, move the cursor to the desired topic and press the ENTER key. This opens another HELP window containing either text or an additional list of topics.

Some words or phrases in the descriptive text within the HELP windows may be highlighted. You can get additional information on these topics by placing the cursor on the highlighted text and pressing the ENTER key.

Use the END command to close the HELP window and return to the FSEDIT Menu window.

Option 2: Screen Modification and Field Identification

Select option 2 from the FSEDIT Menu window to create a customized display for your application. Customization is a three-step process:

1. **Modifying the display.** Redesign the display by moving fields, adding fields, or adding descriptive text.

2. **Defining fields.** Specify the attributes of repeated fields or fields for values calculated in a Screen Control Language program. This step is necessary only when you add repeated or computed fields, which are described in the next section.

3. **Identifying fields.** Specify the location of the field for each data set variable or computed value.

Step 1: Modifying the Display

The first window opened when you select option 2 from the FSEDIT Menu window is the FSEDIT Modify window. In this window you design a customized display for your application. Variable fields can be labeled more descriptively, rearranged, and even deleted. You can add comments to help users enter data in the proper format.

The FSEDIT Modify window initially contains the display format for the FSEDIT window (either the default format if a new screen entry is being created, or the previous customized format if an existing screen entry is used.) During this first step, the entire contents of the FSEDIT Modify window is unprotected, so you can type over any area in the display, including the variable names. You can move, delete, or insert any lines in the display. You can move variable fields and add any special comments or instructions that would make data entry easier.

If the modified display format you create has more lines than the number of rows in the FSEDIT window, a multiscreen application is created. Users must scroll to view the fields and text that do not fit in the first screen. Option 5 in the FSEDIT Menu window permits you to specify the initial height of the FSEDIT window.

Creating Fields

There are three important requirements for variable fields in a customized display:

□ Each field must be designated with underscore (_) characters.

□ Each variable field must be preceded and followed by at least one blank space, unless the field begins in the leftmost column.

□ If a field continues to the next set of underscores, an asterisk (*) must be placed in the last position of a series of underscores, whether the next set is on the same line or on the next line.

Note: The restriction of using an underscore as the field pad character applies only when you are identifying fields to the FSEDIT procedure. This rule does not affect the final appearance of the display. If you want to use a pad character other than the default underscore to mark the location of a variable field, use option 4 from the FSEDIT Menu window to change the PAD attribute for the field.

The number of underscores you use for a field determines the field width, the number of characters that can be entered in that field. The default width of each variable field depends on how the variable is stored in the data set and whether the variable has an associated output format:*

Variable Type	Default Width
character	the larger of
	□ the width of the variable in the data set
	□ the width of the variable's format or informat (whichever is longer), if one has been assigned.
numeric	either
	□ the width of the variable's format or informat (whichever is longer), if one has been assigned
	□ the default width of 12 (because BEST12. is the default numeric format).

---

* See *SAS Language: Reference* for a complete discussion of SAS variable attributes.

You are free to modify the default field widths when you create a customized display. For example, many numeric fields do not require the full default width of 12 positions. However, you should take care that the width of the field is appropriate for the width of the corresponding variable. Otherwise users of your application may be unable to enter the full range of valid variable values in the fields.

Special Fields

In addition to variable fields, you can create two different types of special fields:

repeated fields
repeat the values from other variable or computed fields. Repeated fields effectively provide multiple fields for a single variable. Changes made in a variable field appear in any repeated fields for that variable, and changes made in a repeated field affect the variable field as well as any other repeated fields for that variable.

Repeated fields are useful in multiscreen applications when you want certain fields to appear on more than one screen.

computed fields
display temporary values calculated or defined when a Screen Control Language program executes. Although computed fields do not have an associated variable in the input data set, they can be referenced in an SCL program and used for calculations.

These special fields are defined in the same manner as variable fields, with a series of underscores preceded and followed by either a blank or the edge of the window.

FSEDIT Modify Window Commands

When designing a display in the FSEDIT Modify window, you can use all of the SAS/FSP global commands and all of the SAS text editor commands. These commands are listed in Chapter 18. The text editor commands are described in detail in Chapter 19, "SAS Text Editor Commands," in *SAS Language: Reference*.

Note: Because the Modify window uses the SAS text editor, you can use the editor's spell checking feature. To check the spelling of the descriptive text in the window, use the SPELL ALL command. Refer to Chapter 19 in *SAS Language: Reference* for details.

Color and Highlighting

If your terminal or workstation supports color and highlighting, you can alter the attributes of the text in your customized display. Simply use the special keys on your terminal that control text color and highlighting as you enter or modify information.

When your application is used, the color information is ignored if the user's device does not support color. If you have used a color that is not available on the user's device, the procedure substitutes the available color that most closely matches the specified color.

Special Topic: Systems without Special Color Keys

For operating systems where terminals do not provide special keys to set text color and highlighting characteristics, the SAS System recognizes combinations of the ESC key and a letter or number key as commands to change text color or highlighting.

The following list shows the key sequences that select the color of subsequent text:

ESC A	gray	ESC K	black	ESC P	pink
ESC B	blue	ESC M	magenta	ESC R	red
ESC C	cyan	ESC N	brown	ESC W	white
ESC G	green	ESC O	orange	ESC Y	yellow

For example, to type text in cyan, press the ESC and then the C key. The next characters entered are displayed in cyan.

The following list shows the key sequences that select the highlighting of subsequent text:

ESC 0	turns off all highlighting
ESC 1	turns on high intensity
ESC 2	turns on underlining
ESC 3	turns on reverse video
ESC 4	turns on blinking.

Note: Some operating systems may require a different prefix key rather than ESC. If ESC does not work on your system, ask your SAS Software Consultant for the correct prefix.

Exiting the FSEDIT Modify Window
Execute the END command to close the FSEDIT Modify window. Before the window is closed, the FSEDIT procedure displays the following question:

```
Did you create any computational or repeated fields (Y or N) ? _
```

Your response determines whether you go directly to the field identification step or enter the field definition step first.

If you have added any special (computed or repeated) fields, type a Y in the space provided. You then enter the field definition step (step 2), where you can define the fields you have added. Otherwise, type an N in the space provided. The procedure takes you directly to the field identification step (step 3).

Step 2: Defining Fields

When you indicate in the FSEDIT Modify window that you have created special fields, the FSEDIT Names window is opened when the FSEDIT Modify window is closed. In the FSEDIT Names window you define the characteristics of special fields. Display 13.3 shows the inital FSEDIT Names window display.

Display 13.3
*The FSEDIT
Names Window*

```
┌─FSEDIT Names────────────────────────────────────────────────────┐
│ Command ===>                                                     │
│                                                                  │
│   Name      Type  Format         Informat                        │
│                                                                  │
│   _____   _   _____     _____                     │
│   _____   _   _____     _____                     │
│   _____   _   _____     _____                     │
│   _____   _   _____     _____                     │
│   _____   _   _____     _____                     │
│   _____   _   _____     _____                     │
│   _____   _   _____     _____                     │
│   _____   _   _____     _____                     │
│   _____   _   _____     _____                     │
│   _____   _   _____     _____                     │
│   _____   _   _____     _____                     │
│   _____   _   _____     _____                     │
│   _____   _   _____     _____                     │
│   _____   _   _____     _____                     │
│   _____   _   _____     _____                     │
│                                                                  │
└──────────────────────────────────────────────────────────────────┘
```

All the entries in the FSEDIT Names window are initially blank. Special fields added during customization are unknown to the FSEDIT procedure until they are defined in the FSEDIT Names window. Special fields are used to hold repeated values or computed values from the program. Do not confuse defining special fields with adding variables to an existing SAS data set.

Defining Special Fields

The rules for defining special fields are similar to the rules for defining SAS variables when creating a new data set:

□ Give each special field a name in the Name field. The name must follow SAS naming conventions. For repeated fields, use the exact name of the variable being repeated.

□ Indicate the type of each special field in the Type field. Use one of the following characters:

For computed fields: N for numeric fields
                         $ (or C) for character fields

For repeated fields: R (the field automatically takes the type of the
                         original variable field).

If you do not specify a value in the Type field, the default type is N (numeric computed).

□ Optionally, assign each special field a format and an informat. Repeated fields can have different formats and informats from the original variable field.

Note: For repeated fields, the first occurrence of the field in the display is treated as the original field, the next occurrence is treated as the first repeat, and so forth.

FSEDIT Names Window Commands
In addition to the global commands listed in Chapter 18, you can use the
following commands in the FSEDIT Names window step to scroll information,
duplicate selected lines, and exit, going directly into the field identification step.

Scrolling

BACKWARD
BOTTOM
FORWARD
TOP

Duplicating

REPEAT
SELECT

Other

END
HELP
KEYS

Command Descriptions
Descriptions of each of the special FSEDIT Names window commands follow:

BACKWARD
> scrolls toward the top of the window.

BOTTOM
> scrolls to the bottom of the window.

END
> exits the field definition step and enters the field identification step.

FORWARD
> scrolls toward the bottom of the window. You can scroll forward only if
> you have filled all lines currently displayed or if there are more special
> field names to be displayed.

HELP
> displays information about defining special fields in the FSEDIT Names
> window.

KEYS
> opens the KEYS window for browsing and editing function key
> definitions. See the description of the KEYS command in the FSEDIT
> window for details.
> **Note:** FSEDIT procedure windows share the same keys entry.
> Changes you make with this command from the FSEDIT Names window
> will affect the other windows also.

REPEAT
> indicates the target line on which you want a selected line to be
> repeated. After executing the SELECT command, type REPEAT on the
> command line, position the cursor on the desired line, and press ENTER.
> The selected line is then copied to the indicated target line. Unless the
> field type is R (repeated), you receive an error message warning you that
> the copy is the second occurrence of the field name. To cancel the error,
> change the name on the copied line.

SELECT

>indicates a line whose contents you want to be repeated on another line. Type SELECT on the command line, position the cursor on the line you want to repeat, and press ENTER. The selected line is remembered; any REPEAT command issued subsequently copies the selected line to the desired target line.

TOP

>scrolls to the top of the window.

Exiting the FSEDIT Names Window

When you have defined all computational and repeated fields, execute the END command to leave the field definition step. Once all special fields are defined to the procedure, you enter the field identification step where you identify the location of all special fields and any variable fields that the FSEDIT procedure has lost track of.

Step 3: Identifying Fields

The FSEDIT Identify window is opened automatically when the FSEDIT Names window is closed, or when the FSEDIT Modify window is closed if no special fields were created during display modification. When the FSEDIT Identify window is opened, the status of each field, whether a data set variable field or a special field, is determined to be one of the following:

identified   The procedure knows the field's location in the display.

unidentified   The procedure does not know the field's location in the display and prompts you to specify the location.

unwanted   The procedure knows that the variable is omitted from the display and does not prompt you for it. (For example, if you use a VAR statement to select variables to display when you invoke the FSEDIT procedure, all variables in the data set that are not specified in the VAR statement are deemed unwanted by the FSEDIT procedure.)

Before you can exit the field identification step, all fields must be either identified or defined as unwanted. When the FSEDIT procedure knows the location of all variable fields, the following message is displayed:

```
NOTE: All fields are identified.
```

If the FSEDIT procedure does not know the location of a variable field, or if you have added any special fields, you receive a prompt to identify the location of the unidentified fields.

Unidentified Fields

Fields in a customized display can become unidentified in several ways:

□   If you perform extensive editing when you modify the display, the FSEDIT procedure may lose track of the location of some variables. Previously identified fields may become unidentified.

□   If you add a variable to the data set used in the application, you must create a field for the variable in the display in order to have the new variable recognized by the FSEDIT procedure. (When you use a customized display, new fields are not automatically added for new data set variables.) A field you create for the new variable is initially unidentified.

□ If you add special fields, they are always initially unidentified. The FSEDIT procedure knows their names but not their locations.

For each unidentified field, you receive a prompt like the following:

```
Please put cursor on field: _____ and press ENTER ... or UNWANTED
```

To indicate that you are not using a particular variable in the application, execute the UNWANTED command. To identify the location of a variable field or a special field that is being used in the application, position the cursor on any underscore in the appropriate field and press ENTER. Continue to identify fields until you receive the message that all fields are identified.

For example, if you receive the prompt

```
Please put cursor on field: ADDR1 and press ENTER ... or UNWANTED
```

you can do one of the following:

1. Execute the UNWANTED command. (The command can be assigned to a function key.) The FSEDIT procedure then knows that the variable ADDR1 is purposely excluded from the display, so it does not prompt you again to identify ADDR1's location.

2. Position the cursor on the underscores for the appropriate variable field (ADDR1 in this example), and press ENTER. The variable ADDR1 changes from unidentified to identified. The FSEDIT procedure then knows ADDR1's location.

Changing a Field from Unwanted to Identified

If you change your mind about making a variable unwanted, you can use the DEFINE command. Follow DEFINE with the variable name; then position the cursor on the variable field and press ENTER.

If you want to change the status of several variables, you can use the WANTED command. When you execute the WANTED command without specifying any variable names, all unwanted variables become unidentified. The FSEDIT procedure then prompts you to identify the location of all unidentified variable fields.

Notice the difference between these two commands: DEFINE changes a single variable directly from unwanted to identified. WANTED changes one or all variables from unwanted to unidentified. You must then identify the location of each variable's field or define the variable as unwanted again.

FSEDIT Identify Window Commands

In addition to the global commands listed in Chapter 18, you can use the following commands in the FSEDIT Identify window:

Identifying Fields

DEFINE *variable*
UNWANTED ·   (replaces the Version 5 HOME command)
WANTED ⟨*variable*⟩   (replaces the Version 5 FREE command)

Scrolling

=*variable*
LEFT
RIGHT

Other

END
HELP
KEYS

Command Descriptions

Descriptions of each of the special FSEDIT Identify window commands follow:

=*variable*

> locates identified variables. To determine the location of a variable field in the display, type an equal sign on the command line, followed by the variable name, and press ENTER. If the specified variable is an identified variable in the customized display, the cursor then moves to the field for the variable.

DEFINE *variable*

> changes the status of a variable from unwanted to identified. Follow DEFINE with the name of the variable, position the cursor on any underscore of the field for that variable, and press ENTER. Remember to use the actual name of the variable instead of a label you may have given the variable in the customized display.

END

> ends the field identification step, closes the FSEDIT Identify window, and returns to the FSEDIT Menu window. This command is not valid until all fields have been identified or defined as unwanted. If any fields are not currently identified, the FSEDIT procedure prompts you to identify their locations before ending the field identification step.

HELP

> displays information about the process of identifying fields in the FSEDIT Identify window.

KEYS

> opens the KEYS window for browsing and editing function key definitions. See the description of the KEYS command in the FSEDIT window for details.
>
> **Note:** FSEDIT procedure windows share the same keys entry. Changes you make with this command from the FSEDIT Identify window affect the other windows also.

LEFT

> moves to the previous screen of an observation in multiscreen applications.

RIGHT

> moves to the next screen of an observation in multiscreen applications.

UNWANTED

> indicates that a variable field is unwanted and will not be used in this application. To indicate an unwanted variable, execute the UNWANTED command when prompted for the location of the variable field.
>
> **Note:** The UNWANTED command performs the same function as the HOME command did in the field identification step for Version 5 SAS/FSP software.

WANTED ⟨*variable*⟩

> changes the status of a specified variable from unwanted to unidentified. If you do not specify a particular variable, all unwanted variables are changed to unidentified variables. Once a variable becomes unidentified rather than unwanted, the FSEDIT procedure prompts you to identify its location.
>
> **Note:** The WANTED command (when used without a variable name) performs the same function as the FREE command did in the field identification step for Version 5 SAS/FSP software.

Exiting the FSEDIT Identify Window

You cannot exit the field identification step until you have identified the locations of the fields for all wanted variables and have received the following message:

```
NOTE: All fields are identified.
```

After receiving this message, you can execute the END command to close the FSEDIT Identify window and return to the FSEDIT Menu window.

Option 3: Edit Program Statements and Compile

Select option 3 from the FSEDIT Menu window to create, compile, and save a Screen Control Language program for your FSEDIT application. This option opens the FSEDIT Program window, in which you can use all of the SAS text editor commands to enter and edit SCL program statements. Use the END command to compile and save the SCL program in the current screen entry, close the FSEDIT Program window, and return to the FSEDIT Menu window.

Using Screen Control Language

Screen Control Language (SCL) allows you to add power and flexibility to your FSEDIT applications. You can write SCL programs that

- □ cross-validate values entered in FSEDIT window fields with other variable values in the same SAS data set

- □ cross-validate values entered in FSEDIT window fields with variable values in other SAS data sets

□ manipulate field values based on user input

□ manipulate values in other SAS data sets

□ manipulate external (non-SAS) files

□ provide custom messages and help based on user input.

See Chapter 10, "Enhancing Data Entry Applications Using Screen Control Language," for examples of using SCL with FSEDIT applications. For complete documentation of SCL, see *SAS Screen Control Language: Reference.*

Option 4: Assign Special Attributes to Fields

Select option 4 from the FSEDIT Menu window to define the attributes of each field in the FSEDIT display. This option opens the FSEDIT Attribute window. Use the END command to close the FSEDIT Attribute window and return to the FSEDIT Menu window.

Field Attributes

Field attributes make it easier for users of your application to enter and edit data correctly. Each field has the following attributes:

INITIAL	provides an initial value of the field.
MAXIMUM	determines the maximum value for the field.
MINIMUM	determines the minimum value for the field.
REQUIRED	controls whether a value must be entered in the field when a new observation is added.
CAPS	controls whether text in the field is forced to uppercase.
FCOLOR	selects text color when the field contains a valid value.
ECOLOR	selects text color when the field contains an invalid value.
FATTR	selects the text highlighting attribute when the field contains a valid value.
EATTR	selects the text highlighting attribute when the field contains an invalid value.
PAD	determines the pad character for the field.
PROTECT	controls whether the field value can be edited.
JUSTIFY	determines text alignment for the field.
NONDISPLAY	controls whether text in the field is visible.
NOAUTOSKIP	determines cursor behavior for the field.

FSEDIT Attribute Window Frames

The FSEDIT Attribute window is divided into a series of frames, one for each field attribute. Each frame of the FSEDIT Attribute window defines the status of a particular attribute for all the fields in the customized display. Each frame uses the customized display format created for the application.

Scrolling in the FSEDIT Attribute Window

Field attribute frames are stored in the order shown in the preceding list. You can move from one field attribute frame to another using the BACKWARD and FORWARD commands. You can also display the frame for a particular attribute by typing its name on the command line and pressing ENTER.

For multiscreen applications, each field attribute frame is also divided into screens. Use the LEFT and RIGHT commands to display fields on successive screens. Use the END command to close the FSEDIT Attribute window and return to the FSEDIT Menu window.

Attribute Frame Descriptions

Descriptions of each of the attribute frames follow:

INITIAL

> assigns initial values to fields. Values entered in the fields of this frame are displayed instead of pad characters in the corresponding fields for all new observations added to the data set. Initial values assigned in this frame do not affect existing values in the data set.

MAXIMUM

> designates the maximum value allowed for fields. If a data value is entered that is greater than the maximum value for that field, an error condition occurs.
>
> This attribute is valid for character fields as well as numeric fields. For character fields, the "greater than" comparison is based on the operating system's character collating sequence.
>
> By default, users of your application can use the OVERRIDE command to override the error condition caused by entering a value greater than the specified maximum. This allows the value to be stored in the data set. You can prevent this by indicating in the Override on errors: field of the FSEDIT Parms window that overriding is disallowed. See "Option 5: Modification of General Parameters" later in this chapter for details.

MINIMUM

> designates the minimum value allowed for fields. If a data value is entered that is less than the minimum value for that field, an error condition occurs.
>
> This attribute is valid for character fields as well as numeric fields. For character fields, the "less than" comparison is based on the operating system's character collating sequence.
>
> By default, users of your application can use the OVERRIDE command to override the error condition caused by entering a value less than the specified minimum. This allows the value to be stored in the data set. You can prevent this by indicating in the Override on errors: field of the FSEDIT Parms window that overriding is disallowed. See "Option 5: Modification of General Parameters" later in this chapter for details.

REQUIRED

> indicates required fields. When the FSEDIT application is used to add a new observation to the data set, all required fields must be given a value before the user can leave the observation. A blank or missing value is not considered a valid value unless, in the case of numeric variables, it is a special missing value.

(REQUIRED continued)

Type an R in the first position of a field of this frame to indicate a required field.

By default, users of your application can use the OVERRIDE command to override the error condition caused by attempting to leave an observation without providing a value for a required field. You can prevent this by indicating in the Override on required: field of the FSEDIT Parms window that overriding is disallowed. See "Option 5: Modification of General Parameters" later in this chapter for details.

▶ *Caution*................. ***Do not assign this attribute to a field that is also assigned the PROTECTED attribute.***

Doing so will put users of your application in the paradoxical situation of having to enter a value in a field that does not allow data entry. ▲

CAPS

indicates fields in which entered values are automatically capitalized (converted to all uppercase characters). This attribute has no effect on fields for numeric variables.

Type a C in the first position of a field of this frame to indicate that the field value is automatically capitalized. By default, all fields initially have this attribute when you create a new custom display. To allow lowercase letters to remain lowercase in a field for which the CAPS attribute is currently specified, type an underscore or blank space over the C in the field.

FCOLOR

indicates the color of each field. If the user's device does not support extended color attributes, this information is ignored.

Type the character corresponding to the desired color in each field of this frame. See the list of color codes later in this section. The initial color code for all fields is Y (yellow).

ECOLOR

indicates the color of the field when an error condition involving the field is detected. You can use this attribute to draw attention to data entry errors. If the user's device does not support extended color attributes, this information is ignored.

Type the character corresponding to the desired color in each field of this frame. See the list of color codes later in this section. The initial color code for all fields is R (red).

FATTR

indicates the highlighting attribute of each field.

Type the character corresponding to the desired highlighting attribute in each field of this frame. See the list of highlighting attribute codes later in this section. There is no default highlighting attribute.

EATTR

indicates the highlighting attribute of each field when an error condition involving the field is detected. You can use highlighting to draw attention to data entry errors. If the user's device does not support extended highlighting attributes, this information is ignored.

Type the character corresponding to the desired highlighting attribute in each field of this frame. See the list of highlighting attribute codes later in this section. The initial highlighting attribute code for all fields is H (high intensity).

PAD

specifies the character used to display fields in which no value has been entered.

Type the desired pad character in the first position of each field of this frame. (After you press ENTER, all positions in the field are filled with the specified pad character.) The initial pad character for all fields is the underscore (_).

When the FSEDIT procedure processes the value entered in a padded field, it converts any pad characters remaining in the field to blanks. Therefore, it is best to choose a pad character that is not likely to be contained in a value for that field.

Note: To include pad characters in field values, you can edit the field value after initial data entry. For example, if you include an underscore character in text entered in a field that is padded with underscores, the entered underscore is converted to a blank when the value is processed. However, padding is not used after a value is entered in the field, so you can then immediately edit the field value to restore the desired underscore.

PROTECT

indicates protected fields. Values in protected fields in existing observations cannot be changed. When new observations are added, values cannot be entered in protected fields.

Type a P in the first position of a field of this frame to indicate a protected field.

▶ *Caution*................*Do not assign this attribute to a field that is also assigned the REQUIRED attribute.*

Doing so will put users of your application in the paradoxical situation of having to enter a value in a field that does not allow data entry. ▲

JUSTIFY

indicates the alignment of values in fields.

Type one of the following values in the fields of this frame:

L   aligns values against the left side of the field.

R   aligns values against the right side of the field.

C   centers values in the field.

If you leave a field in this frame blank, the corresponding field in the application display is right-aligned if numeric type or left-aligned if character type (unless the $CHAR. format is used).

NONDISPLAY

indicates fields in which values are not visible. This attribute does not prevent values from being entered in a field; it prevents values typed in a field from appearing on the display. This attribute is useful for protecting fields that contain passwords or other sensitive information.

Type an N in the first position of a field of this frame to prevent values from being displayed in the corresponding field of the application display.

NOAUTOSKIP

indicates fields that the cursor does not leave unless explicitly moved. By default, when the user types a character in the last position of a field the cursor jumps to the first position in the next field. When this attribute is specified, the cursor does not automatically jump to the next field.

Type an N in the first position of a field of this frame to prevent automatic cursor skipping from the corresponding field of the application display.

Codes for Color and Highlighting Attributes

The following codes are valid for the FCOLOR and ECOLOR field attributes:

B blue	G green	W white	A gray
R red	C cyan	K black	N brown
P pink	Y yellow	M magenta	O orange

When your application is used, the color attributes are ignored if the user's device does not support color. If you specify a color that is not available on the user's device, the procedure substitutes the available color that most closely matches the specified color.

The following codes are valid for the FATTR and EATTR field attributes:

H   high intensity
U   underlining
R   reverse video
B   blinking

Most monochrome devices support only high intensity and underlining. If a user's device does not support the highlighting attributes you specify, the highlighting attribute assignments are simply ignored. You can, therefore, assign these field attributes even though the application may not always be used on a device that allows users to take advantage of color and highlighting.

Option 5: Modification of General Parameters

Select option 5 from the FSEDIT Menu window to view or modify the current parameter settings for your FSEDIT application. This option opens the FSEDIT

Parms window. Use the END command to close the FSEDIT Parms window and return to the FSEDIT Menu window.

Display 13.4 shows the FSEDIT Parms window for a typical application.

Display 13.4
Parameter
Modification

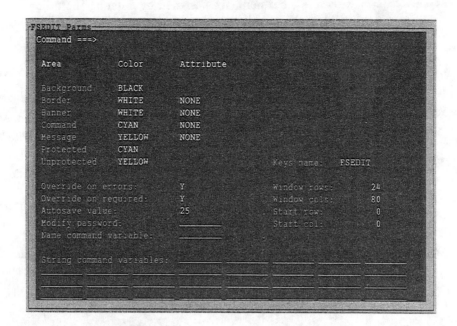

Parameter Fields

To change one of the general parameters of the FSEDIT session, modify the value in the corresponding parameter field. (If the field has a current value, simply type over it.) Descriptions of the available parameter fields follow:

Color

On devices that support color, you can change the default colors of protected and unprotected text and other window features. The following values are valid in the Color fields:

BLUE	GREEN	WHITE	GRAY
RED	CYAN	BLACK	BROWN
PINK	YELLOW	MAGENTA	ORANGE

If a specified color is not available on a user's device, the procedure substitutes the available color that most closely matches the specified color. Some devices do not allow changing the background color; for these devices, the background color parameter is ignored.

Note: If you change the color values in the Protected and Unprotected fields of this window, the specified colors override the colors you used when you created the custom display for the application in the FSEDIT Modify window.

Highlighting attribute

On devices that support extended highlighting attributes, you can assign a highlighting attribute to specified areas in the window. Note that you are not allowed to assign a highlighting attribute for the background or for protected or unprotected fields. The other areas accept highlighting

(Highlighting continued)

attributes, but none are assigned by default. The following values are valid in the Highlight fields:

H   high intensity
B   blinking
U   underlining
R   reverse video

When the FSEDIT window is displayed, any parameter that specifies a highlighting attribute not available on the device is ignored.

Keys name

This parameter identifies the keys entry containing function key assignments for the application. The default is FSEDIT, which selects the default entry FSEDIT.KEYS. The FSEDIT procedure searches for the specified entry in the following catalogs in the order shown:

1. the catalog identified in the SCREEN= option of the PROC FSEDIT statement or the *screen-name* parameter of the FSEDIT command

2. SASUSER.PROFILE (or WORK.PROFILE if the SASUSER library is not allocated)

3. SASHELP.FSP.

If the specified entry is not found, the default FSEDIT key definitions are used.

Override on errors

This parameter determines whether users of your application are allowed to use the OVERRIDE command to exit an observation even though one or more fields contain invalid values (such as a value outside the acceptable range assigned by the MINIMUM and MAXIMUM attributes).

Specify Y in this field if you want to allow the OVERRIDE command in value error situations. Specify N to prevent users from exiting an observation without supplying a value within an acceptable range. Y is the default.

Override on required

This parameter determines whether users of your application are allowed to use the OVERRIDE command to exit an observation even though one or more fields that have been assigned the REQUIRED attribute contain no value.

Specify Y in this field if you want to allow the OVERRIDE command in required error situations. Specify N to prevent users from exiting an observation without supplying values for all required fields. Y is the default.

Autosave value

The AUTOSAVE parameter determines how frequently the data set used by the application is automatically saved. By default, AUTOSAVE is set to 25, which means that the data set is automatically saved after each group of 25 observations is entered, edited, or deleted.

The AUTOSAVE parameter can also be set using the AUTOSAVE command.

Modify password
You can protect your customized application by assigning it a password. Once you assign a value in the password parameter field, users of the application must specify the password with the MODIFY command in order to modify the screen entry. Also, once you assign a password, the MODIFY option is no longer valid in the PROC FSEDIT statement.

Name command variable
You can assign a default variable to search with the LOCATE command in your application. If you specify a search variable here, users do not have to execute a NAME command before using the LOCATE or LOCATE: commands in the FSEDIT window.

String command variables
You can specify up to 29 variables to search for embedded text with the SEARCH command in your application. If you specify search variables here, users do not have to execute a STRING command before using the SEARCH or SEARCH@ commands in the FSEDIT window.

Rows and columns
You can specify the height and width (in rows and columns) of the FSEDIT window for your application. You can position the FSEDIT window within the display by specifying the row and column for the upper-left corner of the window.

Commands Versus Parameter Settings

Values for the NAME, STRING, and AUTOSAVE parameters, described above, are saved when the FSEDIT Menu window is closed. Users can override the stored parameter values (for the duration of an FSEDIT session) by executing the NAME, STRING, or AUTOSAVE commands in the FSEDIT window. If a user opens the FSEDIT Menu during an FSEDIT session, any changes made with the NAME, STRING, and AUTOSAVE commands in the FSEDIT window are automatically saved with the customized information.

Option 6: Browse Program Statements

Select option 6 from the FSEDIT Menu window to browse the current contents of the FSEDIT Program window. When you open the FSEDIT Program window with this option, all the SAS text editor browsing commands are valid, but editing the SCL program is prohibited. Use the END command to close the FSEDIT Program window and return to the FSEDIT Menu window.

Creating Application-Specific Key Definitions

The FSEDIT procedure allows you to specify a customized set of function key assignments. This gives you control over which commands the function keys execute in your application.

By default, the FSEDIT procedure uses the function key assignments defined in the FSEDIT.KEYS entry in the SASHELP.FSP catalog. This is one of the standard catalogs defined automatically when a SAS session is initiated. The SASHELP.FSP catalog is shared by all SAS users at your site, so when you use the KEYS command in the FSEDIT window, the procedure creates a copy of the FSEDIT.KEYS entry in your personal PROFILE catalog (SASUSER.PROFILE, or WORK.PROFILE if the SASUSER library is not allocated). This copy is then used in subsequent FSEDIT sessions.

You can use the KEYS= option with the PROC FSEDIT statement to select a different keys entry for your FSEDIT session. When you use the KEYS= option, the procedure searches the following catalogs in the order shown for the specified keys entry:

1. the SAS catalog identified in the SCREEN= option, if that option was also used with the PROC FSEDIT statement

2. SASUSER.PROFILE (or WORK.PROFILE if the SASUSER library is not allocated)

3. SASHELP.FSP.

If the specified keys entry is not found, a blank keys entry with the specified name is created in the catalog identified in the SCREEN= option, or in your personal PROFILE catalog if the SCREEN= option was not used with the PROC FSEDIT statement.

When you use the MODIFY command to create a new screen entry, the keys entry used at the time the screen entry is created is recorded in the Keys name: parameter field in the FSEDIT Parms window. (See "Option 5: Modification of General Parameters" earlier in this chapter for details of the FSEDIT Parms window.) If you do not use the KEYS= option in the PROC FSEDIT statement that initiates the FSEDIT session, the keys entry name is FSEDIT.

Once a screen entry is created, the keys entry name specified in the screen entry parameter takes precedence over one specified in a KEYS= option. For example, assume that you have previously created a screen entry named DISPLAY.SCREEN in the MASTER.CUSTOM catalog, and that the Keys name parameter specified in the screen entry is MYKEYS. If you then submit the following statements, the procedure uses the keys entry MYKEYS.KEYS (specified in the screen entry) rather than the EDKEYS.KEYS entry (specified in the KEYS= option).

```
proc fsedit data=master.subscrib
     screen=master.custom.display.screen
     keys=edkeys;
run;
```

The procedure looks for the keys entry MYKEYS.KEYS in the MASTER.CUSTOM catalog, then in SASUSER.PROFILE (or WORK.PROFILE), then in SASHELP.FSP. If it is not found, a blank keys entry is created.

Note: The FSEDIT New window always uses the keys entry specified in the KEYS= option or the default entry FSEDIT.KEYS, not the one specified in the screen entry.

You can change the associated keys entry during an FSEDIT session using option 5 in the FSEDIT Menu window. Use the MODIFY command to open the FSEDIT Menu window; then select option 5 to open the FSEDIT Parms window. Enter the name of the desired keys entry in the Keys name: field. The new value takes effect immediately. If the specified entry is not found in the current screen catalog (or in your PROFILE catalog or SASHELP.FSP), a new blank keys entry is created in the screen catalog if one has been identified; otherwise, the entry is created in your personal PROFILE catalog.

Chapter **14** The FSLETTER Procedure

Overview

The FSLETTER procedure allows you to create, edit, and print letters and other documents. When creating and editing documents in the FSLETTER window, you can use all the features of the SAS text editor, including the spelling checker.

Your FSLETTER documents can include named fields. When the document is printed, you can fill in these fields manually or the procedure can fill the fields automatically using values from a SAS data set. This is convenient for creating and maintaining form letters, for example. You can print individual copies of the document or automatically print a copy for every observation in a data set.

You can enter the FSLETTER procedure from the FSBROWSE and FSEDIT procedures. See Chapter 12, "The FSBROWSE Procedure," and Chapter 13, "The FSEDIT Procedure," for details of the LETTER, EDIT, and SEND commands that allow you to do this.

Terminology

You will encounter the following terms in the discussion of the FSLETTER procedure. Refer to the Glossary at the end of this book if you are unsure of the meaning of these terms:

field

field attributes

form

letter entry

FSLETTER Procedure Syntax

You can use the following statements to invoke the FSLETTER procedure:

□   The PROC FSLETTER statement is required.

> **PROC FSLETTER** LETTER=*SAS-catalog*⟨*.catalog-entry*⟩
> ⟨DATA=*data-set*⟩
> ⟨PRINTFILE=*fileref* | *'actual-filename'*⟩;

□   The following statement is optional.

> **WHERE** *expression;*

Statement Descriptions

The following is a brief description of each of the FSLETTER procedure statements:

PROC FSLETTER   initiates the FSLETTER procedure and names the SAS catalog in which documents created with the procedure are stored.

WHERE   specifies a condition or set of conditions that observations in an input data set must meet in order to be used for filling variable fields. This statement is valid only when the DATA= option is used in the PROC FSLETTER statement to identify the data set.

Requirements

You must specify a SAS catalog when you initiate the FSLETTER procedure. Documents created using the procedure are stored in this catalog.

FSLETTER Command

The FSLETTER procedure can also be initiated by entering the following command on the command line of any SAS System window:

FSLETTER 〈? | *SAS-catalog*〈.*catalog-entry*〉〉

PROC FSLETTER Statement

The PROC FSLETTER statement initiates the FSLETTER procedure and specifies the SAS catalog in which documents created with the procedure are stored. It allows you to specify a data set used to fill variable fields when the document is printed, as well as an external file in which procedure output is stored.

Refer to "FSLETTER Procedure Syntax" earlier in this chapter for a complete list of the arguments that can be used with the PROC FSLETTER statement.

PROC FSLETTER Statement
Requirements

You must use the LETTER= argument in the PROC FSLETTER statement. This argument identifies the catalog in which documents, forms, and editor parameters created using the FSLETTER procedure are stored. If the specified catalog does not exist, it is created. The argument can also be used to specify a particular entry to edit. The procedure terminates with an error message if this argument is omitted.

Valid forms of the LETTER= argument are

LETTER=*SAS-catalog*⟨*.catalog-entry*⟩
CATALOG=*SAS-catalog*⟨*.catalog-entry*⟩
CAT=*SAS-catalog*⟨*.catalog-entry*⟩
C=*SAS-catalog*⟨*.catalog-entry*⟩

The general form of the *SAS-catalog* value is

⟨*libref.*⟩*catalog-name*

If you specify a one-level name, it is treated as a catalog name in the default library, WORK. Remember that the contents of the WORK library are erased at the end of each SAS session. Use a two-level catalog name to permanently store your work. You must use a two-level catalog name if you want to specify a catalog entry name.
The general form of the *catalog-entry* value is

entry-name⟨*.entry-type*⟩

If you omit the catalog entry name, the FSLETTER DIRECTORY window is opened showing the current contents of the specified catalog. If you supply an entry name in addition to a catalog name, the procedure opens the appropriate window for editing the entry:

□   If the entry type is LETTER, or if the entry type is omitted, an FSLETTER window is opened.

□   If the entry type is FORM, a FORM window is opened.

□   If the entry is FSLETTER.EDPARMS, an EDPARMS window is opened.

The procedure terminates with an error message if an entry name is specified with an entry type that is anything other than EDPARMS, FORM, or LETTER.

PROC FSLETTER Statement Options

The following options can be used in the PROC FSLETTER statement:

DATA=*data-set*⟨*(data-set-options)*⟩
     names an existing SAS data set used to fill fields in the document. The FSLETTER procedure terminates with an error message if the specified data set does not exist.
     Note: This option is valid only if you also specify the name of an existing letter entry in the LETTER= argument.
     When you use this option, the procedure does not initiate an interactive FSLETTER session. A pause occurs while a copy of the document is printed for each observation in the data set; then the procedure ends.
     You can follow the data set name with a list of data set options enclosed in parentheses. The following data set options are valid with the DATA= option:

DROP   RENAME
KEEP   WHERE

See Chapter 15, "SAS Data Set Options," in *SAS Language: Reference, Version 6, First Edition* for descriptions of these data set options.

PRINTFILE=*fileref* | '*actual-filename*'
PRTFILE=*fileref* | '*actual-filename*'
PRINT=*fileref* | '*actual-filename*'
DDNAME=*fileref* | '*actual-filename*'
DD=*fileref* | '*actual-filename*'

specifies the fileref or the actual name of an external (non-SAS) file to which procedure output is directed. By default, procedure output is sent to the destination specified in the associated form entry. When this option is used, output is sent to the specified file instead.

If you use a fileref, you must have previously assigned the fileref to an external file with the FILENAME statement. If you use an actual filename, enclose it in quotes.

WHERE Statement

The WHERE statement defines criteria that observations in the data set named in the DATA= option of the PROC FSLETTER statement must meet in order for the procedure to print a copy of the document for the observation. By default, the FSLETTER procedure prints a copy of the document for each observation in the data set.

Note: The WHERE statement is valid only when the DATA= option is used in the PROC FSLETTER statement.

WHERE Statement Syntax

The general form of the WHERE statement is

WHERE *expression*;

where *expression* is any valid WHERE expression involving one or more of the variables in the input data set. Refer to the description of the WHERE statement in Chapter 9 of *SAS Language: Reference* for details of the operators and operands that are valid in WHERE expressions.

Using the WHERE Statement

When you use the DATA= option in the PROC FSLETTER statement, the FSLETTER procedure by default generates a copy of the document for every observation in the data set. If you do not need a copy for every observation, you can use the WHERE statement to generate copies for only those observations that meet a specified condition or list of conditions.

For example, to print form letters for only those observations in which the variable YEAR in the data set has a value less than 5, follow the PROC FSLETTER statement with the following statement:

```
where year<5;
```

In this case, the FSLETTER procedure uses only those observations that meet the specified criterion. No documents are printed for observations that do not satisfy the condition.

FSLETTER Command

The FSLETTER command provides a handy way to initiate an FSLETTER session from any SAS System window. The command allows you to specify the letter catalog (and, optionally, the catalog entry) or to select the desired catalog from a list of all available catalogs.

FSLETTER Command Syntax

The general form of the FSLETTER command is

FSLETTER ⟨? | *SAS-catalog*⟨*.catalog-entry*⟩⟩

FSLETTER Command Arguments

The following arguments can be used with the FSLETTER command:

?

opens a selection window from which you can choose the catalog used by the FSLETTER procedure. The selection list in the window includes all catalogs in all SAS data libraries identified in the current SAS session (all data libraries with defined librefs).

To select a catalog, position the cursor on the desired catalog name and press ENTER.

SAS-catalog⟨*.catalog-entry*⟩

specifies the catalog in which documents, forms, and editor parameters for the FSLETTER session are stored and, optionally, the specific entry. The complete form of the argument is

⟨*libref.*⟩*catalog-name*⟨*.entry-name*⟨*.entry-type*⟩⟩

You can specify a one-, two-, three-, or four-level name:

□ If a one-level name is specified, it is treated as a catalog name in the default library, WORK. If the specified catalog does not already exist in the WORK library, it is created.

Remember that all catalogs in the WORK library are erased when you end your SAS session.

□ If a two-level name is specified, it is treated as *libref.catalog-name.* If the specified catalog does not already exist in the specified library, it is created.

□ If a three-level name is specified, it is treated as *libref.catalog-name.entry-name.* The entry type is assumed to be LETTER. If the specified catalog does not already exist in the specified library, it is created.

□ If a four-level name is specified, the fourth level should be EDPARMS, FORM, or LETTER. Any other valid catalog entry type causes an error message. Invalid catalog entry types are ignored; LETTER is used instead. If the specified catalog does not already exist in the specified library, it is created.

If you use a one- or two-level name, the procedure initially opens the FSLETTER DIRECTORY window, from which you can select an entry in the specified catalog. If you use a three- or four-level name, the procedure opens the appropriate window for creating or editing the specified entry:

□ If the entry type is LETTER, or if the entry type is omitted, an FSLETTER window is opened.

□ If the entry type is FORM, a FORM window is opened.

□ If the entry is FSLETTER.EDPARMS, an EDPARMS window is opened.

If an entry name is specified with an entry type that is anything other than EDPARMS, FORM, or LETTER, the procedure terminates with an error message.

If you do not specify either of these arguments, the procedure opens the selection window described for the ? argument.

Using the FSLETTER Command

The FSLETTER command is a convenient way to invoke the FSLETTER procedure because it can be issued in any SAS System window. When you end an FSLETTER session initiated with the FSLETTER command, you return to whatever window was active when the command was issued.

Using the FSLETTER Procedure

The process of producing a document using the FSLETTER procedure involves the following steps:

1. **Selecting catalog entries.**
   The FSLETTER procedure provides two ways to choose which catalog entry to create or edit:

   □ You can specify a complete catalog entry name in the LETTER= option of the PROC FSLETTER statement or in the FSLETTER command. In this case, the FSLETTER window is opened for creating or editing the specified entry.

   □ You can specify only a catalog name in the LETTER= option of the PROC FSLETTER statement or in the FSLETTER command. In this case, the FSLETTER DIRECTORY window is opened. From this window you can view the current entries in the specified catalog and select entries to browse or edit. You can also print existing documents from the FSLETTER DIRECTORY window.

2. **Creating and editing documents.**
Documents are created and edited in the FSLETTER window. This window uses the SAS text editor, which provides a variety of commands and features that simplify the process of entering and editing the text of your document.
You can define fields in your document that allow you to enter information that changes from one copy of the document to the next. Fields are filled when the document is printed.

3. **Assigning field attributes.**
If you include fields in your document, you can open the FSLETTER ATTR window from the FSLETTER window to define the attributes of any fields in the document. Field attributes control whether field values are given special handling when the document is printed.

4. **Printing documents.**
Documents are prepared for printing in the FSLETTER SEND window. In this window you fill any fields in the document and make final editing changes before sending the document to a printer or to an external file.

Note: The process is different if you use the DATA= option in the PROC FSLETTER statement. In that case, the procedure is not interactive; it prints a copy of the document for each observation in the specified data set without opening any windows.
You can also create form entries and editor parameter (EDPARMS) entries with the FSLETTER procedure. The process of creating these entries involves the first two of the steps listed above, except that these entry types use their own special windows rather than the FSLETTER window:

□ Form entries are created and modified in the FORM window.

□ Editor parameter entries are created and modified in the EDPARMS window.

The remainder of this chapter describes the various FSLETTER procedure windows and the commands that are valid in each.

Selecting Catalog Entries

You can select the entry to create or edit by specifying a catalog entry name with the catalog name in the LETTER= option of the PROC FSLETTER statement or in the FSLETTER command. In that case, the initial window in the FSLETTER session is the appropriate window for the type of entry (FSLETTER, FORM, or EDPARMS).
If you specify only a catalog name when you invoke the FSLETTER procedure, the initial window in the FSLETTER session is the FSLETTER DIRECTORY window. The FSLETTER DIRECTORY window allows you to manipulate catalog entries in various ways. You can create new entries or display existing entries for editing, browsing, or printing. You can also rename, delete, and copy entries.
Display 14.1 shows an FSLETTER DIRECTORY window for a catalog containing letter, form, and editor parameter entries.

Display 14.1
Typical Catalog
Directory
Displayed in the
FSLETTER
DIRECTORY
Window

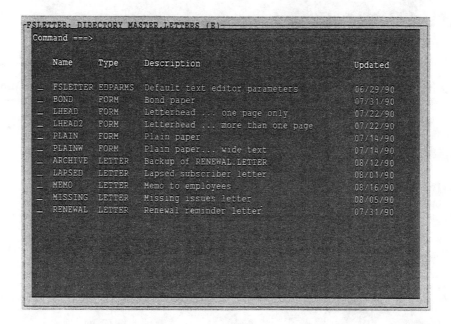

In the FSLETTER DIRECTORY window, you can execute commands from either the command line (or the action bar, if the PMENU facility is active) or from one of the selection fields to the left of each entry name. The following sections describe the commands available in each case.

FSLETTER DIRECTORY Window Selection Field Commands

Selection field commands consist of single characters. Enter the commands in the selection field next to the entry you want to process. (The selection field is the underscore to the left of each entry name in the FSLETTER DIRECTORY window.)

The following commands are valid in the selection fields:

B   opens the appropriate window for browsing the catalog entry.

D   marks the catalog entry for deletion. You are then prompted to verify that you indeed want to delete the entry. Use the V command to proceed with the deletion, or press ENTER to cancel it.

E   opens the appropriate window for editing the catalog entry.

P   opens the FSLETTER SEND window for printing the document. (This command is valid only for letter entries.)

R   renames the catalog entry or changes its description.

V   verifies a deletion. (This command is valid only after a D command has been executed.)

Executing More than One Command

You can rename or delete several entries at one time. For example, if you want to rename five entries, you can place an R in the selection fields of all five entries, press ENTER, make your changes, and then press ENTER again. You can use the same technique to delete multiple entries. You can also execute R and D commands for separate entries at the same time.

FSLETTER DIRECTORY Window Commands

In addition to the global commands listed in Chapter 18, "Command Reference," you can use the following commands in the FSLETTER DIRECTORY window. Commands specific to the FSLETTER DIRECTORY window are indicated below with an asterisk and are described in this section. The other commands are described in "Auxiliary Window Commands" later in this chapter.

Scrolling

BACKWARD ⟨HALF | PAGE | MAX | n⟩
BOTTOM
FORWARD ⟨HALF | PAGE | MAX | n⟩
HSCROLL HALF | PAGE | n
LEFT ⟨HALF | PAGE | MAX | n⟩
RIGHT ⟨HALF | PAGE | MAX | n⟩
TOP
VSCROLL HALF | PAGE | n

Searching

BFIND ⟨character-string | 'character-string'⟩
BLOCATE ⟨value | 'value'⟩
BLOCATE: ⟨partial-value | 'partial-value'⟩
FIND ⟨character-string | 'character-string'⟩
KEYFIELD ⟨field-name⟩
LOCATE ⟨value | 'value'⟩
LOCATE: ⟨partial-value | 'partial-value'⟩
RFIND
RLOCATE

Managing Catalog Entries

* COPY ⟨SAS-catalog.⟩entry-name⟨.entry-type⟩ ⟨new-entry-name⟩
* DELETE entry-name.entry-type
* END
* LISTDIR
* RENAME current-entry-name⟨.entry-type⟩ new-entry-name ⟨'new-description'⟩
* REPLACE ⟨SAS-catalog.⟩entry-name⟨.entry-type⟩ ⟨new-entry-name⟩
* SEND letter-name⟨.LETTER⟩ ⟨ALL⟩ ⟨DATA=data-set⟨(data-set-options)⟩⟩
        ⟨FILE=fileref | 'actual-filename' ⟨APPEND | REPLACE⟩⟩

Opening Other Windows

* BROWSE letter-name⟨.LETTER⟩ | form-name.FORM | FSLETTER.EDPARMS
* EDIT letter-name⟨.LETTER⟩ | form-name.FORM | FSLETTER.EDPARMS

Managing Data Sets

* CLOSE
* DATA ⟨data-set⟨(data-set-options)⟩⟩
* WHERE ⟨⟨ALSO⟩ expression⟩ | ⟨UNDO | CLEAR⟩

Command Descriptions

Descriptions of the special FSLETTER DIRECTORY window commands follow. Refer to Chapter 5, "Preparing Letters Using The FSLETTER Procedure," for examples of using these commands.

BROWSE *letter-name*⟨.LETTER⟩ | *form-name*.FORM | FSLETTER.EDPARMS
  opens a window for browsing the specified entry:

  □ If the entry type is LETTER, or if no entry type is specified, an
    FSLETTER window is opened for browsing the specified
    document. For information on using the FSLETTER window, see
    "Creating and Editing Documents" later in this chapter.

  □ If the entry type is FORM, a FORM window is opened for
    browsing the specified form. For information on using the FORM
    window, see Chapter 17, "SAS Display Manager Windows," in
    SAS Language: Reference.

  □ If the entry is FSLETTER.EDPARMS, an EDPARMS window is
    opened for browsing the default editor parameter file. For
    information on using the EDPARMS window, see "Setting Text
    Editor Parameters" later in this chapter.

  An error occurs if you specify an entry type other than LETTER,
  FORM, or EDPARMS.

CLOSE
  closes the data set opened with the DATA command. After the data set is
  closed, the FSLETTER procedure no longer uses it to fill fields during
  printing.

COPY *entry-name*⟨.entry-type⟩ *new-entry-name*
COPY *libref.catalog-name.entry-name*⟨.entry-type⟩ ⟨*new-entry-name*⟩
  makes a copy of a specified catalog entry.
    You can copy an entry in the current catalog by specifying its name
  and type, followed by a new name for the copy being created. The new
  entry will have the same type as the existing entry. If you omit the type,
  LETTER is assumed.
    You can copy an entry from another catalog by specifying the
  complete four-level name of the entry to be copied. (If you give only the
  first three levels, the entry type is assumed to be LETTER.) You can omit
  the new name unless the catalog already contains an entry with the same
  name.
    If you specify an existing entry as a new name, the COPY command
  fails so that you do not accidentally write over it. To deliberately
  overwrite the existing file, use the REPLACE command instead.

DATA ⟨*data-set*⟨(*data-set-options*)⟩⟩
  opens the specified SAS data set for filling fields in documents.
    While the data set is open, any fields in a document that have the
  same name or alias as variables in the specified data set are filled
  automatically from the data set when a document is printed. If you use
  the P selection field command or the SEND command without the ALL
  option, a copy is printed for only the first observation in the data set. If
  you use the SEND command with the ALL option, copies of the
  document are printed for each observation in the specified data set.

(DATA continued)

You can add a list of data set options following the data set name. The list must be enclosed in parentheses. The following data set options are valid with the DATA command:

DROP	RENAME
KEEP	WHERE

Refer to Chapter 15 in *SAS Language: Reference* for descriptions of these data set options.

Use the CLOSE command to close the data set opened with the DATA command if you no longer want fields filled from the data set.

DELETE *entry-name.entry-type*
deletes a catalog entry. You must specify both the name and the type of the entry you want to delete.

This command uses a two-step process designed to help you avoid accidental deletions. When you issue a DELETE command, the system positions the cursor on the selection field for the entry and prompts you to verify that you want the deletion executed. To delete the entry, type V (for verify) in the selection field and press ENTER. If you do not want the entry deleted, press ENTER without entering anything in the selection field.

EDIT *letter-name*⟨.LETTER⟩ | *form-name*.FORM | FSLETTER.EDPARMS
opens a window for creating or editing the specified entry:

□ If the entry type is LETTER, or if no entry type is specified, an FSLETTER window is opened for editing the specified document. If the specified entry does not exist, the FSLETTER window is initially blank. The entry is not created until you enter text and save the document or close the FSLETTER window. (No entry is created when you close a blank FSLETTER window.)

For information on using the FSLETTER window, see "Creating and Editing Documents" later in this chapter.

□ If the entry type is FORM, a FORM window is opened for creating or editing the specified form. For information on using the FORM window, see Chapter 17 in *SAS Language: Reference*.

□ If the entry is FSLETTER.EDPARMS, an EDPARMS window is opened for creating or editing the default editor parameter file. For information on using the EDPARMS window, see "Setting Text Editor Parameters" later in this chapter.

An error occurs if you specify an entry type other than LETTER, FORM, or EDPARMS.

END
closes the FSLETTER DIRECTORY window and ends the FSLETTER procedure. If a data set opened by the DATA command is still open, it is closed.

Note: The FSLETTER DIRECTORY window cannot be closed while any FSLETTER windows opened during the current FSLETTER session are still open. If any FSLETTER windows are still open, the END command moves to the next FSLETTER window in the current session rather than closing the FSLETTER DIRECTORY window.

LISTDIR

sends a listing of the entries in the current catalog to the SAS log.

RENAME *current-entry-name*⟨*.entry-type*⟩ *new-entry-name* ⟨*'new-description'*⟩

allows you to change the name or description of an existing catalog entry.

Follow the RENAME command with the current name of the entry and the desired new name for the entry. If you omit the *entry-type* element of the current name, the type is assumed to be LETTER. (You cannot specify a new type for the catalog entry.) Optionally, you can also specify a new description for the entry. The *new-description* argument can be up to 40 characters long and must be enclosed in quotes.

To change the description without changing the entry name, specify the same name for both the *current-entry-name* and *new-entry-name* arguments.

REPLACE *entry-name*⟨*.entry-type*⟩ *new-entry-name*

REPLACE *libref.catalog-name.entry-name*⟨*.entry-type*⟩ ⟨*new-entry-name*⟩

makes a copy of a specified catalog entry. This command behaves like the COPY command, except that it overwrites an existing entry with the same name as the *new-entry-name* argument. See the description of the COPY command for details.

SEND *letter-name*⟨*.LETTER*⟩ ⟨ALL⟩ ⟨DATA=*data-set*⟨(*data-set-options*)⟩⟩
⟨FILE=*fileref* | *'actual-filename'* ⟨APPEND | REPLACE⟩⟩

prints the specified letter entry. The entry must exist in the current catalog. By default, the SEND command opens the FSLETTER SEND window, where you can fill in fields and make final editing changes before the document is printed.

If a SAS data set is currently open, any fields in the document with names or aliases that match variable names in the open data set are filled automatically with values from the data set. If the data set was opened with a DATA command, the field values come from the first observation in the data set. If the data set is open because the FSLETTER DIRECTORY window was opened by a LETTER command in an FSBROWSE or FSEDIT session, the field values come from the observation displayed in the FSBROWSE or FSEDIT window when the LETTER command was issued.

If you include the ALL argument with the SEND command, a copy of the document is produced for every observation in the open data set (or for every observation that satisfies the WHERE condition, if a WHERE command has been issued). When you use the ALL option, the FSLETTER SEND window is not opened. After a pause, a message appears in the FSLETTER DIRECTORY window's message line informing you that the documents have been sent.

Note: The ALL argument is valid only when a data set is currently open.

(SEND continued)

You can also use the DATA= option in the SEND command to produce a copy of the document for each observation in a specified data set. The DATA= option is useful in the following circumstances:

□ when you want to produce copies of an individual document without using the DATA command to open a data set for the FSLETTER session.

□ when you want to produce copies of an individual document for a data set other than the one currently open. (The DATA= option has no effect on any other data set that may currently be open.)

The DATA= option produces a copy of the document for each observation in the data set; it is not necessary to use the ALL option with the DATA= option. When you use the DATA= option, the FSLETTER SEND window is not opened. After a pause, a message appears on the FSLETTER DIRECTORY window's message line informing you that copies of the document have been sent.

You can add a list of data set options following the data set name in the DATA= argument. The list must be enclosed in parentheses. The following data set options are valid with the DATA= option:

DROP	RENAME
KEEP	WHERE

Refer to Chapter 15 in *SAS Language: Reference* for descriptions of these data set options.

Unless you issue a PRTFILE command or use the PRINTFILE= option in the PROC FSLETTER (or PROC FSBROWSE or PROC FSEDIT) statement that initiates the session, output is sent to the destination specified in the form associated with the document being printed. You can use the FILE= option in the SEND command to route output to an external file instead. The FILE= option is useful in the following situations:

□ when you want to send an individual document to an external file while leaving the printer as the default output destination

□ when you want to send an individual document to an external file other than the currently designated print file.

You can identify the external file using either a fileref or its actual filename. If you use a fileref, you must have previously assigned the fileref to the external file using a FILENAME statement. If you use an actual filename, it must be enclosed in quotes.

By default, each new document sent to the file replaces any text previously in the file. (If you use the ALL or DATA= options to produce copies of a document for observations in a SAS data set, all copies are sent to the same file.) To have the output from the current SEND command appended to the existing text instead of overwriting it, add the APPEND option to the SEND command. The REPLACE option specifies the default behavior.

WHERE ⟨⟨ALSO⟩ *expression*⟩ | ⟨UNDO | CLEAR⟩

imposes one or more sets of conditions that observations in the open data set must meet in order for a copy of the document to be produced for that observation. *Expression* is any valid WHERE expression involving one or more variables in the open data set. Refer to the description of the WHERE statement in Chapter 9 of *SAS Language: Reference* for details of the operators and operands that are valid in WHERE expressions.

Note: The WHERE command is valid only when a data set is open for the FSLETTER session.

The complete set of conditions imposed by the WHERE command is called a temporary WHERE clause. The conditions can be modified or canceled during the FSLETTER session.

The WHERE command has several forms:

WHERE *expression* applies the conditions specified in *expression* as the new temporary WHERE clause, replacing any clause previously in effect.

WHERE ALSO *expression* adds the conditions specified in *expression* to the existing temporary WHERE clause.

WHERE UNDO removes the most recently added set of conditions from the temporary WHERE clause.

WHERE cancels the current temporary WHERE clause.
WHERE CLEAR

Creating and Editing Documents

Documents are entered or edited in the FSLETTER window. FSLETTER windows can be opened for editing in the following ways:

□ by specifying the name of a letter entry in the LETTER= argument of the PROC FSLETTER statement or in the FSLETTER command

□ by issuing an EDIT command (or by using the E selection field command) in the FSLETTER DIRECTORY window

□ by issuing an EDIT command in another FSLETTER window

□ by issuing an EDIT command in an FSBROWSE or FSEDIT window.

If the letter entry you specify when you open the FSLETTER window is not in the current catalog, an empty FSLETTER window is opened for entering text. If the specified entry already exists, it is displayed for editing. All text in the FSLETTER window is unprotected. Using editing keys and commands, you can write new documents and edit existing ones.

The FSLETTER window uses the SAS text editor, so all the standard text editor commands are available. See Chapter 8, "SAS Text Editor," in *SAS Language: Reference* if you need an introduction to the features of the SAS text editor. You can customize many features of the text editor to suit your own tastes and needs. Refer to "Setting Text Editor Parameters" later in this chapter for a discussion of the features you can control.

Choosing a Form

When you create a new document, you should choose a form to associate with it. *Forms* are SAS catalog entries of type FORM that contain instructions for formatting the text in your document when it is printed. In addition, the line length specified in the form determines the width of the text entry area in the FSLETTER window. Refer to Chapter 20, "Forms," for additional information on forms.

Newly created documents are assigned the default form FSLETTER.FORM. You can change the form assignment using the FORM command in the FSLETTER window. When you change the form assignment, the procedure first looks for the new form in the current catalog (the one where the current document resides). If the specified entry is not there, the procedure looks in your personal PROFILE catalog (SASUSER.PROFILE, or WORK.PROFILE if the SASUSER library is not allocated). If the specified entry is not there, the procedure looks last in the SASHELP.FSP system catalog. If the specified entry still is not found, an error message is returned. In this case, the current form assignment is not changed.

Defining Fields

The FSLETTER procedure allows you to define *fields* in your documents. Fields are areas in which values can change for each copy of a document. A field appears in the text of a document as an ampersand (&) followed by a valid SAS name.

The length of each field in your document should be equal to the largest number of characters expected for that value. The field length is determined by the number of characters in the field name (including the ampersand). To extend a field, you can follow the field name with a series of underscores (_). The underscores serve to increase the field length, but they are not part of the field name.

You can use the automatic variables &DATE and &DATE7 as FSLETTER fields. These variables provide the current date when the document is printed. Because the variable names already begin with an ampersand, the field text should begin with two ampersands (&&DATE and &&DATE7). The variables provide the current date in WORDDATE. and DATE7. formats, respectively. If you use &&DATE, add underscores to extend the field to 18 characters (the maximum possible length for date values in the WORDDATE. format).

Display 14.2 shows a portion of a document displayed in the FSLETTER window. This portion of the document contains six different fields; FULLNAME appears twice.

Display 14.2
FSLETTER
Document
Containing Fields

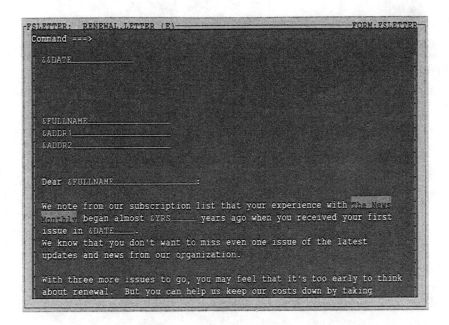

You define fields in the FSLETTER window, but you do not supply values for the fields until you print the document from the FSLETTER SEND window. See "Printing Documents" later in this chapter for details. The FSLETTER procedure can also fill the fields automatically using values from observations in a SAS data set. See "Printing Documents" later in this chapter for details.

Using Color and Highlighting Attributes

If your terminal or workstation supports color and highlighting, you can change the color and highlighting of characters as you type (or overtype) them. Simply use the special keys on your terminal that control text color and highlighting as you enter the text. The attributes are stored with the document; therefore, they remain in effect the next time the document is displayed.

Special Topic: Systems without Special Color Keys

For operating systems where terminals do not provide special keys to set text color and highlighting characteristics, the SAS System recognizes combinations of the ESC key and a letter or number key as commands to change text color or highlighting.

The following list shows the key sequences that select the color of subsequent text:

ESC A	gray	ESC K	black	ESC P	pink
ESC B	blue	ESC M	magenta	ESC R	red
ESC C	cyan	ESC N	brown	ESC W	white
ESC G	green	ESC O	orange	ESC Y	yellow

For example, to type text in cyan, press the ESC and then the C key. The next characters entered are displayed in cyan.

(continued on next page)

(continued from previous page)

The following list shows the key sequences that select the highlighting of subsequent text:

ESC 0   turns off all highlighting
ESC 1   turns on high intensity
ESC 2   turns on underlining
ESC 3   turns on reverse video
ESC 4   turns on blinking.

Note: Some operating systems may require a different prefix key rather than ESC. If ESC does not work on your system, ask your SAS Software Consultant for the correct prefix.

You can use color and highlighting in documents for two different purposes:

□   to control the appearance of elements of the text

□   to control the way text is printed.

Using Color and Highlighting to Enhance Displayed Text

You can change the default text color and highlighting attributes to alter the appearance of the document in the FSLETTER and FSLETTER SEND windows. For example, you can use a different color or highlighting attribute for the fields in the document so that they stand out more clearly when the text is displayed in the FSLETTER SEND window for data entry.

Using Color and Highlighting to Signal Printing Instructions

The form associated with the document may interpret certain colors or highlighting (or combinations of color and highlighting) as signals to use a particular printer feature when the document is printed. For example, the form can interpret the combination of red and reverse video as a signal that text with those attributes should be underlined or italic when printed.

You can edit the form entry to select which attributes select printing features for your documents. For details of how the color and highlighting attributes that signal printing instructions are defined in the form entry, see the discussion of the FORM window in Chapter 17 of *SAS Language: Reference.*

You can use the global FONT command in the FSLETTER window to check which color and highlighting attributes are defined as printing instructions for the current form. Refer to Chapter 18 for more information on the FONT command.

FSLETTER Window Commands

In addition to the SAS text editor commands described in Chapter 19, "SAS Text Editor Commands," in *SAS Language: Reference* and the global commands described in Chapter 18 of this book, you can use the following commands when editing a document in the FSLETTER window:

Managing Letter Entries

```
ATTR
COPY ⟨libref.catalog-name.⟩entry-name⟨.LETTER⟩
DES description
EDPARMS
FORM form-name
SAVE ⟨letter-name⟩
SEND ⟨ALL⟩ ⟨DATA=data-set⟨(data-set-options)⟩⟩
        ⟨FILE=fileref | 'actual-filename' ⟨APPEND | REPLACE⟩⟩
```

Opening Additional Windows

```
BROWSE letter-name⟨.LETTER⟩ | form-name.FORM | FSLETTER.EDPARMS
EDIT letter-name⟨.LETTER⟩ | form-name.FORM | FSLETTER.EDPARMS
```

Closing the Window

```
CANCEL
END
```

Managing Data Sets

```
CLOSE
DATA ⟨data-set⟨(data-set-options)⟩⟩
WHERE ⟨⟨ALSO⟩ expression⟩ | ⟨UNDO | CLEAR⟩
```

Command Descriptions

Descriptions of the special FSLETTER window commands follow. Refer to Chapter 5 for examples of using these commands.

ATTR

opens the FSLETTER ATTR window, in which the field attributes for the current document can be viewed or modified.

Assigning an attribute to a field tells the FSLETTER procedure to take certain actions when it encounters the field in the FSLETTER SEND window. See "Assigning Field Attributes" later in this chapter for more information.

BROWSE *letter-name*⟨.LETTER⟩ | *form-name*.FORM | FSLETTER.EDPARMS

opens an additional window for browsing the specified entry:

□ If the entry type is LETTER, or if no entry type is specified, another FSLETTER window is opened for browsing the specified document.

□ If the entry type is FORM, a FORM window is opened for browsing the specified form. For information on using the FORM window, see Chapter 17 in *SAS Language: Reference*.

(BROWSE continued)

□ If the entry is FSLETTER.EDPARMS, an EDPARMS window is opened for browsing the default editor parameter file. For information on using the EDPARMS window, see "Setting Text Editor Parameters" later in this chapter.

An error occurs if you specify an entry type other than LETTER, FORM, or EDPARMS.

The new window opened by the BROWSE command becomes the active window. You can use the SWAP command to move between the windows opened in the current FSLETTER session. Use the END command to close the new window and return to the previous one.

CANCEL

cancels all changes made to the current document since the FSLETTER window was opened (or since the last SAVE command), closes the current FSLETTER window, and returns you to the window from which the FSLETTER window was opened.

CLOSE

closes the data set opened with the DATA command. After the data set is closed, the FSLETTER procedure no longer uses it to fill fields during printing.

COPY ⟨*libref.catalog-name.*⟩*entry-name*⟨*.LETTER*⟩

copies the specified letter entry into the current document. You can use text editor line target commands (A or B, for after or before) to copy the document in at a specific position within the current text. Otherwise, the copied document is appended to the end of the current document.

If the document being copied in uses a different form than the current document, the document being copied is flowed (if necessary) using the line length information in the current document's form.

DATA ⟨*data-set*⟨*(data-set-options)*⟩⟩

opens the specified SAS data set for filling fields in documents.

While the data set is open, any fields in a document that have the same name or alias as variables in the specified data set are filled automatically from observations in the data set when the document is printed.

You can add a list of data set options following the data set name. The list must be enclosed in parentheses. The following data set options are valid with the DATA command:

DROP	RENAME
KEEP	WHERE

Refer to Chapter 15 in *SAS Language: Reference* for descriptions of these data set options.

Use the CLOSE command to close the data set opened with the DATA command if you no longer want fields filled from the data set.

DES *description*

assigns a description of up to 40 characters to a document. The description does not need to be enclosed in quotes. The description is displayed with the name of the document in the FSLETTER DIRECTORY window.

EDIT *letter-name*⟨.LETTER⟩ | *form-name*.FORM | FSLETTER.EDPARMS

opens an additional window for creating or editing the specified entry:

□ If the entry type is LETTER, or if no entry type is specified, an FSLETTER window is opened for editing the specified document. If the specified entry does not exist, the FSLETTER window is initially blank. The entry is not created until you enter text and save the document or close the FSLETTER window. (No entry is created when you close a blank FSLETTER window.)

□ If the entry type is FORM, a FORM window is opened for creating or editing the specified form. For information on using the FORM window, see Chapter 17 in *SAS Language: Reference*.

□ If the entry is FSLETTER.EDPARMS, an EDPARMS window is opened for creating or editing the default editor parameter file. For information on using the EDPARMS window, see "Setting Text Editor Parameters" later in this chapter.

Note: The parameter settings in the FSLETTER.EDPARMS entry do not affect the current document. The FSLETTER.EDPARMS entry determines the initial parameters for newly created documents. Use the EDPARMS command to change parameter settings for the current document.

An error occurs if you specify an entry type other than LETTER, FORM, or EDPARMS.

The new window opened by the EDIT command becomes the active window. You can use the SWAP command to move between the windows opened in the current FSLETTER session. Use the END command to close the new window and return to the previous one.

EDPARMS

opens an EDPARMS window and displays the text editor parameter settings for the current document. Any changes you make take effect when the EDPARMS window is closed. The parameter settings are stored in the letter entry and remain in effect the next time you edit this document.

See "Setting Text Editor Parameters" later in this chapter for more information on using the EDPARMS window.

Note: Changes made in the EDPARMS window opened by the EDPARMS command do not affect the default parameter settings in the FSLETTER.EDPARMS entry for the catalog.

END

saves the document currently displayed, closes the FSLETTER window, and returns you to the window from which the FSLETTER window was opened.

FORM *form-name*

changes the form entry assigned to a document. The form name is recorded in the letter entry.

When you specify a new form name, the FSLETTER procedure looks first for a form entry with the specified name in the current catalog (the catalog opened when the procedure was initiated). If the form is not present in the current catalog, the procedure looks for it in your personal PROFILE catalog (SASUSER.PROFILE, or WORK.PROFILE if the SASUSER library is not allocated). If the form is not there, the procedure looks for it in the SASHELP.FSP system catalog. If the form still is not found, the procedure returns an error message. In this case, the current form assignment is not changed.

If the new form specifies a different line width than the current form uses, a requestor window appears asking if you want the document to be flowed to the new line width. Respond with a Y to flow the text or with an N to wrap the text. If you choose N, lines of text are split if the new line length is smaller, or blanks are added to pad the lines if the new line length is larger.

SAVE ⟨*letter-name*⟩

stores the current version of the document in the catalog, leaving the document displayed for further editing. If you do not specify a name for the entry, the text is saved under its original name in the catalog. Specify a different name to store the current document under another name in the catalog.

It is wise to issue SAVE commands occasionally while entering text to guard against loss of work due to interruptions in computing services. Any document that has been modified is automatically saved when you use the END or SEND commands.

SEND ⟨ALL⟩ ⟨DATA=*data-set*⟨(*data-set-options*)⟩⟩
⟨FILE=*fileref* |*"actual-filename"* ⟨APPEND | REPLACE⟩⟩

closes the FSLETTER window and prints the current letter entry. By default, the SEND command opens the FSLETTER SEND window, where you can fill in fields and make final editing changes before the document is printed.

If a SAS data set is currently open, any fields in the document with names or aliases that match variable names in the open data set are filled automatically with values from the data set. If the data set was opened with a DATA command, the field values come from the first observation in the data set. If the data set is open because the FSLETTER window was opened by an EDIT command in an FSBROWSE or FSEDIT session, the field values come from the observation displayed in the FSBROWSE or FSEDIT window when the EDIT command was issued.

If you include the ALL argument with the SEND command, a copy of the document is produced for every observation in the open data set (or for every observation that satisfies the WHERE condition, if a WHERE command has been issued). When you use the ALL option, the FSLETTER SEND window is not opened.

Note: The ALL argument is valid only when a data set is currently open.

You can also use the DATA= option in the SEND command to produce a copy of the document for each observation in a specified data set. The DATA= option is useful in the following circumstances:

□ when you want to produce copies of an individual document without using the DATA command to open a data set for the FSLETTER session.

□ when you want to produce copies of an individual document for a data set other than the one currently open. (The DATA= option has no effect on any other data set that may currently be open.)

The DATA= option produces a copy of the document for each observation in the data set; it is not necessary to use the ALL option with the DATA= option. When you use the DATA= option, the FSLETTER SEND window is not opened.

You can add a list of data set options following the data set name in the DATA= argument. The list must be enclosed in parentheses. The following data set options are valid with the DATA= option:

DROP	RENAME
KEEP	WHERE

Refer to Chapter 15 in *SAS Language: Reference* for descriptions of these data set options.

Unless you issue a PRTFILE command or use the PRINTFILE= option in the PROC FSLETTER (or PROC FSBROWSE or PROC FSEDIT) statement that initiates the session, output is sent to the destination specified in the form associated with the document being printed. You can use the FILE= option in the SEND command to route output to an external file instead. The FILE= option is useful in the following situations:

□ when you want to send an individual document to an external file while leaving the printer as the default output destination

□ when you want to send an individual document to an external file other than the currently designated print file.

You can identify the external file using either a fileref or its actual filename. If you use a fileref, you must have previously assigned the fileref to the external file using a FILENAME statement. If you use an actual filename, it must be enclosed in quotes.

By default, each new document sent to the file replaces any text previously in the file. (If you use the ALL or DATA= options to produce copies of a document for observations in a SAS data set, all copies are sent to the same file.) To have the output from the current SEND command appended to the existing text instead of overwriting it, add the APPEND option to the SEND command. The REPLACE option specifies the default behavior.

WHERE ⟨⟨ALSO⟩ *expression*⟩ | ⟨UNDO | CLEAR⟩

imposes one or more sets of conditions that observations in the data set must meet in order to fill fields in printed documents. *Expression* is any valid WHERE expression involving one or more of the variables in the input data set. (Refer to the description of the WHERE statement in Chapter 9 of *SAS Language: Reference* for details of the operators and operands that are valid in WHERE expressions.) No documents are created for observations that do not satisfy the specified conditions.

Note: The WHERE command is valid only when a data set is open for the FSLETTER session.

The complete set of conditions imposed by the WHERE command is called a temporary WHERE clause. The conditions can be modified or canceled during the FSLETTER session.

The WHERE command has several forms:

WHERE *expression*	applies the conditions specified in *expression* as the new temporary WHERE clause, replacing any clause previously in effect.
WHERE ALSO *expression*	adds the conditions specified in *expression* to the existing temporary WHERE clause.
WHERE UNDO	removes the most recently added set of conditions from the temporary WHERE clause.
WHERE WHERE CLEAR	cancels the current temporary WHERE clause.

Assigning Field Attributes

After entering the document text and defining variable fields, you can use the FSLETTER ATTR window to assign attributes to each field. Use the ATTR command in the FSLETTER window to open the FSLETTER ATTR window. Although you assign field attributes while editing the document, the attributes do not take effect until the second step of the printing process.

The FSLETTER ATTR window is partitioned into a series of frames. Each frame contains the field attributes for a particular field. The attribute frames are displayed in the order in which the fields appear in the document. If the same field name is used more than once in the document, each occurrence has a separate attribute frame. Display 14.3 shows a sample field attribute frame.

Display 14.3
Sample Field
Attribute Frame

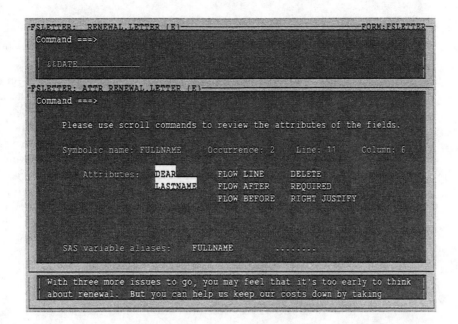

Use the FORWARD and BACKWARD commands to move among the attribute frames for the document.

The attributes for each frame are choice groups. To turn on an attribute for a field, move the cursor to the term in the attribute frame that corresponds to the desired attribute; then press ENTER. The term is highlighted in reverse video to show that it is turned on. To turn off a currently selected attribute, move the cursor to the highlighted term and press ENTER. The highlighting is removed to show that the attribute is turned off.

Field Attribute Descriptions

The following attributes can be assigned in the FSLETTER ATTR window:

DEAR

modifies the field value by excluding all but the first and last elements of the value.

To assign this attribute, move the cursor to the DEAR item and press ENTER. The item is highlighted in reverse video. To turn off the attribute, move the cursor to the highlighted item and press ENTER.

This attribute is designed to convert names in the form *title first-name last-name* into *title last-name* for use in the salutations of letters. For example, if the name **Mr. John E. Doe** is entered in a field assigned the DEAR attribute, the field value is converted to **Mr. Doe** when the document is printed.

Note: The DEAR attribute does not automatically provide the *Dear* element of the salutation. You must provide that in text:

Dear &NAME_____ :

The DEAR attribute can be used in conjunction with the LASTNAME attribute. If the LASTNAME and DEAR attributes are both assigned, the LASTNAME attribute is processed first so that the field value is in the proper order for the DEAR attribute.

DELETE

deletes the line containing the field if the line is blank when the letter is printed.

To assign this attribute, move the cursor to the DELETE item and press ENTER. The item is highlighted in reverse video. To turn off the attribute, move the cursor to the highlighted item and press ENTER.

Assign the DELETE attribute if there is a possibility that one or more observations will not have a value for the field or that the field will not be needed for a particular document. For example, some letters require more address lines than others. Suppose your document provides three fields for the address. Some letters require only two address lines, so you can assign the DELETE attribute to the last address field. If the field is blank, the FSLETTER procedure deletes the line allotted for the field when the letter is printed. If you do not assign the DELETE attribute to the field, a blank line appears in its place when the letter is printed.

FLOW AFTER

removes extra spaces beginning at the first character following the field and ending with the first blank line after the field. If the field ends the line and paragraph, any following blank lines between the line containing the field and the next nonblank line are removed. If the next nonblank line is on a following page, the blank lines are not removed.

To assign this attribute, move the cursor to the FLOW AFTER item and press ENTER. The item is highlighted in reverse video. To turn off the attribute, move the cursor to the highlighted item and press ENTER.

FLOW BEFORE

takes out extra spaces beginning after the last nonblank character preceding the field and ending with the first blank line after the field. If the field starts the line, any preceding blank lines between the line containing the field and the previous nonblank line are removed.

To assign this attribute, move the cursor to the FLOW BEFORE item and press ENTER. The item is highlighted in reverse video. To turn off the attribute, move the cursor to the highlighted item and press ENTER.

FLOW LINE

takes out extra spaces beginning after the last nonblank character preceding the field and ending with the end of the line containing the field.

To assign this attribute, move the cursor to the FLOW LINE item and press ENTER. The item is highlighted in reverse video. To turn off the attribute, move the cursor to the highlighted item and press ENTER.

LASTNAME

modifies the field value by moving the first element of the value that is followed by a comma to the end of the value.

To assign this attribute, move the cursor to the LASTNAME item and press ENTER. The item is highlighted in reverse video. To turn off the attribute, move the cursor to the highlighted item and press ENTER.

This attribute is designed for use with fields containing names stored in the form *last-name, first-name*. Since records are often kept by last name, this attribute is helpful when using a SAS data set to fill in field values. For example, if the LASTNAME attribute is assigned to a field, and the value entered in the field is

```
Doe, Mr. John E.
```

the value printed in the document is

```
Mr. John E. Doe
```

Note: The LASTNAME attribute has no effect if the field value does not contain a comma. Thus, you can still enter values in the normal order in fields that have been assigned the LASTNAME attribute.

REQUIRED
:   indicates that the field must be filled in before you can leave the first step of the printing process.

    To assign this attribute, move the cursor to the REQUIRED item and press ENTER. The item is highlighted in reverse video. To turn off the attribute, move the cursor to the highlighted item and press ENTER.

    You must use the CANCEL command to end the first printing step without supplying a value for a required field.

RIGHT JUSTIFY
:   indicates that the field value should be right-aligned in the space reserved for the field. By default, values are left-aligned.

    To assign this attribute, move the cursor to the RIGHT JUSTIFY item and press ENTER. The item is highlighted in reverse video. To turn off the attribute, move the cursor to the highlighted item and press ENTER.

SAS variable aliases
:   specifies names for the variables used to fill in the field from a SAS data set. You can assign up to two aliases for the field name. By default, the SAS System assigns the field name as the first alias (unless the field name is a SAS automatic variable).

FSLETTER ATTR Window Commands

In addition to the global commands described in Chapter 18, you can use the following commands in the FSLETTER ATTR window. Commands with special meanings in the FSLETTER ATTR window are marked with an asterisk and are described in this section. The remaining commands are described in "Auxiliary Window Commands" later in this chapter.

Scrolling

```
* BACKWARD
* BOTTOM
* FORWARD
  HSCROLL HALF | PAGE | n
  LEFT ⟨HALF | PAGE | MAX | n⟩
  RIGHT ⟨HALF | PAGE | MAX | n⟩
* TOP
```

Searching

BFIND ⟨*character-string* | '*character-string*'⟩
BLOCATE ⟨*value* | '*value*'⟩
BLOCATE: ⟨*partial-value* | '*partial-value*'⟩
FIND ⟨*character-string* | '*character-string*'⟩
KEYFIELD ⟨*field-name*⟩
LOCATE ⟨*value* | '*value*'⟩
LOCATE: ⟨*partial-value* | '*partial-value*'⟩
RFIND
RLOCATE

Closing the Window

* CANCEL
* END

Command Descriptions

Descriptions of the special FSLETTER ATTR window commands follow:

BACKWARD
    displays the attribute frame for the previous field.

BOTTOM
    displays the attribute frame for the last field in the document.

CANCEL
    closes the FSLETTER ATTR window without recording any changes to
    the previous field attribute settings.

END
    closes the FSLETTER ATTR window and records any changes you made
    to field attribute settings while the window was open.

FORWARD
    displays the attribute frame for the next field.

TOP
    displays the attribute frame for the first field in the document.

Printing Documents

The FSLETTER procedure provides two ways to print documents:

□ noninteractively. When you use the DATA= option in the PROC FSLETTER
statement, or the ALL or DATA= options in the SEND command, the
procedure prints copies of a document for each observation in a SAS data
set. In this case, no windows are opened.

□ interactively. When you use the SEND command without the ALL or
DATA= options, the procedure opens the FSLETTER SEND window. In this
case, you can enter and edit field values manually and make final editing
changes before the document is printed.

Printing documents from the FSLETTER SEND window is a two-step process:

1. Fill in the fields in the document.
   Note: This step is skipped if the document does not contain fields.

2. Perform final editing and release the document.

The remainder of this section explains how the FSLETTER SEND window is used to prepare documents for printing.

Step 1: Filling Fields

In this step, you fill in the fields in the document. (If your document does not contain fields, you go directly to step 2.) During this step, you can enter text only in the fields; all other text is protected. As you fill in each field, press the ENTER key to position the cursor at the beginning of the next field. If you fill a field, the cursor moves automatically to the next field.

If a data set is open when you open the FSLETTER SEND window, the fields in the document are automatically filled using the values from the data set. If the data set was opened by the DATA command, the values come from the first observation in the data set. If the data set is open because the FSLETTER session was invoked from the FSBROWSE or FSEDIT windows, the values come from the observation displayed in the FSBROWSE or FSEDIT window when you entered the FSLETTER session.

Once you have filled in the fields, use the END command to proceed to the second step of the process.

FSLETTER SEND Window Commands: Step 1

The FSLETTER SEND window uses the SAS text editor. In the first step of sending a document, you can use any of the text editor commands described in Chapter 19 of *SAS Language: Reference* and the global commands described in Chapter 18 of this book, plus the following commands:

CANCEL
END

Command Descriptions

Descriptions of the special FSLETTER SEND window commands for the first step of the printing process follow:

CANCEL
> closes the FSLETTER SEND window without printing the document and returns you to the previous FSLETTER window, or to the FSLETTER DIRECTORY window if no other FSLETTER windows are open. Use the CANCEL command if you decide after opening the FSLETTER SEND window that you do not want to print the document.

END
> enters the final editing step of the printing process.

Step 2: Final Editing

At the beginning of this step, any field attributes you assigned earlier take effect. For example, fields with the LASTNAME and DEAR attributes are rearranged, any flowing is done, and unused underscores in fields are deleted. All text in the FSLETTER SEND window is unprotected; you can type over any part of the document, field values as well as text.

In this step you can make any final editing changes required for the document. Changes you make in the FSLETTER SEND window are not recorded in the stored copy of the document.

When you are ready to print the document, execute the END command again. The document is sent, and you return to the previous FSLETTER window, or to the FSLETTER DIRECTORY window if no other FSLETTER windows are open.

By default, the document is sent to the destination defined in the form associated with the document. You can use the PRTFILE= option in the PROC FSLETTER statement, the PRTFILE command in the FSLETTER window, or the FILE= option in the SEND command to route the output to an external file instead.

Note: If you want to route output to an external file, you must select the output file before you enter the FSLETTER SEND window. Once you open the FSLETTER SEND window, you cannot use the PRTFILE command to change the output destination for the current document.

FSLETTER SEND Window Commands: Step 2

The FSLETTER SEND window uses the SAS text exitor. In the second step of sending a document, you can use any of the text editor commands described in Chapter 19 of *SAS Language: Reference* and the global commands described in Chapter 18 of this book, plus the following commands:

CANCEL
END

Command Descriptions

Descriptions of the special FSLETTER SEND window commands for the second step of the printing process follow:

CANCEL
closes the FSLETTER SEND window without printing the document and returns you to the previous FSLETTER window, or to the FSLETTER DIRECTORY window if no other FSLETTER windows are open. Use the CANCEL command if you decide after you fill fields that you do not want to print the current document.

END
closes the FSLETTER SEND window, sends the document to the specified printer or file, and returns to the previous FSLETTER window, or to the FSLETTER DIRECTORY window if no other FSLETTER windows are open.

Notice that if your document has fields this is the second execution of the END command after you open the FSLETTER SEND window. The first END command enters the final editing step.

Setting Text Editor Parameters

The working environment for entering, editing, or browsing text in the FSLETTER window is provided by the SAS text editor. The appearance and behavior of the SAS text editor in the FSLETTER window is determined by the settings of a collection of parameters associated with the document being edited.

To review or customize the text editor environment for a document you are currently composing or for a previously created document that you are now editing, issue the following command while the document is displayed in the FSLETTER window:

    edparms

This command opens the EDPARMS window to display the text editor parameters in effect for the current document. Display 14.4 shows the EDPARMS window for a typical FSLETTER document.

Display 14.4
EDPARMS
Window Showing
Parameter Settings
for an FSLETTER
Document

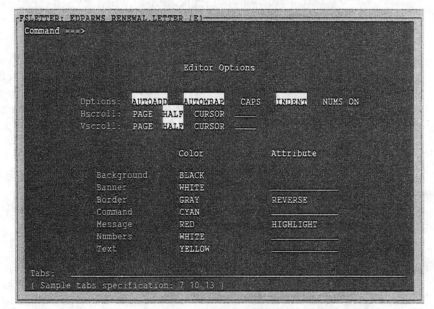

You can change the current parameter settings in the EDPARMS window. Some of the parameter settings in the EDPARMS window are choice groups. To turn on these parameters, move the cursor to the corresponding term in the EDPARMS window and press ENTER. The term is highlighted in reverse video to show that the parameter is turned on. To turn off a parameter, position the cursor on the highlighted term and press ENTER. The highlighting is removed to show that the parameter is turned off. Other parameter settings are fields in which you enter the desired parameter values. The following section describes the parameters available in the EDPARMS window.

The set of editor parameters displayed by the EDPARMS command is associated with the displayed document only. Any parameter changes you make apply only to the current letter entry. The changes take effect when you close the EDPARMS window.

Parameter Descriptions

The following text editor parameters are used in the FSLETTER window. The default settings of these parameters are determined by the values in the FSLETTER.EDPARMS entry when the document is created. Refer to "Creating Default Parameter Settings" later in this chapter for details.

AUTOADD

> controls the automatic insertion of new lines as you scroll forward past existing text. If the AUTOADD parameter is off, you must execute a specific command, such as the I (insert) line command, to insert new lines of text in the FSLETTER window.

AUTOWRAP

> controls whether a word that will not fit on the current line is automatically moved (wrapped) to the next line.
>
> If the AUTOWRAP parameter is turned on, you can enter text continuously, without moving the cursor to the next line. You can also use the INCLUDE command to bring a file with a longer line length into the text editor without truncating any text. When the INDENT parameter is also set on, you can wrap text that is indented.

CAPS

> determines whether or not all text subsequently entered or modified is translated into uppercase characters when you press ENTER or a function key, or when you move the cursor from the line you are working on. If the CAPS parameter is turned on, character strings for the FIND and CHANGE command are also translated into uppercase. Enclose your character string in quotes if you do not want lowercase characters in the string translated into uppercase. When the CAPS parameter is turned off, all text is left as entered.

INDENT

> allows indention at the left margin to remain when text is flowed or automatically wrapped to the next line.

NUMS ON

> turns on line numbering for the FSLETTER window. If your window already contains text when you turn on line numbering, all text is shifted to the right, and the line numbers appear on the left side of the window. When line numbers are displayed, you can use them to execute text editor line commands. (See Chapter 19 in *SAS Language: Reference* for details of text editor line commands.)

Hscroll

> specifies the default horizontal scrolling amount for the LEFT and RIGHT commands. Specify one of the following amounts:
>
> HALF   scroll half the current window width.
>
> PAGE   scroll the entire current window width.
>
> CURSOR   scroll to the current cursor position.
>
> *n*   scroll the specified number of columns.

Tabs

sets default tab stops for the text editor.

Specify the tab stop for each column explicitly in the field provided. For example, the following values set tab stops at columns 1 (default), 25, 40, and 55:

```
25 40 55
```

Move your cursor to a tab stop by pressing your keyboard's TAB key.

Vscroll

specifies the default vertical scrolling amounts for the BACKWARD and FORWARD commands. Specify one of the following amounts:

HALF   scroll half the current window height.

PAGE   scroll the entire current window height.

CURSOR   scroll to the current cursor position.

n   scroll the specified number of lines.

Colors and Attributes

control the color and highlighting attributes of selected areas of the FSLETTER window.

The following values are valid in the Color fields:

BLUE	GREEN	WHITE	GRAY
RED	CYAN	BLACK	BROWN
PINK	YELLOW	MAGENTA	ORANGE

If a specified color is not available on a user's device, the procedure substitutes the available color that most closely matches the specified color. Some devices do not allow changing the background color; for these devices, the background color parameter is ignored.

The following values are valid in the Attribute fields. (You can abbreviate the values by entering only the first letter; the procedure fills in the complete value when you press ENTER):

HIGHLIGHT	high intensity
BLINKING	blinking
UNDERLINE	underlined
REVERSE	reverse video

Any parameter that specifies a highlighting attribute not available on the device is ignored. You cannot specify a highlighting attribute for the background.

EDPARMS Window Commands

In addition to the global commands described in Chapter 18, you can use the following commands in the EDPARMS window. Commands with special meanings in the FSLETTER ATTR window are marked with an asterisk and are described in this section. The remaining commands are described in "Auxiliary Window Commands" later in this chapter.

Scrolling

> BACKWARD ⟨HALF | PAGE | MAX | n⟩
> BOTTOM
> FORWARD ⟨HALF | PAGE | MAX | n⟩
> HSCROLL HALF | PAGE | n
> LEFT ⟨HALF | PAGE | MAX | n⟩
> RIGHT ⟨HALF | PAGE | MAX | n⟩
> TOP
> VSCROLL HALF | PAGE | n

Closing the Window

> * CANCEL
> * END

Command Descriptions

Descriptions of the special EDPARMS window commands follow:

CANCEL

> closes the EDPARMS window without recording any changes made in the window and returns you to the window from which the EDPARMS command was issued. Use this command when you decide not to change the current parameter settings after you have opened the EDPARMS window.

END

> closes the EDPARMS window, records any changes you made to the parameter settings in the letter entry, and returns you to the window from which the EDPARMS window was opened.

Using Text Editor Commands

Another way to change the text editor environment while editing a particular document is to use global text editor commands. There is a corresponding text editor command for each of the parameters in the EDPARMS window.

Parameter	Text Editor Command
AUTOADD	AUTOADD ⟨ON	OFF⟩
AUTOWRAP	AUTOWRAP ⟨ON	OFF⟩
CAPS	CAPS ⟨ON	OFF⟩
INDENT	INDENT ⟨ON	OFF⟩
NUMS ON	NUMS ⟨ON	OFF⟩
Hscroll	HSCROLL HALF	PAGE	CURSOR	MAX	n
Tabs	TABS n
Vscroll	VSCROLL HALF	PAGE	CURSOR	MAX	n
Colors and Attributes	COLOR area color ⟨highlight⟩

If you open the EDPARMS window after issuing one of these commands, you see that the parameter settings in the EDPARMS window change to reflect the parameter status specified in these commands.

Creating Default Parameter Settings

Whenever you create a new document, the initial text editor parameter settings are copied from a catalog entry named FSLETTER.EDPARMS. The default FSLETTER.EDPARMS entry is stored in the SASHELP.FSP system catalog. You can customize the default parameter entry for a catalog using the FSLETTER procedure.

To create a custom FSLETTER.EDPARMS entry, issue the following command in an FSLETTER window or in the FSLETTER DIRECTORY window:

```
edit fsletter.edparms
```

If the current catalog does not already contain an FSLETTER.EDPARMS entry, a copy of the FSLETTER.EDPARMS entry from the SASHELP.FSP system catalog is created in the current catalog and then opened for editing.

This command opens an EDPARMS window, like the one in Display 14.4 (except that the window title does not include the word EDPARMS). However, the parameter settings in this window have no effect on existing documents. Instead, these parameter settings become the default settings for any new documents created in the current catalog. You can change the parameters in FSLETTER.EDPARMS whenever you want without affecting existing letter entries.

You may find it convenient to create different FSLETTER.EDPARMS entries for different catalogs. If you keep letters in one catalog, reports in another, and questionnaires in another, you can create a different FSLETTER.EDPARMS entry for each catalog to store appropriate parameter settings for each kind of text.

When you create a new document, the FSLETTER procedure locates the default text editor parameter values by looking for the FSLETTER.EDPARMS entry first in the current catalog, then in your personal PROFILE catalog (SASUSER.PROFILE, or WORK.PROFILE if the SASUSER library is not allocated). If the entry does not exist in either of those catalogs, the FSLETTER procedure uses the default FSLETTER.EDPARMS entry in the SASHELP.FSP system catalog.

Thus, you may also want to create a custom FSLETTER.EDPARMS entry in your personal PROFILE catalog. That entry then provides default parameter values for any catalog that does not have its own FSLETTER.EDPARMS entry.

Copying Parameter Entries to New Catalogs

You do not have to create a new FSLETTER.EDPARMS entry each time you create a new catalog. If you do not want to use the default text editor parameters in the SASHELP.FSP catalog or in your personal PROFILE catalog, you can copy your custom FSLETTER.EDPARMS entry from one catalog to another.

Suppose that you have defined an FSLETTER.EDPARMS entry in an existing catalog named MASTER.LETTERS and that you have created a new catalog named MASTER.LETTERS2. You can issue the following command in the

FSLETTER DIRECTORY window for the MASTER.LETTERS2 catalog to copy the
FSLETTER.EDPARMS entry from the old catalog into the new catalog:

```
copy master.letters.fsletter.edparms
```

Auxiliary Window Commands

The commands used for scrolling work the same way in the FSLETTER
DIRECTORY, FSLETTER ATTR, and EDPARMS windows. The same search
commands work in the FSLETTER DIRECTORY and FSLETTER ATTR windows.
These commands are listed and defined in this section. As a reminder, a
command list is given for each window in which they are valid.

In addition to the global commands described in Chapter 18, you can use the
following commands in the FSLETTER DIRECTORY, FSLETTER ATTR, and
EDPARMS windows to scroll information and to control default scrolling:

BACKWARD ⟨HALF | PAGE | MAX | *n*⟩
BOTTOM
FORWARD ⟨HALF | PAGE | MAX | *n*⟩
HSCROLL HALF | PAGE | *n*
LEFT ⟨HALF | PAGE | MAX | *n*⟩
RIGHT ⟨HALF | PAGE | MAX | *n*⟩
TOP
VSCROLL HALF | PAGE | *n*

You can use the following commands in the FSLETTER DIRECTORY and
FSLETTER ATTR windows to search for specified character strings:

BFIND ⟨*character-string* | *'character-string'*⟩
BLOCATE ⟨*value* | *'value'*⟩
BLOCATE: ⟨*partial-value* | *'partial-value'*⟩
FIND ⟨*character-string* | *'character-string'*⟩
KEYFIELD ⟨*field-name*⟩
LOCATE ⟨*value* | *'value'*⟩
LOCATE: ⟨*partial-value* | *'partial-value'*⟩
RFIND
RLOCATE

Command Descriptions
Descriptions of the special commands for the FSLETTER DIRECTORY,
FSLETTER ATTR, and EDPARMS windows follow:

BACKWARD ⟨HALF | PAGE | MAX | *n*⟩
>   scrolls vertically toward the top of the window. The following scroll
>   amounts can be specified:

HALF	scrolls upward by half the number of lines in the window.
PAGE	scrolls upward by the number of lines in the window.
MAX	scrolls upward to the top of the window.
n	scrolls upward the specified number of lines.

If you do not explicitly specify a scrolling increment, the default increment is the amount specified in the VSCROLL command. The default VSCROLL amount is HALF.

BFIND ⟨*character-string* | *'character-string'*⟩

searches backward for the specified character string in the field identified using the KEYFIELD command. Enclose the search string in quotes if it contains special characters, embedded blanks, or lowercase characters.

The BFIND command, unlike the BLOCATE command, looks for the string anywhere in the field, not just at the beginning.

If you want to search forward from the cursor position toward the bottom of the window rather than backward toward the top, use the FIND command.

Use the BFIND command without arguments to search backward for the character string specified in a previous BFIND or FIND command.

BLOCATE ⟨*value* | *'value'*⟩
BLOCATE: ⟨*partial-value* | *'partial-value'*⟩

searches backward for the specified value in the field identified using the KEYFIELD command. Enclose the search value in quotes if it contains special characters, embedded blanks, or lowercase characters.

The BLOCATE command searches only for an exact match. If you want to specify only the first part of a value, use the BLOCATE: command. If you want to search for a match in any part of the value instead of just at the beginning, use the BFIND command instead.

If you want to search forward from the cursor position toward the bottom of the window rather than backward toward the top, use the LOCATE command.

Use the RLOCATE command to find the next occurrence of the value specified.

BOTTOM

scrolls to the bottom of the information displayed in the window.

FIND ⟨*character-string* | *'character-string'*⟩

searches for the specified character string in the field identified using the KEYFIELD command. Enclose the search string in quotes if it contains special characters, embedded blanks, or lowercase characters.

The FIND command, unlike the LOCATE command, looks for the string anywhere in the field, not just at the beginning.

If you want to search backward from the cursor position toward the top of the window rather than forward toward the end, use the BFIND command.

Use the RFIND command to find the next occurrence of the string specified.

FORWARD ⟨HALF | PAGE | MAX | *n*⟩

scrolls vertically toward the bottom of the window. The following scroll amounts can be specified:

HALF   scrolls downward by half the number of lines in the window.

PAGE   scrolls downward by the number of lines in the window.

(FORWARD continued)

MAX   scrolls downward to the bottom of the window.

n   scrolls downward the specified number of lines.

If you do not explicitly specify a scrolling increment, the default increment is the amount specified in the VSCROLL command. The default VSCROLL amount is HALF.

HSCROLL HALF | PAGE | *n*
specifies the default horizontal scroll amount for the LEFT and RIGHT commands. Specify one of the following scroll amounts:

HALF   scroll half the width of the window.

PAGE   scroll the full width of the window.

n   scroll the specified number of columns.

KEYFIELD ⟨*field-name*⟩
identifies the field that is searched when you next execute a FIND, LOCATE, BFIND, or BLOCATE command. Indicate the field you want searched by supplying the field name as an argument in the KEYFIELD command or by typing KEYFIELD on the command line, positioning the cursor on the desired field, and pressing ENTER.
For example, to search for all the entries named RENEWAL in the Name field of the FSLETTER DIRECTORY window, you must first identify Name as the field you want searched. Type KEYFIELD on the command line, position the cursor anywhere on the Name field, and press ENTER. Then issue the following command to locate the first entry in the catalog with the name RENEWAL:

```
locate renewal
```

Use the KEYFIELD command without arguments to display the current key field value on the window's message line.

LEFT ⟨**HALF | PAGE | MAX |** *n*⟩
scrolls the window horizontally by the specified amount. The following scroll amounts can be specified:

HALF   scrolls by half the window width.

PAGE   scrolls by the full window width.

MAX   scrolls to the left margin of the window.

n   scrolls the specified number of columns.

If you do not explicitly specify a scrolling increment, the default increment is the amount specified in the HSCROLL command. The default HSCROLL amount is HALF.

LOCATE ⟨*value* | *'value'*⟩
LOCATE: ⟨*partial-value* | *'partial-value'*⟩

> searches for the next occurrence of the specified value in the field identified using the KEYFIELD command. Enclose the search value in quotes if it contains special characters, embedded blanks, or lowercase characters.
>
> The LOCATE command searches only for an exact match. If you want to specify only the first part of a value, use the LOCATE: command. If you want to search for a match in any part of the value instead of just at the beginning, use the FIND command instead.
>
> If you want to search backward from the cursor position toward the top of the window rather than forward toward the end, use the BLOCATE command.
>
> Use the RLOCATE command to find the next occurrence of the value specified.

RFIND

> re-executes the most recent FIND command, locating the next occurrence of the character string.

RIGHT ⟨HALF | PAGE | MAX | *n*⟩

> scrolls the window horizontally by the specified amount. The following scroll amounts can be specified:

> HALF   scrolls by half the window width.

> PAGE   scrolls by the full window width.

> MAX   scrolls to the right margin of the window.

> *n*   scrolls the specified number of columns.

> If you do not explicitly specify a scrolling increment, the default increment is the amount specified in the HSCROLL command. The default HSCROLL amount is HALF.

RLOCATE

> re-executes the most recent LOCATE or BLOCATE command, locating the next occurrence of the value.

TOP

> scrolls to the top of the information displayed in the window.

VSCROLL HALF | PAGE | *n*

> specifies the default vertical scroll amount for the FORWARD and BACKWARD commands. Specify one of the following scroll amounts:

> HALF   scroll half the height of the window.

> PAGE   scroll the full height of the window.

> *n*   scroll the specified number of rows.

Chapter 15 The FSLIST Procedure

Overview

The FSLIST procedure allows you to browse external (non-SAS) files within a SAS session. Because the files are displayed in an interactive window, the procedure provides a highly convenient mechanism for examining file contents. In addition, you can copy text from the FSLIST window into any window that uses the SAS text editor.

FSLIST Procedure Syntax

Use the PROC FSLIST statement to invoke the FSLIST procedure:

PROC FSLIST FILEREF=*fileref* | '*actual-filename*' | UNIT=*nn* ⟨*options*⟩;

☐ You must specify either the FILEREF= or UNIT= argument with the PROC FSLIST statement.

☐ *Options* can be one or more of the following:

CAPS | NOCAPS
CC | FORTCC | NOCC
HSCROLL=HALF | PAGE | *n*
NUM | NONUM
OVP | NOOVP

FSLIST Command

The FSLIST procedure can also be initiated by entering the following command on the command line of any SAS System window:

FSLIST 〈? | *fileref* | *'actual-filename'* 〈CC | FORTCC | NOCC 〈OVP | NOOVP〉〉〉

PROC FSLIST Statement

The PROC FSLIST statement initiates the FSLIST procedure and specifies the external file to browse. Statement options allow you to modify the default behavior of the procedure.

PROC FSLIST Statement Requirements

The PROC FSLIST statement must include an argument that specifies the external file to be opened for browsing. The file can be identified either by its actual filename (including a path specification on operating systems where that is required) or by a *fileref*, a SAS nickname for the file. You can use the FILENAME statement to associate a fileref with an actual filename. See "External Files" in Chapter 1, "Introduction to SAS/FSP Software," for an example of the FILENAME statement. Complete details are provided in Chapter 9, "SAS Language Statements," in *SAS Language: Reference, Version 6, First Edition*.

Either one of the following arguments can be used to specify the file:

FILEREF=*fileref* | *'actual-filename'*
DDNAME=*fileref* | *'actual-filename'*
DD=*fileref* | *'actual-filename'*
> specifies the fileref or the actual filename of the external file to be browsed. If you supply a filename, it must be enclosed in quotes.

UNIT=*nn*
> defines the FORTRAN-style logical unit number of the external file to be browsed. This is useful when the file to be browsed has a fileref of the form FT*nn*F001, where *nn* is the logical unit number specified in the UNITS= argument. For example, you can specify

```
proc fslist unit=20;
```

> instead of

```
proc fslist fileref=ft20f001;
```

> This form of fileref was used for a variety of SAS System output files in Version 5 SAS software under the MVS, CMS, and VSE operating systems. For example, the SAS log was written to a file with the fileref (DDname) FT11F001.

PROC FSLIST Statement Options

The following options can be used with the PROC FSLIST statement:

CAPS
NOCAPS

> controls how search strings for the FIND command are treated:
>
> > CAPS
> >
> > > translates search strings into uppercase unless they are enclosed in quotes. For example, with this option in effect, the command
> > >
> > > ```
> > > find nc
> > > ```
> > >
> > > would locate occurrences of **NC**, but **nc** would not be considered a match. To locate lowercase characters, enclose the search string in quotes:
> > >
> > > ```
> > > find 'nc'
> > > ```
> >
> > NOCAPS
> >
> > > no translation is performed; the FIND command locates only those text strings that exactly match the search string.
>
> The default is NOCAPS. You can use the CAPS command in the FSLIST window to change the behavior of the procedure while browsing a file.

CC
FORTCC
NOCC

> indicates whether carriage-control characters are used to format the display. You can specify one of the following values for this option:
>
> > CC
> >
> > > use the native carriage-control characters of the host operating system.
> >
> > FORTCC
> >
> > > use FORTRAN-style carriage control. The first column of each line in the external file is not displayed; the character in this column is interpreted as a carriage-control code. The FSLIST procedure recognizes the following carriage-control characters:
> > >
> > > | | |
> > > |---|---|
> > > | + | skip zero lines and print (overprint) |
> > > | blank | skip one line and print (single space) |
> > > | 0 | skip two lines and print (double space) |
> > > | - | skip three lines and print (triple space) |
> > > | 1 | go to new page and print. |
> >
> > NOCC
> >
> > > treat carriage-control characters as regular text.
>
> The default is NOCC.
>
> **Note:** Under some operating systems, FORTRAN-style carriage control is the native carriage control. For these systems, the FORTCC and CC options produce the same behavior. The FORTCC option in

(CC continued)

Release 6.06 of SAS/FSP software produces the same behavior as the CC option did in earlier releases of Version 6.

HSCROLL=*n* | HALF | PAGE
indicates the default horizontal scroll amount for the LEFT and RIGHT commands. The following values are valid:

n   sets the default scroll amount to *n* columns.

HALF   sets the default scroll amount to half the window width.

PAGE   sets the default scroll amount to the full window width.

The default is HSCROLL=HALF. You can use the HSCROLL command in the FSLIST window to change the default scroll amount.

NUM
NONUM

controls the display of line sequence numbers in files that have a record length of 80 and contain sequence numbers in columns 73 through 80. NUM displays the line sequence numbers; NONUM suppresses them. The default is NONUM.

OVP
NOOVP

indicates whether the carriage-control code for overprinting is honored:

OVP   causes the procedure to honor the overprint code and print the current line over the previous line when the code is encountered.

NOOVP   causes the procedure to ignore the overprint code and print each line from the file on a separate line of the display.

The default is NOOVP. The OVP option is only valid when the CC or FORTCC option is also used.

FSLIST Command

The FSLIST command provides a handy way to initiate an FSLIST session from any SAS System window. The command allows you to use either a fileref or an actual filename to specify the file to browse. It also allows you to specify how carriage-control information is interpreted.

FSLIST Command Syntax

The general form of the FSLIST command is

FSLIST ⟨? | *fileref* | *'actual-filename'* ⟨CC | FORTCC | NOCC ⟨OVP | NOOVP⟩⟩⟩

FSLIST Command Arguments

You can specify one of the following arguments with the FSLIST command:

?

opens a selection window from which you can choose the external file to browse. The selection list in the window includes all external files identified in the current SAS session (all files with defined filerefs).

To select a file, position the cursor on the corresponding fileref and press ENTER.

fileref

identifies the external file to be browsed by its assigned fileref.

If you specify a fileref that is not currently defined, a selection window is opened showing all available filerefs. An error message in the selection window indicates that the specified fileref is not defined.

'actual-filename'

identifies the external file to be browsed by its complete operating system file specification (called the fully qualified pathname under some operating systems). The filename must be enclosed in quotes.

If the specified file is not found, a selection window is opened showing all available filerefs.

If you do not specify any of these three arguments, a selection window is opened showing the available filerefs (as if you had used the ? argument).

FSLIST Command Options

If you use a *fileref* or *'actual-filename'* argument with the FSLIST command, you can also use the following options. These options are not valid with the ? argument, or when no argument is used:

CC
FORTCC
NOCC

indicates whether carriage-control characters are used to format the display. You can specify one of the following values for this option:

CC   use the native carriage-control characters of the host operating system.

FORTCC   use FORTRAN-style carriage control. See the discussion of the PROC FSLIST statement's FORTCC option earlier in this chapter for details.

NOCC   treat carriage-control characters as regular text.

The default is NOCC.

OVP
NOOVP

indicates whether the carriage-control code for overprinting is honored. OVP causes the overprint code to be honored; NOOVP causes it to be ignored. The default is NOOVP. The OVP option is only valid when the CC or FORTCC option is also used.

Using the FSLIST Procedure

The FSLIST procedure displays an external file in the FSLIST window. The commands available in this window allow you to

□ scroll the display both vertically and horizontally

□ search for a string of characters

□ display line numbers and column rulers

□ display the hexadecimal values of file characters

□ change the colors used in the display.

The FSLIST procedure displays files for browsing only, You cannot edit files in the FSLIST window. You can, however, use the global MARK and STORE commands to copy text from the FSLIST window into a paste buffer. This text can then be pasted into any window that uses the SAS text editor, including the FSLETTER window in SAS/FSP software.

FSLIST Window Commands

In addition to the global commands described in Chapter 18, "Command Reference," you can use the following commands in the FSLIST window:

Scrolling

n
BACKWARD ⟨*n* | HALF | PAGE | MAX⟩
BOTTOM
FORWARD ⟨*n* | HALF | PAGE | MAX⟩
HSCROLL ⟨*n* | HALF | PAGE⟩
LEFT ⟨*n* | HALF | PAGE | MAX⟩
RIGHT ⟨*n* | HALF | PAGE | MAX⟩
TOP
VSCROLL ⟨*n* | HALF | PAGE⟩

Searching

BFIND ⟨*search-string* ⟨PREFIX | SUFFIX | WORD⟩⟩
CAPS ⟨ON | OFF⟩
FIND *search-string* ⟨NEXT | FIRST | LAST | PREV | ALL⟩ ⟨PREFIX | SUFFIX | WORD⟩
RFIND

Controlling the Display

COLOR *area color* ⟨*highlighting*⟩
COLUMN ⟨ON | OFF⟩
HEX ⟨ON | OFF⟩
NUMS ⟨ON | OFF⟩

File Management

BROWSE *fileref* | '*actual-filename*' ⟨CC | FORTCC | NOCC ⟨OVP | NOOVP⟩⟩
END

Copying Text

(The following commands are documented in Chapter 18, "SAS Display Manager Commands," in *SAS Language: Reference*.)

MARK
STORE
UNMARK

Other

HELP ⟨*command*⟩
KEYS

Command Descriptions

Descriptions of the special FSLIST window commands follow. Refer to Chapter 6, "Browsing External Files Using the FSLIST Procedure," for examples of using these commands.

n

> scrolls the window so that the specified line of text is at the top of the window. Type the desired line number on the command line and press ENTER. If the *n* value is greater than the number of lines in the file, the last line of the file is displayed at the top of the window.

BACKWARD ⟨*n* | HALF | PAGE | MAX⟩

> scrolls vertically toward the first line of the file. The following scroll amounts can be specified:

> *n*   scrolls upward the specified number of lines.

> HALF   scrolls upward by half the number of lines in the window.

> PAGE   scrolls upward by the number of lines in the window.

> MAX   scrolls upward until the first line of the file is displayed.

> If the scroll amount is not explicitly specified, the window is scrolled by the amount specified in the most recent VSCROLL command. The default VSCROLL amount is PAGE.

BFIND ⟨*search-string* ⟨PREFIX | SUFFIX | WORD⟩⟩

> locates the previous occurrence of the specified string in the file, starting at the current cursor position and proceeding backward toward the beginning of the file. The *search-string* value must be enclosed in quotes if it contains embedded blanks.

> If a FIND command has previously been issued, you can use the BFIND command without arguments to repeat the search in the opposite direction.

> The CAPS option and the CAPS ON command cause search strings to be converted to uppercase for the purposes of the search, unless the strings are enclosed in quotes. See the discussion of the FIND command for details.

(BFIND continued)

By default, the BFIND command locates any occurrence of the specified string, even where the string is embedded in other strings. You can use any one of the following options to alter the command's behavior:

PREFIX   causes the search string to match the text string only when the text string occurs at the beginning of a word.

SUFFIX   causes the search string to match the text string only when the text string occurs at the end of a word.

WORD   causes the search string to match the text string only when the text string is a distinct word.

You can use the RFIND command to repeat the most recent BFIND command.

BOTTOM
scrolls downward until the last line of the file is displayed.

BROWSE *fileref* | *'actual-filename'* ⟨CC | FORTCC | NOCC ⟨OVP | NOOVP⟩⟩
closes the current file and displays the specified file in the FSVIEW window. You can specify either a fileref previously associated with a file or an actual filename enclosed in quotes.

The BROWSE command also accepts the same carriage-control options as the FSLIST command. See "FSLIST Command Options" earlier in this chapter for details.

CAPS ⟨ON | OFF⟩
controls how the FIND, BFIND, and RFIND commands locate matches for a search string. By default, the FIND commands locate only those text strings that exactly match the search string as it was entered. When the CAPS attribute is turned on, the FIND commands translate search strings into uppercase for the purposes of searching (displayed text is not affected), unless the strings are enclosed in quotes. Quoted strings are not affected.

For example, after you issue a CAPS ON command, the following commands both locate occurrences of **NC** but not occurrences of **nc**:

```
find NC
find nc
```

If you omit the ON or OFF argument, the CAPS command acts as a toggle, turning the attribute on if it was off or off if it was on.

COLOR *area color* ⟨*highlighting*⟩
sets the color and highlighting attributes of areas of the FSLIST window. This is a global display manager command; see Chapter 18, "SAS Display Manager Commands," in *SAS Language: Reference* for a list of valid values for the *area, color,* and *highlighting* arguments. In addition to the

areas listed for the global command, the following areas can be specified when the command is used in the FSLIST window:

NUMBERS the column of line numbers displayed at the left side of the window when the NUMS ON command is used

TEXT the text of the external file.

COLUMN ⟨ON | OFF⟩
displays a column ruler below the message line in the FSLIST window. The ruler is helpful when you need to determine the column in which a particular character is located.

If you omit the ON or OFF specification, the COLUMN command acts as a toggle, turning the ruler on if it was off and off if it was on.

END
closes the FSLIST window and ends the FSLIST session.

FIND *search-string* ⟨NEXT | FIRST | LAST | PREV | ALL⟩
⟨PREFIX | SUFFIX | WORD⟩
locates an occurrence of the specified string in the file. The string must be enclosed in quotes if it contains embedded blanks.

The text in the search string must match the text in the file in both character and case. For example, the command

```
find raleigh
```

will not locate the text **Raleigh** in the file. You must instead use

```
find Raleigh
```

When the CAPS option is used with the PROC FSLIST statement or when a CAPS ON command is issued in the window, the search string is converted to uppercase for the purposes of the search, unless the string is enclosed in quotes. In that case,

```
find raleigh
```

will only locate the text **RALEIGH** in the file. You must instead use

```
find 'Raleigh'
```

to locate the text **Raleigh**.

You can modify the behavior of the FIND command by adding any one of the following options:

ALL reports the total number of occurrences of the string in the file in the window's message line and moves the cursor to the first occurrence.

FIRST moves the cursor to the first occurrence of the string in the file.

LAST moves the cursor to the last occurrence of the string in the file.

(FIND continued)

NEXT   moves the cursor to the next occurrence of the string in the file.

PREV   moves the cursor to the previous occurrence of the string in the file.

The default behavior is NEXT.

By default, the FIND command locates any occurrence of the specified string, even where the string is embedded in other strings. You can use any one of the following options to alter the command's behavior:

PREFIX   causes the search string to match the text string only when the text string occurs at the beginning of a word.

SUFFIX   causes the search string to match the text string only when the text string occurs at the end of a word.

WORD   causes the search string to match the text string only when the text string is a distinct word.

After you issue a FIND command, you can use the RFIND command to repeat the search for the next occurrence of the string, or the BFIND command to repeat the search for the previous occurrence.

FORWARD ⟨n | HALF | PAGE | MAX⟩

scrolls vertically toward the end of the file. The following scroll amounts can be specified:

n   scrolls downward the specified number of lines.

HALF   scrolls downward by half the number of lines in the window.

PAGE   scrolls downward by the number of lines in the window.

MAX   scrolls downward until the last line of the file is displayed.

If the scroll amount is not explicitly specified, the window is scrolled by the amount specified in the most recent VSCROLL command. The default VSCROLL amount is PAGE. Regardless of the scroll increment, this command will not scroll beyond the last line of the file.

HELP ⟨command⟩

opens a HELP window providing information about the FSLIST procedure and about the commands available in the FSLIST window. To get information about a specific FSLIST window command, follow the HELP command with the name of the desired command. Use the END command to close the HELP window and return to the FSLIST window.

HEX ⟨ON | OFF⟩

controls the special hexadecimal display format of the FSLIST window. When hexadecimal format is turned on, each line of characters from the file occupies three lines of the display. The first is the line displayed as characters; the next two lines of the display show the hexadecimal value of the host system's character codes for the characters in the line of text.

The hexadecimal values are displayed vertically, with the most significant byte on top.

If you omit the ON or OFF specification, the HEX command acts as a toggle, turning hexadecimal format on if it was off and off if it was on.

HSCROLL ⟨*n* | HALF | PAGE⟩

sets the default horizontal scrolling amount for the LEFT and RIGHT commands. The following scroll amounts can be specified:

n	sets the default scroll amount to the specified number of columns.
HALF	sets the default scroll amount to half the number of columns in the window.
PAGE	sets the default scroll amount to the number of columns in the window.

The default HSCROLL amount is HALF.

KEYS

opens the KEYS window for browsing and editing function key definitions for the FSLIST window. The default key definitions for the FSLIST window are stored in the FSLIST.KEYS entry in the SASHELP.FSP catalog. If you change any key definitions in the KEYS window, a new FSLIST.KEYS entry is created in your personal PROFILE catalog (SASUSER.PROFILE, or WORK.PROFILE if the SASUSER library is not allocated). When the FSLIST procedure is initiated, it looks for function key definitions first in the FSLIST.KEYS entry in your personal PROFILE catalog. If that entry does not exist, the default entry in the SASHELP.FSP catalog is used.

LEFT ⟨*n* | HALF | PAGE | MAX⟩

scrolls horizontally toward the left margin of the text. This command is ignored unless the file width is greater than the window width. The following scroll amounts can be specified:

n	scrolls left the specified number of columns.
HALF	scrolls left by half the number of columns in the window.
PAGE	scrolls left by the number of columns in the window.
MAX	scrolls left until the left margin of the text is displayed at the left edge of the window.

If the scroll amount is not explicitly specified, the window is scrolled by the amount specified in the most recent HSCROLL command. The default HSCROLL amount is HALF. Regardless of the scroll increment, this command will not scroll beyond the left margin of the text.

NUMS ⟨ON | OFF⟩

controls whether line numbers are shown at the left side of the window. By default, line numbers are not displayed. If line numbers are turned on, they remain at the left side of the display when text in the window is scrolled right and left.

If you omit the ON or OFF argument, the NUMS command acts as a toggle, turning line numbering on if it was off or off if it was on.

RFIND

repeats the most recent FIND command, starting at the current cursor position and proceeding forward toward the end of the file.

RIGHT ⟨n | HALF | PAGE | MAX⟩

scrolls horizontally toward the right margin of the text. This command is ignored unless the file width is greater than the window width. The following scroll amounts can be specified:

n   scrolls right the specified number of columns.

HALF   scrolls right by half the number of columns in the window.

PAGE   scrolls right by the number of columns in the window.

MAX   scrolls right until the right margin of the text is displayed at the right edge of the window.

If the scroll amount is not explicitly specified, the window is scrolled by the amount specified in the most recent HSCROLL command. The default HSCROLL amount is HALF. Regardless of the scroll increment, this command will not scroll beyond the right margin of the text.

TOP

scrolls upward until the first line of text from the file is displayed.

VSCROLL ⟨n | HALF | PAGE⟩

sets the default vertical scrolling amount for the FORWARD and BACKWARD commands. The following scroll amounts can be specified:

n   sets the default scroll amount to the specified number of lines.

HALF   sets the default scroll amount to half the number of lines in the window.

PAGE   sets the default scroll amount to the number of lines in the window.

The default VSCROLL amount is PAGE.

Chapter 16 The FSVIEW Procedure

Overview

The FSVIEW procedure allows you to browse or edit a SAS data set displayed as a table of rows and columns. You can also use it to create a new SAS data set.

The procedure provides tools for customizing an FSVIEW application. For example, you can redesign the display by changing the size, position, and colors of the FSVIEW window. You can also add computed variables that display values calculated from other variables in the data set.

The FSVIEW procedure replaces the FSPRINT procedure included in SAS/FSP software prior to Release 6.06.

Terminology

You will encounter the following terms in the discussion of the FSVIEW procedure. Refer to the Glossary at the end of this book if you are unsure of the meaning of these terms:

control level

format

formula

formula entry

informat

FSVIEW Procedure Syntax

You can use the following statements to invoke the FSVIEW procedure:

□ The PROC FSVIEW statement is required.

PROC FSVIEW ⟨DATA=*data-set*⟩ | ⟨NEW=*data-set* ⟨LIKE=*data-set*⟩⟩
⟨FORMULA=*SAS-catalog*⟨.*formula-entry*⟩⟩
⟨*options*⟩;

where *options* can be one or more of the following:

AUTOADD
BROWSEONLY
DEBUG

EDIT | MODIFY
NOADD
NODELETE
NOMSG

Note: For compatibility with earlier releases of SAS/FSP software, PROC FSPRINT is accepted as an alias for PROC FSVIEW.

□ The following statements are optional.

FORMAT *variable-list format* ⟨. . . *variable-list-n format-n*⟩;

ID *variable* ⟨. . . *variable-n*⟩;

INFORMAT *variable-list informat* ⟨. . . *variable-list-n informat-n*⟩;

VAR *variable* ⟨. . . *variable-n*⟩;

WHERE *expression*;

Note: The optional statements should not be used when you use the NEW= option in the PROC FSVIEW statement. (The ID and VAR statements cause errors; the FORMAT, INFORMAT, and WHERE statements are ignored.) When you load a formula entry, the features defined in the entry take precedence over the features specified in the FORMAT, ID, INFORMAT, and VAR statements.

Statement Descriptions

The following is a brief description of each of the FSVIEW procedure statements:

PROC FSVIEW   initiates the FSVIEW procedure.

FORMAT   associates formats with variables in the input data set.

ID   specifies the variable or variables used to identify observations in lieu of observation numbers.

INFORMAT   associates informats with variables in the input data set.

VAR   specifies the names and order of variables in the display.

WHERE   specifies a condition or set of conditions that observations in the input data set must meet in order to be displayed.

Requirements

Unless you are using the FSVIEW procedure to create a new SAS data set, it must have an input data set. By default, the procedure uses the most recently created data set (the data set identified by the system variable _LAST_) as its input data set. If you do not specify a data set name and no data set has previously been created in the current SAS session, the procedure terminates with an error message.

FSVIEW Command

The FSVIEW procedure can also be initiated by entering the following command on the command line of any SAS System window:

FSVIEW ⟨? | *data-set* ⟨*formula-name*⟩⟩

where

□ *data-set* is the input data set to be displayed

□ *formula-name* is the associated formula entry.

Note: FSPRINT is also accepted as an alias for FSVIEW.

PROC FSVIEW Statement

The PROC FSVIEW statement initiates the FSVIEW procedure. It allows you to specify the data set to be browsed or edited and to identify a formula entry containing formulas for computed variables and other information used to customize the FSVIEW session. Additional statement options allow you to modify the display or change the default behavior of the procedure.

▶ *Caution* .... *The FSVIEW procedure edits a SAS data set in place.*
The FSVIEW procedure does not leave an unedited copy of the original. If you need to preserve the original data, be sure to make a copy of the data set before you begin editing. ▲

Refer to "FSVIEW Procedure Syntax" earlier in this chapter for a complete list of the options that can be used with this statement.

PROC FSVIEW Statement Options

The following options can be used with the PROC FSVIEW statement:

AUTOADD

> turns on the autoadd feature. A new observation is displayed when the FSVIEW window is opened. Another new observation is added automatically whenever you enter values in the previous new observation and press ENTER.
>
> The AUTOADD option is ignored if you also specify the NOADD option with the PROC FSVIEW statement.

BROWSEONLY
BRONLY

> prevents editing of data sets during the FSVIEW session. This option disables the MODIFY command so that data sets opened for browsing cannot be switched to editing and also disables the EDIT command so that additional FSVIEW windows cannot be opened for editing.

DATA=*data-set*⟨(*data-set-options*)⟩
:   names the SAS data set to edit or browse. By default, the FSVIEW procedure displays the data set most recently created.

    If you specify both the DATA= option and the NEW= option in the same PROC FSVIEW statement, the DATA= option is ignored.

    You can add a list of data set options following the data set name. The list must be enclosed in parentheses. The FIRSTOBS= and OBS= options are ignored; all other data set options are valid. Refer to Chapter 15, "SAS Data Set Options," in *SAS Language: Reference, Version 6, First Edition* for a listing and descriptions of data set options.

DEBUG
:   turns on the Screen Control Language (SCL) source-level debugger. The debugger is useful for finding and correcting errors in formulas. See *SAS Screen Control Language: Reference, Version 6, First Edition* for information on using the debugger.

EDIT
MODIFY
:   opens the initial FSVIEW window for editing the data set. By default, the initial FSVIEW window is opened for browsing.

    This option is ignored if the BROWSEONLY option is also used. If the data set cannot be opened for editing, it is opened for browsing instead.

FORMULA=*SAS-catalog*⟨.*formula-entry*⟩
:   names a SAS catalog or specific formula entry containing formulas for computed variables and other FSVIEW session parameters to be associated with the data set, or where the procedure can store formulas and parameter settings defined during the current FSVIEW session.

    The general form of the *SAS-catalog* value is

    ⟨*libref.*⟩*catalog-name*

    If the specified catalog does not already exist, it is created.

    If you specify only a one-level name, it is treated as a catalog name in the default library, WORK. You must use a two-level catalog name if you want to specify a formula entry name.

    The general form of the *formula-entry* value is

    entry-name⟨.FORMULA⟩

    If you specify a two-level formula name with anything other than FORMULA as the second level (entry type), the specified type is ignored; FORMULA is used instead.

    When an entry name is provided, the procedure attempts to load the specified entry when the initial FSVIEW window is opened. If the entry is not found, the FSVIEW session is initiated with default FSVIEW window characteristics. A formula entry with the specified name is created when you end the FSVIEW session or use the SAVE FORMULA command.

LIKE=*data-set*⟨(*data-set-options*)⟩
:   names an existing SAS data set whose structure is copied when a new SAS data set is created. (This option must be used in conjunction with the NEW= option.) When the FSVIEW NEW window is opened, the

(LIKE= continued)

variable names and attributes of the data set specified with the LIKE= option are displayed.

You can add a list of data set options following the data set name. The list must be enclosed in parentheses. Refer to Chapter 15 in *SAS Language: Reference* for a listing and descriptions of data set options.

MODIFY

See the EDIT option.

NEW=*data-set⟨(data-set-options)⟩*

creates a new SAS data set. The FSVIEW procedure terminates with an error message if a data set with the specified name already exists.

When this option is used, the procedure begins by opening the FSVIEW NEW window, in which the names and attributes of the variables in the new data set are defined. Use the LIKE= option in conjunction with the NEW= option to initialize the FSVIEW NEW window with the variable names and attributes of an existing data set. After the structure of the new data set is defined, the FSVIEW window is opened so that observations can be added. For details, see "Creating New SAS Data Sets" later in this chapter.

If you specify both the NEW= option and the DATA= option in the same PROC FSVIEW statement, the DATA= option is ignored.

You can add a list of data set options following the data set name. The list must be enclosed in parentheses. Refer to Chapter 15 in *SAS Language: Reference* for a listing and descriptions of data set options.

NOADD

prevents the addition of observations to any data set edited during the current FSVIEW session. This option disables the AUTOADD and DUP commands so that no new observations can be added.

NODELETE
NODEL

prevents the deletion of observations from any data set edited during the current FSVIEW session. This option disables the DELETE command so that observations cannot be deleted.

NOMSG

routes any messages generated by the FSVIEW procedure to the SAS log rather than to the MESSAGE window.

FORMAT Statement

The FORMAT statement associates formats with variables in the input data set. *Formats* are patterns the SAS System uses to determine how variable values are displayed. The formats can be either SAS formats or custom formats you have defined with the FORMAT procedure.

Note: If you load an existing formula entry, the formats recorded in the formula entry take precedence over the formats specified in the FORMAT statement. If you use the NEW= option in the PROC FSVIEW statement, the FORMAT statement is ignored.

FORMAT Statement Syntax

The general form of the FORMAT statement is

FORMAT *variable-list format* ⟨*. . . variable-list-n format-n*⟩;

where *variable-list* consists of one or more variable names from the input data set.

Using the FORMAT Statement

You can use a single FORMAT statement to assign the same format to several variables or to assign different formats to different variables. You can use any number of FORMAT statements with each PROC FSVIEW statement.

Variable formats specified in a FORMAT statement take precedence over formats defined in the data set itself. Formats assigned in a FORMAT statement remain in effect only for the duration of the procedure; the FORMAT statement does not affect any variable format assignments stored in the data set. You can use the FORMAT command in the FSVIEW window to override formats specified in the FORMAT statement.

Format widths determine the width of the columns for the associated variables in the FSVIEW display.

Refer to *SAS Language: Reference* for more detailed information on formats and on the FORMAT statement. See the *SAS Procedures Guide, Version 6, Third Edition* for information on defining your own formats with the FORMAT procedure.

ID Statement

The ID statement specifies one or more variables whose values identify observations in the FSVIEW window. By default, the FSVIEW procedure uses observation numbers to identify observations. Observation numbers are not displayed when ID variables are used. The values of the ID variables appear at the beginning of each row and remain on the left side of the window when the other variable columns are scrolled horizontally.

Note: If you load an existing formula entry, the ID variables recorded in the formula entry take precedence over the ID variables specified in the ID statement. The FSVIEW procedure terminates with an error message if you use the ID statement in conjunction with a PROC FSVIEW statement that includes the NEW= option.

ID Statement Syntax

The general form of the ID statement is

ID *variable* ⟨*. . . variable-n*⟩;

If you specify more than one variable, any valid form of variable list can be used. See *SAS Language: Reference* for details on variable lists.

Using the ID Statement

The FSVIEW procedure does not show more than the first 60 characters of ID variables. If the ID variable column exceeds this length, it is truncated.

If you want to know an observation's number when it is identified by an ID variable, use the OBS command. See "Browsing and Editing SAS Data Sets" later in this chapter for details.

Use the COLOR command to select the color for ID variables and for the ID variable column heading. See "Using the FSVIEW Procedure" later in this chapter for details.

INFORMAT Statement

The INFORMAT statement associates informats with variables in the input data set. *Informats* are patterns the SAS System uses to determine how values entered in variable columns are interpreted. The informats can be either SAS informats or custom informats you have defined with the FORMAT procedure.

Note: If you load an existing formula entry, the informats recorded in the formula entry take precedence over the informats specified in the INFORMAT statement. If you use the NEW= option in the PROC FSVIEW statement, the INFORMAT statement is ignored.

INFORMAT Statement Syntax

The general form of the INFORMAT statement is

> **INFORMAT** *variable-list informat* ⟨. . . *variable-list-n informat-n*⟩;

where *variable-list* consists of one or more variable names from the input data set.

Using the INFORMAT Statement

You can use a single INFORMAT statement to assign the same informat to several variables or to assign different informats to different variables. You can use any number of INFORMAT statements with each PROC FSVIEW statement.

Variable informats specified in an INFORMAT statement take precedence over informats defined in the data set itself. Informats assigned in an INFORMAT statement remain in effect only for the duration of the procedure; the INFORMAT statement does not affect any variable informat assignments stored in the data set. You can use the INFORMAT command in the FSVIEW window to override informats specified in the INFORMAT statement.

When using INFORMAT statements with the FSVIEW procedure, you should take care that the informats you assign to variables are compatible with the formats for those variables. That is, the output produced by the format should be valid input for the informat. Otherwise, you complicate the process of editing variable values. For example, suppose the data set displayed by the FSVIEW procedure contains a variable AMOUNT that is assigned the informat 10.2 and the format DOLLAR10.2. Because of the format, values in the column for the variable AMOUNT are displayed with commas and a leading dollar sign, so the value 1250 would be displayed as $1,250.00. However, if you edit this value (for example, changing it to $1,150.00) and press ENTER, an error condition occurs. The 10.2 informat does not allow the dollar sign ($) or comma characters in entered values. An appropriate informat for this variable is COMMA., which does allow these characters.

Refer to *SAS Language: Reference* for more detailed information on informats and on the INFORMAT statement. See the *SAS Procedures Guide* for information on defining your own informats with the FORMAT procedure.

VAR Statement

The VAR statement selects which variables appear in the display and in what order. By default, the FSVIEW procedure displays all the variables from the data set in the FSVIEW window and arranges the variable columns in the order in which the variables appear in the data set (except for any variables used as ID variables).

Note: If you load an existing formula entry, the variables and variable order recorded in the formula entry take precedence over the list and order of variables specified in the VAR statement. The FSVIEW procedure terminates with an error message if you use the VAR statement in conjunction with a PROC FSVIEW statement that includes the NEW= option.

VAR Statement Syntax

The general form of the VAR statement is

> **VAR** *variable* ⟨*. . . variable-n*⟩;

When more than one variable name is supplied, any valid form of variable list can be used. See *SAS Language: Reference* for details of variable lists.

Using the VAR Statement

Columns of variable values appear in the order specified in the VAR statement. The number of columns visible at any given time depends on the width of the variable values and the current width of the FSVIEW window.

If the same variable name appears in both the ID and VAR statements, the variable is used only as an ID variable.

During an FSVIEW session, use the SHOW and DROP commands to control the display of variables. The SHOW command can add variables to the display even if they are not listed in the VAR statement. See "Using the FSVIEW Procedure" later in this chapter for details.

Use the COLOR command to select the colors for displayed variables and column headings. See "Using the FSVIEW Procedure" later in this chapter for details.

WHERE Statement

The WHERE statement defines criteria that observations in the input data set must meet in order to be displayed by the procedure. By default, the FSVIEW procedure displays all the observations in the data set.

Note: If you use the NEW= option in the PROC FSVIEW statement, the WHERE statement is ignored.

WHERE Statement Syntax

The general form of the WHERE statement is

WHERE *expression*;

where *expression* is any valid WHERE expression involving one or more of the variables in the input data set. Refer to the description of the WHERE statement in Chapter 9 of *SAS Language: Reference* for details of the operators and operands that are valid in WHERE expressions.

Using the WHERE Statement

The WHERE statement is useful when you want to view only a subset of the observations in a SAS data set. For example, to view only observations for which the variable YEAR has a value less than 5, you would follow your PROC FSVIEW statement with the following statement:

```
where year<5;
```

In this case, the FSVIEW procedure displays only those observations that meet the specified criterion. Observations that do not satisfy the condition are not shown and cannot be edited.

Conditions imposed by a WHERE statement (or, equivalently, by a WHERE= data set option) are called permanent WHERE clauses because they remain in effect for the duration of the FSVIEW session and cannot be canceled or modified while the procedure is active.

When you use a WHERE statement in conjunction with the PROC FSVIEW statement, the behavior of the FSVIEW procedure is affected in the following ways:

□ The word *Subset* appears in parentheses following the FSVIEW window title to indicate that a permanent WHERE clause is in effect.

□ Observation numbers may not be sequential because some observations may be excluded.

□ You cannot use the SORT command to sort the displayed observations.

□ You cannot scroll a particular observation to the top of the FSVIEW window by typing the corresponding observation number on the command line.

FSVIEW Command

The FSVIEW command provides a handy way to initiate an FSVIEW session from any SAS System window. The command allows you to specify the data set to be displayed or to select the desired data set from a list of all available data sets. It also provides the option of specifying a formula entry containing computed variable formulas and window characteristics for the FSVIEW session.

FSVIEW Command Syntax

The general form of the FSVIEW command is

FSVIEW ⟨? | *data-set* ⟨*formula-name*⟩⟩

FSVIEW Command Arguments

You can specify the following arguments with the FSVIEW command:

?
> opens a selection window from which you can choose the data set to be displayed by the FSVIEW procedure. The selection list in the window includes all data sets in all SAS data libraries identified in the current SAS session (all data libraries with defined librefs).
>
> To select a data set, position the cursor on the desired data set name and press the ENTER key.

data-set
> specifies the data set to be displayed by the FSVIEW procedure. The general form of the argument is
>
> ⟨*libref.*⟩*data-set-name*⟨(*data-set-options*)⟩
>
> If you omit the libref, the default library, WORK, is assumed.
>
> If you specify a data set that does not exist, a selection window is opened showing all available data sets. An error message in the selection window indicates that the specified data set does not exist.
>
> If you omit this argument and do not specify ? for a selection window, the data set most recently created (the one identified in the system variable _LAST_) is selected. If no data set has previously been created in the current SAS session, a selection window is opened showing all available data sets. An error message in the selection window indicates that no default data set is available.
>
> You can add a list of data set options following the data set name. The list must be enclosed in parentheses. The FIRSTOBS= and OBS= options are ignored; all other data set options are valid. See Chapter 15 in *SAS Language: Reference* for a listing and descriptions of data set options.

formula-name
> specifies a formula entry associated with the FSVIEW session. The general form of the argument is
>
> ⟨*libref.*⟩*catalog-name*⟨*.entry-name*⟨*.FORMULA*⟩⟩

(formula-name continued)

You can specify a one-, two-, three-, or four-level name:

□ If a one-level name is specified, it is treated as a catalog name in the default library, WORK. If the specified catalog does not already exist in the WORK library, it is created. The procedure does not attempt to load a formula entry when the FSVIEW session is initiated. When you end the FSVIEW session, a formula entry is created using the data set name as the formula entry name.

   Remember that all catalogs in the WORK library are erased when you end your SAS session.

□ If a two-level name is specified, it is treated as *libref.catalog-name*. If the specified catalog does not already exist in the specified library, it is created. The procedure does not attempt to load a formula entry when the FSVIEW session is initiated. When you end the FSVIEW session, a formula entry is created in the specified catalog using the data set name as the formula entry name. (If an entry with that name already exists in the catalog, it is replaced without warning.)

   For example, suppose you initiate an FSVIEW session with the following command:

```
fsview master.subscrib master.custom
```

When you end the FSVIEW session, the formula entry MASTER.CUSTOM.SUBSCRIB.FORMULA is created.

□ If a three-level name is specified, it is treated as *libref.catalog-name.entry-name*. The entry type is assumed to be FORMULA. The procedure attempts to load the specified formula entry when the FSVIEW session is initiated. If the specified formula entry is not found, the FSVIEW session is initiated without an associated formula entry. A formula entry with the specified name (and entry type of FORMULA) is created when you end the FSVIEW session.

□ If a four-level name is specified, the fourth level (entry type) should be FORMULA. Any other value for the type is ignored; FORMULA is used instead. The procedure attempts to load the specified formula entry when the FSVIEW session is initiated. If the specified formula entry is not found, the FSVIEW session is initiated without an associated formula entry. A formula entry with the specified name is created when you end the FSVIEW session.

Using the FSVIEW Command

The FSVIEW command always opens the data set for browsing. Use the MODIFY command to allow editing of the displayed entries.

The FSVIEW command is a convenient way to invoke the FSVIEW procedure because it can be issued in any SAS System window. When you end an FSVIEW session initiated with the FSVIEW command, you return to whatever window was active when the command was issued. Thus, the command is particularly useful when you want to view the contents of a data set while another interactive windowing procedure is executing.

The FSVIEW command does not allow you to specify procedure options such as BROWSEONLY and NOADD. You must use the PROC FSVIEW statement rather than the FSVIEW command if you want to invoke the procedure with these options, or if you want to establish default procedure characteristics with the FORMAT, ID, INFORMAT, VAR, or WHERE statements.

Using the FSVIEW Procedure

You can use the FSVIEW procedure to perform the following tasks:

□ browse and edit existing SAS data sets

□ create new SAS data sets

□ duplicate existing SAS data sets

□ define formulas to create computed variables or manipulate data set variables

□ customize the FSVIEW environment by setting general parameters

□ create data entry or data browsing applications.

The remainder of this chapter describes the windows and commands you use to accomplish these tasks.

Browsing and Editing SAS Data Sets

In the FSVIEW procedure, observations are displayed in the FSVIEW window. Figure 16.1 identifies important features of the FSVIEW window.

Figure 16.1
FSVIEW Window
Features

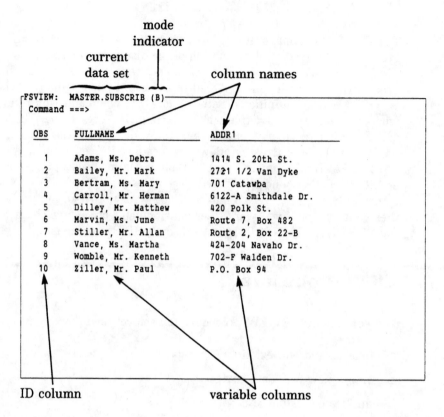

Note: If the data set is compressed, the observation number column is labeled ROW instead of OBS.

By default, the FSVIEW procedure opens the input data set for browsing. Use the MODIFY command if you want to edit the data set. (If you use the PROC FSVIEW statement to start the procedure, you can add the EDIT or MODIFY option to directly open the data set for editing.) If you use the procedure to create a new data set, the FSVIEW window is opened for editing after the structure of the new data set has been defined in the FSVIEW NEW window.

▶ *Caution* . . . . *The FSVIEW procedure edits a SAS data set in place.*

The FSVIEW procedure does not leave an unedited copy of the original. If you need to preserve a copy of the original data, be sure to copy the data set before you begin editing. ▲

How Control Level Affects Editing

The editing behavior of the FSVIEW procedure depends on the control level selected when the data set or data view is opened. The *control level* is the degree to which the procedure can restrict access to the data set.

The FSVIEW procedure supports two levels of control:

RECORD   locks only the observation currently being edited. With this control level, you can open multiple FSVIEW windows for browsing or editing the same data set. Using SAS/SHARE software, other users can edit the same data set simultaneously.

MEMBER   locks the entire data set. No other window or user can open the data set while this control level is in effect.

By default, the FSVIEW procedure selects a control level of RECORD when it opens a SAS data set. You can specify the control level with the MODIFY command in the FSVIEW window, or by using the CNTLLEV= data set option with the data set name in the PROC FSVIEW statement, FSVIEW command, or BROWSE or EDIT command. The MODIFY command is described later in this section. The CNTLLEV= data set option is described in Chapter 15 of *SAS Language: Reference.*

Editing with RECORD-Level Control

When the RECORD control level is selected, you must first lock an observation for editing before you can change variable values in that observation. To lock an observation, move the cursor to the line for the desired observation and press ENTER. The line is highlighted to indicate that it is locked. (You can use the HI command to control the type of highlighting used.) Once the observation is locked, you can change values in the variable columns. Scroll right or left to display additional columns. If you have formulas defined for any data set variables, the values of the variables with formulas are updated only when observations are locked.

The lock on the current observation is released when you lock a different observation for editing. In addition, the lock is released when any of the following commands cause the currently locked observation to scroll out of the window:

FORWARD   *n*
BACKWARD   AUTOADD
TOP   DUP
BOTTOM

The lock is always released when you issue any of the following commands:

DELETE
SORT
WHERE

Editing with MEMBER-Level Control

When the MEMBER control level is selected, the FSVIEW procedure obtains exclusive control over the data set. In this case, all observations are available for editing. It is not necessary to select an individual observation before editing; simply move the cursor to the desired observation and enter the new value in the desired variable column.

Opening Multiple FSVIEW Windows

After entering the FSVIEW procedure, you can use the BROWSE, EDIT, and NEW commands to open additional FSVIEW windows to concurrently browse or edit other SAS data sets. The multiple FSVIEW windows may overlap visually, but each is completely independent of the others. (See Display 16.1.)

Display 16.1
Displaying Two
SAS Data Sets
Concurrently

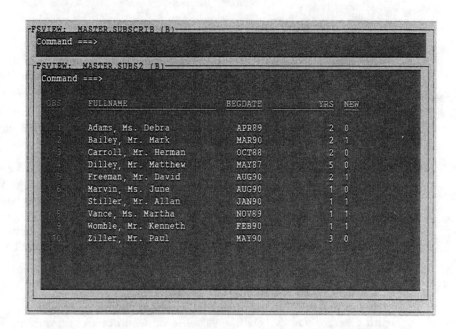

Opening additional FSVIEW windows within the current FSVIEW session using the EDIT or BROWSE commands consumes fewer computer resources than starting additional FSVIEW sessions using the FSVIEW command.

If you invoke the FSVIEW procedure with a PROC FSVIEW statement, some of the PROC FSVIEW statement options affect the behavior of the additional FSVIEW windows:

□   If you use the BROWSEONLY option, the MODIFY and EDIT commands are not allowed in any FSVIEW windows opened during the FSVIEW session.

□   If you use the NOADD option, the AUTOADD and DUP commands are not allowed in any FSVIEW windows opened during the FSVIEW session.

□   If you use the NODELETE option, the DELETE command is not allowed in any FSVIEW windows opened during the FSVIEW session.

FSVIEW Window Commands

In addition to the global commands discussed in Chapter 18, "Command Reference," you can execute the following commands when editing a data set with the FSVIEW procedure. When browsing, you can use all the following commands except those identified as editing commands:

Scrolling

n
=*variable*
BACKWARD ⟨HALF | PAGE | MAX | *n*⟩
BOTTOM
FORWARD ⟨HALF | PAGE | MAX | *n*⟩
HSCROLL *n*
LEFT ⟨MAX | *n*⟩
RIGHT ⟨MAX | *n*⟩
TOP
VSCROLL HALF | PAGE | *n*

Managing the Data Set

AUTOSAVE ⟨*n*⟩
BROWSE *data-set*⟨*(data-set-options)*⟩ ⟨FORMULA=*SAS-catalog*⟨*.formula-entry*⟩⟩
CANCEL
CREATE *data-set*⟨*(data-set-options)*⟩ ⟨REPLACE⟩ ⟨*variable-list* | ALL | ?⟩
EDIT *data-set*⟨*(data-set-options)*⟩ ⟨FORMULA=*SAS-catalog*⟨*.formula-entry*⟩⟩
END
MODIFY ⟨RECORD | MEMBER⟩
NEW *data-set*⟨*(data-set-options)*⟩ ⟨LIKE=*data-set*⟨*(data-set-options)*⟩⟩
    ⟨FORMULA=*SAS-catalog*⟨*.formula-entry*⟩⟩
SAVE
WHERE ⟨⟨ALSO⟩ *expression*⟩ | ⟨UNDO | CLEAR⟩

Editing the Data Set

(The commands in this group are valid only when the FSVIEW window is opened for editing.)

AUTOADD | ADD ⟨ON | OFF⟩
CURSOR ⟨*variable*⟩
DELETE | DEL ⟨*obs* ⟨. . . *obs-n*⟩⟩
DUP ⟨*n* ⟨*obs*⟩⟩
INITIAL ⟨*obs* | CLEAR⟩
PROTECT ON | OFF ⟨*variable* ⟨. . . *variable-n*⟩⟩
SORT ⟨ASCENDING | DESCENDING⟩ *variable*
    ⟨. . . ⟨ASCENDING | DESCENDING⟩ *variable-n*⟩

Managing Formulas

DEFINE ⟨*variable-name* ⟨$⟩ ⟨⟨*format*⟩⟨,⟨*informat*⟩⟨,*label*⟩⟩⟩⟩⟨= *formula*⟩⟩
FORMULA ⟨*formula-name*⟩
RESET ⟨ALL | *variable* ⟨. . . *variable-n*⟩⟩
REVIEW
SAVE FORMULA ⟨*formula-name*⟩

Changing the Display

COLOR *area color* ⟨*highlight*⟩
DROP ⟨*variable* ⟨. . . *variable-n*⟩⟩
FORMAT *variable-list* '*format*' ⟨. . . *variable-list-n* '*format-n*'⟩
HI ⟨ON | OFF⟩ | ⟨*color* ⟨*highlight*⟩⟩ | ⟨RESET ⟨ALL⟩⟩
INFORMAT *variable-list* '*informat*' ⟨. . . *variable-list-n* '*informat-n*'⟩
MOVE *variable* | *variable-range* ⟨*target-variable*⟩
RENAME *current-variable-name new-variable-name*
SETWSZ ⟨CLEAR⟩
SHOW ID | VAR *variable* ⟨. . . *variable-n*⟩

Other

HELP ⟨*command*⟩
KEYS
OBS
PARMS

Command Descriptions

Descriptions of the special FSVIEW window commands follow. Refer to Chapter 4, "Browsing and Editing SAS Data Sets Using the FSVIEW Procedure," and to Chapter 9, "Creating Data Entry Applications Using the FSVIEW Procedure," for examples of using these commands.

n

scrolls the FSVIEW window vertically so that the specified observation occupies the top line. Type the desired observation number on the command line; then press ENTER. You receive an error message if you specify a value that is greater than the highest observation number.

The *n* command is still valid when ID variables are used in place of observation numbers to identify observations. However, the command is not valid when the access method used to read the data set does not support access by observation number. The command is also invalid while a permanent or temporary WHERE clause is in effect.

=*variable*

scrolls the FSVIEW window horizontally so that the column for the specified variable is visible.

AUTOADD ⟨ON | OFF⟩
ADD ⟨ON | OFF⟩

(editing command; not valid while browsing a data set)

turns the autoadd feature on or off. While the autoadd feature is on, a new observation is always displayed. If observation numbers are used in the ID column, the new observation is identified with the word NEW.

Note: The AUTOADD command is not allowed if the FSVIEW session is initiated with a PROC FSVIEW statement that includes the NOADD option.

By default, all values in the new observation are missing. You can use the INITIAL command to store the current contents of an existing observation; the stored values are then copied into new observations when they are displayed by the autoadd feature.

By default, the cursor is positioned on the column for the leftmost variable in the FSVIEW window whenever a new observation is displayed. You can use the CURSOR command to specify the variable on which the cursor is positioned when the new observation is displayed.

The new observation is not actually added to the displayed data set until you add values and press ENTER or until you issue any FSVIEW command other than LEFT or RIGHT. While entering values, you can use the LEFT and RIGHT commands to scroll among the variable columns without adding the new observation to the data set. After the observation is added, another new observation is displayed.

If the new observation has not been modified when you issue the END command, the observation is not added to the data set.

When the AUTOADD command is used without the ON or OFF arguments, it acts as a toggle, turning the autoadd feature on if it is currently off or off if it is currently on.

Note: In previous Version 6 releases of SAS/FSP software, the ADD command added a single blank observation at the end of the data set. ADD is now an alias for AUTOADD.

AUTOSAVE ⟨*n*⟩

specifies how frequently the FSVIEW procedure automatically saves the data set. The *n* value determines how many modifications must be made before an automatic save is performed. By default, the procedure saves the data set automatically whenever 25 observations have been modified since the last save.

To check the current autosave parameter value, issue the AUTOSAVE command without specifying an *n* value.

You can change the default autosave value for an FSVIEW application by changing the value in the Autosave value: field in the FSVIEW Parameters window. See "Customizing the FSVIEW Environment" later in this chapter for details.

Regardless of the Autosave parameter value, you can save the data set at any time using the SAVE command.

BACKWARD ⟨HALF | PAGE | MAX | *n*⟩

scrolls vertically toward the top of the window. The following scroll amounts can be specified:

HALF   scrolls upward by half the number of lines in the window.

PAGE   scrolls upward by the number of lines in the window.

MAX   scrolls upward until the first observation is at the top of the window.

n   scrolls upward the specified number of observations.

If the scrolling increment is not explicitly specified, the window is scrolled by the amount specified with the VSCROLL parameter. The default VSCROLL amount is HALF.

BOTTOM

scrolls forward until the last observation in the data set is displayed at the bottom of the window.

BROWSE *data-set*⟨*(data-set-options)*⟩ ⟨FORMULA=*SAS-catalog*⟨*.formula-entry*⟩⟩

opens another FSVIEW window and displays the specified SAS data set for browsing. The current FSVIEW window remains open, but the new FSVIEW window becomes the active window. All FSVIEW procedure browsing commands are valid in the new window (except for those disabled with PROC FSVIEW statement options). When you use the END command to close the new window, you return to the FSVIEW window from which the BROWSE command was issued.

The additional FSVIEW window may overlay the current one. To control where the additional window appears, use the global WREGION command before issuing the BROWSE command. You can use the global SWAP command to move among concurrent FSVIEW windows. Refer to Chapter 18 for descriptions of the WREGION and SWAP commands.

(BROWSE continued)

You can use the MODIFY command to change the new window from browsing to editing, unless the procedure is initiated by a PROC FSVIEW statement that includes the BROWSEONLY option.

You can add a list of data set options following the data set name. The list must be enclosed in parentheses. The FIRSTOBS= and OBS= options are ignored; all other data set options are valid. Refer to Chapter 15 in *SAS Language: Reference* for a listing and descriptions of data set options.

You can add the FORMULA= argument to the BROWSE command to associate a formula entry with the displayed data set. The syntax for the FORMULA= argument is the same as for the PROC FSVIEW statement's FORMULA= option.

CANCEL

closes the FSVIEW window and saves the data set without recording any updated information in the associated formula entry. (Changes to variable values are recorded; changes to formulas and to other general parameters are not.) If only one FSVIEW window is open in the current FSVIEW session, the CANCEL command also ends the FSVIEW procedure.

COLOR *area color* ⟨*highlight*⟩

sets the color and highlighting attributes of different areas of the window. You can specify the following areas:

VAR	variable value columns (except for ID variables)
VARNAME	variable names used as column headings (except for ID variables)
ID	ID value columns (or observation number column if ID variables are not used)
IDNAME	ID variable names used as column headings (or observation number column heading if ID variables are not used).

The following values are valid for the *color* argument:

BLACK	CYAN	MAGENTA	RED
BLUE	GRAY	ORANGE	WHITE
BROWN	GREEN	PINK	YELLOW

The following values are valid for the *highlight* argument:

H (high intensity)	U (underlined)
R (reverse video)	B (blinking)

In addition to the areas specific to the FSVIEW procedure, you can specify colors and attributes for the following FSVIEW window areas using the global COLOR command:

BACKGROUND   BORDER   MESSAGE
BANNER   COMMAND

Refer to Chapter 18, "SAS Display Manager Commands," in *SAS Language: Reference* for more information on the COLOR command.

CREATE *data-set*⟨*(data-set-options)*⟩ ⟨REPLACE⟩ ⟨*variable-list* | ALL | ?⟩
creates a new SAS data set using some or all of the variables from the data set currently displayed. The new data set duplicates both the structure and contents of the displayed data set. You can select which variables are included in the new data set in any of the following ways:

□   by listing the desired variable names as command arguments.

□   by using the ALL argument to select all variables in the displayed data set.

□   by using the ? argument to open the FSVIEW VARLIST window. In this window you can select the desired variables from a list of all available variables in the displayed data set. Refer to "Selecting Variables for FSVIEW Operations" later in this chapter for more information on using the FSVIEW VARLIST window.

    Note: The FSVIEW VARLIST window is also opened if you issue a CREATE command that does not include any variable names or the ALL or ? arguments.

Both computed variables and data set variables can be selected. Computed variables in the displayed data set become data set variables in the created data set.

You can add a list of data set options following the data set name. The list must be enclosed in parentheses. Refer to Chapter 15 in *SAS Language: Reference* for a listing and descriptions of data set options.

By default, the CREATE command fails with an error message if the named data set already exists. Specify the REPLACE option if you want the new data set to replace an existing data set with the same name. If you use the REPLACE option, it must come before the variable name arguments.

CURSOR ⟨*variable*⟩
(editing command; not valid while browsing a data set)
specifies the variable column on which the cursor is positioned when a new observation is displayed. (New observations are created by the autoadd feature or the DUP command.) By default, the cursor is positioned on the leftmost variable column in the FSVIEW window when the new observation is added.

You can specify the desired variable name as an argument for the CURSOR command, or you can type CURSOR on the command line, position the cursor on the desired variable column, and press ENTER.

DEFINE ⟨*variable-name* ⟨$⟩ ⟨(⟨*format*⟩⟨,⟨*informat*⟩⟨,*label*⟩⟩)⟩ ⟨=*formula*⟩⟩
defines a formula for a computed variable or for an existing data set
variable.

When you use the DEFINE command alone or with only the
variable-name argument, the FSVIEW Define window is opened. In this
window you can enter all the information necessary to define the
formula. You can also use this form of the command to open the
FSVIEW Define window to edit an existing formula. See "Defining
Formulas" later in this chapter for more information on using the
FSVIEW Define window.

If the variable name you specify does not exist in the displayed data
set, the FSVIEW procedure creates a computed variable. When creating
a computed variable, the procedure assumes by default that the variable
is numeric. To create a character variable, add the $ argument following
the variable name if you are specifying the formula in the DEFINE
command argument. (Do not use the $ argument if you want to open the
FSVIEW Define window.)

You can supply the formula as an argument with the DEFINE
command. In this case, the FSVIEW Define window is not opened.
Separate the formula from the variable name with an equal sign (=).

Formulas are not limited to SAS expressions. They can also include
any valid Screen Control Language functions or statements except those
valid only in SAS/AF software and the following statements:

ERRORON
ERROROFF
PROTECT
UNPROTECT
CURSOR

Refer to *SAS Screen Control Language: Reference* for details of including
Screen Control Language in FSVIEW formulas.

Note: When you assign a formula to a variable (either a data set
variable or a computed variable), the corresponding variable column in
the FSVIEW window is protected. You cannot change the values of a
variable that has an associated formula.

You can specify a format, informat, and label for the variable in the
DEFINE command. The arguments for these values must be enclosed in
parentheses and must appear before the equal sign that begins the
formula definition. The values must be specified in the order
format, informat, label. You can omit any of the values as long as you
include the necessary commas.

If you omit the *format* argument when defining a computed variable,
the default format is BEST12. for numeric variables or $8. for character
variables. If you omit the *informat* argument, the default informat is 12.
for numeric variables and $8. for character variables.

You can also use the *format, informat,* and *label* arguments to change
the format, informat, or label of an existing variable. For an existing
variable, you can supply these arguments without supplying a formula.
(The arguments must still be enclosed in parentheses.) For data set
variables, these arguments change the format, informat, and label
recorded in the formula entry but do not affect any format, informat, or
label for the variable recorded in the data set itself.

DELETE ⟨*obs* ⟨. . . *obs-n*⟩⟩
DEL ⟨*obs* ⟨. . . *obs-n*⟩⟩

    (editing command; not valid while browsing a data set)

        deletes one or more observations from the data set you are editing.

▶ *Caution* . . . . *The DELETE command deletes observations from the displayed data set, not just from the FSVIEW window.*

You cannot recover the contents of a deleted observation. ▲

    Note: The DELETE command is not allowed if the FSVIEW session is initiated with a PROC FSVIEW statement that includes the NODELETE option.

    To delete a single observation, follow the DELETE command with the observation number for the observation to be deleted. You can also type DELETE (or DEL) on the command line, position the cursor on the observation to be deleted, and press ENTER.

    To delete multiple observations, follow the DELETE command with a list of observation numbers. Separate the observation numbers with at least one space. For example, issue the following command to delete observations 5 and 10:

```
delete 5 10
```

    To delete a range of observations, specify the first and last observation numbers of the range, separated by a dash. For example, the following command deletes all observations between 5 and 10, inclusive:

```
delete 5-10
```

DROP ⟨*variable* ⟨. . . *variable-n*⟩⟩

    excludes one or more variables from the FSVIEW window. The DROP command affects only the display, not the actual data set.

    If you issue the DROP command without arguments, the FSVIEW VARLIST window is opened for you to select the variables to be dropped. Refer to "Selecting Variables for FSVIEW Operations" later in this chapter for more information on using the FSVIEW VARLIST window.

    To exclude a single variable, follow the DROP command with the name of the variable to be dropped. You can also type DROP on the command line, position the cursor on the variable column to be dropped, and press ENTER.

    To exclude multiple variables, follow the DROP command with a list of variable names. Separate the variable names with at least one space. For example, the following command drops the variables X and Z from the display:

```
drop x z
```

(DROP continued)

You can indicate a range of variables by specifying the first and last variables to be dropped, separated by a dash. For example, the following command drops all the variables between X and Z, inclusive:

```
drop x-z
```

Note: At least one variable, in addition to any ID variables specified, must remain displayed.

Use the SHOW command to redisplay dropped variables.

DUP ⟨*n* ⟨*obs*⟩⟩

(editing command; not valid while browsing a data set)

copies the specified observation *n* times and adds the new observation(s) to the displayed data set. The FSVIEW window is automatically scrolled forward so the new observations appear at the top of the window.

Note: The DUP command is not allowed if the FSVIEW session is initiated with a PROC FSVIEW statement that includes the NOADD option.

You can select the observation to copy by supplying its number as the *obs* argument in the DUP command. To specify the *obs* argument, you must also specify the *n* argument (the number of times you want the observation duplicated). For example, the following command duplicates observation 5 one time:

```
dup 1 5
```

You can also select the observation to copy by typing DUP on the command line, positioning the cursor on the desired observation, and pressing ENTER. By default, the observation is duplicated once. To duplicate the same observation again, leave the cursor on the command line and execute the DUP command again. Alternatively, you can follow the DUP command with the desired number of copies. For example, if the cursor is on the command line, the following command duplicates the most recently duplicated observation three times:

```
dup 3
```

If the cursor is positioned on an observation, that observation is duplicated three times.

By default, the cursor is positioned on the leftmost displayed variable column of the first added observation. You can use the CURSOR command to select a particular variable to which the cursor is moved when the duplicate observation is displayed.

EDIT *data-set*⟨*(data-set-options)*⟩ ⟨FORMULA=*SAS-catalog*⟨*.formula-entry*⟩⟩

opens another FSVIEW window and displays the specified data set for editing. The current FSVIEW window remains open, but the new FSVIEW window becomes the active window. All FSVIEW window commands are valid in the new window. When you use the END command to close the new window, you return to the FSVIEW window from which the EDIT command was issued.

Note: The EDIT command is not valid if the FSVIEW session is initiated by a PROC FSVIEW statement that includes the BROWSEONLY option.

The additional FSVIEW window may overlay the current one. To control where the additional window appears, use the global command WREGION before issuing the EDIT command. You can use the SWAP command to move among concurrent FSVIEW windows. Refer to Chapter 18 for descriptions of the SWAP and WREGION commands.

You can add a list of data set options following the data set name. The list must be enclosed in parentheses. The FIRSTOBS= and OBS= options are ignored; all other data set options are valid. Refer to Chapter 15 in *SAS Language: Reference* for a listing and descriptions of data set options.

END

saves any changes you make to the displayed data set (if it is open for editing), updates the formula entry (if a formula name or formula catalog has been specified), closes the current FSVIEW window, and returns to the previous FSVIEW window.

If only one FSVIEW window is open, the END command ends the FSVIEW procedure.

FORMAT *variable-list 'format'* ⟨. . . *variable-list-n 'format-n'*⟩

changes the format of one or more variables for display purposes only. The FORMAT command does not alter any formats stored with the variables in the data set. Formats specified in the FORMAT command take precedence over ones defined in the displayed data set or assigned in FORMAT statements.

The format name can be any SAS format, or it can be a custom format you define with the FORMAT procedure. The format name must be enclosed in quotes.

You can specify multiple variables either individually or as a range. Separate two variable names with a dash to indicate a range. For example, the following command alters the display formats of variables X and Z only:

```
format x z 'date7.'
```

The following command alters the display format of all the variables between X and Z, inclusive:

```
format x-z 'date7.'
```

You can assign multiple formats in a single FORMAT command. For example, the following command assigns different display formats to the variables X and Z:

```
format x 'date7.' z 'monyy5.'
```

FORMULA ⟨*formula-name*⟩
>   reads in a formula entry.
>
>   The general form of the *formula-name* argument is
>
>   ⟨⟨*libref.*⟩*catalog-name.*⟩*entry-name*⟨.FORMULA⟩
>
>   You can specify a one-, two-, three-, or four-level name:
>
>   □   If a one-level name is specified, it is treated as an entry name in
>   the current formula catalog. The entry type is assumed to be
>   FORMULA. If no catalog has been previously specified in a
>   FORMULA command, in the FORMULA= option of the PROC
>   FSVIEW statement, or in the *formula-name* argument of the
>   FSVIEW command, the procedure looks for the specified entry in
>   your personal PROFILE catalog (SASUSER.PROFILE, or
>   WORK.PROFILE if the SASUSER library is not allocated.)
>
>   □   If a two-level name is specified, the second level must be
>   FORMULA. Any other value causes an error message. The name
>   is treated as an entry name in the current formula catalog. If no
>   formula catalog has been previously specified, the procedure
>   looks for the specified entry in your personal PROFILE catalog.
>
>   □   If a three-level name is specified, it is treated as
>   *libref.catalog-name.entry-name*. The entry type is assumed to be
>   FORMULA. You receive an error message if the specified libref
>   is undefined or if the specified catalog does not exist.
>
>   □   If a four-level name is specified, the fourth level must be
>   FORMULA. Any other value causes an error message. You
>   receive an error message if the specified libref is undefined or if
>   the specified catalog does not exist.

If you omit the *formula-name* argument altogether, the procedure
looks for an entry with the default name. The default formula name is
the name used in the previous FORMULA command. If no previous
FORMULA command has been issued, the default name is the name
specified in the FORMULA= option of the PROC FSVIEW statement or
in the *formula-name* argument of the FSVIEW command when the
procedure was initiated. If no formula name was specified when the
procedure was invoked, the name of the displayed data set is used as the
default formula entry name. The procedure looks for the default entry in
the current formula catalog. If no formula catalog has previously been
specified, the procedure looks for the default entry in your personal
PROFILE catalog.

If the specified formula entry exists, it replaces the formula entry
currently used for the FSVIEW window. All current formula definitions
are removed.

If the specified entry does not currently exist, no entry is read in
and a warning message is issued. An entry with the specified name is
created when you issue an END command to close the FSVIEW window
or when you issue a SAVE FORMULA command without specifying
another formula name.

The FORMULA command is valid even if you do not use the
FORMULA= option in the PROC FSVIEW statement or the

formula-name argument in the FSVIEW command when you initiate the
FSVIEW session.

FORWARD ⟨HALF | PAGE | MAX | *n*⟩
    scrolls vertically toward the bottom of the window. The following scroll
    amounts can be specified:

HALF   scrolls downward by half the number of lines in the window.

PAGE   scrolls downward by the number of lines in the window.

MAX   scrolls downward until the last observation is at the bottom
               of the window.
                   Note: See the discussion of the BOTTOM command
               earlier in this section for details of the restrictions that apply.

n   scrolls downward by the specified number of observations.

    If the scrolling increment is not explicitly specified, the window is
scrolled by the amount specified in the VSCROLL parameter. The default
VSCROLL amount is HALF.
    Note: Regardless of the scroll increment specified, the FSVIEW
procedure does not scroll beyond the last observation in the data set.

HELP ⟨*command*⟩
    displays information about the FSVIEW procedure or about a specific
    FSVIEW command. Used alone, the HELP command opens a HELP
    window from which you can make selections to view additional
    information about various FSVIEW topics. To get assistance with a
    particular FSVIEW command, follow the HELP command with the name
    of the command for which you want more information.
        You can also use the HELP command to request information about a
    specific variable in an FSVIEW window. To display help on a variable,
    type HELP on the command line, position the cursor anywhere in a
    variable column, and press ENTER (or position the cursor and press the
    HELP function key). A window is opened showing the name, observation
    number, format, and informat for the specified variable. Press ENTER to
    close the variable HELP window.
        Note: You can replace the SAS System's default help information
    with custom information for an FSVIEW application. Use the SETHELP
    command to assign a catalog entry containing the custom help
    information to be displayed when a HELP command is issued in the
    FSVIEW window. See Chapter 18 for details of the SETHELP command.

HI ⟨ON | OFF⟩
HI ⟨*color* ⟨*highlight*⟩⟩
HI ⟨RESET ⟨ALL⟩⟩
    controls the highlighting status of an individual row or of the entire
    window, or sets the highlighting characteristics for an individual row or
    for the entire window.
        To turn highlighting on for an unhighlighted row or to turn it off for
    a highlighted row, use the HI command. Type HI on the command line,
    position the cursor on the row that you want the command to affect, and
    press ENTER (or position the cursor on the desired row and press the
    function key to which the HI command has been assigned).

(HI continued)

To turn highlighting on for all unhighlighted rows, use the HI ON command. To turn it off for all highlighted rows, use the HI OFF command.

To set default highlighting characteristics for the window, follow the HI command with the desired color and (optionally) an attribute. The following values are valid for the *color* argument:

BLACK	CYAN	MAGENTA	RED
BLUE	GRAY	ORANGE	WHITE
BROWN	GREEN	PINK	YELLOW

The following values are valid for the *highlight* argument:

H (high intensity)	U (underlined)
R (reverse video)	B (blinking)

To change the highlighting characteristics for an individual row, type HI on the command line, followed by the new color and (optionally) the new attribute, position the cursor on the desired row, and then press ENTER.

To reset all rows to the default color and highlighting attribute, use the HI RESET ALL command.

To reset the highlight characteristics of an individual row to the default, type HI RESET on the command line, position the cursor on the desired row, and then press ENTER.

HSCROLL *n*

sets the default horizontal scrolling amount for the LEFT and RIGHT commands. For *n*, specify the number of variable columns to scroll. The default amount is one column.

INFORMAT *variable-list* 'informat' ⟨. . . *variable-list-n* 'informat-n'⟩

changes the informat of one or more variables in the FSVIEW window. The INFORMAT command does not alter any informats stored with the variables in the data set. Informats specified with the INFORMAT command take precedence over ones defined in the data set assigned in INFORMAT statements.

The informat name can be any SAS informat, or it can be a custom informat you define with the FORMAT procedure. The informat name must be enclosed in quotes.

You can list multiple variable names individually or as a range. Separate two variable names with a dash to indicate a range. For example, the following command selects the informats for the variables X and Z only:

```
informat x z 'date7.'
```

The following command selects the informat for all the variables between X and Z, inclusive:

```
informat x-z 'date7.'
```

You can also assign multiple informats in a single INFORMAT command. For example, the following command selects different informats for the variables X and Z:

```
informat x 'date7.' z 'monyy5.'
```

INITIAL ⟨*obs* | CLEAR⟩

(editing command; not valid while browsing a data set)

selects an observation whose contents are used as initial values for added observations. By default, all variables in a new observation added by the autoadd feature are initialized with missing values. You can use this command to record the current variable values from an existing observation for use as initial values for new observations.

The values of the selected observation are recorded in the formula entry. The recorded values are then used to initialize autoadded observations. Any subsequent changes you make to the observation designated in the INITIAL command do not affect the stored values used to initialize new observations.

You can identify the desired observation by specifying its observation number as the *obs* argument in the INITIAL command, or you can type INITIAL on the command line, position the cursor on the desired observation, and press ENTER.

Use the INITIAL CLEAR command to reset the initial variable values for new observations to missing values.

KEYS

opens the KEYS window for browsing and editing function key definitions for the FSVIEW window. Function key definitions are stored in catalog entries of type KEYS.

The default function key definitions for the FSVIEW window are stored in the FSVIEW.KEYS entry in the SASHELP.FSP system catalog. If you are using this default set of key definitions when you issue the KEYS command and you change any key definitions in the KEYS window, a new copy of the FSVIEW.KEYS entry is created in your personal PROFILE catalog (SASUSER.PROFILE, or WORK.PROFILE if the SASUSER library is not allocated). The changes you make are recorded in your personal copy of the keys entry.

LEFT ⟨MAX | *n*⟩

scrolls the FSVIEW window to the left in increments of variable columns. The following scroll amounts can be specified:

MAX   scrolls to the leftmost variable column.

n   scrolls to the left the specified number of variable columns.

If the LEFT command is used without arguments, the FSVIEW window is scrolled by the amount specified in the HSCROLL parameter. The default HSCROLL amount is one column.

MODIFY ⟨RECORD | MEMBER⟩

changes the FSVIEW window from browsing to editing, or changes the control level of an FSVIEW window already open for editing.

Note: The MODIFY command is not allowed if the FSVIEW session is initiated with a PROC FSVIEW statement that includes the BROWSEONLY option.

(MODIFY continued)

The data set can be opened for editing with a control level of either RECORD or MEMBER. (Refer to "How Control Level Affects Editing" earlier in this chapter for more information on control levels.) You can specify a control level using the RECORD or MEMBER arguments with the MODIFY command. If you do not use either argument, the default control level is RECORD (unless you use the CNTLLEV=MEMBER data set option with the data set name when you open the FSVIEW window).

When the FSVIEW window is open for editing, you can use the MODIFY RECORD and MODIFY MEMBER commands to change the current control level for the window.

The MODIFY command fails if the specified control level would cause a locking conflict. For example, you cannot specify MODIFY MEMBER if the same data set is open with a control level of RECORD in another FSVIEW window.

MOVE *variable* | *variable-range* ⟨*target-variable*⟩
moves a variable column or a range of variable columns.
Note: The MOVE command only affects the order of variables in the FSVIEW window, not the actual position of the variables in the data set.

To move a single variable, type MOVE on the command line, followed by the name of the variable to be moved; then place the cursor on the variable you want the moved variable to follow and press ENTER.

To move a range of variables, specify the name of the first and last variables of the range separated by a dash. All variables in the range must be of the same class, either ID or VAR. Indicate the variable you want the range to follow by specifying the variable name as the *target-variable* argument in the MOVE command. For example, the following command moves the variables VAR1 through VAR3 to the right of the variable VAR6:

```
move var1-var3 var6
```

You can also move a range of variables by typing MOVE and the variable range on the command line, positioning the cursor on the desired target variable, and pressing ENTER.

To move only one variable and specify the target variable as a command argument, you must supply the name of the moved variable as a range. For example, the following command moves the variable VAR2 after the variable VAR6:

```
move var2-var2 var6
```

NEW *data-set*⟨*(data-set-options)*⟩ ⟨LIKE=*data-set*⟨*(data-set-options)*⟩⟩
⟨FORMULA=*SAS-catalog*⟨*.formula-entry*⟩⟩
opens the FSVIEW NEW window for creating a new data set.
Note: An error message is returned if the data set you specify in the NEW command already exists. You cannot use the NEW command to alter variable names or attributes in an existing data set.

In the FSVIEW NEW window you enter the names of your variables, the type, length, and (if desired) a label, format, and informat. See

"Creating New SAS Data Sets" later in this chapter for more information on using the FSVIEW NEW window. After you define the structure of the data set, an additional FSVIEW window is opened for entering values in the new data set.

You can add a list of data set options following the data set name. The list must be enclosed in parentheses. Refer to Chapter 15 in *SAS Language: Reference* for a listing and descriptions of SAS data set options.

You can add the LIKE= option to specify an existing data set whose variable names and attributes are copied into the FSVIEW NEW window when it is opened. The data set name in the LIKE= option can also be followed by a list of data set options.

You can add the FORMULA= option to specify a formula to be associated with the new FSVIEW window that is opened for the data set. The rules for the *formula-name* argument are the same as in the FORMULA= option of the PROC FSVIEW statement. See "PROC FSVIEW Statement Options" earlier in this chapter for details.

OBS

displays the number of the observation on which the cursor is currently positioned. This is useful when observation numbers are not displayed because an ID variable is used. Type OBS on the command line, position the cursor on an observation, and press ENTER. Or position the cursor on the desired observation and press the function key to which you assigned the OBS command.

PARMS

opens the FSVIEW Parameters window, from which general parameters for the FSVIEW session can be reviewed and modified. Refer to "Customizing the FSVIEW Environment" later in this chapter for more information on the parameters that can be set in the FSVIEW Parameters window.

PROTECT ON | OFF ⟨*variable* ⟨. . . *variable-n*⟩⟩

(editing command; not valid while browsing a data set)

prevents changes to the values in one or more variable columns when the data set is edited.

You must follow the PROTECT command with either the ON or OFF argument, depending on whether you want to turn the protection feature on or off for the column. You can select the column you want the command to affect by specifying the variable name as an argument for the command, or by typing PROTECT ON or PROTECT OFF on the command line, positioning the cursor on the desired column, and pressing ENTER.

Note: You cannot use the PROTECT OFF command to turn off protection for computed variables or for data set variables that have associated formulas.

You can control the protection feature for multiple columns with a single PROTECT command. You can provide a list of variable names, separated by spaces, as arguments for the command, or you can select a range of variable columns by specifying the names of the first and last variables in the range separated by a dash. For example, the following command turns on protection for the variables X and Z:

```
protect on x z
```

(PROTECT continued)

The following command turns on protection for all variables between X and Z, inclusive:

```
protect on x-z
```

RENAME *current-variable-name new-variable-name*
changes the name for a specified variable column for the purposes of the FSVIEW window display only. The variable name in the data set is not changed; only the name used for the variable column in the FSVIEW window is changed. The new name is stored in a formula entry rather than in the data set itself.

Like the original variable name, the new name is limited to eight characters. All the other rules for SAS names also apply.

If the renamed variable is used in any formulas, the formulas are updated to reflect the new name.

RESET ⟨ALL | *variable* ⟨. . . *variable-n*⟩⟩
deletes some or all formula definitions. For computed variables, resetting the formula deletes the variable column from the FSVIEW window.

You can remove the formula definitions for more than one variable with a single RESET command. You can provide a list of variable names, separated by spaces, as arguments for the command, or you can select a range of variables by specifying the names of the first and last variables in the range separated by a dash. For example, the following command resets formula definitions for the variables X and Z:

```
reset x z
```

The following command resets formula definitions for all variables between X and Z, inclusive:

```
reset x-z
```

Use the RESET ALL command to remove all current formula definitions.

REVIEW
opens the FSVIEW REVIEW window in which all current formula definitions are displayed. See "Defining Formulas" later in this chapter for more information on using the FSVIEW REVIEW window.

If no formulas are currently defined, the FSVIEW REVIEW window is not opened. Instead, a message is printed in the FSVIEW window's message line indicating that no formula definitions exist.

RIGHT ⟨MAX | *n*⟩
scrolls the FSVIEW window to the right in increments of variable columns. The following scroll amounts can be specified:

MAX   scrolls to the rightmost variable column.

n   scrolls to the right the specified number of variable columns.

If the RIGHT command is used without arguments, the FSVIEW window is scrolled by the amount specified in the HSCROLL parameter. The default HSCROLL amount is one column.

SAVE

stores all changes made to the data set since the last time it was saved. See also the AUTOSAVE command.

SAVE FORMULA ⟨*formula-name*⟩

stores all current formula definitions, general parameter settings, and FSVIEW window characteristics in a formula entry.

The general form of the *formula-name* argument is

⟨⟨*libref.*⟩*catalog-name.*⟩*entry-name*⟨.FORMULA⟩

You can specify a one-, two-, three-, or four-level name:

□ If a one-level name is specified, it is treated as an entry name in the current formula catalog. The entry type is assumed to be FORMULA. If no catalog has been previously specified in a FORMULA or SAVE FORMULA command, in the FORMULA= option of the PROC FSVIEW statement, or in the *formula-name* argument of the FSVIEW command, the procedure stores the specified entry in your personal PROFILE catalog (SASUSER.PROFILE, or WORK.PROFILE if the SASUSER library is not allocated).

□ If a two-level name is specified, the second level must be FORMULA. Any other value causes an error message. The name is treated as an entry name in the current formula catalog. If no formula catalog has been previously specified, the procedure stores the specified entry in your personal PROFILE catalog.

□ If a three-level name is specified, it is treated as *libref.catalog-name.entry-name*. The entry type is assumed to be FORMULA. You receive an error message if the specified libref is undefined. If the specified catalog does not exist, it is created.

□ If a four-level name is specified, the fourth level must be FORMULA. Any other value causes an error message. You receive an error message if the specified libref is undefined. If the specified catalog does not exist, it is created.

If you omit the *formula-name* argument altogether, the procedure stores the entry using the default name. The default formula name is the name used in the previous FORMULA command. If no FORMULA command has been issued, the default name is the name specified in the FORMULA= option of the PROC FSVIEW statement or in the *formula-name* argument of the FSVIEW command when the procedure was initiated. If no formula name was specified when the procedure was invoked, the name of the displayed data set is used as the default formula entry name. The procedure stores the default entry in the current formula catalog. If no formula catalog has previously been specified, the procedure stores the default entry in your personal PROFILE catalog.

SETWSZ ⟨CLEAR⟩

records the current size and position of the FSVIEW window in the formula entry. The SETWSZ CLEAR command removes any previously recorded size and position information.

SHOW ID | VAR *variable* ⟨. . . *variable-n*⟩

adds dropped variables to the FSVIEW window and controls how they are displayed. Dropped variables are variables excluded from the FSVIEW window using the DROP command, or variables that were omitted from the VAR and ID statements when the procedure was initiated.

You must follow the SHOW command with an argument indicating whether the variables are to be displayed as ID variables or as scrolling variables. ID variables remain on the left side of the window as you scroll the other variable columns horizontally.

New scrolling variables are added to the right of existing scrolling variable columns. The first ID variable added replaces the observation number column. Additional ID variables are added to the right of existing ID variable columns, before the first scrolling variable column.

Note: The combined width for all ID variables cannot exceed 60 columns. A single ID variable having a length greater than 60 is truncated to 60 characters. If multiple ID variables are used, only those variables that can be displayed in 60 columns without truncation appear in the FSVIEW window. Any additional ID variables are not visible.

You can add more than one variable with a single SHOW command. You can provide a list of variable names, separated by spaces, as arguments for the command, or you can specify a range of variable columns by specifying the names of the first and last variables in the list, separated by a dash. For example, the following command adds the variables X and Z as scrolling variables:

```
show var x z
```

The following command adds all variables between X and Z, inclusive, as scrolling variables:

```
show var x-z
```

In addition to adding variables that are currently dropped from the window, you can use the SHOW command to change current ID variables into scrolling variables and vice versa. For example, suppose that the FSVIEW window currently displays an ID variable named PRICE that you want to scroll with the other variables. Use the following command to redefine it as a scrolling variable:

```
show var price
```

Similarly, to change a scrolling variable into an ID variable, use the SHOW command to redefine it as an ID variable.

You can also issue the SHOW ID or SHOW VAR commands with no variables specified to open the FSVIEW VARLIST window. The FSVIEW VARLIST window provides a selection list from which the variables to be added can be chosen. See "Choosing Variables for FSVIEW

Operations" later in this chapter for more information on using the FSVIEW VARLIST window.

SORT ⟨ASCENDING | DESCENDING⟩ *variable*
⟨... ⟨ASCENDING | DESCENDING⟩ *variable-n*⟩
(editing command; not valid while browsing a data set)
sorts the data set by the specified variables and saves the data set. If you have deleted any observations from the data set, the remaining observations are renumbered sequentially when you execute the SORT command.

▶ *Caution* . . . . *The SORT command sorts the data set itself, not just the displayed values.*
The FSVIEW procedure sorts a data set in place. It does not leave an unsorted copy of the original. If you need to preserve a copy of the original data, make a copy of the data set before using the SORT command. ▲

Note: The SORT command is not valid while a permanent or temporary WHERE clause is in effect.

By default, the procedure sorts the data set in ascending order of each specified variable. To sort a data set in descending order of a particular variable, precede the variable name with the DESCENDING option. You must specify the DESCENDING option separately for each variable. For example, the following command sorts the data in descending order by STATE and in descending order by CITY within STATE:

```
sort descending state descending city
```

You can also use the ASCENDING option to explicitly indicate the default sorting order.

Note: If the sort fails for any reason, the FSVIEW procedure is immediately terminated to preserve the contents of the data set.

TOP
scrolls the FSVIEW window vertically so that the first observation in the data set appears at the top of the window.

VSCROLL HALF | PAGE | *n*
sets the default vertical scrolling amount for the FORWARD and BACKWARD commands. The following scroll amounts can be specified:

HALF   scroll half the number of lines in the window.

PAGE   scroll the full number of lines in the window.

n   scroll the specified number of lines.

The default amount is HALF.

WHERE ⟨⟨ALSO⟩ *expression*⟩ | ⟨UNDO | CLEAR⟩
imposes one or more sets of conditions that observations in the data set must meet in order to be displayed. *Expression* is any valid WHERE expression involving one or more of the variables in the input data set. Refer to the description of the WHERE statement in Chapter 9 of *SAS Language: Reference* for details of the operators and operands that are valid in WHERE expressions. Observations that do not satisfy the specified conditions cannot be displayed or edited.

(WHERE continued)

The complete set of conditions is called a temporary WHERE clause. The conditions can be modified or canceled during the FSVIEW session. In contrast, the WHERE statement defines a permanent WHERE clause that cannot be changed or canceled during the FSVIEW session and which is not affected by WHERE commands. See "WHERE Statement" earlier in this chapter for details.

The word *Where...* appears in the upper-right corner of the window whenever a temporary WHERE clause is in effect.

The WHERE command has several forms:

WHERE *expression*	applies the conditions specified in *expression* as the new temporary WHERE clause, replacing any clause previously in effect.
WHERE ALSO *expression*	adds the conditions specified in *expression* to the existing temporary WHERE clause.
WHERE UNDO	deletes the most recently added set of conditions from the temporary WHERE clause.
WHERE WHERE CLEAR	cancels the current temporary WHERE clause.

If you edit values in an observation so that it no longer meets the conditions of the WHERE clause, that observation can still be displayed and edited. However, a warning message is printed whenever the observation is displayed, indicating that the observation no longer meets the WHERE conditions.

If you use the ADD or DUP command to add a new observation and enter values that do not meet the WHERE conditions, that observation cannot be displayed or edited once you scroll to another observation.

Creating New SAS Data Sets

You can use the FSVIEW procedure to create new SAS data sets. You name the variables and specify their attributes in the FSVIEW NEW window. After you exit the FSVIEW NEW window, the data set is created with one observation filled with missing values. An FSVIEW window is then automatically opened for editing so that you can enter values in the new data set.

See Chapter 4 for a detailed example of using this feature.

Opening the FSVIEW NEW Window

You can open the FSVIEW NEW window in two different ways:

□ by using the NEW= option in the PROC FSVIEW statement when you invoke the procedure

□ by using the NEW command after you enter the procedure.

Using the NEW= Option

When you invoke the FSVIEW procedure with the NEW= option rather than the DATA= option in the PROC FSVIEW statement, the FSVIEW NEW window is opened when the FSVIEW procedure is initiated.

For example, the following statements initiate an FSVIEW session and open the FSVIEW NEW window to create the new data set MASTER.QTR1REV:

```
proc fsview new=master.qtr1rev;
run;
```

Display 16.2 shows the initial FSVIEW NEW window display.

Display 16.2
The FSVIEW NEW
Window

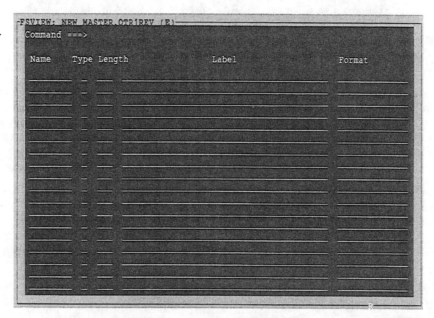

You define the variables in the fields provided. When you execute the END command, the data set is created, and the FSVIEW window is automatically opened for editing so that you can add observations and enter variable values.

Note: After you execute the END command to close the FSVIEW NEW window, you cannot return to that window to make changes to information in the data set.

Using the NEW Command

You can execute the NEW command from an FSVIEW window to define a new data set within an FSVIEW session.

For example, the following command opens the FSVIEW NEW window to define the data set MASTER.QTR1REV:

```
new master.qtr1rev
```

The display in this case is the same as shown in Display 16.2. However, when you use the END command to close the FSVIEW NEW window and create the new data set, an additional FSVIEW window is opened for you to add observations and enter values for the new data set. The new FSVIEW window may overlay the one from which the NEW command was issued.

Creating a Data Set Like an Existing One

If you want to create a SAS data set that is identical or similar in structure to an existing one, you can save time by letting the SAS System do some of the work. Instead of entering all the variable information, use the LIKE= option to identify an existing SAS data set. When the FSVIEW NEW window is opened, the variable names and attributes of the data set you specified in the LIKE= option are automatically displayed.

The display contains all the information necessary to create a SAS data set with exactly the same structure as the one specified. (Only the structure of the specified data set is copied, not the contents.) You have the option of making changes to the variable names and attributes before creating the new data set. You can also delete a variable entirely by blanking out its name.

As discussed earlier, you open the FSVIEW NEW window in one of two ways: either with the NEW= option when you invoke the FSVIEW procedure or with the NEW command when you open an additional FSVIEW window. You can use the LIKE= option with both of these methods.

In the PROC FSVIEW statement, the LIKE= option must always be used in conjunction with the NEW= option. For example, the following statements initiate an FSVIEW session, open the FSVIEW NEW window to create the data set MASTER.QTR2REV, and fill in the fields of the FSVIEW NEW window with the names and attributes of the variables in the data set MASTER.QTR1REV:

```
proc fsview new=master.qtr2rev
     like=master.qtr1rev;
run;
```

The following command performs the same tasks, but from within an active FSVIEW session:

```
new master.qtr2rev like=master.qtr1rev
```

Closing the FSVIEW NEW Window

Execute the END command to close the FSVIEW NEW window, create the SAS data set, and open the FSVIEW window so that you can enter values for each observation. Execute the CANCEL command to close the FSVIEW NEW window without creating a data set.

FSVIEW NEW Window Commands

In addition to SAS/FSP global commands, you can use the following commands in the FSVIEW NEW window to scroll information, to duplicate selected lines, or to exit with the choice of creating a data set or canceling it.

Scrolling

BACKWARD ⟨HALF | PAGE | *n*⟩
BOTTOM
FORWARD ⟨HALF | PAGE | *n*⟩
LEFT
RIGHT
TOP
VSCROLL HALF | PAGE | *n*

Duplicating

REPEAT
SELECT

Exiting

CANCEL
END

Command Descriptions

A description of each of the FSVIEW NEW window commands follows:

BACKWARD ⟨HALF | PAGE | n⟩

> scrolls vertically toward the top of the window. The following scroll amounts can be specified:

> HALF   scrolls upward by half the number of lines in the window.

> PAGE   scrolls upward by the number of lines in the window.

> n   scrolls upward the specified number of lines.

> If you do not explicitly specify an amount to scroll, the default increment is the amount specified in the VSCROLL command. The default VSCROLL amount is HALF.

BOTTOM

> scrolls downward until the last line containing a variable definition is displayed.

CANCEL

> closes the FSVIEW NEW window and ends the FSVIEW session. The new data set is not created.

END

> closes the FSVIEW NEW window, creates the SAS data set defined in the window, and opens an FSVIEW window for editing observations in the newly created data set.

FORWARD ⟨HALF | PAGE | n⟩

> scrolls vertically toward the bottom of the window. You can scroll forward only if you have filled the last blank variable definition line currently displayed or if there are more variables to be displayed. The following scroll amounts can be specified:

> HALF   scrolls downward by half the number of lines in the window.

> PAGE   scrolls downward by the number of lines in the window.

> n   scrolls downward the specified number of lines.

> If you do not explicitly specify an amount to scroll, the default increment is the amount specified in the VSCROLL command. The default VSCROLL amount is HALF.

LEFT

> displays the FORMAT column when the INFORMAT column is displayed or vice versa.

REPEAT

indicates the target line on which you want a selected line repeated. After executing the SELECT command, type REPEAT on the command line, position the cursor on the desired line, and press ENTER. The selected line is then copied to the indicated target line.

RIGHT

displays the INFORMAT column when the FORMAT column is displayed or vice versa.

SELECT

indicates a line whose contents you want repeated on another line. Type SELECT on the command line, position the cursor on the line you want to repeat, and press ENTER. The selected line is remembered; any REPEAT command issued subsequently copies the selected line to the indicated target line.

TOP

scrolls upward until the first variable definition line is displayed.

VSCROLL HALF | PAGE | n

sets the default vertical scrolling amount for the window. The following scroll amounts can be specified:

HALF   scroll half the number of lines in the window.

PAGE   scroll the full number of lines in the window.

n   scroll the specified number of lines.

Duplicating Existing SAS Data Sets

The FSVIEW procedure allows you to create a new data set that duplicates both the structure and the contents of the one currently displayed in the FSVIEW window. You use the CREATE command to create new data sets. See "FSVIEW Window Commands" earlier in this chapter for details of the CREATE command.

The new data set can incorporate some or all of the variables from the currently displayed data set. (Dropped variables cannot be used.) Computed variables in the displayed data set become data set variables in the new data set. The current computed values of the variables are stored as the values of the new variables. If a temporary or permanent WHERE clause is in effect, only those observations from the displayed data set that satisfy the WHERE conditions are copied to the new data set.

There are two ways to specify which variables in the displayed data set are used in the new data set:

□ You can list the desired variable names as arguments for the CREATE command (or use the ALL argument to copy all variables).

□ You can issue a CREATE command with no variable names listed or with the ? argument. This form of the command opens the FSVIEW VARLIST window, from which you can select the variables to include in the new data set. The FSVIEW VARLIST window is explained in the following section.

Selecting Variables for FSVIEW Operations

The CREATE, DROP, and SHOW commands in the FSVIEW window allow you to open the FSVIEW VARLIST window to select which variables from the displayed data set are involved in the specified operation. The FSVIEW VARLIST window is a convenient alternative to entering variable names as command arguments.

Display 16.3 shows a typical FSVIEW VARLIST window.

Display 16.3
Using the FSVIEW VARLIST Window

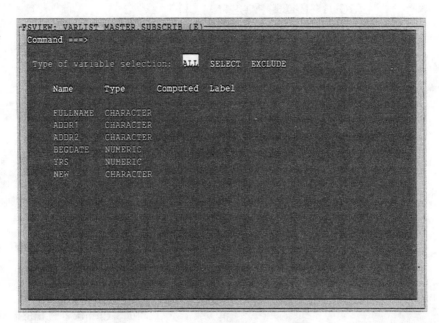

The window includes a list of all the variables in the FSVIEW window along with a three-item choice group: ALL, SELECT, and EXCLUDE. The items correspond to the three ways to use this window:

ALL   use all the variables in the variable list.

SELECT   use only selected variables from the variable list.

EXCLUDE   use all except selected variables from the variable list.

To choose one of these selection methods, move the cursor to the corresponding term and press ENTER. The selection is highlighted in reverse video.

If you choose SELECT or EXCLUDE, you can mark selections in the list of variables. To select variables from the list, move the cursor anywhere on the row for a variable and press ENTER. The selected line is highlighted, and an asterisk appears to the left of the variable name. If you choose SELECT, the marked variables are used in the operation. If you choose EXCLUDE, all variables except those marked are used in the operation.

After you have selected variables, use the END command to carry out the operation, or use the CANCEL command to cancel the operation.

FSVIEW VARLIST Window Commands

In addition to the global commands described in Chapter 18, you can use the following commands in the FSVIEW VARLIST window:

Scrolling

BACKWARD ⟨HALF | PAGE | MAX | n⟩
BOTTOM
FORWARD ⟨HALF | PAGE | MAX | n⟩
HSCROLL HALF | PAGE | n
LEFT ⟨HALF | PAGE | MAX | n⟩
RIGHT ⟨HALF | PAGE | MAX | n⟩
TOP
VSCROLL HALF | PAGE | n

Exiting the Window

CANCEL
END

Command Descriptions

Descriptions of the special FSVIEW window commands follow:

BACKWARD ⟨HALF | PAGE | MAX | n⟩
 scrolls vertically toward the top of the variable selection list. The following scroll amounts can be specified:

 HALF   scrolls upward by half the number of lines in the window.

 PAGE   scrolls upward by the number of lines in the window.

 MAX   scrolls upward to the top of the selection list.

 n   scrolls upward the specified number of lines.

 If you do not explicitly specify an amount to scroll, the default increment is the amount specified in the VSCROLL command. The default VSCROLL amount is HALF.

BOTTOM
 scrolls to the bottom of the selection list.

CANCEL
 closes the FSVIEW VARLIST window and cancels the operation that opened the window.

END
 closes the FSVIEW VARLIST window and carries out the operation that opened the window using the variables selected in the FSVIEW VARLIST window.

FORWARD ⟨HALF | PAGE | MAX | n⟩
 scrolls vertically toward the bottom of the variable selection list. The following scroll amounts can be specified:

 HALF   scrolls downward by half the number of lines in the window.

 PAGE   scrolls downward by the number of lines in the window.

MAX scrolls downward to the bottom of the selection list.

n scrolls downward the specified number of lines.

If you do not explicitly specify an amount to scroll, the default increment is the amount specified in the VSCROLL command. The default VSCROLL amount is HALF.

HSCROLL HALF | PAGE | *n*

specifies the default horizontal scroll amount for the LEFT and RIGHT commands. Specify one of the following scroll amounts:

HALF scroll half the width of the window.

PAGE scroll the full width of the window.

n scroll the specified number of columns.

The default HSCROLL amount is HALF.

LEFT ⟨HALF | PAGE | MAX | *n*⟩

scrolls the contents of the window to the left. The following scroll amounts can be specified:

HALF scrolls by half the width of the window.

PAGE scrolls by the full width of the window.

MAX scrolls to the left margin of the window.

n scrolls the specified number of columns.

If you do not explicitly specify an amount to scroll, the default increment is the amount specified in the HSCROLL command. The default HSCROLL amount is HALF.

RIGHT ⟨HALF | PAGE | MAX | *n*⟩

scrolls the contents of the window to the right. The following scroll amounts can be specified:

HALF scrolls by half the width of the window.

PAGE scrolls by the full width of the window.

MAX scrolls to the right margin of the window.

n scrolls the specified number of columns.

If you do not explicitly specify an amount to scroll, the default increment is the amount specified in the HSCROLL command. The default HSCROLL amount is HALF.

TOP

scrolls to the top of the selection list.

VSCROLL HALF | PAGE | *n*

specifies the default vertical scroll amount for the FORWARD and BACKWARD scrolling commands. Specify one of the following scroll amounts:

HALF   scroll half the number of lines in the window.

PAGE   scroll the number of lines in the window.

n   scroll the specified number of lines.

The default VSCROLL amount is HALF.

Defining Formulas

The FSVIEW procedure allows you to define formulas that perform computations and otherwise manipulate variables. *Formulas* are SAS expressions that calculate values for variables in the FSVIEW window. You can define formulas for variables in the data set, or you can create computed variables to display the formula results.

The effect of a formula assigned to a data set variable depends on whether the FSVIEW window is open for browsing or editing. If the window is open for browsing, the result of computations performed by the assigned formula is displayed in the variable's column in the FSVIEW window, but the variable value in the data set is not affected. If the window is open for editing, the result of the formula computations replaces the value stored in the data set as well as in the FSVIEW window.

Computed variables exist only in the FSVIEW window to show the result of computations performed by a formula; they are not added to the displayed data set. However, within the FSVIEW window computed variables can be manipulated just like data set variables. The only exception is that you cannot use the SORT command to sort the data set according to the values of a computed variable.

When you assign a formula to a variable (either a data set variable or a computed variable), the corresponding variable column in the FSVIEW window is protected. You cannot edit the values of variables with assigned formulas.

Use the DEFINE command to define formulas. The FSVIEW procedure provides two ways to use the DEFINE command:

□ Use the DEFINE command alone or with only the *variable-name* argument to open the FSVIEW Define window. In this window you can enter all the information necessary to define the formula. You can also use this form of the command to open the FSVIEW Define window to edit an existing formula. See "Defining Formulas in the FSVIEW Define Window" later in this section for more information on using the FSVIEW Define window.

□ Supply the formula as an argument with the DEFINE command. Separate the formula from the variable name with an equal sign (=).

Formulas are stored in SAS catalog entries with the type FORMULA. See "Creating FSVIEW Applications" later in this chapter for more information on formula entries.

How Formulas Are Evaluated

Formulas are evaluated in the order that the corresponding variables appear in the FSVIEW window. It is the order of the variables, not the order in which the formulas are defined, that determines the evaluation order. Formulas are evaluated first for any ID variables, then for the remaining variables in left-to-right order. After the formulas for displayed variables are evaluated, any formulas assigned to variables that are dropped from the FSVIEW window are evaluated, in the order in which the variables are dropped.

If you use a computed variable in the formula definition for another variable, it is important that the variable named in the formula appear in the FSVIEW window to the left of the variable for which the formula is defined. Otherwise, the value of the variable in the formula is missing when the formula is evaluated.

When the FSVIEW window is displayed or redrawn, the formulas are evaluated for all displayed observations. When an observation is edited, formulas are evaluated for the edited observation only.

Using Screen Control Language in Formulas

Formulas can also include any valid Screen Control Language functions or statements except those valid only in SAS/AF software and the following statements:

ERRORON
ERROROFF
PROTECT
UNPROTECT
CURSOR
CONTROL ALWAYS

The MODIFIED, ERROR, and CUROBS functions are valid.

Each formula you define is treated as a block of SCL code. When you define a formula, the FSVIEW procedure internally adds a label for the formula and a RETURN statement so that each formula can be treated as a separate SCL block. (The label is the same as the variable name.) The SCL code segments are compiled individually when the formulas are defined.

For example, suppose you define a computed variable named MODSTAT with the following formula:

```
modstat=modified(begdate)
```

The SCL block for the MODSTAT variable would be stored as follows:

```
MODSTAT: modstat=modified(begdate);RETURN;
```

The blocks are executed in the order in which the corresponding variables appear in the FSVIEW window, as explained earlier in this section.

Refer to *SAS Screen Control Language: Reference* for details of including Screen Control Language in FSVIEW formulas.

Defining Formulas in the FSVIEW Define Window

When you execute a DEFINE command in the FSVIEW window without specifying a formula for the variable, the FSVIEW Define window is opened for you to enter the formula definition and other variable attributes. Display 16.4 shows the FSVIEW Define window opened for a variable named ENDDATE:

Display 16.4
FSVIEW Define Window for the Variable ENDDATE

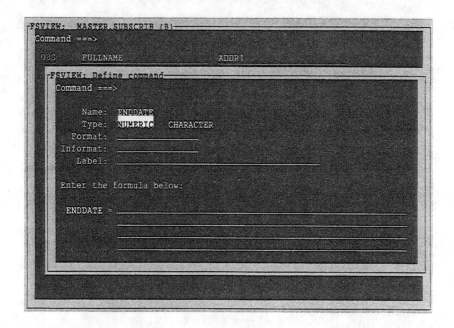

The FSVIEW Define window includes the following fields:

Name

    the name of the variable with which this formula is associated. You can change the name in this field while the FSVIEW Define window is open to change the variable for which the formula is defined. If you specify the name of a variable with an existing formula definition, the remaining fields in this window are filled with values from the current definition.

Type

    the variable type. To select a type, position the cursor on the corresponding term and press ENTER. The default is NUMERIC.

Format

    the format that determines how the variable is displayed. The format also determines the width of the variable's column in the FSVIEW window. If you do not specify a format, a default is used:

        □ BEST12. for numeric variables

        □ $8. for character variables.

Informat

the informat that determines how values entered in the variable's column in the FSVIEW window are interpreted. If you do not specify an informat, a default is used:

□ 12. for numeric variables

□ $8. for character variables.

Label

a descriptive label up to 40 characters long. (The FSVIEW procedure does not display variable labels.)

At the bottom of the window are four lines for entering the formula. The FSVIEW Define window supplies the variable name and the equal sign that begin the definition.

When you define formulas in the FSVIEW Define window, they can consist of more than one statement. If you use multiple statements, separate the statements with semicolons. The definition can include as many statements as you can fit in the space provided.

The following section describes the commands you can use in the FSVIEW Define window.

FSVIEW Define Window Commands

In addition to the global commands described in Chapter 18, you can use the following commands in the FSVIEW Define window:

CANCEL
COMPILE
END

Command Descriptions

Descriptions of the special FSVIEW Define window commands follow:

CANCEL

closes the FSVIEW Define window without recording the formula or variable attributes entered in the window. Once you open the FSVIEW Define window, you must use this command to close the window without entering a formula definition.

COMPILE

compiles the current formula and reports whether it is a valid SAS expression.

END

compiles the current formula. If the formula is valid, the FSVIEW Define window is closed, the formula definition is recorded in the formula entry, and you return to the FSVIEW window. If the formula contains errors, an error message is displayed and the FSVIEW Define window remains open.

Reviewing Formula Definitions

You can browse existing formula definitions in the FSVIEW REVIEW window. Use the REVIEW command in the FSVIEW window to open the FSVIEW REVIEW window. Display 16.5 shows a FSVIEW REVIEW window containing two formula definitions.

Display 16.5
Viewing Formulas in the FSVIEW REVIEW Window

```
┌FSVIEW: REVIEW MASTER.SUBSCRIB (B)─────────────────
│ Command ===>
│
│ ENDDATE= intnx('month',begdate,(yrs*12)-1)
│
│ REMAIN=int((enddate-date())/30)
│
│ *** END OF TEXT ***
```

The FSVIEW REVIEW window displays the formulas for browsing only. You cannot make changes to the formulas in this window. The formula definitions are listed in the order in which they are entered.

FSVIEW REVIEW Window Commands

The FSVIEW REVIEW window uses the SAS text editor. All text editor browsing commands are valid in this window. Refer to Chapter 19, "SAS Text Editor Commands," in *SAS Language: Reference* for more information on the commands that can be used.

Use the END command to close the FSVIEW REVIEW window and return to the FSVIEW window.

Customizing the FSVIEW Environment

You can control some of the characteristics of the FSVIEW session by specifying values for parameters in the FSVIEW Parameters window. Use the PARMS command to open the FSVIEW Parameters window. Display 16.6 shows the FSVIEW Parameters window with the default parameter settings.

Display 16.6
The FSVIEW
Parameters
Window

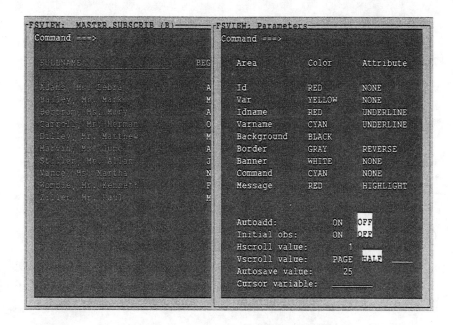

You can change the current parameter settings in the FSVIEW Parameters window. Some of the parameter settings in the FSVIEW Parameters window are choice groups. To turn on these parameters, move the cursor to the term for the desired parameter status and press ENTER. The selected term is highlighted. Other parameter settings are fields in which you enter the desired parameter values. The following section describes the parameters available in the FSVIEW Parameters window.

If you create a formula entry for the FSVIEW session, all the parameter settings from the FSVIEW Parameters window are recorded and will be in effect the next time that formula entry is loaded.

Parameter Descriptions

The following parameters can be controlled using the FSVIEW Parameters windows:

Autoadd

> controls whether new observations are automatically added to the displayed data set. This parameter reflects the current status of the autoadd feature, which can also be controlled with the AUTOADD command in the FSVIEW window.

Autosave value

> controls how frequently the data set is automatically saved. An automatic save is performed whenever the number of modifications (additions, deletions, or changes) specified in this parameter have been made since the last save. The default value is 25.
>
> If you use the AUTOSAVE command in the FSVIEW window, the value you specify with that command appears in the field for this parameter.

Cursor variable

> controls which variable column the cursor is positioned on when a new observation is added by the autoadd feature or the DUP command.

(Cursor variable continued)

If you use the CURSOR command in the FSVIEW window, the variable you specify with that command appears in the field for this parameter.

Hscroll value

controls how many columns are scrolled when a LEFT or RIGHT command does not specify an explicit scroll amount. The default value is 1.

If you use the HSCROLL command in the FSVIEW window, the value you specify with that command appears in the field for this parameter.

Vscroll value

controls how many observations are scrolled when a FORWARD or BACKWARD command does not specify an explicit scroll amount. The following default scroll amounts can be specified:

HALF   scroll half the number of lines in the window.

PAGE   scroll the number of lines in the window.

n   scroll the specified number of lines. Enter the desired value in the space provided; then press ENTER to select this value. The value is highlighted in reverse video when it is selected.

The default value is HALF.

If you use the VSCROLL command in the FSVIEW window, the value you specify with that command is shown in the field for this parameter.

Colors and Attributes

control the color and highlighting of various areas of the FSVIEW window. If you use the COLOR command in the FSVIEW window, the colors and highlighting attributes you specify in that command appear in these parameters.

The following values are valid in the Color fields:

BLUE	GREEN	WHITE	GRAY
RED	CYAN	BLACK	BROWN
PINK	YELLOW	MAGENTA	ORANGE

If a specified color is not available on a user's device, the procedure substitutes the available color that most closely matches the specified color. Some devices do not allow changing the background color; for these devices, the background color parameter is ignored.

The following values are valid in the Attribute fields. (You can abbreviate the values by entering only the first letter; the procedure fills in the complete value when you press ENTER):

HIGHLIGHT	high intensity
BLINKING	blinking
UNDERLINE	underlined
REVERSE	reverse video

Any parameter that specifies a highlighting attribute not available on the device is ignored. You cannot specify a highlighting attribute for the background.

One parameter in the FSVIEW Parameters window is displayed for information only; its value cannot be changed:

Initial obs

indicates whether initial values have been recorded to fill added observations. This parameter is set on when you use the INITIAL command in the FSVIEW window. The INITIAL command records values from an existing observation so that they can be copied into new observations added by the autoadd feature.

FSVIEW Parameters Window Commands

In addition to the global commands described in Chapter 18, you can use the following commands in the FSVIEW Parameters window:

CANCEL
END

Command Descriptions

Descriptions of the special FSVIEW Parameters window commands follow:

CANCEL

closes the FSVIEW Parameters window without recording any changes to the previous parameter settings.

END

closes the FSVIEW Parameters window and applies the parameter settings contained therein to the FSVIEW window.

Creating FSVIEW Applications

If you are an applications developer, you can use the FSVIEW procedure as the basis for data entry and editing applications. The FSVIEW procedure allows you to tailor the application environment to suit the needs of your users. Customization can include

□ redesigning the display

□ defining formulas to create computed variables or manipulate data set variables

□ setting general parameters that control the behavior of the FSVIEW session.

The feature of the FSVIEW procedure that makes this customization possible is the formula entry. *Formula entries* are SAS catalog entries of type FORMULA that are created by the FSVIEW procedure to record the following information about the FSVIEW session:

□ the names and order of variables in the FSVIEW window.

□ the format and informat of the variables.

□ any formula definitions for the variables.

□ the format and informat of the variables.

□ any formula definitions for the variables.

□ the current size and position of the FSVIEW window. (These values can be reset with the SETWSZ command.)

□ the current FSVIEW window colors.

□ the initial values for variables in added observations. (These values can be reset with the INITIAL command.)

□ the current settings of all general parameters: Autoadd, Autosave value, Hscroll value, Vscroll value, and Cursor variable.

The formula entry also records which observations and variables are currently displayed in the FSVIEW window when the formula entry is saved.

Creating and Updating Formula Entries

If you specify a catalog name or a complete formula name when you open an FSVIEW window (by using the FORMULA= option in the PROC FSVIEW statement, the *formula-name* argument in the FSVIEW command, or the FORMULA= option in the BROWSE, EDIT, and NEW commands in the FSVIEW window), a formula entry is created automatically when the FSVIEW window is closed. You can also create a formula entry by issuing a SAVE FORMULA command in the FSVIEW window. If you specify a catalog name only, the FSVIEW procedure uses the name of the displayed data set as the formula name.

Loading Formula Entries

To load an existing formula entry when you invoke the FSVIEW procedure, use the FORMULA= option in the PROC FSVIEW statement or the *formula-name* argument in the FSVIEW command. You can also use the FORMULA= option in the BROWSE, EDIT, and NEW commands in the FSVIEW window to load a formula entry for additional FSVIEW windows opened during the FSVIEW session. You can use the FORMULA command in an open FSVIEW window to change the formula entry used for the window or to load a formula entry if none was used when the window was originally opened. (The FORMULA command is valid even when you do not specify a formula catalog when you invoke the FSVIEW procedure.)

Part 5
Reference: Global Features

Chapter 17 Overview: Part 5

Introduction

Chapters 18 through 20 provide information on features of SAS/FSP software that are common to all procedures. These features include

□ global commands

□ the PMENU facility

□ forms for printing.

Refer to Part 4, Chapters 11 through 16, for descriptions of specific SAS/FSP procedures. Refer to Parts 2 and 3, Chapters 2 through 10, for examples of how the procedures are used.

Guide to Global Features

Table 17.1 explains the function of each of the global features discussed in this part of the book. It also directs you to the chapter that documents each feature.

Table 17.1
Guide to Global Features

Topic	Description	Chapter
Global commands	commands that can be used in all windows opened by SAS/FSP procedures	18
The PMENU facility	menu system for executing commands in windows opened by SAS/FSP procedures	19
Forms	catalog entries that define printer characteristics for printouts produced by SAS/FSP software	20

Chapter **18** Command Reference

Overview

Four classes of commands are available in the windows provided by SAS/FSP procedures:

SAS display manager commands
> valid in all SAS System windows, including all SAS/FSP windows. These commands are described in Chapter 18, "SAS Display Manager Commands," in *SAS Language: Reference, Version 6, First Edition.*

SAS/FSP software global commands
> valid in all SAS/FSP windows. These commands are described in this chapter.

SAS text editor commands
> valid in windows that use the SAS text editor, including selected SAS/FSP windows. These commands are described in Chapter 19, "SAS Text Editor Commands," in *SAS Language: Reference.*

Procedure-specific commands
> valid only in particular SAS/FSP windows. These commands are described in the individual reference chapters for each procedure (Chapters 12 through 16 in this book).

This chapter gives an overview of these classes of commands and provides specific details of the SAS/FSP global commands.

Executing Commands in SAS/FSP Windows

Three methods are available for executing commands in SAS/FSP windows:

□ Type the command on the command line and press ENTER. (See the examples in this book.)

□ Assign the command to a function key. (See the discussion of assigning commands to function keys in Chapter 7, "SAS Display Manager System," in *SAS Language: Reference.*)

□ Use the PMENU facility. (See Chapter 19, "The PMENU Facility.")

The SAS text editor provides an additional method:

□ Type a text editor line command over a line number and press ENTER. (See Chapter 8, "SAS Text Editor," in *SAS Language: Reference.*)

SAS System Global Commands

Two of the classes of commands available in SAS/FSP windows are provided by SAS System facilities outside of SAS/FSP software: SAS display manager commands and SAS text editor commands.

SAS Display Manager Commands

Display manager global commands are valid in all SAS/FSP windows, with the following exceptions:

□ The WSAVE command is invalid in most SAS/FSP windows. However, some SAS/FSP procedures provide facilities for defining default window characteristics.

□ Scrolling commands are not global. Scrolling commands vary from window to window within SAS/FSP software because the commands are adapted to the specific environment of each window. Scrolling commands for each SAS/FSP window are described in Chapters 12 through 16.

Display manager commands are described in Chapter 18 of *SAS Language: Reference.*

Among the new display manager commands for Release 6.06 are the following commands to call SAS/FSP procedures from any SAS System window:

□ FSBROWSE

□ FSEDIT

□ FSLETTER

□ FSLIST

□ FSVIEW.

These display manager commands are described in detail in the reference chapters for each procedure (Chapters 12 through 16 in this book).

SAS Text Editor Commands

The SAS text editor is an editing and browsing facility available throughout the SAS System, including the following SAS/FSP windows:

□ FSEDIT Modify and FSBROWSE Modify

□ FSEDIT Program and FSBROWSE Program

□ FSLETTER

□ FSLETTER SEND

□ FSVIEW REVIEW.

Using the SAS text editor in SAS/FSP windows is very similar to using the editor in the PROGRAM EDITOR or the NOTEPAD windows in base SAS software. SAS text editor commands are described in Chapter 19 of *SAS Language: Reference*.

SAS/FSP Software Global Commands

In addition to the global commands provided by base SAS software facilities, SAS/FSP windows have several global commands that relate to special SAS/FSP software features such as controlling multiple windows within a procedure. The following sections describe SAS/FSP software global commands, as well as display manager global commands that are especially useful in SAS/FSP windows.

Moving from Window to Window

Use display manager window call commands to open or move to specific display manager windows. For example, to move from an FSLETTER window to the LOG window, execute the following command:

    log

To move among all currently open windows, use the following command:

NEXT ⟨*window-name*⟩
        moves to the next open window, or to a specified window. If no window is specified, the order of selection is determined by the order in which the windows were opened.

(NEXT continued)

To move to a specific window, follow the NEXT command with the name of the desired window. For example, to move an open FSLETTER window from any other window, execute the following command:

```
next fsletter
```

You can abbreviate the window names. For example, the following command moves to the next open SAS/FSP window:

```
next fs
```

Managing Concurrent Windows

The FSLETTER and FSVIEW procedures allow concurrent windows (multiple windows opened from a single invocation of the procedure). The following commands are useful for managing windows in FSLETTER or FSVIEW sessions that open more than one window:

SWAP

moves the cursor to the next concurrent window and activates that window. In the FSLETTER procedure, this command can also move the cursor from an FSLETTER window to the FSLETTER DIRECTORY window without closing the FSLETTER window.

WREGION ⟨*start-row start-column rows columns*⟩
WREGION CLEAR

specifies the area of the display that the next window of a multiwindow FSLETTER or FSVIEW session will occupy. Specify the starting row and column for the window and the window's size in rows and columns.

Note: The area of the window available for procedure output is four lines and two columns less than the amount you specify in the *rows* and *columns* arguments. Remember that the top and bottom window borders, command line, and message line occupy a total of four lines, and the left and right window borders occupy a total of two columns.

For example, the following command causes the next window to occupy the bottom half of the current window (assuming that the current window occupies a 24-line-by-80-column display):

```
wregion 13 1 12 80
```

Display 18.1 shows the result of issuing the preceding command before opening a second FSLETTER window in an FSLETTER session.

Use the WREGION CLEAR command to clear any previous WREGION setting and return to the default format in which windows partially overlap in a staggered pattern.

Use the WREGION command with no argument to display the current region setting on the window's message line.

WSIZE

> displays the size and position of the current window on the window's message line. The WSIZE command is useful for determining the current window dimensions before you execute a WREGION command.

Display 18.1
Using the
WREGION
Command

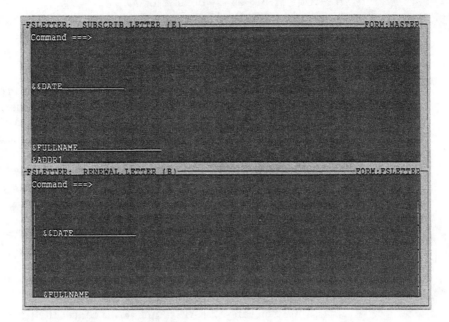

Printing

The following commands are used for taking pictures of windows and for obtaining information about the current form for printing.

FONT

> opens the FONT window and displays the font control information from the current form. The listing tells what color and highlighting attributes the form interprets as signals to change printing characteristics. The FONT window is for browsing only; to change the font information, you must open the FORM window and edit the form entry. See Chapter 20, "Forms," for more information.
>
> **Note:** The FONT window is not opened if no font control information is defined in the current default form. Instead, a message is printed on the window's message line indicating that the form contains no font information.

FORMNAME ⟨*form-name*⟩
FORMNAME CLEAR

> specifies the default form containing instructions for printing images captured with the SPRINT command. The SAS System's default form is DEFAULT.FORM. This command allows you to specify a different default. See Chapter 20 for additional information on forms.
>
> When a form is required, the SAS System looks for the specified form first in the current catalog (if a catalog is currently open). If the form is not there, the system looks in your personal PROFILE catalog (SASUSER.PROFILE, or WORK.PROFILE if the libref SASUSER is not defined) and then, finally, in the SASHELP.FSP catalog.

(FORMNAME continued)

Use the FORMNAME CLEAR command to return to using DEFAULT.FORM as the default form.

Use the FORMNAME command with no argument to display the current default form name on the window's message line.

PRTFILE ⟨*fileref* | '*actual-filename*' ⟨APPEND | REPLACE⟩⟩
PRTFILE CLEAR

specifies a file to which the procedure sends documents created with the FSLETTER procedure or screen images captured with the SPRINT command. By default, output is sent to the printer destination specified in the current form. You can use this command to route the output to an external file instead.

You identify the file using either a previously assigned fileref or the actual filename. Quotes are required when you specify an actual filename rather than a fileref. For a discussion of assigning filerefs to external files, see Chapter 1, "Introduction to SAS/FSP Software."

With the filename or fileref, you can also specify either the APPEND or REPLACE option to determine how the file is handled if it already exists. The default is REPLACE, which causes text sent to an existing file to overwrite the current contents of the file. Use the APPEND option to have the new text appended to the file instead.

Use the PRTFILE CLEAR command to cancel the previous PRTFILE specification and route information to the printer again.

Use the PRTFILE command with no argument to display the name of the current print file on the window's message line.

SPRINT ⟨FORM=*form-name*⟩ ⟨FILE=*fileref* | '*actual-filename*'⟩ ⟨NOBORDER⟩
SPRINT FREE

takes a picture of the current window (except for the command and message lines). Unless you use the NOBORDER option, the image includes the window border.

The form used to define output characteristics can be specified using either a FORMNAME command or the FORM= option. Use a FORMNAME command before using the SPRINT command to set the default form for all images. Use the FORM= option with the SPRINT command to use a form other than the current default for an individual image.

By default, the image goes to the printer destination specified in the form. Use a PRTFILE command before using the SPRINT command if you want all images sent to a file instead of to the printer. Use the FILE= option with the SPRINT command to route a single image to an external file instead of to the printer, or to route a single image to a file other than the one specified with the PRTFILE command. Changing output destinations within a procedure automatically frees the previous print file or print queue.

Note: Once you have sent SPRINT output to a file, any additional SPRINT output you send to that file must use the same form.

The print queue or print file used by the SPRINT command is freed when you end the procedure from which you captured images. Use the SPRINT FREE command to free the print queue or print file before ending the procedure. You can use the SPRINT command to capture images from several procedures in a single print file or print queue. In this case, the print file or print queue cannot be freed until you end all the procedures that sent output to the file.

Controlling the Procedure Environment

The following commands control the default behavior of various features of SAS/FSP procedures:

DEBUG ⟨ON | OFF⟩
> turns the Screen Control Language source-level debugger on or off. If you omit the argument, the debugger is turned on. The debugger cannot be turned off while it is active.
>
> The SCL debugger is a tool for identifying and correcting problems in Screen Control Language programs and FSVIEW formulas. See *SAS Screen Control Language: Reference, Version 6, First Edition* for information on the SCL debugger.

MSG ⟨ON | OFF | CLOSE⟩
> controls access to the MESSAGE window. In SAS/FSP software you can intercept messages sent to the SAS log and display them in the MESSAGE window instead.
>
> The following options can be used:

ON   turns on the interception of messages. This option also opens the MESSAGE window if it is not currently open.

OFF   turns off the interception of messages. This option does not close the MESSAGE window.

CLOSE   turns off the interception of messages and closes the MESSAGE window.

> Use the MSG command with no arguments to move to the MESSAGE window and make that the active window.

SETPMENU ⟨*libref.catalog-name.*⟩*pmenu-name*
> identifies the source of PMENU information for the current window. Action bar and pull-down menu characteristics are stored in catalog entries of type PMENU. This command assigns a particular PMENU entry to the current window.
>
> If you omit the *libref* and *catalog-name* arguments, the procedure looks for the PMENU entry first in the current catalog (if a catalog is currently open), then in your personal PROFILE catalog, and finally in the system catalog SASHELP.FSP.
>
> You can use the PMENU procedure in base SAS software to create custom action bars and pull-down menus for SAS/FSP windows. Refer to the *SAS Procedures Guide: Version 6, Third Edition* for more information on the process of creating custom action bars and menus.
>
> This command does not turn on the PMENU facility; it only identifies the PMENU entry for the current window. Use the PMENU command to activate the PMENU facility if it is not active by default at your site.

SETCR ⟨STAY | HTAB | VTAB | NEWL | CMDPN RET | NORET MOD | NOMOD⟩
defines the behavior of the ENTER key. You can use the command with
or without arguments, but if you use arguments you must supply one
from each of the following three groups:

Cursor Movement
determines the behavior of the cursor when the ENTER key is
pressed. The following selections are valid:

STAY	cursor does not move.
HTAB	cursor moves to the next unprotected field on the current line. If there are no more unprotected fields on the current line, the cursor moves to the first unprotected field on a line below the current field.
VTAB	cursor moves to the next unprotected field below the current field.
NEWL	cursor moves to the first unprotected field on a line below the current line.
CMDPN	cursor moves to the command line.

Control Passing
determines whether control passes to the application when the
ENTER key is pressed. The following selections are valid:

RET	returns control to the application.
NORET	does not return control to the application.

Field Modification
determines whether a field is marked as modified when the
ENTER key is pressed on that field, even if the field value has
not been changed. The following selections are valid:

MOD	marks the field as modified.
NOMOD	does not mark the field as modified unless the field value is changed.

SETHELP ⟨*libref.catalog-name.*⟩*help-entry*⟨*.entry-type*⟩
identifies the source of help information for the current window. When
you issue the HELP command in a window, the SAS System opens a
HELP window and displays information from a catalog entry of the type
HELP or CBT. This command assigns a particular HELP or CBT entry to
the current window.
If you omit the *libref* and *catalog-name* arguments, the procedure
looks for the specified entry first in the current catalog (if a catalog is
currently open), then in your personal PROFILE catalog
(SASUSER.PROFILE or WORK.PROFILE), and finally in the system
catalog SASHELP.FSP. The *entry-type* value can be either CBT or HELP.
If you omit the type, the procedure looks for an entry of type CBT.
You can use the BUILD procedure in SAS/AF software to create
custom help entries for SAS/FSP windows. You can create either HELP
or CBT entries, depending on the level of interactivity you want to

provide. HELP entries simply provide text. CBT entries can provide more sophisticated assistance, including topic selection lists and nested windows. Refer to *SAS/AF Software: Usage and Reference, Version 6, First Edition* for more information on creating HELP and CBT entries.

SHOWTYPE ⟨*entry-type* | ALL⟩

selects the type of catalog entry listed in a catalog directory. By default, catalog directories list all entries in the specified catalog, regardless of type. You can use this command to restrict the listing to only one type of entry.

For example, issue the following command in the FSLETTER DIRECTORY window to show only those entries with type LETTER:

```
showtype letter
```

Use the following command to display all types of entries.

```
showtype all
```

Use the SHOWTYPE command with no argument to display the current default type on the window's message line.

TYPE ⟨*entry-type*⟩

specifies the entry type the procedure assumes when the type is not explicitly specified in a command. Each procedure that uses catalog entries assumes a different default type. You can use this command to change the default type to suit your needs.

For example, if you issue the following command in the FSLETTER. DIRECTORY window, the FSLETTER procedure by default assumes that you are copying an entry of type LETTER:

```
copy renewal renewal2
```

Use the TYPE command when you want the procedure to assume a different entry type.

Use the TYPE command with no argument to display the current default type on the window's message line.

SAS/FSP Software Global Command Reference List

The following commands are global in all SAS/FSP windows. Commands that are specific to SAS/FSP software or that have additional uses within SAS/FSP software are marked with an asterisk. These commands are discussed in this chapter. All others are display manager global commands and are discussed in Chapter 18 of *SAS Language: Reference*.

Window Call	AF	LIBNAME
	CATALOG	LISTING
	DIR	LOG
	FILENAME	MANAGER | MGR
	FOOTNOTES	MENU
	* FSBROWSE	* MSG
	* FSEDIT	NOTEPAD
	FSFORM	OPTIONS
	* FSLETTER	OUTPUT
	* FSLIST	PGM
	* FSVIEW	SETINIT
	* HELP	TITLES
	KEYS	VAR
Window Position	WDEF	* WREGION
	WGROW	WSHRINK
	WMOVE	* WSIZE
Window Management	AUTOPOP	PREVWIND
	BYE | ENDSAS	RESHOW
	COLOR	SCROLLBAR
	* DEBUG	* SETCR
	HOME	* SETHELP
	ICON	* SETPMENU
	KEYDEF	* SHOWTYPE
	NEXT	* SWAP
	PMENU	* TYPE
	PREVCMD | ?	X
		ZOOM
Cut and Paste Facility	CUT	PLIST
	MARK	SMARK
	PASTE	STORE
	PCLEAR	UNMARK
Printing	* FONT	* PRTFILE
	* FORMNAME	* SPRINT

Chapter **19** The PMENU Facility

Overview

In addition to executing commands from the command line or with function keys, you can use the PMENU facility to execute commands from menus in SAS/FSP windows. If you use some procedures only occasionally or if you forget the syntax of a command, the PMENU facility provides an alternative to entering commands on the command line.

Using the PMENU Facility

If the PMENU facility is not active by default at your site, you can turn it on for all SAS System windows with the following command:

```
pmenu on
```

When the PMENU facility is active, an *action bar* is displayed. The action bar consists of a number of *items*, which correspond to the actions or classes of actions that can be executed in the current window.

Making Selections from the Action Bar

Display 19.1 shows an example of an FSEDIT window with an action bar.

Display 19.1
Action Bar for the
FSEDIT Window

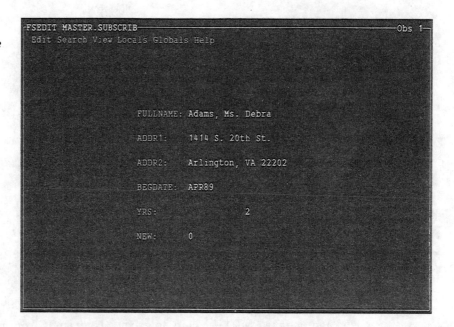

```
─FSEDIT MASTER.SUBSCRIB─────────────────────────────────────────────Obs 1─
  Edit Search View Locals Globals Help




                    FULLNAME: Adams, Ms. Debra

                    ADDR1:    1414 S. 20th St.

                    ADDR2:    Arlington, VA 22202

                    BEGDATE:  APR89

                    YRS:                   2

                    NEW:     0


```

To choose an action from the action bar, position the cursor on the desired item.
Use the TAB key or cursor keys to move from one item in the action bar to the
next. If your device supports a mouse, you can also use that to move the cursor.
To execute your item, press the ENTER key or the mouse button.

When you make a selection from an action bar, the SAS System responds in
one of the following ways:

□   If the item corresponds to a single command, that command is executed.

□   If the item corresponds to a label for a class of commands, a pull-down
    menu is opened below the item. The pull-down menu provides an additional
    list of actions from which to choose.

Making Selections from Pull-Down Menus

Display 19.2 shows the pull-down menu for the View item in the FSEDIT
window action bar.

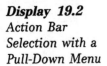

Display 19.2
Action Bar
Selection with a
Pull-Down Menu

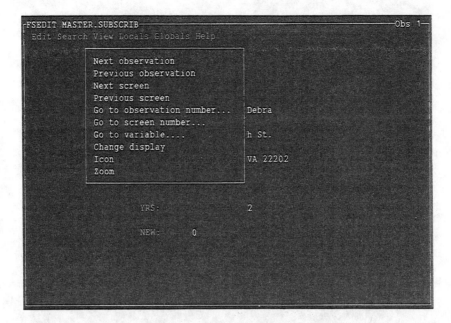

The process for selecting items from pull-down menus is the same as for choosing items from the action bar. Move the cursor to the desired item, and press ENTER or the mouse button. To close the menu without making a selection, move the cursor anywhere outside the menu borders and press ENTER or the mouse button.

When you make a selection from a pull-down menu, the SAS System responds in one of the following ways:

□ If the item corresponds to a command that requires no additional information, that command is executed.

□ If the item corresponds to a command that requires additional information such as values for arguments, a *dialog box* is opened. Dialog boxes are special data entry windows that allow you to provide supplemental information for the command. Items that open dialog boxes are indicated with an ellipsis (...) in the pull-down menus.

□ If the item corresponds to a label for a class of actions, another pull-down menu is opened. Subordinate pull-down menus provide the same three types of items as the first menu.

The View menu in Display 19.2 contains all three types of items:

□ The Next observation and Previous observation items correspond to the individual commands FORWARD and BACKWARD. When you select one of these items, the corresponding command is executed.

□ The Change display item is a label for another class of actions. When you select this item, another pull-down menu is opened from which you can make further selections.

□ The Go to observation number... item corresponds to the *n* (observation number) command. This command requires additional information—the number of the observation to be displayed. When you select this item, a dialog box is opened in which you can enter the desired observation number.

Using Dialog Boxes

Display 19.3 shows the dialog box that is opened when you select Go to observation number... in the View menu.

Display 19.3
Pull-Down Menu
with a Dialog Box

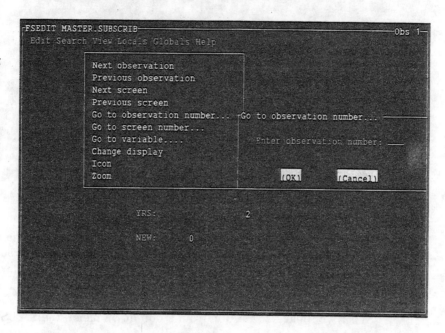

Dialog boxes are data entry windows with special features:

fields	areas in which you enter values for the operation.
pushbuttons	highlighted terms that trigger actions when you press the ENTER key or the mouse button while the cursor is located on them.

All dialog boxes include the following two pushbuttons:

OK	closes the dialog box and carries out the specified operation using the values provided in the fields.
Cancel	closes the dialog box without performing the specified operation.

selection lists	lists of terms from which you can select values by moving the cursor to the desired item and pressing the ENTER key or the mouse button.

To specify information in a dialog box, enter the desired values in the fields provided; then move the cursor to the OK pushbutton and press ENTER or the mouse button. If you decide after the dialog box is opened that you do not want to execute the command, move the cursor to the Cancel pushbutton and press ENTER or the mouse button. You can also cancel the command by moving the cursor anywhere outside the dialog box and pressing ENTER or the mouse button.

For example, to use the dialog box in Display 19.3, you enter the desired observation number in the space provided. Once you have filled in the field, you move the cursor to the OK pushbutton at the bottom of the box and press ENTER or the mouse button to move to the specified observation.

Turning Off the PMENU Facility

To turn the PMENU facility off for all windows, choose the Globals selection from the action bar; then select the Global options item in the Globals menu. That opens another pull-down menu. From the Global options menu, choose the Action bar off item.

You can also turn the action bar off in selected windows while the PMENU facility remains active in others. Open the Globals menu and select the Command item. That opens another pull-down menu. From the Command menu, choose the Command line item to turn off the action bar for the current window. Use the command COMMAND to reinstate the action bar.

Note: If you want to issue a single command, another choice in the Command menu is the Command window item. This opens a special dialog box in which you can issue commands without turning on the command line.

With the action bar turned off in a particular window (or from the Command window), you can enter the following command to turn the PMENU facility off:

```
pmenu off
```

This command turns the PMENU facility off for all windows.

Creating Your Own Menus

You can use the PMENU procedure in base SAS software to create custom action bars and menus for your SAS/FSP applications. For details about the process of creating menus, refer to the *SAS Procedures Guide, Version 6, Third Edition*.

The menu system you design is stored in catalog entries of type PMENU. You use the SETPMENU command to associate a PMENU entry with a SAS/FSP window. The SETPMENU command is described in Chapter 18, "Command Reference."

Chapter 20 Forms

Overview

When the SAS System prints text or writes text to an external file, it may need information about the type of printer used and the way the text is to be formatted. This information is stored in a *form*, a SAS catalog entry of the type FORM. Forms are a feature of base SAS software.

When you do not explicitly select a particular form, a default form is used. Several default forms are supplied with the SAS System. For example, the FSLETTER procedure uses the default form FSLETTER.FORM. The SPRINT command uses the default form DEFAULT.FORM.

You can create custom forms to define the exact formatting and printer features you want to use for your output. This chapter gives a brief overview of the process of creating and editing forms. Complete details can be found in *SAS Language: Reference, Version 6, First Edition.*

Creating and Modifying Forms

Forms are created and edited in the FORM window. This window has several frames in which you provide information such as the type of printer, desired margins, and items specific to controlling the appearance of your text.

You can create or edit a form entry from any SAS System window by issuing the FSFORM command:

FSFORM ⟨*SAS-catalog.*⟩*form-name*

If you omit the catalog name, the system looks for the entry in your personal PROFILE catalog (SASUSER.PROFILE, or WORK.PROFILE if the SASUSER library is not allocated). If the specified form does not currently exist, the FORM window is opened for you to create a new form.

You can also create or edit a form entry by issuing an EDIT command in any SAS/FSP window that allows the EDIT command:

EDIT *form-name*.FORM

Specifying an entry type of FORM causes the EDIT command to open the FORM window for editing the specified form in the currently designated catalog.

You can browse FORM entries by issuing a BROWSE command in any SAS/FSP window that allows the BROWSE command:

BROWSE *form-name*.FORM

This opens the FORM window for browsing only.

FORM Window Frames

The FORM window includes the following frames:

Printer Selection
> allows you to select the type of printer from a list of available printer types. Your choice of printer in this frame determines the initial values for all the other frames.
>
> This frame appears only if you are creating a new form. Once you select a printer, you cannot return to this frame to change the printer type.

Text Body and Margin Information
> allows you to specify page formats such as margins, line size, and number of lines per page.

Carriage Control Information
> allows you to specify whether carriage-control information is created with the output text and, if so, at what points in the output.

Print File Parameters
> allows you to specify operating-system-specific features of the print file.

Font Control Information
> allows you to define which text characters are interpreted as control characters and to specify which color and highlighting attributes are used in your text to select special printer features.

Printer Control Language
> allows you to compose lists of control sequence codes that are sent to your printer.

If you are creating a new form, the first frame displayed when the FORM window is opened is the Printer Selection frame. This frame is only displayed when a new form is created; it cannot be displayed again once a printer is selected. If you are editing an existing form entry, the first frame displayed is Text Body and Margin Information.

You define the form by supplying values for fields in the frames. Many of the fields in the frames have default values, which you can modify to change the characteristics of the form.

FORM Window Commands

You can use the following commands in the FORM window. Refer to Chapter 17, "SAS Display Manager Windows," in *SAS Language: Reference* for additional details.

CANCEL
> cancels any changes made when editing an existing form. When you are defining a new form, the CANCEL command closes the window and does not save the form entry.

DES ⟨*'description-string'*⟩
>   displays or changes the description that appears in the catalog directory.

END
>   saves any changes made to the form entry and closes the FORM window.

=*n*
>   moves you to the frame specified by *n*, where *n* can be the following:

> | | |
> |---|---|
> | 1 | Text Body and Margin Information |
> | 2 | Carriage Control Information |
> | 3 | Print File Parameters |
> | 4 | Font Control Information |
> | 5 | Printer Control Language |

>   You cannot use this command to return to the Printer Selection frame.

NEXTSCR
>   scrolls forward to the next FORM frame.

PREVSCR
>   scrolls back to the previous FORM frame. You cannot use the PREVSCR command to return to the Printer Selection frame.

Using Forms

There are two cases when forms are required in SAS/FSP software:

□   when you print a document using the FSLETTER procedure (including when the procedure is called from the FSEDIT or FSBROWSE procedures)

□   when you print a screen image captured by the SPRINT command.

For documents created with the FSLETTER procedure, the associated form name is stored in the letter entry for the document. You use the FORM command in the FSLETTER window to associate a form with a document. The default form name is FSLETTER.FORM. The system searches the following catalogs in the order shown for the specified form entry:

1. the current letter catalog

2. your personal PROFILE catalog (SASUSER.PROFILE, or WORK.PROFILE if the SASUSER library is not allocated)

3. the system catalog SASHELP.FSP

For the SPRINT command, the form name is retained by the system. The default form name is DEFAULT.FORM. You use the global FORMNAME command to change the current form. The syntax of the FORMNAME command is

FORMNAME ⟨*form-name* | CLEAR⟩

You can also select a form for an individual SPRINT command using the command's FORM= option. See Chapter 18, "Command Reference," for more information on the FORMNAME and SPRINT commands.

The system searches the following catalogs in the order shown for the specified form entry:

1. the current catalog, if one is open (for example, the letter catalog for the FSLETTER procedure)

2. your personal PROFILE catalog (SASUSER.PROFILE, or WORK.PROFILE if the SASUSER library is not allocated)

3. the system catalog SASHELP.FSP

Creating Personal Default Forms

If the default forms for your site (the forms stored in the system catalog SASHELP.FSP) do not meet your needs, you can create personalized default forms. For example, you may need to choose a printer type or destination that is different from the default.

Because of the search sequence used to locate forms, the most logical place to store personal default forms is in SASUSER.PROFILE, your personal SAS profile catalog. The SAS System looks in the profile catalog after checking the local catalog, so you can still have different default forms in selected catalogs. The SAS System looks in the profile catalog before checking the system catalog, so forms in the profile catalog take precedence over those in the system catalog, SASHELP.FSP.

To provide custom default forms, create the following two form entries in your SASUSER.PROFILE catalog:

FSLETTER.FORM   default printing instructions for documents created with the FSLETTER procedure.

DEFAULT.FORM   default printing instructions for screen images captured using the SPRINT command.

Glossary

access method
See *engine*.

action bar
a horizontal list of menu items displayed in place of a window's command line when the PMENU facility is active.

computed variable
a variable in an FSVIEW window whose value is calculated by a formula.

control level
the degree to which a procedure can control access to observations in a SAS data set. Two control levels are currently supported:

RECORD   allows the procedure to have exclusive access to only one observation at a time.

MEMBER   allows the procedure to have exclusive access to the entire data set.

dialog box
a data entry window opened when certain items are selected from a pull-down menu. Menu items that open dialog boxes have an ellipsis (...) following the item name. Dialog boxes are used when additional information is required to perform the action indicated in the menu item.

engine
a set of internal instructions the SAS System uses to read from or write to files.

external file
a file maintained by the host operating system rather than by the SAS System.

field
an area in a SAS/FSP window in which values can be entered or edited, or in which computed values are displayed.

field attributes
a set of characteristics that define the way the contents of a field are treated when values are entered or displayed in the field.

fileref
a SAS nickname used to identify an external file in lieu of its actual filename. Filerefs can be assigned with the FILENAME statement.

form
form entry
a SAS catalog entry of type FORM containing information used to format printed output.

format

a pattern that the SAS System uses to determine how a variable value should be displayed. The SAS System provides a set of standard formats and also allows you to define your own custom formats.

formula

an expression that calculates the value for a computed variable or manipulates the value of a data set variable in the FSVIEW window. Formulas can consist of more than one statement and can also include any of the elements of Screen Control Language that are valid in SAS/FSP software.

formula entry

a SAS catalog entry of type FORMULA containing formulas for computed variables and other general parameters of an FSVIEW session. Only one formula entry at a time can be associated with a data set, but the associated formula entry can be changed during an FSVIEW session.

FSBROWSE application
FSEDIT application

an FSBROWSE or FSEDIT session with an associated screen entry that employs one or more of the following:.

☐ a custom display format

☐ special field attributes

☐ a Screen Control Language program

☐ custom window parameters.

FSVIEW application

an FSVIEW session with an associated formula entry that employs one or more of the following:

☐ a custom display format

☐ computed variables

☐ special variable attributes

☐ custom window parameters.

global command

a command valid in all SAS System windows or in all windows for a given SAS software product.

informat

a pattern that the SAS System uses to determine how values entered in variable fields should be interpreted. The SAS System provides a set of standard informats and also allows you to define your own custom informats.

letter entry
a SAS catalog entry of type LETTER containing the text of a document prepared with the FSLETTER procedure. The letter entry also stores

☐ the attributes of any fields in the document

☐ the name of the associated form for printing the document

☐ the general text editor parameters in effect when the document was last edited.

libref
a SAS nickname used to identify a SAS data library. A libref is the first element of all SAS filenames. Librefs can be assigned with the LIBNAME statement.

parameter
a window or procedure characteristic that can be controlled by the user. The FSBROWSE, FSEDIT, FSLETTER, and FSVIEW procedures provide windows for setting the values of general parameters. These parameter settings are stored in the catalog entries used by the procedure.

pull-down menu
a list of menu items displayed vertically in a rectangular box when a menu item is selected in an action bar or in another pull-down menu.

SAS catalog
a SAS file used to store a special class of data objects called catalog entries. A single SAS catalog can contain several different types of catalog entries.

SAS catalog entry
a member of a SAS catalog. SAS procedures use catalog entries to store a variety of utility information. Each catalog entry has an associated type, and most procedures that use catalog entries can use only a particular type of entry. See also *form entry, formula entry, letter entry,* and *screen entry.*

SAS data file
a SAS file consisting of a collection of data values arranged in a rectangular form and a descriptor portion that identifies the values to the SAS System.

SAS data library
the highest level of organization for SAS files. All SAS files reside in SAS data libraries. The physical structure of the SAS data library depends on the host operating system. SAS data libraries are identified to the SAS System with nicknames called librefs.

SAS data set
a SAS file that allows the SAS System to access stored data as rows of observations and columns of variables. SAS data sets include SAS data files, which physically contain the information in this form, and SAS data views, which contain directions that allow the SAS System to access information from other files as if it were stored in this form.

SAS data view

a SAS file that allows the SAS System to access a database management system table or a PROC SQL view as if it were a SAS data file.

SAS file

a file maintained by the SAS System rather than by the host operating system. All SAS files are stored in SAS data libraries.

screen

a division of the information presented by an FSBROWSE or FSEDIT session. When the data set contains more variables than can fit in the FSBROWSE or FSEDIT window, or when the defined size of a custom display is larger than the current window dimensions, the information to be displayed is divided into discrete window-sized units called screens. Use the LEFT and RIGHT commands to move among screens in an FSBROWSE or FSEDIT window.

Screen Control Language (SCL)

a programming language provided in SAS/AF and SAS/FSP software to manipulate variable values and control windows. In SAS/FSP software, SCL can be used in FSBROWSE, FSEDIT, and FSVIEW applications.

screen entry

a SAS catalog entry of type SCREEN containing information about the custom features of an FSBROWSE or FSEDIT application. If the application includes a Screen Control Language program, that is also stored in the screen entry.

Index

Special Characters